WHAT IS NECESSARY
IN THESE URGENT TIMES

RUDOLF STEINER (1910)

WHAT IS NECESSARY
IN THESE URGENT TIMES

Eighteen Lectures Held in Dornach
January 9 – February 22, 1920

TRANSLATED BY RORY BRADLEY

INTRODUCTION BY CHRISTOPHER BAMFORD

RUDOLF STEINER

SteinerBooks

CW 196

SteinerBooks

Anthroposophic Press

610 Main Street
Great Barrington, Massachusetts 01230
www.steinerbooks.org

Translation from the German by Rory Bradley

This book is volume 196 in the Collected Works (CW) of Rudolf Steiner, published by SteinerBooks, 2010. It is a translation of *Geistige und soziale Wandlungen in der Menschheitsentwickelung*, published by Rudolf Steiner Verlag, Dornach, Switzerland, 1992.

Library of Congress Cataloging-in-Publication Data

Steiner, Rudolf, 1861-1925.
  [Geiste und soziale wandlungen in der menschheitsentwickelung. English]
  What is necessary in these urgent times : eighteen public lectures given in Dornach, January 9-February 22, 1920 / Rudolf Steiner ; translated by Rory Bradley ; introduction by Christopher Bamford.
      p. cm. — (The collected works of Rudolf Steiner ; v. 196)
  Includes bibliographical references and index.
  ISBN 978-0-88010-631-3
  1. Liberty. 2. Social psychology. 3. Social history. I. Title.
  JC571.S78813 2008
  323.44–dc22
                                    201034373

Printed in the United States

CONTENTS

3.
Knowledge of the Human Being through Knowledge of the World

DORNACH, JANUARY 11, 1920

The head organization and the trunk-limb system in the human being. Activity of the Moon forces in the head organization; activity of the Earth and Sun forces in the trunk-limb system. Two evolutionary phases of humanity before the Mystery of Golgotha: the old pagan and the old Hebrew cultures, and their effects today. The necessity of a newly developed morality based on Christianity. The wish for a new spirituality in the development of humanity. The opponents of the new spirituality.

4.
The Necessity for the Development of New Social Forms

DORNACH, JANUARY 16, 1920

Human soul development in the post-Atlantean age. How humanity is becoming younger; the lowering of the age at which we have the ability for development in our present era. The coming end of the development of physical humanity on Earth. The experience of revelations through the physical brain in ancient times and the modern necessity to turn to spiritual science. Czernin about Austria. The threefold social organism. Lloyd George as a typical representative of modern humanity. The inappropriateness of Olympic games in our time. The necessity for the development of new social forms. Opposition to Anthroposophy.

5.
Initiation Science in the Light of Modern Thinking

DORNACH, JANUARY 17, 1920

Our ability to develop until age twenty-eight; the science of initiation is the only possibility for the further progress of humanity. One-sidedness of Anglo-American initiates. Initiation science calls on activation of the individual instead of working through group hypnosis. Trust for one another is the most important social motive of the future. Since the sixteenth century, thought-forms have had no significance in the supersensible world. The evolution of speech; the increasing effect of Ahriman in speech. Report on opponents.

6.

Conditions for Understanding Supersensible Experiences

DORNACH, JANUARY 18, 1920

How the forces of the dead work in the physical world. Present and future relationship of the living and the dead to the Earth. Truthfulness in relation to sense experiences as a requirement for understanding supersensible experiences. National interests hinder truthful thinking. Mutual trust as the main principle of social living. Trust in the path of knowledge of initiation science. Thinking as interwoven with the light; the experience of crossing the threshold. Development of independent thinking through an active "I"-experience. About the Dornach building.

pages 80–96

7.

Thinking, Feeling, and Willing in Social Life

DORNACH, JANUARY 30, 1920

The necessity of a spiritual impulse for our time. Johannes Scherr and his call for "Ideal-Realism." The unreceptivity of people today for the spiritual world. The thinking, feeling, and willing life of the human being. Modern thinking as a development of the picture-experiences of our soul during Moon existence. The re-forming and re-organization of natural materials into works of art, machines, etc., as actions with meaning in the future. The intervention of Ahriman. Raphael's art works. The necessity of a spiritual understanding of the Mystery of Golgotha. The destiny of Europe and of the whole Earth.

pages 97–110

8.

The Nature of the Threefold Social Organism

DORNACH, JANUARY 1, 1920

Significant requirements of the present and future. How dream-like elements creep into thinking. The separation of spiritual life, rights-and-political life, and economic life in the threefold social organism. Talents and gifts are a resonance of the supersensible life before birth. The significance after death of our actions in economic life and political life. Influences of Lucifer and Ahriman; how to overcome them. Humanity stands between the alternatives of Bolshevism and threefolding. The history and destiny of Europe .

pages 111–124

12.
Transforming Social Life through
a New Understanding of Christianity
DORNACH, FEBRUARY 8, 1920

The change in the human soul condition and the view of the necessities of social life in the course of the ages. The migration of Atlanteans to Europe and Asia. In Asia, the spiritual developed in the soul without involvement of the bodily nature. In Europe, the spiritual developed through the instrument of the body. The coming of Christianity from Asia to Europe. Around the mid-fifteenth century, the gradual smoke-screening of the cosmic spirit and the nature spirit in European bodies, and the loss of the understanding of Christianity. Differences in the constitutions of Western and Eastern people today. War catastrophes occur because of the rejection of a new understanding of Christianity. Lloyd George and Woodrow Wilson. Direct understanding from person to person is achieved through spiritual forces. A new understanding of the Mystery of Golgotha. Transformation of casualness and sleepiness into mobility and industriousness of the inner soul life.

13.
Memory, Intelligence, and the Senses in Relation
to the Spiritual World
DORNACH, FEBRUARY 13, 1920

Ancient Mysteries and modern colleges. Ancient knowing and the connection of the human being with the cosmos. The metamorphosis of human soul life. Memory: strongly dependent on the bodily constitution; individual. Intelligence: less dependent on the bodily constitution; reflection through the body. Activity of the senses: least dependent; the process of seeing, as an example. Relationship of the "I" to memory, intelligence, and sense perception. The development of memory from the Moon condition; intelligence from the Sun condition; sense activity from the Saturn condition. Disposition of the various senses during the Saturn, Sun, Moon and Earth developments. Perception of the "I" by soul activities through the body. The life of angels in human memory; archangels in human intelligence; and archai in human sense activity. The relationship of the soul to spiritual substances (angels, archangels, archai) and the relationship of the body to food. The necessity to awaken consciousness. Practical effects in education. About opponents.

14.

The Metamorphosis of Feeling, Desiring, and Wanting

DORNACH, FEBRUARY 14, 1920

The connection of the three soul activities (memory, intelligence, sense activity) with the physical body; disposition in the consciousness form of earlier Earth conditions; connection to the hierarchies. The lower soul capabilities: feeling, desiring, wanting. Their significance for future Earth conditions. The playing into the upper capabilities by those below. Since the fifteenth century, the goal of freeing the upper soul abilities from those below. The future drying-up of the physical body and the lower soul capabilities; filling the higher soul capacities with revelations from the spiritual world. The social world as result of the lower soul abilities. The social order of Lenin and Trotsky determined by the drying higher soul. The danger of human civilization becoming paralyzed or rigid. The necessity of threefolding in public affairs: the separation of the state from the spiritual and the economical life.

15.

A Spiritual Contemplation of Threefolding

DORNACH, FEBRUARY 15, 1920

The human physical organization points to the earthly, to the past and the future. The head organization as metamorphosis of the trunk and limb organization of the previous earthly life; the present trunk and limb organization as the foundation for the head organization of the future earthly life. Tendencies from the fourth post-Atlantean culture appearing in our fifth culture through the head organization of the reincarnating human being. The necessity for human beings to feel themselves placed in time as a twofold being. Anthroposophy instead of merely anthropology. Cooperation among the French nation, the English state, and the German folk for the welfare of Europe. The evolution of the French into a unified nation in contrast to the Germans. The legal-political nature of the French; the predestination of the Germans and the understanding for the spiritual to develop; the economic life of the English-Americans. Necessity to recognize threefolding in an historical connection. The defamation of Monsieur Ferrière

16.

The Development of Imperialism: I

DORNACH, FEBRUARY 20, 1920

Untruthfulness in relation to historical manifestations in our time. Old Oriental imperialism. The ruler as a god; the Paladine as a higher being. The second form of imperialism: ruler and Paladine as god-sent. Church hierarchies as an image of the heavenly. Everything is viewed as symbol, as sign. The splitting of the second form of imperialism into two variations: Church communities and communities of the realm. Pope and emperor. Protestantism as protest against the real significance of the god-sent human being. What was preserved from the first form of imperialism in the Catholic Church, the manner in which Mohammedanism spread, and the despotism of Russian Czarism. The third form of imperialism: Anglo-American economic imperialism. Parliamentarianism, the will of the people, and the monarchy. The empty phrase, instead of signs and symbols. A colonial realm as a reality existing as an empty phrase. The task of the third phase of imperialism: to acknowledge the spiritual beside physical reality.

pages 232–247

17.

The Development of Imperialism: II

DORNACH, FEBRUARY 21, 1920

The foundation for a new spiritual life in Anglo-American imperialism. Economic life as the only reality in the emptiness. Beside the physical reality of economics a spiritual reality must be added. Existence of the prerequisite of this knowledge among the Western peoples. The inability in the Middle Ages to come to spiritual realities through symbols; lack of clarity about social organization. The German imperial rule since 1871 as illusion; the reality that developed out of it: the political conditions since November 1918. The secret societies of the English-speaking world. Empty phrases in exoteric, public life; symbolism that has become meaningless in esoteric societies. The outer power of the secret societies. The threefold impulse brings truth in the place of empty phrases or meaninglessness. Symbols in spiritual manifestations; Habsberger and Hohenzoller. Empty phrases and meaninglessness: Woodrow Wilson's book, The State.

pages 248–262

18.

The Development of Imperialism: III

DORNACH, FEBRUARY 22, 1920

The historical development of imperialism. First stage: will of the ruler as absolute power-factor. Second stage: consideration of persons, objects, deeds, etc., as symbols, as signs. The arising of personal judgment and the possibility for discussion and critique. Third stage: empty phrases and meaninglessness in relation to the soul life. Woodrow Wilson's codex of emptiness and empty words. Demand for a transformation of human thinking and feeling. Describing in pictures, not through definitions and judgments. The Roman Catholic Church as shadow-picture of the first stage of imperialism. Enmity between the Catholic Church and the secret societies. The state as shadow-picture of the second stage. Future call for a knowledge of the spiritual, brought about by feeling shame for recognized meaninglessness. The threefolding of the social organism. The social organism as a living being. Responsibility of the English-speaking world to bring real spirituality into outer economic imperialism. Actualization of an invisible kingdom of Christ through the will of the individual human being living in free spiritual life. Opposition to spiritual science.

pages 263–280

INTRODUCTION

CHRISTOPHER BAMFORD

Think about these things, for they are matters of great importance.
Lecture Twelve

Behold I make all things new. Revelations 21:5

Not unexpectedly, in the vast range of Rudolf Steiner's Collected Works (more than 360 volumes), unacknowledged jewels of all kinds often lie hidden in plain sight, awaiting only our discovery of them. Frequently such ignored treasures are to be found in humbler pastures—"routine" lectures to members, for instance—that suddenly astonish us by their freshness, intimacy, insights, and directness of expression. Reading them, besides being transformed and inspired, we come to know Steiner in a different way: to sense the human being himself and the way that the passionate conviction of his heart bears moving witness to his great love of humanity and the Earth, as well as to his compassionate care for the all-too-human individuals who make up his students, the members of the Anthroposophical Society.

Put in another way: in the Collected Works, there are first of all the basic texts, which lay the essential, necessary foundations for any future work. Out of these arise the manifold peaks of spiritual research, whose profound insights penetrate to the very essence of spiritual reality. Less read are the more esoteric valleys, explored by hardier souls, which unveil the invisible forces at work in the hidden crannies of human and cosmic evolution. Finally, lying in between these, are many other lectures and lecture courses, to which, sadly, too few people have attended, for frequently they contain a kind of wisdom not found elsewhere; and sometimes, as in the present case, have a translucency and conviction that gives them extraordinary transformational power. In such cases, it is nearly always the context—the living, earthly reality—that accounts for their power. Rudolf Steiner is faced with a situation and he must rise to it.

In the present instance, the situation is complex. It is, in some sense, a moment of overlapping crises. Among these, two above all stand out. First, the revelatory and world-changing nature of the recently ended conflict (World War I), which made it a spiritual and ethical necessity for Anthroposophy and the Anthroposophical Society itself to change and turn outward; and second, the related phenomenon of the sudden influx of young people born around the turn of the century—the end of the Kali Yuga—who embodied the spiritual capacities able to respond, as older people were not, to what the Archangel Michael had made available since 1879. These factors implicitly and explicitly frame the message of *What Is Necessary in These Urgent Times*.

The lectures themselves were given to members of the Anthroposophical Society in Dornach, Switzerland, during January and February 1920, a mere eighteen months after the war had limped to its conclusion. The great symbolic "Temple of Anthroposophy," the first Goetheanum, which would burn down over New Year 1922-23, was nearing completion, but still needed funding and continued effort. Attending the lectures were older members who lived in the community, as well as some younger people, workers on the building, and visitors from far and wide, including a contingent of English members, whom Steiner several times addresses directly and who were visiting for the first time since the end of the war.

The war, in fact, overshadows all else. As both symptom and reality, it was the first phenomenon underlying these lectures, for it defined that present moment, the great crisis. It framed it. Its very scale had left an immense void—a sense of meaninglessness that put all previous understandings into question. After all, almost ten million people had died during the conflict: six thousand a day, for fifteen hundred days; and the duplicity of the Versailles Peace Treaty had made the apparent uselessness of the carnage even worse. It seemed to confirm the pervasive feeling that Western civilization as it had been was over: bankrupt. Thus, although no one knew how to bring it about, unconsciously many people recognized that all things had now to be made new and that the old ways of doing things was over.

Europe, and particularly Germany and Central Europe—what remained of the old Hapsburg Empire—was traumatized and disoriented. No one knew where to turn. Social, economic, and political chaos reigned. In desperation, seeking the illusion of certainties, people everywhere turned to competing ideologies, which soon began to take the place of clear, independent thinking. Three of these, above all, vied for supremacy. Marxist communism, which seemed to promise a new, international program for universal social justice; Anglo-American capitalism, which, while offering freedom (which communism seemed to deny), did so only on the condition of embracing an even more fervid materialism; and fascism, nascent in France, Italy, and (most perniciously) Germany, which seemed to offer a viable, even familiar, if conservative alternative, one that promised to safeguard and even enhance the older nationalistic values of family, nation, and traditional ways of life.

At the same time, more thoughtful observers well understood that the war had revealed more than simply the folly of "statesmen," national ambitions, and existing ideologies. Those who could read more deeply into the signs of the times saw clearly that modern Western values—the very values that had seemed in the nineteenth century to ensure endless progress into a material paradise—had not just been called into question, but shown up for what they truly were: a sham.

Among those who saw what was at issue, Rudolf Steiner was perhaps the most prescient. Already, in 1917, in anticipation of the inevitable, long-expected peace, he had met in Berlin with a well-placed German diplomat, Otto von Lerchenfeld, to prepare a plan to be instituted upon the termination of hostilities. Together they prepared two "Memoranda" outlining a radically new approach to the nation's political, economic, and cultural life, one that would never allow a similar conflict to arise.

The Memoranda argued that the time of the unitary, centralized, militarized, national-political state—the dead weight of which had led to the conflict—was over. Peace and justice required a radical re-thinking and re-ordering of society. *Culturally*, it was imperative that individual, spiritual freedom be protected, supported, encouraged, and enhanced in all possible ways. Spiritual or cultural freedom is, after all, the source of all future, evolutionary good in the form of new ideas that come to expression through art, science, philosophy, and other transformative pursuits. *Economically*, too, freedom was also necessary for the circulation, production, distribution, and consumption of goods and services: not spiritual freedom, but *freedom in community*, that is, freedom of association. Finally, *politically*, the separate and distinct freedoms of cultural and economic life required as their basis the essential freedom assured by equality under the law. All of which is to say that, just as the human is a threefold being of body, soul, and spirit and composed of three systems—a metabolic system, a respiratory/circulatory system, and a nerve-sense system—with three functions (willing, feeling, and thinking), so also human society, too, is a threefold organism. Thus, Steiner gave new meaning to the motto of the French Revolution, *"Liberté, Egalité, Fraternité"*—"Freedom" in the spiritual-cultural sphere, "Equality" in the legal-rights sphere, and "Fraternity" (or association) in the economic sphere.

Although the Memoranda were read in the highest circles, in the press of events surrounding the end of hostilities, nothing came of them at an official level. Once the war was over, however, and the ensuing chaos set in, it was clear to Steiner that what they contained must be taken up. This meant that Anthroposophy would have to transform itself. It would have to engage its mission in a new way. It had done so before. During the first, "Theosophical," phase, the esoteric foundations had been laid. Once these were established, new art forms (drama, eurythmy, architecture, painting, and sculpture) had been created to bring the fruits of esotericism into culture in artistic form. But now, with the stakes extraordinarily high, the spiritual world called for initiation knowledge to engage and permeate society in a larger sense. A consequence of this would be a much more open face for Anthroposophy, which, as the years unfolded, would be increasingly in the glare of public scrutiny.

The years following 1918 thus witnessed a proliferation of social initiatives, whose success would depend both on Rudolf Steiner's ability to convince the public and on the ability of Anthroposophists to follow him. The epistemology and insights of spiritual science would have to be translated into accessible, jargon-free language that ordinary people through the exercise of healthy thinking could understand. At the same time, everyone concerned would have to develop the presence of mind to act with dedication and responsibility. It would be a struggle on two fronts, internal and external. Both would prove difficult.

The difficulties began already in 1919, which saw the beginning of the work to make "The Movement for the Threefolding of the Social Organism" into a popular, political movement. The Association for the Threefold Social Organism was formed. Cultural and spiritual renewal was the order of the day. Books and lectures were published. Steiner traveled indefatigably, giving public lectures to large numbers of people. All this effort fell initially on fertile soil. Eighty thousand copies of *Towards Social Renewal* were sold in the first year. Soon, however, it would become clear that Steiner's effort to transform society would fail. While his and his collaborators' heroic labors (almost daily meetings with workers, managers, and owners, as well as finance ministers and other powerful people) had some initial success, in the long run the odds were against them. There was too much confusion and too many competing philosophies and ideologies.

Yet, growing out of the Threefold Social Movement, the first Waldorf school was born. Among the first to heed the call for social renewal had been Emil Molt, owner and director of the Waldorf Astoria cigarette factory in Stuttgart. In April 1919, Steiner talked to the factory workers about the threefold social order. Following his talk, Molt asked Steiner whether he would take on the establishment and leadership of a school for the worker's children: in September, the first Waldorf school opened its doors. Thus, the threefold seed germinated the foundation of cultural renewal through education. At the same time, other initiatives—exemplary of the threefold idea—were also planned.

The year of these lectures, 1920, also saw the creation of other "model institutions," public corporations that exemplified the threefold principles. Businesses were formed to promote economic and spiritual undertakings. Meanwhile, as the Waldorf school continued to develop, Rudolf Steiner, understanding education to be the key to cultural transformation, expanded his lecturing activity to include cultural renewal in a larger sense, including the renewal of the natural sciences, as well as the traditional academic disciplines. Practical efforts were also undertaken to renew the sciences themselves. Laboratories were created. Medicine, too, was seen as central and, at the request of doctors, Steiner gave the first medical course (thus initiating what would become anthroposophical medicine). "University" or higher education, liberal arts courses, too, were initiated.

Despite all this activity, however, not all was well. Chaos in the social world was rising to dangerous levels. The businesses took up much more of Steiner's time than he anticipated. Though it had been easy to raise investment capital in his name, it did not take long for the economic future of the companies to begin to look dim. At the same time, hardly a week went by without some public attack on Anthroposophy and on Steiner personally. Considerable time had to be taken up in responding. More consequentially still, an undercurrent of misunderstanding (even lack of understanding) began to rumble through the Anthroposophical Society, especially among older members, who were more fixed in their ways, and less able to adapt to the changing circumstances and the new approach to spiritual science that these demanded.

Here we may note that a second phenomenon, related to the war but in a sense separate from it, had begun to intrude into these "new circumstances"—a clue to which has already been presented in the turn toward spiritual-scientific courses oriented toward "University" education. With the war's end, a whole new generation of highly idealistic, intelligent young people had begun to turn to Anthroposophy for an answer to the social-political, cultural-educational, and spiritual chaos that they saw stemmed directly from the inertia of materialist, sclerotic, habitual, soulless, and dead thinking that, as they understood it, stifled all creativity, spirituality, and true communion.

Unlike the "homeless souls" who joined Steiner in 1900, when he started teaching, this new generation came to Anthroposophy innocently, out of their hearts' needs, without any connection either to traditional esotericism or to the remarkable spiritual happenings of the last third of the nineteenth century. They knew little if anything about Spiritualism, Theosophy, Masonry, Ritual Magic, or any of the other movements from which the first Anthroposophists were drawn. Therefore, they did not think of themselves primarily as aspirant "occultists." If they were anything, they were spiritually open *activists*. They sought to become spiritual, social, scientific, and philosophical *pioneers*. They wanted to change the world and change themselves. They saw that if it were allowed to continue unchecked, "life as usual" would result only in the progressive dehumanization of humanity, the destruction of the Earth, and the alienation of the gods—and the consequent loss of any and all transcendent purpose to life. They understood—as we do still today—that a radical change in human "being" was necessary.

To them, the older generation of Anthroposophists seemed to come entirely from another world, another culture, with which they could find little shared ground—and the feeling was mutual.

Naturally, however, Steiner welcomed the opportunity to speak to the new generation. He had been waiting for this moment, for these young people, all his life. Whatever and whoever else he was, Steiner himself had always possessed a radical side. Like these young people who were now coming to him, he had no patience for conventional values and conventional thinking. Conventionality—synonymous with sleep—was one of the few things that irritated him. He saw conventionality as a symptom of a potentially fatal disease, one carried preeminently by the bourgeoisie, whose unthinking espousal of egotism, utility, and comfort as primary virtues dominated not only social and cultural life, but also and above all, academic, artistic, scientific, and even religious life.

Steiner, after all, had always sought to lay the ground for a *global transformation* that would overcome all egotistic divides: between subject and object, self and other, individual and community, spirit and matter, nature and cosmos, and cosmos and divinity. As *The Philosophy of Freedom* (1894) makes very clear, he never separated the necessary epistemological transformation in *how we know* (monism or non-dualism) from either the ethical transformation of *how we act* (ethical individualism) or its social consequences in *how we live together* (basically, a kind of anarchism). It does not take much to read Steiner's non-dualist, individualist, quasi-anarchist philosophy between the lines of his biography. One finds his radical affinities delineated quite explicitly in his *Autobiography* as he unfolds his sympathies: with Nietzsche's "transvaluation of all values;" Max Stirner's radical individualism, as well as the "individualistic anarchism" of his friend and fellow Stirnerian J. H. Mackay; and, finally, his commitment to teaching at the leftist Worker's College.

However, when the spiritual world graciously offered him the opportunity to work through Theosophy, Steiner had to temper this social-cultural side of his mission. Certainly, the vast and initiatory field of opportunity opened up by Theosophy (and the other esoteric movements that flowed into it) more than compensated for what he had to give up in terms of social activism. Yet, we can be sure that when young people, drawn to Anthroposophy out of the same radical, activist mood of soul that more than forty years before had led him to it, he was enormously heartened, as is evident in his total commitment to working with them.

What is remarkable is that from Steiner's beginning to teach in 1900, it took about twenty years for a new generation of young people to be drawn to him. Those who came to him in 1918–1922 were born at about the time that he began to teach. This was not a coincidence. For Steiner, 1900 marked a supremely important moment in human evolution: the end of the Kali Yuga, the Dark Age. Those born after that date were different from those born before it. To be able to grasp his teaching truly as he intended it, a person, in fact, would ideally have to have grown to maturity in the post-Kali Yuga period when, on a higher turn of the evolutionary spiral, the return to a new Age of Light would already be in process and humanity would begin crossing what he called "the threshold into the spiritual world." Therefore, when those whose destiny it was to do so stood before him, he understood with perfect clarity that here were people truly prepared to receive his teaching. The older members would just have to struggle to keep up. But there is more to it than that.

For, coincident with these changes, and integral to our ability to deal with them, there was a second cosmic-spiritual phenomenon that is central both to the particular lectures printed here and to Anthroposophy in general: namely, the accession to the regency of evolving human consciousness by the archangel Michael, which occurred according to the traditional teaching (and was confirmed by Rudolf Steiner) in November 1879.

Steiner therefore had always taught that we now live in the "Michael Age." During the period of these lectures, however, and coincident with the arrival of a new generation of students, he began to place his own striving and the deepest meaning of the teaching and practice of Anthroposophy explicitly and even with the force of a vow under the sign and aegis of the archangel Michael. Michael, he taught, is the spirit of inner strength, making it possible for human beings to go beyond the duality of an abstract spirituality on the one hand and a literalized material world on the other in order to see *matter penetrated everywhere by spirit.*

All this was very much in Steiner's mind and heart at this time (1920) as he sought to welcome the new "Michaelites"—the new generation—and help the older members adjust to the new reality. Indeed, immediately before the series of lectures printed here (i.e., during November and December of 1919), Steiner gave the lectures to members in Dornach, *The Mission of the Archangel Michael* (CW 194).

As he was doing so, in the universities and colleges in Germany, Switzerland, and Austria, anthroposophical student groups were springing into being. To receive these "Michaelites," by summer of 1920, a Union for Anthroposophical College Work would be founded and "college" courses held in the Goetheanum. All this youthful activity was not well received by the older members, who felt the foundations of their world and their understanding of Anthroposophy shaking. For Steiner, who saw the influx of new life as "epoch-making in the Anthroposophical Society," this resistance on the part of older members proved to be a problem. He would have to do all he could to bring them into the new way of thinking.

This was easier said than done. The conflict between the older members and the new, young people was real. The young people prized their freedom and independence. They wanted to pursue the "free spiritual life" offered by Anthroposophy in their own way and did not shy away from expressing their dissatisfaction and unhappiness with the mood, tenor, and spirit of the Anthroposophical Society as they found it. Indeed, very soon, they sought to organize their own society, and already by March 1920 (just after the lectures printed here) they circulated a "Call for the Foundation of a Youth Branch." In April of that same year, one of their members, Otto Palmer, made their case at the Goetheanum. He began quite bluntly:

If you want to understand this movement rightly, you must see it above all as a protest that has come alive among the youth against the old life of the branches . . . . In fact, something in the youth feels the need not to see Anthroposophy as a mere Sunday afternoon decoration. Rather, it wants to lead what we are given in Anthroposophy into life and translate it into practice.

As these lectures demonstrate, Rudolf Steiner could not agree more.

Against this complex background, then, Rudolf Steiner continues his "Michael" lectures, speaking to members in the new, direct "Michaelic" manner, seeking to build a bridge to the rising consciousness, to the new way of doing Anthroposophy, by addressing, in perhaps a general way, but with great earnestness and with heartfelt passion, "What is necessary in these urgent times." His purpose is, in a manner of speaking, a call: Awake! Face reality! Act! Clearly, what was necessary then (in 1920) is still necessary now. The external conditions may have changed, but it takes little imagination to see that the crisis for human consciousness remains essentially the same.

All the immediate contextual themes, mentioned above, reverberate in what he has to say. The tone is relaxed and intimate. Steiner is talking to his friends, his students: one senses the love he feels for those he is addressing and for the suffering human beings on whose behalf he is doing so. Beyond and above that—indeed, permeating all he says—is his commitment to the greater evolutionary necessity that humanity consciously and dedicatedly accept the responsibility the spiritual world places upon it.

As he tells it—and history continues to demonstrate—the situation is critical. Action and a new inner determination are called for. Yet Steiner never loses his sense of humor or his compassion and equilibrium. His tone is continuously warm. In this he is helped by the fact that, unlike the better known, more tightly focused lecture courses, which build their insights in an almost architectonic way, the lectures here are looser and have a more conversational tone. Daily matters are dealt with, as well as high questions of initiation science. There is a sense of improvisation. Rather than following a strictly predetermined path, Rudolf Steiner speaks directly from his heart, from what concerns him—which is what he feels should also concern his listeners.

We may say then that Steiner is not here speaking from "initiation consciousness," but from the clear waking consciousness of an initiate. There is a great value in this, and it would be quite wrong to have the impression that Rudolf Steiner is not as serious as in his "great" lecture courses. Far from it, he is most serious, even earnest, and he has a theme—indeed a double theme—which, simply stated, is the critical importance for our time of spiritual, initiation knowledge— that is, of Anthroposophy. This knowledge must become existential. It must become social understanding. It must be acted upon. It cannot remain either a theory or system, or simply a matter of "inner" experiences, but must become living knowledge, the ongoing context of our lives, not just a once-a-week devotion.

The message thus is clear. We must learn not just to pay lip service to spiritual reality, but to act out of it, knowing that, as human beings, we are an integral part of an evolving spiritual cosmos that demands no less of us. Because this is so—and this is an important teaching, too—as he circles around different aspects of his themes, he always places his call to action in an evolutionary, historical context. In fact, he does so to such an extent, and with such insistency, that we may say that the pressing need to act *consciously* out of our historical, evolutionary moment constitutes a third theme. Such a historically awake, contextual response in terms of our actual lives—as the lectures stress repeatedly—is the only basis upon which humanity can avert the dangers that now threaten the entire course of evolution.

In these lectures, then, Rudolf Steiner has deep concerns, and he wants to share them, to wake up his listeners, his friends, to what is truly important. At the same time, precisely because he is with friends, he will not hesitate to interrupt the flow of his message and speak directly about what is on his mind—such as fundraising and how to deal with attacks on Anthroposophy. Thus, much ground is covered, and many themes central to Anthroposophy are brought together.

Steiner begins by stressing the importance of spiritual or "initiation" knowledge throughout the course of human history, and especially at times of crisis when ordinary (habitual, automatic) human thinking cannot rise to the questions that humanity faces. Initiates of such knowledge are always present. They are with us today, though many people "balk when they hear of the necessity of incorporating initiation science into our contemporary consciousness." However, initiation consciousness is not all the same—there is a difference between East and West—and not all initiation consciousness is pure, or unaffected by time and place.

Generally speaking, for instance, the new "humanitarian ideal," then, as still today, emerging in the consciousness of the Anglo-Saxon West, may be viewed as being inspired by such initiatory sources. At the same time, we can also sense another, less pure motive working behind this ideal: that of world domination by the English-speaking peoples and Anglo-American culture. To recognize this, Steiner says, is to face reality—which is what the times require. Yet most people prefer to bury their head in the sand.

The same is true with regard to what emanates from the East. Rabindranath Tagore, a great mystical poet, may espouse radical ideals and write beautiful verses, but he is not an initiate. Eastern initiates, in fact, do not speak. They work in silence. Yet they too have a goal. Their goal is to end earthly civilization: that is, to tear souls from the reincarnational cycle so that they pursue their further evolution solely in the spiritual world. But such a goal, however, is clearly antithetical to the deed of Christ, which forever united the earthly and the spiritual.

Such quandaries remain unknown to most people. At the same time, most people are equally unaware that much of what is good in any culture arises instinctually from the unconscious. Therefore, at the boundaries of the East, in Germany, for instance, Goethe, Fichte, Schiller, Hegel, Herder, and so on—aristocrats of the spirit, bearers of civilization—are ignored. They are hardly known or read. Germans, like everyone else, are losing their "instincts"—instincts, which geniuses like Goethe separated from traditional culture, so that now they lie fallow, unfructifed by the spirit. The same is true of Eastern Europe proper, where in Russia an ossified orthodoxy still holds sway. In other words, human beings everywhere are asleep. The situation is dire. As Steiner says prophetically, Asia too could well fall prey to Western dominance, thereby strengthening the urge to escape from the Earth.

Thus "we stand in the midst of various forces." But what do we have to confront them with? Our spiritual life is razor thin; it is nothing but rhetoric. To work together socially, as human beings, we have only intellectualism (judgmentalism) and emotionalism (basically animalistic drives). Both of these remove us from reality. But *it is precisely the task of spiritual science to awaken us to reality, to bring us to a true understanding of life!* To do so, however, we must understand the Earth and the human being in their whole spiritual-evolutionary context. Without such a holistic vision, nothing can be understood: neither society, nor the war, nor capitalism, nor the human future.

Continuing, Steiner turns next to two major forces disrupting human life and turning it away from reality: the pervasive presence of illusions and the ever-present possibility of degeneration into wickedness or evil. Both are related to the mystery of illness and death; both require a spiritual perspective to be understood. To do so, however, we distinguish *life* from *consciousness* as we know it, which arose only relatively late in our evolution. The farther back we go, in fact, the more life-processes are active, and the dreamier and less "conscious" consciousness is. Indeed, prior to the previous, pre-earthly phase of evolution—called by Steiner the "Moon phase"—there was no consciousness except that of dreamless sleep.

Consciousness, as we know it, comes about through the head— "head-processes"—which are actually death-processes that, while we live, only the life processes in the rest of the organism are able to counteract. Death is thus a necessity for consciousness: "an essential and fundamental law." To understand this, as Steiner explains, we must understand the relationship of the Sun-Earth sphere and the Moon sphere and its forces. In our head, we are Moon beings; with the rest of our body, Sun beings. For, although Moon forces created our head, it receives everything from the Sun. In other words: "The human being's center is a creation of the Moon, into which the Sun flows. The rest of the human organism is a creation of the Sun, in which Moon forces are at work." What this means is that soul-spiritually we are cosmic beings, but because of the Moon forces (which are infused with luciferic powers) we occlude that reality. This gives rise to the capacity for illusion. Yet, without this capacity for illusion—which is also the capacity for mental pictures and imaginations—consciousness is not possible. We would not able to separate ourselves from, and then re-unite in consciousness, with our organism, which is our earthly task. Hence, illusion, like death, is necessary.

Up to this point Steiner has made little mention of the Earth. He has been dealing with the interaction of Sun and Moon—with nearly everything deriving from the Sun and processed as consciousness through the Moon. He has spoken, too, of the Sun-Earth sphere. But actually the Earth is "a kind of interpolation," working in what comes to us from the Sun, so that we are not entirely Sun beings. What difference, then, does the Earth make? It makes us *independent*. Such is the function of gravity. But gravity must be tempered: we cannot only be pulled down. That is, the Sun saves us from becoming entirely one with the Earth. Were we to do so, we would become like wild beasts. To become independent, we need to have the Earth, but at the same time, it opens us up to the possibility of wickedness, the possibility of the overcoming of which lies with the capacities that we receive from the side of the "Sun." Nevertheless, necessarily, the possibility—the temptation—to wickedness exists. Just as we need the capacity for illusion to become intelligent, so too we need the capacity of wickedness to become independent. But that is not all. The evolutionary insertion of will, without which we could not fulfill our human task, gives us a new power. It gives us the possibility of transforming illusion into lying, and wickedness into evil.

Such truths, Steiner says, are important, and without them no accurate picture of the human being is possible. Without knowing and acting out of them in a new way, no new social or human order can be imagined. Too long human beings have acted out of what is old, fixed, and habitual: now everything must be made new. And, for this to happen, Steiner says, we must take into account the Mystery of Golgotha, which represents a critical rupture or turning point in the evolution of the human being as a Sun-Earth and Moon being.

Up to Golgotha, because of the near-universal "openness" of the head organization of human beings, cultures had a unified character.

"Ancient wisdom"—accessed through the "open heads" of initiates and less powerfully by ordinary people—permeated humanity, connecting it to the cosmos. Ancient wisdom was cosmic knowledge. It taught little about human beings themselves, for they had not fully arrived at independent Earth-consciousness. Then, approaching Golgotha, divine revelation was given to the ancient Hebrew people. This revelation, addressed to the whole human bodily organization, rather than the head, was focused on the human: how Israel could best serve Yahweh. In other words, according to Steiner, humanity was addressed; but only collectively, not yet individually. This meant that, when the Mystery of Golgotha occurred, "pagan" or ancient wisdom could grasp the cosmic aspect, which gave rise to Gnosticism; while the Hebrew tradition could understand the collective-human aspect, which then formed the notion of the Church, which in turn led to that of the nation. But, as yet, no way of understanding the individual aspect was available. That would come only with the evolution of the Christian Mystery—for whose sake, from one point of view, Anthroposophy came into being.

After all, the Mystery of Golgotha demonstrated (as *An Outline of Esoteric Science* also showed) that cosmic and human evolutions are one; and that knowledge of the cosmos or nature and knowledge of the human being are similarly one, and they culminate in the individual human being. To take account of this reality obviously not only transforms the nature of the sciences, but also of culture and society generally—for if you take the individual, not the collective, as primary, then power has no place. As Steiner puts it:

> When one human being stands before another, it is impossible to found anything on the basis of power; it is only possible to found something on the basis of things that can develop in the human being, so that the other person has some worth. We all have a worth to discover and develop within ourselves that will allow us to accomplish something for the sake of humanity; and each of us must simultaneously develop within ourselves a receptivity that allows us to recognize this worth in others.

In other words: instead of power, receptivity and trust are primary. This is how the meaning of the Mystery of Golgotha is built up. "It must be built on what Christ said: Everything that you do to another, you do to me. The Christ came into the midst of humanity so that every individual human being would be able to recognize the worth of all other human beings." To realize this, which is the meaning of spiritual life, we must be able to free ourselves all from exterior, worldly powers. And to accomplish this, we must learn to separate thinking and speaking, so that we are no longer mindlessly filled with "empty phrases," "word husks," but speak to one another in fresh words crafted from the direct intuition of wordless thinking. Then we will be able to recognize the spiritual gift that is another human being.

As always, Steiner relates these insights to the larger evolutionary movements of which they are a part. With great vigor and freshness, he repeatedly adduces phenomena to buttress his argument that now everything must be made new—that old forms and ways of thinking, old attitudes and assumptions, some of which go back millennia, must be let go of if the human-cosmic-divine enterprise is to flourish and fulfill its proper end. He tells us for instance how human spiritual-and-physical plasticity has changed over time: how in the ancient Indian epoch (8167-5567 B.C.E.), human beings continued to develop into their fifties, and how progressively this was gradually reduced until now we no longer develop after our twenty-eighth year. In other words, our heads have become increasingly hardened, or as he puts it "mummified," so that now a different means—a purely spiritual means—of spiritual knowing is necessary. But it is not only how we think we know that depends on a malleability that we no longer possess; our social thinking suffers from the same barren atavism. Just as *The Philosophy of Freedom* outlined a new way of knowing out of the spirit, a radical new social structure—the Threefold Social order—must now be created out of the spirit. Just how radical it is, is suggested by the remark that "this threefold social order will create its own states and borders...."

But people are all asleep! We, too, must make ourselves anew; or we will remain perpetually twenty-seven-year-olds. Today, we must make ourselves into what—less consciously—we were by nature in past ages. To do this, we cannot go back, but must recreate ourselves out of the spirit. And our spiritual lives must penetrate all aspects of life. Anthroposophy cannot be a Sunday-only observance. It must fill every moment of every day.

On the one hand, this is easy: "There exists a spiritual revelation, a supersensory revelation—and we need only turn ourselves toward it." On the other, it is extraordinarily difficult because the dead weight of habit and the past all mitigate against it. Yet it must be done—and done individually, one by one. This is new. Previously, initiation science worked through the collective. For this reason, as Steiner insists, now "initiation science always centers absolutely on the individual." It can only gain ground by addressing each individual and appealing to his or her powers of conviction. Thus addressed, the true work of cooperation can begin. We can begin to act not by rote and dead phrase, but out of the spirit. Here, again, trust becomes "the most important social motive of the future. If we cannot learn to trust each other as individuals, "humanity will fall into the abyss." As Steiner puts it, "There is no third path." Either we learn to trust one another, or we fall into a path that can lead only to the war of all against all. Anything else is simply an abstraction. Only radical trust in each other and the spiritual world can free us from the bonds of habit and dead speech. Again, as Steiner says, "The necessary task of forging a true place for thought in the world must nowadays begin in a battle with language." Simply stated, we must learn to think before we speak, and to realize that thinking and speaking are different activities and that speaking must serve, and be continuously formed and reformed—in, by, and through thinking.

Again, this is easier said than done, and requires, above all, that we grasp and existentially realize that we are spiritual beings, who, in addition to incarnated lives on Earth between birth and death, experience life in another form between death and a new birth. Indeed, our lives in the "spiritual" world have a significant consequence on our subsequent earthly lives. From this it follows, as became increasingly important to Steiner, that our earthly lives—and earthly life as a whole—are constantly "acted in" from the spiritual world by discarnate beings, including deceased human beings (the "dead") and various members of the angelic hierarchies. Finally, indeed, as Steiner puts it: "these powers that stream from the spiritual world are the one and only thing that will make it possible to understand all of humanity and the entire course of human evolution on Earth." More than that: we ourselves live with two thirds of our being in the spiritual world; only one third lives on Earth.

It is critical, then, that we maintain the right balance between the Earth and the spiritual worlds. We need to strive in a lively, sensitive way in-between the two. Here, of course, what Steiner calls the luciferic and ahrimanic temptations come into play: Lucifer would draw us away from the Earth; Ahriman would bind us too tightly to it. Our destiny is to become conscious soul-spiritual beings, which we may say requires us to accomplish the difficult task of learning to care for the Earth for the sake of Heaven, the school for which is the life between death and a new birth, about which only initiation science can teach us. However, it is one thing to have such insights; it is another to be able to translate them into the language of healthy human understanding. At the same time, to understand what is said, *we, too, must develop healthy human understanding.* As Steiner says, "People could have plenty of these experiences if they wanted to. They are out there. People are simply not using their healthy human understanding to arrive at them."

Healthy understanding, healthy logic, is in the end the power of truth that will unveil the spiritual world; but, if we let error and falsehood enter, that spiritual world will disappear and understanding will fail. Our words must say what we mean, and mean what we say. At the same time, and perhaps above all, we must learn to trust, which, Steiner stresses again, is the primary virtue.

At another level, we need to realize that thinking is bound to a physical body only as long as we are embodied. Once we leave the physical body, "our thinking lives in the light." But most people today are used to thinking only in relation to the reflected physical world. They know only the reflected body and the reflected "I," because they have only an objectifying, instrumental consciousness. To begin to overcome this "false consciousness," in addition to trust—in fact, as a way of developing it—we must begin to take a selfless interest (to be distinguished from curiosity, which is egotistic) in everything. This, coupled with a healthy understanding that we live in and from a spiritual world from which we receive even our own being as a gift, can go a long way to transforming human life on Earth. At the same time, as Steiner repeatedly stresses, we must become aware of the extent to which our thinking is not only habitual—that is dead—but thoroughly permeated with unwilled, unconscious, dreamlike, Moon-derived, hence luciferic, illusory elements, which, above all, conceal from us the future-creating potential of our thinking. Thinking only of present utility, we fall into the counter-temptation of Ahriman and thereby make things worse by cooperating in Ahriman's collaboration with Lucifer. Only inner development—in the direction of the Christ, of "making all things new" out of conscious spiritual knowledge—can work against this tendency. Otherwise, things will just fall farther apart, and we can only keep futilely gluing them back together.

At this point the question arises of what Anthroposophy—with its Movement for a Threefold Social Order—is doing getting mixed up in politics. On the contrary, Steiner insists, it is demanding precisely the opposite: that spiritual life no longer "be connected to politics at all." Threefolding calls only for a political system in which spiritual, cultural life can be free and independent, and give itself its own form. Legal, cultural-spiritual, and economic spheres have so interpenetrated each other in modern societies that they constitute virtually a single entity dominated by the most powerful forces, today increasingly those of the economic sphere. But once, for instance, the spiritual-cultural sphere is separated out, it can become its own organism, supporting itself in freedom, and thus becoming entirely dependent on human beings' direct relation to the spirit: it can become truly human and work for a human future out of the spirit. The same is true of economic life: separated, it will necessarily develop in the direction of association and "brotherhood" in a truly human way. And if this occurs, the middle sphere of public rights will likewise be based on truly universal all-human values. In this way, gradually, egotism—the influences of Lucifer and Ahriman—in all spheres will slowly be overcome, and humanity will be able to fulfill its mission as the bridge between the spiritual and the earthly worlds: clear, healthy thinking, feeling, and willing will once again be possible.

But for this to happen, human beings—and Anthroposophists first of all—must develop the openness and independence of mind and heart that—unprejudiced by old habits of thought—can recognize how outmoded and inadequate the political, economic, and spiritual structures inherited from the past have become.

To demonstrate one way of thinking about this, in a dense and allusive lecture—lecture nine—Steiner turns in a more esoteric and historical direction. Usually, we think of history as unfolding at significant transformative moments through the impact of "great" individuals and such indeed, at first glance, is the case. Francis Bacon, William Shakespeare, and Jacob Boehme—for instance—were apparently very different individuals whose work initiated a significant and ongoing transformation in modern consciousness. Their influence is self-evident. But that is only half the story, because, in fact, as Steiner puts it, such individuals are often "simply the means and paths through which certain driving spiritual forces reach from the spiritual world into the Earth's history." They are the "doorway through which such forces enter world history" and "leaps" in consciousness occur. This is to say we cannot understand our present moment, if we do not take into account the leap that inaugurated what Steiner calls "the age of the consciousness soul": that is, the leap that began our contemporary, modern scientific "observer-consciousness," which is evolving into what is now generally recognized as its next, "post-modern" stage, within which, of course, many—now outdated or decadent—"modern" traits necessarily still exist.

Modernity, in this sense, is clearly determined first of all by the entry into consciousness of "scientific thinking"—experimentation, "nature on the rack," the value-free study of the material and, biologically speaking, dead world, and hence the radical separation of "science" from the spiritual or religious viewpoint which became isolated, abstracted and therefore remained unchanged. Here Bacon, for instance, is often considered critical. But, viewed from a larger vantage point, Bacon—and thus the attitude of modern science—is, in fact, only symptomatic of a larger shift of perspective away from human reality and toward an abstracted morality of usefulness or utility. In other words, as Steiner puts it, in historical change, it is not the literal content of what an individual says that is important, but the spirit out of which it comes. As if to demonstrate this, he then unfolds the manifold and in some sense disastrous consequences of the Baconian or scientific spirit in different fields—including the religious and political—at the same time showing how its reception differed in Western and Central Europe. It is an interesting and instructive story, but not in itself surprising.

The surprise comes when Steiner turns to Shakespeare, Boehme, and the largely today unknown Jesuit poet Jacobus Baldus (Jakob Bald) and asserts that however different they may seem they all share the same inspiration. More concretely, they all stem from the "same initiated person"—the same initiate. These three who, as Steiner shows, shaped early modern consciousness in so many ways stem from the same one initiate, whose identity he here leaves unclear. Other lectures however make it clear that he is referring to King James I. Readers wishing to further explore this mystery, which is clearly related to the Bacon-Shakespeare controversy, should read Richard Ramsbotham's *Who Wrote Bacon?—William Shakespeare, Francis Bacon and James the First: A Mystery for the Twenty-first Century* (London: Temple Lodge, 2004).

Steiner's point in these lectures is that the impulses that these figures transmitted have atrophied and sickened, that "it is time for a new understanding," especially with regard to the Mystery of Golgotha.

For as always in Rudolf Steiner, a new understanding of Christ is critical to the possibility of a new impulse entering earthly life. Indeed, he likens the crisis of our time to that occurring at the end of the Roman Empire when, following Constantine and out of the soul possibilities of the time, Christianity began to spread and ancient thought to decline. At that moment, then, a certain view of the Christ and the Christian Mystery was formulated—a view that generally speaking still prevails, even though, as it spread westward into and across Europe, it was modified, for whatever changes it received were once again out of "old imaginations" and so it remained more or less the same. All these imaginations are now obsolete. In a word, we need something new—not just in Christianity but in all things, for anachronistic, archaic notions dominate the entire world we live in—spiritual, economic, and political (just consider the question of national boundaries). Though this condition is general, in the case of our relation to Christ—which is the heart of Christianity—it is worse, since the Protestant Reformation further falsified the situation by its over-emphasis on individual, indeed egotistic, inner experiences. Today, immersion in one's inner life, which was still quite appropriate to mystics like Meister Eckhart and Johannes Tauler in the Middle Ages, is no longer sufficient. The "Christ within" must now be fully complemented by the Christ who said, "When two or more are gathered together in my name I am with them." Steiner is very clear about this:

> When someone is alone, the Christ is not there. You cannot find the Christ without first feeling a connection to collective humanity. You must seek the Christ on a path that brings you together with all of humankind…. Being contented solely with one's own inner experiences leads one away from the Christ-impulse… This is precisely the great misfortune of the present moment, that people do not have any interest in collective humanity (not just individual human beings). We only come to really know ourselves when we first understand human beings as such.

"But," he continues, "we cannot understand the human being as such without seeking its origin in the more-than-earthly." Without such knowledge as is presented in *An Outline of Esoteric Science*, which shows the divine-cosmic-spiritual origin and nature of humanity, no true social life is possible and, likewise, no true renewal of Christianity. What is needed is knowledge of human beings as a single being, coeval in a sense with the cosmos, and hence the intimate coworkers and friends of the spiritual and divine, evolutionarily reincarnating, with lives on both sides of the threshold of death, in both the spiritual and the earthly worlds. Without such self-knowledge, which is excluded from our educational system, any program of reform is illusory. To effect any real change, then, we need a vision of the course of human evolution such as initiation science provides. Such is the new spiritual impulse that is seeking "to enter the very foundation of our civilized world." Yet precisely this impulse is under threat from the egotism of nationalisms still conceived essentially as bloodlines. Blood relations certainly taught humanity the beginnings of love—kinship love—but that time is over. Christ did not appear on Earth for any particular national group of this kind: he came for the sake of all humankind. To begin to receive him, then, we too must begin to take an interest in all human affairs. We can no longer be concerned only with our own souls. Indeed, as Steiner puts it in words as relevant now as when he spoke them: "Self-interest is the great misfortune of our times and the solution will only come if people, having experienced the awful things that have occurred in the last few years, truly say to themselves: we must take an interest in the affairs of all humankind."

In other words, our spiritual lives—to the extent that we have them—have become "removed and abstract," disconnected from the reality of our practical lives. Spirituality has become a "Sunday" affair, as if day-to-day life were somehow unworthy, whereas in fact spiritual life has no real value if we do not take it into the everyday, practical world. This is precisely what Anthroposophy means: bringing the spiritual into the practical, for example through the Threefold Social Order. Anthroposophists must therefore "become practical in the most eminent sense of the word, and yet they must also still be able to look into the spiritual world." The two paths are not mutually exclusive. Together, they allow us to face reality—the truth about what is going on—in a conscious way; only a realistic and conscious approach to the problems facing humanity can hope to solve them. Spiritual reality can only be successfully approached in this way: with clear, healthy, thinking human consciousness and a willingness to face the facts. This may not be easy, but, as Steiner says, the alternative is fear and escapism of one form or another.

Stated thus, one may agree and yet not quite see the way forward. And so, as he does so often in these lectures, Steiner gives the task a historical, evolutionary frame. He points first to the different ways in which ancient (Atlantean) wisdom was transmitted and received in the East and in the West. In the East, it was taken up primarily into the soul, but in the West it was absorbed primarily through the body and the brain. Western European peoples understood that the body could take up the spirit—indeed, that the body was spiritual. This was how they first took up Christianity. But gradually they lost this ability and with it Christianity—and the Christ-impulse itself— gradually got lost too, while, at the same, the memory of the body led the European peoples increasingly into materialism. Thus, in the West we now have to find a new way to the spirit and to Christ. This is a historical, evolutionary necessity. It is what we are called to. But to find this new way to the spirit requires that we begin to meet each other out of a full knowledge of the human being as taught by initiation science. We must begin to act out of a spiritual understanding of the connection of the earthly and the supra-earthly worlds.

In other words, we must become aware again, as the ancients were, that human beings are cosmic beings and belong to the cosmos. We must let go of the "self-knowledge" that "exists in the incubator of one's own beloved 'I,'" and realize ourselves as "universal beings." We must begin to understand our so-called higher soul faculties— memory, intelligence, and sense perception—differently and see them clearly both in their experiential, phenomenological reality and in their evolutionary course. Steiner (in lectures thirteen, fourteen, and fifteen) lays the ground for us to do so in simple direct language and carefully chosen examples, charged with insights. Perhaps he has said these things before—in fact, he certainly has—but for this reader at least, here they have a clarity and immediacy that allows them to penetrate consciousness in a different way. Deep, practical soul questions are planted that could last a lifetime.

The questions are practical because they call for practical application, for the overriding concern that motivates Rudolf Steiner's every word in these lectures is the need—individually, socially, and politically, as well as spiritually—for concerted action: to make it new! Initiation science calls us to make a new world. This new world must be cosmopolitan, person-to-person—at once Earth- and Heaven-centered. It must overcome and transform old, ingrained, egotistic habits, such as nationalism. It must finally overcome the dangerous, exclusivist, separatist tendencies of bloodlines, which are now compounded by the arbitrary, historical drawing of national borders. Associations, affinities, cultures must form naturally out of human relationships open to and permeated by participation in and by the spiritual worlds. Above all, this new world must eschew greed and selfishness. It must leave behind the automatisms of egotistic power and dominance. Therefore, most poignantly and relevantly, Steiner ends with three lectures on "imperialism." In these, he is addressing especially the English members of his audience, because it is already clear to him that Anglo-American, free market capitalism will be the vehicle of a "new" imperialism, the dangers of which threaten the healthy evolution of a new global, cosmopolitan—that is, "Michaelic"—polity in multiple ways. If anything demonstrates conclusively the contemporary relevance of these lectures, this is it. Rudolf Steiner is talking to us, today, in the twenty-first century. We ignore his words at our peril.

WHAT IS NECESSARY
IN THESE URGENT TIMES

1

The Science of Initiation
and the Realities of Life

DORNACH, JANUARY 9, 1920

T HE ways in which the science of initiation has intervened, *neces-sarily* intervened, in all that was and is to be known and undertaken in earthly life, can be effectively "read" in the course of human evolution in history—this is what should be taken from the remarks I made before my departure last December† and also from the, shall we say, underlying text of the public lectures† I have recently given. If you are unable to feel the truth of this statement with the whole of your being, then you are asleep and unaware of the actual demands of the present moment. For all intents and purposes, however, most people *are* asleep to the demands of the present, since (we must be very clear on this point) the questions currently put to humanity cannot be answered except out of knowledge that comes from initiation science.

As a result, it is important not only that initiation science was always present in the history of human evolution, that there were always initiates who understood the powers that actually lay behind worldly occurrences and existence—what matters is that there are still such initiates living today. But only a very few people are able to have a clear mental picture of these initiates' relationship to the world. And actually, people now have no desire for this kind of understanding. Instead, they balk when they hear about the necessity of incorporating initiation science into our contemporary consciousness.

Furthermore, we can come to understand the critical nature of this moment in time only when we observe how these initiates are involved differently in various regions of the civilized world. Their relationship to affairs in the East is very different from their relationship to affairs in the West. And those who believe they can get by with absolute statements and judgments applicable to all people and places do not live in reality; they live rather in a world of abstractions. Instead of dealing in absolutes, we must continually examine world occurrences from many different angles and points of view, so that the critical nature of this moment will at the very least be impressed upon the consciousness of a few.

Turning first to what is happening in the West, particularly in the English-speaking world, we find that contemporary public opinion and all that it produces in the world is not dependent simply on what (today I will speak quite firmly, if I may) the uninitiated dream up and tout as their ideals. Indeed, in the English-speaking world there is currently a violent opposition between what the public considers true and what those who are truly initiated consider true behind the scenes.

If we examine the general consciousness in this region of the civilized world—particularly if we examine the best of what results from it—we find a humanitarian ideal present there. There is a drive to centralize human affairs under the purview of humanitarianism and establish institutions that will serve it well. Today we shall not examine the dark corners of this region or all that is hiding there; we shall instead turn our gaze toward the best parts of public life originating in the uninitiated. This is the ambitious pursuit to unite people under the banner of humanitarianism. Behind this outward striving stands the knowledge of the initiated, leading society onwards. And without the public knowing it, without the public even having the opportunity to know it, the directing forces for these efforts flow out of the circle of certain initiated individuals into public opinion and earthly deeds.

Now and then it is possible for a society to better itself with beautiful programs and beautiful ideals. Otherwise, no one would bother to be idealistic in the first place. But living among those idealistic people, unbeknown to them, are more than the things they speak about; there are also certain ways, certain paths by which their affairs can be penetrated by what flows out of the circles of initiates. And so it happened in the last third of the nineteenth century and the beginning of the twentieth century (we shall consider only this time period and not look farther into the past) that well-intentioned people who were, however, uninitiated dreamt of all possible manner of beautiful ideals and united to bring their beautiful ideals to fruition in society. Behind their efforts, behind what was happening at that time, stood initiates who, in the 1880s (as I said, we shall not look farther back than that), were speaking about an impending world war that would change the face of southern and eastern Europe.

If you are able to follow what was spoken and taught within those circles of initiates, you will know that they foretold the terrible, horrendous things that have come crashing over the civilized world in the past five years. These things were by no means a secret to the initiates of the English-speaking world. In all of their discussions about the subject there is a single difference of opinion. On one side are those who support beautiful, exoteric ideals—the ideals of humanitarianism, for example, and all the ways in which the uninitiated have brought it into the world. On the other side are those who very strongly defend the calculated theory that Central European culture must vanish from modern civilization, and that the culture of the English-speaking people must rise to prominence and achieve world domination.

When these things are spoken now, they have much more weight than they might have had if spoken twenty years ago. Twenty years ago, it was possible to brush aside anyone who said such a thing: "He's just whistling 'Dixie'!" But now we can easily see that much of what those initiates foretold has come to pass.

I say this as cautiously as I am able so as to not deviate from describing what is purely factual. But even describing the purely factual, even *this* is extremely discomfiting to the majority of people living today. They want to cast it aside. They refuse to go anywhere near it. There is so much we can do these days to fuel the fires in our souls—we can do work cultivating nationalism or re-establishing former national institutions, we can advocate for the League of Nations—the list goes on and on. People do not want to hear that in fact humanity is presently in the midst of a terrible crisis.

Thus far we have given a brief indication of the difference between what uninitiated people in the West know and what actually drives and guides their decisions and resolutions without their knowing it. We can come to know our part in what happens in the world only if we work to familiarize ourselves with what truly exists. We must discover what the world holds when we do not allow ourselves to be pushed and prodded into actions, but rather attempt to find the paths that enable true freedom of will.

If we turn now to consider the East, we find the same division between uninitiated and initiated people. What sorts of things could you expect an uninitiated person there to say? An uninitiated person in the East sounds a bit like Rabindranath Tagore.† Rabindranath Tagore is a wonderful Eastern idealist who has taken a stand for unusually radical ideals. Everything that he has published or otherwise expressed publicly is quite beautiful. But Tagore's words are the words of an uninitiated person.

Eastern initiates speak in a very different way, according to the old customs of the East: they do not speak at all. They have other ways of realizing their wishes in society. First among these is the wish to prevent any one side from striving for world domination, because they know quite clearly (or believe they know quite clearly) that if any group were to rise to world dominance, it would be the English-American people. They do not want this to happen. To prevent it, they actually want to do away with civilization on Earth entirely. Being extremely familiar with the spiritual world, they are convinced that human beings would progress more satisfactorily if they were to forego their future earthly incarnations. These initiates of the East are not concerned with what will come of Leninism.† They say: "If this institution of Leninism continues to spread, there is no more certain way of ruining life on Earth as we know it." But this would be a favorable occurrence only for those people who, through the work they have done in previous incarnations, are already able to live on without the possibility of incarnating again on Earth.

If you were to say this to a European, it would be considered paradoxical. But these Eastern initiates speak with one another about these matters in the same way that an ignorant European would speak about the difference in taste between pea soup and rice soup. For these initiates, such matters have true reality; they do not lie outside the range of such everyday discussions. If we examine the conditions of the contemporary civilized world and wish to understand them, then we may not disregard the fact that these two influences from East and West are present in reality. And we absolutely cannot work to aid human progress without a complete feeling for the influence that these things have in the course of human evolution. Outward social life as we know it—is it molded by what people think superficially, by the beliefs of those who allow themselves to be ruled by the science of the uninitiated?

If you wish to study this question, I recommend that you pick eight days in May or June of 1914 and read newspaper articles or books published during those eight days; then ask yourself how many were written by people actually present to reality—in other words, how many people in the civilized world do you find who had any knowledge of the buds that were to flower in August in that civilized world? The uninitiated did not allow themselves to even dream of such things! Even today, the uninitiated will not allow themselves to dream about what is currently happening. But what happens in outward life does not result from the knowledge of uninitiated people. A large gap separates what people believe and what really happens in life. We should bring this gap to the forefront of our consciousness; the correct answer to my earlier question is another question: How much do the uninitiated actually know today about life and what holds sway over it?

People talk with one another about life. People come up with theories and ideals and programs, but without having any real familiarity with life. And when something does appear that is truly a product of life, then humanity does not recognize it as such; they regard it, too, as a theory or an absurdity or something of the like.

The influences of the West and the East have very different meanings for life. These separate meanings play their respective parts in a way that is glaringly obvious to those who can observe such things. If the theories, programs, and social outlook of the West were to become dominant, then nothing, really nothing, would come of them, absolutely nothing. That there is even such a thing as a Western civilization, that people living in the West are able to develop institutions and programs, this is not due to the fact that individuals like Spencer[†] or Darwin[†] or other more socially-minded people live there and contribute their ideas; for in reality nothing can be made of these exoteric theories and worldviews. That life still progresses, that it does not merely stagnate, is due solely to the fact that old traditional instincts are still alive in the English-speaking world and that life is actually aligned with these older instincts and not with the new theories. The theories are just decorations that people put on when they want to speak in flowery language about life. What really governs and directs life are the instincts that float to the surface from the unconscious depths of soul. This is something that must be seriously observed and recognized.

We will turn now to the East. What I am referring to as the "East" begins when one crosses the Rhine River, and the farther east one travels, the more life resembles life in the East. Let us examine what we find there.

First of all, we should consider the history in Germany, Russia, and even the Middle East. When we examine Germany from a historical perspective, we find something very strange indeed. We find that though such great spirits as Goethe, Fichte, Schelling, Hegel, and Herder[†] lived among the German people, in actuality the German people have not the slightest idea that such great spirits lived among them. In Germany, members of a small spiritual aristocracy were the sole bearers of civilization. Never did this civilization find a foothold in the general public. Even Goethe was not known in most German circles, until after 1862. I say after 1862 because in Germany it was very difficult to obtain a copy of Goethe's works before that time. His works were not yet free for open publication, and the Cotta family[†] saw to it that they were very hard to come by. Since 1862, Goethe's works have been available for open publication, and they have certainly been read, but they have never quite penetrated into the intellectual life of the German nation.

For this reason alone we can already observe in the German people the first hint of an extreme uncertainty of instinct. For over and against the focused life force, the intense spiritual power that streams outward from people like Herder or Goethe or Fichte, is an extreme uncertainty of human instinct, an uncertainly caused by the fact that in this region of the world, human instincts moved away from older traditions. As time passed in the West, human instincts continued to exist according to older traditions. Here in Germany, they not only moved away from tradition, but they also failed to undergo any sort of true renewal. They were not penetrated with what the spiritual world could have offered to them.

This can be even more clearly discerned in Eastern Europe. Just think about the role that so-called orthodox religion has played there; think about the mark it has left on institutions, how it has lived an earthly life but done nothing, absolutely nothing, for the soul life. The preservation of this Eastern orthodoxy, which has long outlived its relevance, signifies that the human souls living in the East have also encountered this same uncertainty in their lives. Anyone living in Western Europe who has come to know a Russian will be moved by the idiosyncratic relationship that this person has to what is universally human on the one hand and to orthodox religion on the other. For someone who cannot begin to imagine the desperation with which the Russian people have turned to orthodox religion, a Russian individual will seem to be a soul from centuries long ago, still clinging to the keepsakes and accessories of an outdated religion and believing that they might still hold some meaning. This is what characterizes the Russian soul. And consequently this uncertainty of human instinct, this lack of inner unity, flows out into Eastern Europe. The idiosyncratic division that has permeated the Russian people is connected ultimately with this uncertainty of human instinct.

Sometime soon, in the next few decades perhaps, the whole population of Asia could very well fall prey to European conquerors, because the initiates living in Asia are not doing anything to stop it. After all, if Asia does fall prey to European conquerors, it will only make the members of that society all the more ready to extricate themselves from earthly life and forego their future earth incarnations.

We stand in the midst of these two forces. And there are also forces that do not side with one group or the other, but that are working instead toward a true renewal of initiation science. These forces must be called forth, must be delivered into the world from out of the human soul. These days, it only makes sense to speak about life if we allow our words to be filled with the conscious awareness of this fact. We must assume that this is the task that lies before us. To accomplish this task, it must also be continuously shown how individuals living nowadays must work to navigate between extreme intellectualism on the one hand and extreme emotionalism on the other.

Our lives always fluctuate between a tendency toward an ever-escalating, self-defeating intellectualism and a tendency toward an emotionalism that seeks the meaning of life by diving deep into our animalistic drives. Intellectualism has evolved out of our existing spiritual life, which changed due to things that have risen to prominence since the fifteenth century. But this spiritual life is merely a shadow now. This spiritual life is thin. This spiritual life is nothing but rhetoric. And precisely because this spiritual life is thin and shadowy, the powers at work within it are not directed toward what is truly spiritual. Rather they direct themselves toward the human being's instincts, its drives, its animalistic side. Lacking the strength to give the proper impulses to these drives, and thereby spiritualize them, human beings and their shadowy intellectual ideas are, in every moment, divided in their relationship to the soul.

Imagine for a moment that you are making judgments about your fellow human beings. In that moment, you are intellectualizing. Every time that we are judgmental toward our fellow human beings nowadays, we are intellectualizing. Conversely, whenever we work together with our fellow humans in a social partnership, we are emotionalizing, for in these moments we are dominated by our animalistic drives. Everything we seek in the work we do in life is gradually immersed in the realm of our animalistic drives; everything we look for in the judgments that we make in life is gradually immersed in the realm of our intellectualism. People presently have no awareness of this division in their souls. They do not notice how different they are when they judge their fellow human beings or when they work together with them in society.

Eventually, however, intellectual life is self-defeating. It continues to strive well beyond all objectivity and reality. It attributes no actual worth as such to earthly relationships. In the realm of intellectual life, it is entirely possible to articulate beautiful laws and moral codes within a society wherein people are still servants and slaves. I have spoken quite often about precisely this. Even now I can remember a certain report† about coal mine workers from mid-nineteenth century England. Among the many horrible things outlined in this report, one was particularly emphasized—that all week long nine-year-old, eleven-year-old, thirteen-year-old children were sent down into the mines before sunrise and not released from work until after sundown. These poor children never saw the Sun except on Sunday. They were forced to grow up under the Earth's surface in terrible conditions, the details of which I will spare you, for there, too, are many unbelievable things to tell. But still, people sat in drawing rooms heated by the coals taken out of the earth by these children and discussed charity and brotherly love, discussed the importance of looking beyond race, nation, and class.

This is an extreme example of intellectual life. Not once are the doors opened to reality. The individual floats above the rest of humanity. To say that we have a sense of true reality simply means that we know how our every thought is connected with what is happening in the world around us. This is the task of spiritual science—to reawaken this sense of reality in human beings. This is why it is necessary to say publicly the sorts of things I said recently in Basel:† that followers of religion have, over the course of centuries, established a monopoly on everything that can be said about soul and spirit (but "spirit" was abolished in 869,† so nowadays they only talk about "soul"). People who do natural scientific research now are not permitted to look for the spirit in nature. And you must admit: the most perfected example of this particular worldview must be attributed to those extraordinarily clever Jesuits. If any of them were to become a natural scientist, his research would contain absolutely no trace of the spirit! If one then took seriously what this Jesuit had written about nature, one would quite understandably become a materialist in the current spirit of the age.

These days we have to differentiate between what is theoretically true and what is actually true. It is theoretically true that the Jesuits are champions of a spiritual worldview. It is actually true that the Jesuits propagate materialism! It was theoretically true that Newton,[†] in addition to having a mechanistic way of understanding of the world, always took off his hat when he spoke of "God." It is actually true that Newton's mechanistic worldview prefigured the materialism of a later age. In the end it does not matter what one believes theoretically; it matters what exists in the laws of reality. And the intellectual worldview never offers actual laws or proofs of the things it purports. The intellectual worldview leads only to full-fledged Luciferianism. In the end, it luciferizes the world.

Opposite this intellectualism, there is also a strong trend toward emotionalism, toward life driven by instinct, by the animalistic side of humanity, as I mentioned earlier. When we are called upon to actually live in day-to-day existence and not merely to make judgments, this instinct-driven life is what actually predominates. You could say, for example, that it is shameful how we treat the coal miners. This is a judgment you could make. But then there are the actions you take involving the mines! In the moment you cut out those coupons for coal, you become a supporter of the mining industry, but you do not notice or think about it. I want to use this as a metaphor for all that we do in life, because this is precisely the sort of thing that happens all the time these days. People think about things on the one hand, and then go about their daily business on the other, without noticing the violent discrepancy that separates what they think from what they do.

This state of affairs has come about because people are quite comfortable not taking any opportunities to examine more deeply the true nature of life. Everyone wants to be a "good person," and to "live a good life," without really striving to understand life. But it is not possible to live in reality without understanding life. This world war was truly caused by the fact that the former members of the so-called "governments" of the world (and some are still members of those government structures) were far removed from life. Some are still quite far removed. They are quite comfortable right where they are.

What could demonstrate more clearly the current lack of familiarity with the true nature of life, which was the cause of so much in the last few decades, than those "memoirs" that keep appearing on our newsstands and in our book stores? Every week someone new publishes memoirs—first someone from one side of the war, than someone from the other side. We can see in these publications just how much truth there is to the old saying: "You would not believe with what little understanding the world is ruled."†

However, people nowadays do not willingly accept the consequences of such a statement. For example, people nowadays do not want to recognize that you cannot have a true feeling for or knowledge of society unless you first have a true knowledge of the world. It would be possible to study zoology without this complete knowledge of the world because knowledge of the facts and functions of the animal kingdom can be achieved purely through a study of their physical organisms. But the defining characteristic of human beings is that they are organized in such a way as to be left open to receive impulses out of a true spiritual knowledge of the world. Therefore, it is not possible to have any knowledge of society without having a true knowledge of the world as a foundation. We cannot develop the field of sociology without first knowing that everything human beings are striving for in their inner lives is a product of the entire evolution of Earth in its current incarnation (a description of that evolution can be found in my book *An Outline of Esoteric Science*†). We must furthermore know that everything human beings take up now in society will become a seed for all that is still to occur in the ongoing evolution of the Earth.

We cannot understand society without understanding the world in its entirety. It is impossible for human beings to initiate programs or ideas or ideals in day-to-day life without first laying a spiritual foundation for their initiatives; for currently, all over the world, souls have no grasp of the origins of their impulses, initiatives, and ideas.

This leads to strange things, indeed. The outstanding German socialist theorist Karl Kautsky† has just written a book called *The Causes of the World War*. In it, he first addresses the question of guilt. On the very first pages of the book, Kautsky writes something quite peculiar about his understanding of the answer to this question. I would like to preface my discussion of this by pointing out that Kautsky belongs to a group of people that have done everything they can in the past few decades to hammer home the Party doctrine and Party discipline in the proletariat. They have pounded it into people's heads that it is not individual human beings, but rather something more general—like capitalism—that is responsible for what happens in the world. They are the reason you find people all over the place talking not about capitalists, but about capitalism.

With doctrines like these you can certainly stir the pot. You can create political parties. You can make a strong hammer for pounding things into people's heads, such that the Party doctrines eventually become committed beliefs. But as soon as it is necessary for you to start passing judgments in the world (and never mind doing actual work or starting initiatives), then the whole doctrine suddenly goes out the window! Because now who is Kautsky going to blame for the war? He would have to un-write his whole book if he continued his old litanies against that elusive enemy capitalism.

So what does he do? He writes the following—which is very strange, indeed—on the first page of his book.[†] I would like to read just a few words from that book now: "One cannot blame capitalism alone. For capitalism itself is only a theory drawn from the observation of countless individual situations; it is helpful only insofar as it attends to the common thread in these individual occurrences and spins it into a unified theory. But one can fight against a theory only theoretically, not actually. In actuality, we can fight only against individual situations… certain institutions and persons that are the bearers of certain societal functions."

The moment the socialist theorist is called upon to pass judgment on society (and again, never mind actually building an initiative in that society), capitalism suddenly becomes nothing more than an abstraction. Now he is really getting somewhere! But then, when the same Karl Kautsky takes up the threefold nature of reality, capitalism comes marching onto the scene again dressed in high military fashion, and not as an abstraction, but as something actual!—He simply does not notice the difference between an outlook taken from actual observations of day-to-day life and one taken from generally abstract ideas or abstract feelings.

Insight—that is the thing we must seek nowadays as a way of defending ourselves from the pitfalls of illusion we encounter when participating in intellectual life. It is for this reason that I have tried to make you aware of a certain perspective on the things that are happening in the world at present. Tomorrow and the next day I will continue to build on what I have said today.

2

Illusion and Evil

DORNACH, JANUARY 10, 1920

In order to make the transition from the cultural historical consider-ations of yesterday to the perspectives I will discuss tomorrow, I must interrupt with a kind of episodic lecture today, which will perhaps seem to be quite far afield. However, even if it comes in the form of a fairly complicated lecture, these things must also be included in our considerations.

Two forces disrupt human life, both appearing within it in a way that is puzzling, a way that demands to be understood because it falls outside the conventionally accepted course of human life. The first has to do with the fact that human beings are capable of having illu-sions, of surrendering themselves to such illusions. The other has to do with the fact that human beings can also degenerate into wicked-ness. The influence of illusions and the influence of wickedness in human life is one of the great mysteries of our existence.

Now, I have in the past had cause at various times to point out the mystery of these two facts of life.† The mystery, the secret, is only a mystery because thinking about it falls outside of the normal streams of human thought. And all of the thoughts related to the presence of illusions and wickedness in human life are connected to the problem, the mystery, of illness and death, the full depths of which are not actually felt by most human beings (as is the case with all mysteries) because they are accustomed to having illusions, wickedness, and illness and death as part of their lives. The only person who must find these things altogether unintelligible is the one who starts with a materialistic understanding of life. In particular, the materialistically-minded individual will have continually to ask: "How can I reconcile these deviations from the normal and natural course of life—the deviations that occur in sickness and in death?" The laws of nature supposedly at work in all organisms are doubtlessly expressed in the normal, healthy course of life. But sickness and death abnormally disrupt this normal course of life.

In order to develop something healthy within the afflicted world-view of civilized humanity, we must learn to see in time that sickness and death, that wickedness and illusions, can only be understood from the perspective of a spiritual worldview. As a human being, standing in the world as a physical expression of the facts known to you, it must be clear to you that your development would not be possible if the only things at play within your being were the natural laws described in mainstream contemporary science. Consider just for a moment the following from the perspective of healthy human understanding. Think to yourself: The vital life forces within me sometimes become livelier than they are under so-called normal conditions; they become livelier, for example, when I have a fever, livelier than I am able to manage or control. In these instances when you do not rise to the occasion, when you do not win the upper hand over the forces of nature within, you lose consciousness, or at the very least your consciousness moves into an abnormal state.

Anyone wishing to objectively understand life must realize that life and consciousness are two separate things. We are conscious, we have consciousness, when we have control over our life forces. When those life forces overwhelm us, when they reach a fever pitch and we lose our control over them, it becomes impossible to maintain proper consciousness. To put it briefly, this results in the follow-ing conclusion: our life forces as well as those forces that aggravate our lives into fevers and passions cannot also be the forces of our consciousness.

If you step back and consider human evolution as it has played out in the cosmos, you will find that Earth-consciousness (which is what people nowadays usually mean when they speak about general human consciousness and which will also be the sole focus of today's lecture) only appeared later in that evolution. This Earth-consciousness was preceded by other, dimmer forms of consciousness. I have often indicated to you before that this, our planet Earth, was itself preceded by an earlier planetary incarnation called the Moon incarnation. At that time, when human consciousness was bound up with the Moon incarnation of our planet, human beings had only a kind of dream-consciousness. But at that time (as you may already know from my book *An Outline of Esoteric Science*) it was also filled with life forces to a greater extent than today's Earth-consciousness.

And when we go even farther back in time, to even earlier planetary incarnations of our Earth, we find that more and more life processes were active in the human beings alive during those incarnations. Human beings back then lived lives in connection with the whole of the cosmos. But we will not find any form of consciousness present in human beings prior to the Moon-consciousness, except the kind we know of from dreamless sleep—in other words, from the perspective of Earth, there was no consciousness at all prior to Moon-consciousness.

Having evolved through these earlier incarnations, during which they were filled to a greater extent with life forces but consequently could not have Earth-consciousness, human beings have now arrived at a less lively form of being that does possess this Earth-consciousness. We have also spoken in the past about the bodily conditions that make this Earth-consciousness possible.[†] In the center of our consciousness, in our head, we have certain processes continuously occurring. If these head-processes, however, were to extend into the rest of the physical body, they would, by their very nature, move our physical body into a state of death. Our head-processes are effectively the same as the processes that occur in our physical organism when it becomes a corpse. For as long as we are alive, these nervous system processes so similar to the processes of death are held at bay; they are balanced out by the life processes in the rest of our organism. When these nervous system processes try to extend into the rest of our body, the organization of our torso and limbs is the only thing that can restore life to our body. If the organization of our body was dictated only by our head, we would immediately die or be as good as dead.

You can see that it is necessary for the process of dying, of destruction, to play a role in human life. Without the presence and activity of this process of destruction, the illumination of consciousness would not have been possible in human evolution. This must be understood as a necessary part of this particular development. And it is fundamentally foolish to think: Well, God is almighty. He could have done it all differently if He wanted. This would be the same as saying: God is almighty. He could make a three-cornered shape with four corners if He wanted to.—We are dealing with an essential and fundamental law. It is altogether impossible for consciousness to develop without the integration of the death principle into the human organism.

Now, insofar as we live within our physical Earth organism, insofar as we are beings of the Earth, we are also completely integrated into this Earth organism, this earthly existence. The laws of this earthly existence essentially fill our entire organism. It is necessary here to differentiate between the cosmic laws that are, in actuality, laws of the Earth, and the cosmic laws that can be *considered* laws of the Earth. We are touching upon a fairly complicated subject here. Let us imagine this schematically. When we speak of the whole Earth realm, we are dealing with the Earth, with the Sun, and with a few other things. Everything that works and lives in that realm is somehow connected. But in making that statement—that everything that works and lives in that realm is somehow connected—in making that statement we are actually leaving something out. We are leaving out a crucial fact, which centers primarily on the nature of the Moon.

Strangely, we are in fact living in two different spheres, which do indeed work in and through one another, but which are, in their inner nature, fundamentally different. The forces working in us that are related to the Sun and to the Earth are indeed connected with one another, making up one of these two spheres. Inserted then into this Sun-Earth sphere are all the forces working in us that belong to the Moon sphere. Therefore, I will draw this like so: Earth (E), Sun (S), and then a few other things.

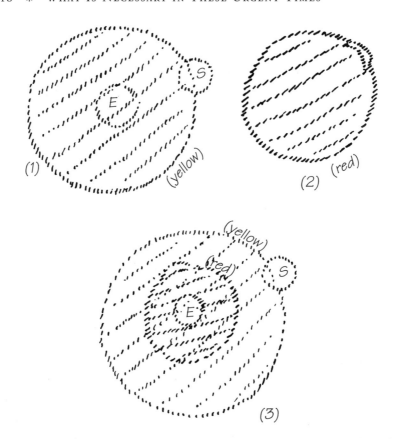

First I will draw the apparent motion of the Earth and the Sun in relation to one another (1). Then, the Moon. If this is the Moon sphere (2) and this is the sphere of the Sun (1), then I must draw the two together (3) in such a way that they fall within the same area while still maintaining the division between the two forces, which cannot be united.

And as human beings, we live in the midst of these two divided spheres. Everything that belongs to the Moon sphere is a remnant, a carry-over from the old Moon incarnation (you can read about this in more detail in *An Outline Esoteric Science*). These things do not belong in any way to what the Earth has become in the process of its evolution. It is a piece left over from the Moon and remains in this incarnation like a foreign body of some sort, and we participate both in it and in the Earth-Sun sphere.

For those who wish to understand earthly existence, it is absolutely necessary to be familiar with the separate individual existences of both the Earth-Sun sphere and the Moon sphere. This fact is connected with something extraordinarily important; so important that modern science has not the slightest awareness of it, and furthermore, were it to learn of this, modern science would most likely view it as absurdly foolish.

Every human being, as it develops as an embryo, is not merely following the direction of the powers released in the body of the mother through the act of conception. To claim that this is true would be the same as saying: Here I have a compass needle that points in a specific direction—the directive powers that cause the compass to point that way must lie within the compass. A physicist would never make such a statement. Every physicist would instead say: The Earth is a big magnet; one pole tugs at one tip of that compass needle, and the other pole tugs at the other tip. In this instance we are perfectly willing to say that everything associated with the needle—its actions, its effectiveness, its position—is dependent upon something greater. It is only when we speak about the human embryo that we try to say that all of the organizing forces causing that embryo to develop are found within the body of the mother; in actuality, cosmic forces streaming into the mother are what is actually at work in developing and shaping the human being. And so it happens that a human being's consciousness-center, the head, is connected with Moon forces, and the rest of the bodily organism is connected with Sun forces. And as humans, we consequently have a divided being. In our head, we are Moon-beings; in the rest of our body, we are Sun-beings. But here the matter becomes far more complicated. If you do not examine it exactly, you will quickly come upon a whole slew of confusions and misunderstanding.

Insofar as the human being is a being with a head, it is a being of the Moon. In other words, the forces of the Moon are integrated into the organization of the human head. Insofar as the human being is a being with a torso and limbs, it is a being of the Sun. In other words, the forces of the Sun are integrated into the organization of the rest of the human body—the torso and limbs.

At the same time, however, when we are awake and conscious in the world, our center—our head—is particularly receptive to everything that comes toward us from the Sun. When sunlight falls upon us, we take it in through our eyes. The head was created by Moon forces, but everything that it receives in the world comes from the Sun. And in the rest of our bodily organism—in the torso and limbs—the human being is a Sun-being, meaning the organization of the torso and limbs was established by the Sun. But everything that is at work in that organism, for as long as it is on the Earth, comes from the .

Taking all of this into consideration, you could say: The human being's center is a creation of the Moon into which the Sun flows. The rest of the human being's organism is a creation of the Sun in which the Moon forces are at work.

You can see that if we do not examine these matters precisely but instead look for more comfortable and familiar concepts, we can easily go astray. It would be very easy for someone to come along and say: The human head is a creation of Moon forces. Another would then say: That is not true; it comes from the Sun, for it is in this part of the human being that the Sun processes take place. Both speakers are correct. But we must come to understand the way in which these two forces interact with one another. I have often said that true reality is not comfortable for us to understand. A few casual concepts will not suffice for a true understanding of reality. We will have to struggle more than a little bit in order to form concepts of reality that actually correspond to it closely. Our Sun-being and our Moon-being are at work in a twofold way within each of us. And everything that happens in the course of our lives cannot be understood unless we see ourselves connected in this twofold manner with the cosmos.

For the tormented people of today (if they feel properly, then they will feel tormented), one of the most important concerns should be the following: that we have lost the old concepts of reality that humanity once knew through atavistic clarity, and that we now stand in the beginning stages of Copernican-ism,† of Galileo-ism!† We must remind ourselves that the ancient Egyptians saw human beings as one part of a vast cosmos and that this cosmos was, to an ancient Egyptian, much more intricately organized than the human being. Today we human beings look out at the cosmos and see one big piece of machinery that we can understand through mathematical formulas. For the modern human being, the planets move across the sky against the backdrop of the fixed stars just as human beings move their arms and legs, according to mathematical formulas that can be reckoned and figured! But in all that is out there in the cosmos as well as all that encompasses the human being, there lives an organization that includes both soul and spirit. And for as long as we do not recognize the presence of soul and the suffusion of spirit in the cosmos, we can understand nothing of human life, which is itself but one part of the ensouled and spirit-penetrated cosmos.

I would like to suggest that, in this, we are living within the Moon sphere. Living with us in this Moon sphere is everything associated with luciferic powers. And these luciferic powers, by moving through our center, through the organization of our head, are what enable the Sun to take part in our earthly existence. The luciferic penetrates throughout the whole of our head being. But it is as foreign to earthly existence as the sphere of the Moon itself. Our central nervous system is not organized by the same powers that give organization to our heart, lungs and stomach; and by the same token, the luciferic forces that exist in us are not given form by our earthly soul-spirit being. They are infused into us along with the elements of the Moon.

Very few people know anything more about the influence of these Moon elements in earthly life than what they hear from poets about magical moonlit nights, nighttime love affairs carried out by moonlight. We are familiar with the affinity of these fanciful outpourings for moonlight, which plays a large role in love life, if it is the higher form of love life—the romantic life. Yet this is but the faintest shadow of what comes to us from the Moon. The sphere of the Moon does not play into our everyday existence only through the fanciful things that occur between two lovers on magical moonlit nights. On the contrary, deep-seated forces play into our lives from the sphere of the Moon—forces that are removed from everyday life, from those things that human beings affix to the Earth, just as by and large amorous play on magical moonlit nights is removed from ordinary everyday life. And the most extreme thing that can play into our lives from out of this altogether foreign sphere is the power of illusion that human beings are capable of developing. If the forces of the Moon sphere were not in us, then as human beings we would not be capable of having illusions.

Without this capacity of having illusions, we would not be able to free ourselves from our life forces, from the organizational life of our physical organism, and we would not be able to ascend to that brilliancy of consciousness that we need as human beings. In order to reach that brilliancy of consciousness, it is necessary that we be able to live in mental pictures and imaginations that entirely disengage from our everyday organism. It is then our task to unify them with our everyday organism. It is up to us to not allow these illusions to tear themselves away from reality, but rather to relate them to that reality in the proper manner. In order to have concepts that have no relationship to our physical senses, we must be capable of generating these illusions. It is simply necessary that human beings be capable of having these illusions. And this ability to have illusions is also connected to our ability to do something other than languishing in a feverish or powerless state; it allows us to ascend to an illuminated consciousness. And if we let slip the reins sometimes, if we do not stay in control of our illusions, but instead allow them control over us, then this is simply a necessary side-effect of the fact that we absolutely must be capable of having these illusions.

So now I have, on the one hand, shown you the cosmic-human origins of our ability to generate illusions, and on the other hand, I directed your attention to one aspect of the world in which something we might call a natural necessity merges with something we might call an inner human activity—for the mechanistic manner in which people typically consider things in the world now, both of these things break down entirely.

Now for the other sphere. You will perhaps have noticed that I made a slight revision in what I had said, and since you are probably exceptionally attentive, you will no doubt have inwardly reproached me for the fact that I retouched my words in this manner. Namely, I first said: "Interwoven are the Earth-Sun sphere and the Moon sphere." Later, I spoke only of the Sun sphere. In one sense, I was right to do so. Everything that is at work in our central nervous system, including what comes toward us from the Earth, is always a product of the Sun. Even the illuminated surfaces of the objects in the world are only reflected sunlight. And thus, everything that plays a role in this sphere, including those things that are a part of the Earth (insofar as they are conveyed to our conscious life), is a product of the Sun.

But not everything. I could allow that statement to stand only up to this point. It is true to say that everything that you process in your consciousness is connected with the Sun sphere. But the fact that you will register as a certain weight when you step onto a scale—that fact comes from the Earth. In truth, however, the Sun sphere (which up until now I was able to describe as one unified sphere) is differentiated in its interior. The Earth is a kind of interpolation into this Earth-Sun sphere. And, in that this Earth is an interpolation into the Earth-Sun sphere, it is at work in what comes toward us from the Sun. Its presence in that sphere means that we are not purely Sun-beings. This point clearly shows that we must always remember to consider the cosmos not as a mechanistic object; we must see that it is ensouled and inspirited.

Because as human beings we are tied into the Earth-Sun sphere, we necessarily and naturally follow closely the true Earth forces in the unconscious forces working within us. In our conscious actions, we follow what the Sun sends to the Earth. But if we investigate (which is very difficult to do) what is connected with everything that causes us to weigh a certain amount when we stand on a scale, we find that it is not simply the gravity that Newton described—rather, it is also caused by everything that we experience as playing a role in our moral life. When it comes to the Sun, the poet was right when he said: "It shines on the good the same as the bad."[†] It makes no difference to the Sun.

But if you investigate the Earth by spiritual-scientific means, you will find that it does make a difference. The Earth is the outward expression of certain forces that want to lift themselves away from our collective planetary system. Just as the Moon wanted to sneak its way in, so does the Earth desire to make itself scarce.[†] The Earth forces want out; they want to be independent. We humans would not have a very particular and very important thing if we did not live under the influence of these Earth forces: We would not have any feeling of independence. If you were not pulled downward by Earth's gravity and were instead able to float about in the elements, you would never arrive at independence. Only because you are constantly being tugged at by the Earth (if I may use this expression, which is meant as the expression of a fact and not a theory)—through that constant attraction you develop your independence. And this is why the Earth is incorporated into the Earth-Sun sphere—in order to give us independence.

You can again raise an objection here, which in your feeling core you have probably already made: Is the same not true for animals? No, it is not the same. For the animal's head is held on a horizontal spine; the human head is situated with all of its weight over the rest of its physical organism. This makes a difference. This is what causes human beings to have a feeling of independence: the fact that human beings are positioned altogether differently from animals in relation to Earth- and Sun-forces.

The kinds of questions we are asking here can only be approached by asking after the alternative: What would we become if we were left only to the influence of the Earth, removed altogether from the Moon influence?! What would become of us if we were left only to the influence of the Sun?! If human beings were to be left only to the influence of the Sun, we would become a kind of angel, but we would be stupid. This is not to say that angels are stupid. On the contrary, they are brilliant; but we would become a kind of angel that was not brilliant as are the real angels—we would be stupid. For we would be lacking a feeling of independence. We would simply be limbs in the organism of the cosmos. We have our existence on Earth to thank for our independence. If, on the other hand, we were to be only under the influence of the Earth, if the Sun was not active in us, what would we be then?! Beasts, predators, creatures that evolved incredibly wild instincts.

Here is a point at which you can peer deeply into the constitution of the universe, because you will say to yourself: The things at work in the universe cannot all come from just this place or just that place. If all the things at work in the universe came from just one place, the result would be a radically extreme existence of one sort or another. If we were only under the influence of the Earth, then these Earth forces would engender in us incredibly wild instincts. The wild fires of our instincts would rage out of control. If this Earth influence were to have no part in our lives, on the other hand, then we would never become independent beings. We must have the potential of becoming wild animals in order to be able to become independent beings. In order to keep us from becoming wild animals, however, the Sun influence must counteract the Earth influence, must paralyze it. This is what happens. And because it happens in this way, you can catch a glimpse of the origin of evil. Evil and wickedness are simply facts of our Earth existence. We are left open to a kind of radical extreme—the Earth extreme—which, if it alone were allowed to influence us, would make us into wicked creatures, would fill us solely with illusions.

In the case of both wickedness and illusions, the Sun forces of the cosmos are at work in the world. These Sun forces make it possible for us to develop in such a way that we do not lapse into illusions. And these Sun forces also make it possible for us to develop in such a way that we do not lapse into a state of wickedness. The influence of illusion in the world makes it possible for us to become intelligent human beings. If everything enabling us to have illusions were not present in the world, then we would never become intelligent human beings. To express it in cosmic terms: If we were not creations of the Moon, if we were not on the one hand beings capable of having illusions, then we would on the other hand exist as beings incapable of intelligence. If we were not cast down onto the Earth and into the influence of its forces, we would never have the possibility of doing something evil or wicked; but at the same time, we would have no possibility of developing independence in our lives.

You can see that the human being must be able to have illusions in order to be intelligent. Humans have had illusions for a long time. Then came the advent of the human will, which was born into the constitution of the human soul only later in the course of history. At that point people became able to make these illusions into actions that came from the will; for the first time, human beings were capable of lying. For a lie, objectively speaking and separate from its relationship to human beings, is the same thing as an illusion. The only difference is that the person who tells a lie is willfully speaking something that does not originate in reality against the truth of what does exist in reality.

So, what works into human beings from the Moon sphere is simultaneously the creator, the creative being of our intelligence, and also what is enabling us to lie. In ancient times, people recognized this truth and established a proverb based on it. We Germans, when we see a Moon that looks like this ☽, say that the Moon *nimmt zu.* (we might amend the shape of the Moon a little to make it into a *z*) When we see a Moon that looks like this ☾, we say that the Moon *nimmt ab* (we might amend the shape of moon to make it into an *a*).[†] If you go back into the origins of the French language, into the lingering aftereffects of the Roman language, then you would say upon seeing the waning moon: *La lune décroît*—from *décroître*. In that case, the Moon does not describe its own behavior; on the contrary, it says the opposite.[†] The Moon only began to speak the truth to the German people.

For this reason, we have the Latin proverb: The Moon is a liar.[†] But this proverb also has esoteric truth, for the forces that come from the Moon are simultaneously the forces of human lying and deception, and this proverb, the Moon is a liar, has a very, very deep foundation, as you can now see. Only after civilization crossed over into the fifteenth century did the Moon begin to tell the truth to certain languages regarding its physical shape, as materialism also began to speak the truth regarding its physical appearance. But in regard to its inner being, the Moon is still a proper liar.

I tell you this for mnemonic purposes, so that you can remember this deep-seated cosmic-human truth. And you see, one of the best things that we humans have—independence—is inwardly connected with wickedness and evil. And the other—intelligence—is inwardly connected with our ability to have illusions, with the possibility of erring. We as human beings must be capable of development. We must have the possibility to not merely remain in one place. This capacity for development would not be possible if we were not called upon to build anew on the foundation of what has been destroyed. This means that we must bear within us the possibility of illness and death so that we can develop within ourselves the forces for building anew.

These extremely important truths have been completely white-washed by the worldviews of the last several centuries, completely buried by them. If something moves outside of the realm of mathematics and mechanics, it can be called science only when it deals with something that happens on the Earth. Outside of the Earth, only mathematically and mechanically comprehensible concepts are at work in existence. We must first come to understand again that altogether different forces are at work in the space through which the Moon moves and through which the stars follow their course—that they do not simply move in paths directed by impulses intelligible by mechanics. And when you realize that most everyday things are a product of the cosmos, that the most common everyday things cannot be understood unless we consider the human being as a product of the cosmos, then how can you intend to infuse with fruitful thoughts those contemporary worldviews that are supposed to inspire our lives?! Nowadays, human beings are forsaken by the world. They do not even begin to suspect their true connection with it. And they would like to establish themselves as social beings but do not even know with whom or with what, because they have not the slightest idea what they really are.

Yes, until certain questions infiltrate the human soul: How little do we actually know about the world under the influence of the last few centuries; how many things are we missing? Until these questions fill our beings, there is no hope for any kind of social striving. Where they are able to speak mechanically or mathematically, human beings nowadays are still willing to establish connections between certain phenomena. They know that a wide range of things are connected with the cycle of sunspots—epidemics and other such things on the Earth. There are still a few places where human beings on Earth desire some attachment to the experience of the cosmos. But people would prefer to deny that everything which occurs in earthly existence is an experience of the whole cosmos; they would like not to think about it. The things that happen among human beings on the Earth will never be understood if they are not understood cosmically. And we cannot come up with effective ideas for our work on Earth if we do not immerse these ideas in a conscious awareness of our connection with the cosmos.

If we only look at the way things actually play out in history, we are left with a bitter feeling. Were there a wall here with an assortment of shadows flitting back and forth across its surface, you would be able to see where the shadows were coming from. When you look at what has happened on the Earth in the last five or six years, you will not discover where these things come from, though they are also only projections, shadows of the things that are occurring in the whole of the cosmos. And the great questions that are at play nowadays between various regions of the Earth can only be understood when that understanding is filled with cosmic ideality.

I read an article[†] today that expressed hope that the statesmen of Great Britain will find the proper impulse to create peace and order between what is happening in Russia and what is happening in the Western countries. To this end, there was a desire to build up something in between the two—in the downward-spiraling Germany. These hopes will go unfulfilled, for everything that is spoken in this spirit, everything that depends upon the knowledge of those who are creating things out of the old—all of that will come to nothing.

The only thing that is fruitful for the future is what is created entirely out of the new. Once humanity wakes up enough to see the truth of this, it will mark the beginning of salvation from many harmful things in human evolution.

3

KNOWLEDGE OF THE HUMAN BEING
THROUGH KNOWLEDGE OF THE WORLD

DORNACH, JANUARY 11, 1920

THE lecture I offered yesterday contained some things that may seem far afield. Yet if we want to perceive truly the spiritual and social necessities of our time, we must familiarize ourselves with these sorts of concepts about the world. Our thinking and our sensations (indeed, our whole being) must be filled with the feelings that come from these concepts. I would like to briefly summarize the main thrust of yesterday's discussion. It is something that was already known to us in a more abstract way from other perspectives—that the substance of the human being is actually comprised of a twofold organization. We could even go so far as to say it is comprised of a threefold organization, but nowadays we factor in that third intermediary aspect to a far lesser extent.

First we have the organization of the human head and then we have the organization of the rest of the human organism, the limbs and the torso. For those of the present day who demand comfortable and familiar thoughts, this is rather difficult to understand, because people nowadays prefer to have everything neatly divided (and if there are gaps between the divisions, so much the better!). Thus, when one speaks of "the head" and "the rest of the body," people like to imagine it like so: the head goes from here down to the neck, and then everything else is just "the rest." This, of course, is not at all what we mean. In a certain sense, one could say that the entire human being is part of the central organization, the "head being;"

this aspect of our organism simply expresses itself most clearly in the area of the human head. Similarly, the torso and limb organization also extends into the entire human being—these aspects of our being simply express themselves most clearly in the torso and limbs, respectively. We have senses in all the different parts of our body; but we always think of our head, the central part of our organism, when we think of our senses, because the senses concentrated in that area of our physical body are the most highly developed.

From this, you will now understand what I meant earlier when I referred to the multifold organization of the human being. In addition, we saw yesterday that this organization is a necessity arising from some inner powers or circumstances in the human being, but that in fact the human being is also integrated into the cosmos, in one way through the head, and in another, different way through the torso and limbs. The head is the most highly developed part of our body, but actually it does not belong to the Earth and Sun spheres; instead, it is a part of the Moon sphere (this is shown not only by esoteric knowledge, but also by carefully observed embryology). The powers that are at work in our head are the powers of the Moon. And in our torso and limbs, the powers of the Earth and Sun are at work.

The entire course of human evolution on Earth is connected with this twofold nature of human existence. And now the moment has come when we must examine how we can take a step forward in this evolution, a step that is dependent upon how we came to be in a position to activate the physical structure of our human form. In the course of human evolution on Earth, the first thing that we find is everything that played itself out in human spirit and soul life prior to the Mystery of Golgotha. This was the great break in the whole course of human evolution. And if you take together everything that occurred up to the Mystery of Golgotha—the ancient Hebrew, the ancient Jewish cultures—then you will say to yourself: Everything that developed up to the Mystery of Golgotha had a necessarily unified character.

The ancient pagan cultures, which developed along the most varied paths in the wake of the Mystery of Antiquity (as I have described in my book *An Outline of Esoteric Science*), all had a unified character, in certain respects. What do I mean by this? The unified culture to which I am referring existed because humanity was in a primeval state; it existed because during this time period all across the world, primeval revelations came to various peoples simultaneously. But how could such a thing have happened—a primeval revelation occurring everywhere at once? It was possible because in these ancient times, the human center, the human head (if I may indeed refer to it as such), had not yet developed as highly as it has in our time, or, for that matter, as it had by the time of the Mystery of Golgotha. It was, in the sense that I discussed in my lecture yesterday, still very much "alive." It was still filled with the possibility of having dreams that had no relationship to earthly experiences or emotions. It was still able to call up the kinds of dream experiences that the human being (a human being possessing a much, much older consciousness than our own) had during Moon evolution.

This unified human character, this openness in the human head—those who created the primeval revelations used all of this to lead humanity to the place in evolution where it was to be when the Mystery of Golgotha occurred. The things that were revealed and that humanity was able to receive because of the structure of its organism at that time led in those ancient times to a general, all-encompassing wisdom (as opposed to what we know these days) that gradually faded as the years passed. We would not be satisfied these days with the kind of wisdom that they possessed, for it was composed of clairvoyant dream images. These days we want much more defined and clear mental pictures, but these defined, clear mental pictures have not gotten us very far.

An ancient wisdom once permeated all of humanity. Out of this wisdom, much was spoken about the essence that ruled over nature, the powers that controlled nature—but very little was spoken about human beings themselves. Humanity had not yet arrived at its Earth-consciousness. It was still being led by the tether of the higher powers. Humanity might have been wise, but the light of self-consciousness was not yet lit. The Apollonian percept: "Know thyself"† was held up before the people as a beacon to strive for but perhaps never reach, a cry shouted into the future by pioneering Greek spirits. There was a wisdom back then, one that dealt primarily with nature, and especially with the nature of the cosmos.

Then, into these people's lives came the old Hebrew revelation. When you meditate upon this ancient Hebrew revelation, you will find that there is something strange about it. It is entirely different from the ancient pagan revelations that had spread far and wide during the time in which the Hebrew revelation appeared. It was ashamed to participate in the natural, worldly wisdom of the time; it shrank back from it. As far as nature and the world were concerned, the old Hebrew revelation had only one thing to say: "God created them, along with human beings, and it is humanity's task in this world to serve God." The entire ancient Hebrew revelation intended to describe to people how they could best serve Yahweh.

What part of the human body was called upon in this ancient Hebrew revelation? What was not called upon was the part that had received the ancient pagan revelations: the central organism, the head, which could still call up memories of the ancient Moon evolution. When it came to the Hebrew revelation this part could not be called upon. Instead, an appeal had to be made to the rest of the bodily organism, the limbs and torso. But remember, I said yesterday that these other parts of the human organism can still understand and take up what comes from the Moon because they are creations of the Sun. And so, what comes from the Moon is what, in its most extreme form, leads people entirely into illusions and can also lead to inner revelations. This is the unique content of the Hebrew revelation. It is first and foremost concerned only with the human being. The human being stands at the center of this ancient Hebrew revelation.

But during the time prior to the Mystery of Golgotha, humanity had no self-consciousness, no knowledge of the individual human being. Therefore, this ancient Hebrew revelation traveled a path to humanity by way of something else—namely, by way of the Jewish culture, the Jewish people as a collective. The Jewish religion was initially not a religion of individual human beings. It centered not on individuals, but on the collective Hebrew people. It was a "folk religion." It spoke of human beings, but only by way of the collective folk.

By the time of the Mystery of Golgotha, two important things were present in the world: an ancient and fading pagan wisdom that centered on nature and the world, and human self-consciousness in the early form of folk-consciousness. Then, in the context of these things, the Mystery of Golgotha occurred. At the time, it could be understood only by the kinds of wisdom and knowledge already present in the world. We must be careful to distinguish the facts—what happened at the Mystery of Golgotha—from the means by which they could be understood, the means by which they could be felt. The pagans could understand it only with what remained of their natural, worldly wisdom. The Jews could understand it only with the knowledge that had come to them in their revelation. These were the ways in which the Mystery was initially understood. The vestiges of the pagan wisdom expressed itself in the Gnostic interpretations of the events at Golgotha. The awareness that came from the Jewish revelations developed progressively into the Catholic, that is to say the Roman Catholic, interpretation of the Mystery of Golgotha. And in order for the Mystery of Golgotha to be understood at all, it was necessary for the interpretations and understandings of it to travel by way of these two separate earthly streams.

Of course, in time, things developed further. People eventually lost their ability to understand the old pagan wisdom because it was already fading by the time of the Mystery and because it had originated so long before. They became too comfortable with other ideas to continue propagating Gnosticism into future generations. Only a very small part of the ancient pagan understanding of the world remained. This became one of the two streams.

Though the Jewish inheritance was much fresher and more intense, it contained none of the worldly wisdom of the pagans. It spoke only of human beings and of laws imposed upon those humans. It propagated itself in the church of the West. What was left of the ancient pagan wisdom, whose origins could no longer be remembered, remained behind as concepts that would eventually become natural science. Galileo,[†] Giordano Bruno,[†] and Copernicus[†] took up these final vestiges of the ancient pagan wisdom, using them as the seeds for new research into the nature of the world. No wonder, then, that eventually this became something altogether unsettling. Only the very last, abstract vestiges of the ancient pagan wisdom remained to be utilized in understanding the things that were received through the new medium of natural science. And no bridges were to be found between this wisdom and what human beings knew from their experience of the Jewish revelation.

Things moved forward in this way, and it is in this state that they continue to exist to this day. We have now a science that is working with only the very last shards of the last nuggets of ancient pagan wisdom, from which it can derive no means of understanding human beings at all. Consequently, this science reached its zenith in the eighteenth century, foregoing any actual understanding of the human being and choosing instead to understand what happens when you see a human being as the final result in a chain of animal evolution. Not to understand the human being, but rather to understand the most highly developed animal and call that a human being—this was the ideal of that science, working with the last broken shards of the final nuggets of pagan wisdom.

Everything associated with the Jewish revelation gradually lost the possibility of saying anything about the natural world in what it had to offer about the human being. Take a look at theology in the form into which it has now developed and see if you can find anything that would offer a satisfactory explanation for our modern consciousness of even the most simple natural phenomena. It is certainly true that moral considerations could be tacked onto natural phenomena from this tradition. But the moral claim that God sent an earthquake to Messina in order to punish the people there is not acceptable for modern consciousness; and the ability to build bridges between the work of the gods and the things that occur in the natural world has been lost to theology. For that reason, it is, in many respects, nothing more than an empty phrase now; whereas our natural science has in a very grandiose manner laid out a tremendous amount of material that contains countless secrets but can do nothing with them, for it lacks the concepts that would enable it to connect these things with one another. This division led eventually to the development of an altogether new form of consciousness, to the development of things like agnosticism, which claims an enlightened person is one who can assert:[†] Human beings are in no position to know anything of the true nature of things. Human beings are simply not organized in a way that allows them to understand anything about the true nature of things.

Such assertions are opposed to the deep longings and strivings that exist in us, and these longings must fight back against them. Our desire to know things about the world, the organization of our society—all these things rebel against such assertions. In the future we must come to see how we are to move forward, because at the moment, we are stuck in a very old time, hindered by our world conceptions and our ideas. What has Jewish revelation brought into the world? The most recognizable thing that it has brought into the world is the politics of nationalism. After exerting its influence on the Roman Empire, the politics of nationalism has wound its way through history into our own time period. And what are the most influential people in politics currently striving to do in the world? Stir up nationalism! But this is politics that comes from ancient Hebrew culture. In terms of our public life, we have not yet moved on to Christianity. We are still living in the Old Testament. And it is part of our mission in these times to move society toward and into Christianity. But this advancement cannot occur unless it is supported by a similar progression into Christianity in the scientific fields. For that, however, it is essential that we come to truly understand the human being.

Take a moment to reflect on my book *An Outline of Esoteric Science.* In that book, so much is said about cosmic evolution—about the evolution of Saturn, the Sun, the Moon, the Earth, and so on—that the "truly clever" people of our times will become either afraid or anxious, or be prompted to laugh or to become angry. If you consider the book's content more exactly, you will find that everything that is presented as knowledge about the world and the cosmos is simultaneously knowledge about the human being. In all of that knowledge about the world, there also exists knowledge about the human being. The things that human development owes to Saturn, the way that development continued from that point forward, and the way other forms of existence were incorporated into this process—all of this is considered. In the things presented there, you cannot separate knowledge about the world from knowledge about the human being.

But in these times, the union of worldly and human knowledge is a Christian demand in the sciences, just as it is a Christian demand in society, that when considering another person we learn to disregard all other associations and see the other only as a human being. The latter is something about which people have fantasized in empty phrases for a long time, but in reality we have never actually achieved it. In reality, national identity continues to exist as an overwhelming force in the political life of this world, and the human being is constantly subsumed under the consideration of national ties. What must come to replace these considerations of national identity are relationships between individuals built on a true feeling for what the human being is. But the founding of these relationships requires a certain inner strength of spirit, an inner strength of the human soul. And if we ask ourselves: "Did the human being grow stronger in soul during the so-called blessed nineteenth century?" If we ask ourselves this, we find (if we are honest and sincere) that no matter where we choose to look, the human being did not grow stronger, but rather weaker in terms of the intensity of its concepts and ideals. Those of you who know me will understand what is meant by this.

I would like to interrupt my lecture here with a personal anecdote. Several decades ago, I was having a conversation with a man in Vienna who since then has made quite a name for himself as a historian.† We were talking with one another about the development of Germany and the German people. The man articulated his abstract perspective on the matter as follows: "Well, Germany has developed and it is possible that it will just keep developing in the same matter that it has been." I said: "That is just an abstraction; it is not something taken from observations of reality. As far as I am concerned, it is the same thing as saying, 'Here is a plant; it has already produced fruit, and now it will produce new flowers, and then fruit, then flowers, and it will just continue like that forever.' If the plant has already produced flowers and fruit, it is not possible to say, 'It will just keep doing the same thing over and over again.' It is certainly true that the flower's seed could in turn produce something new—a whole new plant. But it is not possible to imagine that from the flower the old plant will again emerge in a new form that would continue in the way it had before."

I went on to say: "The substance, the essence of German existence came to fruit and flower in the time of Goethe, Schiller, Herder, and Hegel. That was a high point. That cannot simply be sustained and continued. Since then we have moved into a period of decadence, since then we have been declining." These were the ideas I expressed back then. I found little understanding, as you might imagine; for by then we had already moved into the time when such ideas were too intense for the human soul to grasp, and I was left to think about how different it must have been even as late as the middle of the nineteenth century. At that time in German development, there was a man who wrote a literary history; Gervinus[†] was his name. You might not like Gervinus very much, for his whole literary history has an extremely radical bent; namely, it ends with Goethe's death and then entreats the following generations to simply continue into the future by writing in the old literary style, as if it were possible for new flowers to grow out of the leaves of a plant. Back then, one could be so radical as to say: "It is all over now that Goethe is dead; if you want to continue to develop, you will have to look for somewhere new to start!" Gervinus was not able to offer all of this, but he at least saw the conclusion of the old and drew a sharp line under it.

It is certainly true that since that time a lot of beautiful poetry has been written in Germany, but it has all been in imitation of the greats. The essence that flowed in Herder, Goethe, and Schille flows no longer, nor does the philosophical essence, the essence that flowed in Hegel or Schelling, the essence that flowed in Fichte. Only once since then has a new tone been brought into the world, and that was when Hammerling,[†] later in his life, wrote *Homunculus*, but that also became a satire.

Even back then, the call for something new, for some true understanding of the beginning of an entirely new civilization, was already waiting at the door. This call for a new beginning needs now to permeate the entire world. For therein lies the only hope of salvation for the future of human evolution. Everything must be wiped out that does not further that evolution. You can clearly observe an outward indication of the kinds of things that need to be wiped out in the desperate way that old world conceptions are again being taken up nowadays. In order to say anything now, these old conceptions are called upon.

One of the leading minds of contemporary Central Europe[†] has made an assertion that clearly comes out of the decadent consciousness of these times and that clearly shows the sort of thing that we cannot keep to in this day and age. This man poses the question: How can we return to moral life? He observes that the need for an older form of morality has shown itself in the last five years. This lie has been victorious in all peoples and nations. The old Hebrew-Yahweh politics have taken such a strong hold on so many peoples, that they now would like to believe that long ago in Palestine there was only one united Jewish nation. And so now all peoples want for themselves the kind of political support that the Jews in Palestine were able to get for themselves back then. They would like everything to be as it was; they would like to govern the world in a way that excludes all the annoyances of Christianity.

The content is lacking. In these desires, people are clutching at things that actually are void of content. Instead of seeking new sources of morality in new, fruitful, spiritual worldviews, people ask: "What is to be the source of a new morality?" And then they answer: "Having power is an indispensable means for achieving something good in the world; therefore, you should strive to gain the power necessary (if you do not already possess it) for doing good." People would like to have something good to do in the world, and they beautifully advise one another to seek the power to do that good. A second justification for this new ethics is as follows: With the power that you already possess, you can do some good. Therefore, you should always use the power you have for the achievement of good.

But first you must have some good to do; first you must be able to recognize what is good! The advice that people give is the opposite of what spiritual science must spread throughout the new human civilization. For spiritual science has nothing to do with trying to found something on the basis of having power. You can only found something on the basis of power when you are working with a group of people collectively. When one human being stands before another, it is impossible to found anything on the basis of power; it is only possible to found something on the basis of the things that can develop in the human being, so that the other person has some worth. We all have a worth to discover and to develop within ourselves that will allow us to accomplish something for the sake of humanity; and each of us must simultaneously develop within ourselves a receptivity that allows us to recognize this worth in others.

This is the only possible means of forming a foundation for the morality of the future: to develop our own individual worth, and to become able to recognize that worth in others. To put this another way: all morality will have to be built on real trust! Because people did not want to move toward this perspective, they could not understand the moral demands found in my book, *The Philosophy of Freedom.*†
In that book, a so-called moral individualism was founded, built on the understanding that when everything that is to be developed in a human being is in fact developed, that individual has no need for external laws and is able to exert some influence on how people will behave when they interact with each other in daily life. At the time the book was published, I said to some people: "Look at what we do when we walk down the road—some on this side, some on the other. Do we need to have laws in order to avoid bumping into each other? The fact that some people walk on the left and others on the right is simply a demand of existence—a demand that people quite sensibly observe." This is what it means to conduct oneself morally—when the things that lie in the very essence of the human being are truly developed and brought into reality. Without this, there will be no moral code of the future.

This is also the only form of morality that would truly be built on a renewed understanding of Christianity. It must be built on what the Christ said: "Whatever you do for another human being, you do for me."† The Christ came into the midst of humanity so that every individual human being would be able to recognize the worth of all other human beings. And if the people of the world were to truly treat each other in this manner, it would provide a foundation for a new morality.

This would also mean that from our modern perspective we would come to a new understanding of the Mystery of Golgotha. This Mystery of Golgotha is a fact, an event. The teachings of the Mystery are not the most important things to come out of that event; for these teachings must change with every passing age. The most important thing to come out of that event is simply the fact that it happened. It is becoming increasingly clear that for the religious faiths of the present, the Mystery of Golgotha is greatly decreasing in significance. They see no value in understanding that event with the consciousness of this age; they see value only in continuing to spread and propagate their teachings. But these teachings are becoming increasingly unable to grasp the meaning of the Mystery of Golgotha. And the result is that now we have a new and strange variety of theology in the world, one in which people no longer speak about the Christ, but simply about the man Jesus of Nazareth—the "simple man"† who wandered about in Palestine like some kind of Socrates. As a result, people cannot understand why the few who do still speak about the Christ speak about him as the pivotal point in the entire development of humanity. It was in that moment that the questions now posed to present-day humanity were first so seriously set down. And it is precisely the seriousness, the gravity of those questions that must now be recognized. But they must be worked with in harmony with the sciences on the one hand, and with society on the other.

These matters are all interwoven. I am sure that it would seem incredibly peculiar to a present-day, traditionally-educated academic if you were to tell him that the field of botany must become "Christian." But it must become Christian, meaning that the spirit that so deeply moved humanity in its inner core must work its way into all things, including botany. And socially-minded people—but only a few of them, only a few groups of these socially-minded people—speak about the idea that Christian attitudes (it might be perhaps better to say "ancient Christian attitudes") must be incorporated into how we conduct ourselves in interactions with other human beings. Apart from this, no particular worth has been placed on infusing social ideas with Christian principles.

There is a third option for how we might come to understand these matters, but finding it would require that we learn both to find the Christ in the world and to ignite within ourselves the ability to understand the Christ once we have found him. In all aspects of our lives—in society as a whole as well as individual encounters—two things must work and develop in conjunction with one another: the first is a certain kind human worth, and the second is the ability to recognize and trust this human worth and to allow our recognition and trust of it to permeate the encounters that we have with other human beings.

Insofar as the people of the nineteenth century understood the presence of a new spiritual impulse toward understanding anew the Mystery of Golgotha, they spoke of "practical Christianity." At that point, Christianity had become about as unpractical as it could be. Now, in the wake of recent developments in human evolution, it is indeed necessary that as many people as possible find the energy to recognize that in fact a new spiritual revelation is attempting to enter the flow of human evolution and to see how this new revelation must be understood by humankind. For as long as we allow our spiritual lives to be pawns to exterior powers in the world (be they the state or some other external power), our spiritual lives will never be afforded the opportunity to take up the impulse of this spiritual revelation.

This is why it is necessary for our spiritual lives to be allowed to stand alone on their own two feet, as we are calling for in the idea of threefolding;[†] only then will our spiritual lives be allowed to develop according to their own impulses. It is out of these impulses that science will be saturated with spiritual methodology, and it is subsequently the spiritual methods in science that will ignite our ability to permeate the social life with spirit. In our social deeds, in this social life, we must teach people to realize and actualize the spiritual.

In order to do this, we must first overcome what we might nowadays call "word husks." For right now, we are living a spiritual life filled with word husks, with empty phrases. It is possible these days to hear a person speak very beautifully of things with a pleasing content and then, upon considering the speaker more closely, to find a soul that is void of any spiritual content. How can this be? Because these days, people all over the world are able string together these empty phrases into something. There is no need actually to have a connection with the things that buzz about, enclosed in word husks.

There is no other way to rediscover a connection with the spiritual but to seek out a guide that will truly enable the human soul to reach the spirit on its own. This guide can be found only when the one who seeks it does so with the understanding that the human being can become what it is meant to become in the world only when it does not remain in the realm of earthly things, physical senses and physical powers; when it develops something within itself that is able to move beyond the merely earthly, beyond those things that can be taken directly from the surrounding physical world. We are born into the world with certain aptitudes; these inborn aptitudes are then developed our schooling, but the driving impulses behind education are vestiges of the past, of older traditions. We must come to understand that in every human being there is a hidden seed that does not come from our material incarnation or from the impulses that lie behind our education and upbringing. We must hold the belief that in every human being alive today is something that can be awakened only by spiritual forces and by maintaining the conviction that these spiritual forces exist.

In the things that currently exist in our upbringing and our life, we can experience only the Yahweh-consciousness. The Christ-consciousness can be awakened when we believe not only in the evolution of humanity, but also in the transformation that will occur in human beings when they believe that something will develop in them that has nothing to do with the aptitudes and predispositions they received from their ancestors, but rather is a part of them because they each have lived through earlier incarnations in previous earthly periods. At one time, the principle of lineage predominated in human existence and outshone the things that were carried over from previous incarnations. Now inherited characteristics are less important, and those characteristics that we carry from previous soul incarnations, and not our blood, have become ever stronger.

This is something that we each can bring to consciousness. And when it truly lives in the consciousness of even one human being, that person will encounter others with a set of feelings entirely different from what is typical nowadays.

With these words, I have described to you (though perhaps haltingly, for they deal with a very broad topic) something we must incorporate into our evolution as human beings. When this demand is made on our lives, it is met with the harshest of judgments in the world. It is opposed bitterly. And I have had cause in the past to tell you about certain oppositions to what we refer to here as the anthroposophical worldview. I would like to tell you about two things of this sort today. Recently I read you a letter[†] by our friend Dr. Stein,[†] who illustrated in a manner refreshing to the heart the story of how a churchman was confronted when his assistant, in an attempt to account for a passage in the Bible that sounded somewhat anthroposophical, went so far as to claim: Even Christ makes mistakes. That is what he said! So not he, the churchman, is making a mistake, but rather Christ!

When I went to Stuttgart, I was told that from within our circle a number of opinions and complaints had been filed about this letter, about how harsh it is to confront an old man in such a manner, one who had even read some of my works. Unfortunately, this is actually so widespread in our circles, that in the very moment someone begins to get involved in making a serious point about something, that person is stabbed in the back by those who, it would seem, like nothing more than to support a factious or sectarian perspective. This is something that I feel I must mention.

The second thing I must tell you about is the slanderous remarks that have now made their way through the German press, remarks whose underhanded sources are well known to me (that in particular I would like to mention here), sources for whom the actual content makes no difference. For when it comes to the people who propagate such things, it is not a matter of whether they believe the things they are spreading; all that matters to them is to fabricate something that will discredit a person or movement that is uncomfortable to them. And so, despite the dim light in this hall,[†] I would like to read this "unenlightened" publication[†] that is currently making the rounds in some of the German press.

"The Theosophist Dr. Steiner as Henchman of the Entente. —The *Mannheimer Generalanzeiger* has received reports from Berlin that the Theosophist Dr. Rudolf Steiner, who has a following of several million people"—I want to make this expressly clear: this sentence, for those who find a means to peer into the deeper chambers of the present, is particularly argumentative, and when the time comes that such attacks are intensified even further, you will see why such attacks are spoken alongside these other slanderous things—"Steiner founded a league in support of the threefolding of the social organism, a league that was originally to be simply a religious-socialist collective, before coming into contact with the Bolshevists and Communists; it now practices a form of unusual and unsavory political agitation. The *Berliner Zeitung* learned the following from reports out of Dresden: According to authentic and irreproachable sources"—I would like to draw your attention to the tone here—"the Society for the Threefold Social Order[†] has found out the name of all those officials who were supposedly active in reactionary movements and are collecting material and testimonies about their actions against the rights of the people, which are then to be delivered to the Entente with the goal of extraditing these individuals. The verity of these accusations makes no difference whatsoever to Herr Steiner and his comrades, and that they are not afraid to make use of altogether false evidence is proven by a passage taken from a letter, which reads: Accusations of theft should be left out, because in those cases it is easier to prove that the accusation is false. Similarly, unbelievable accusations such as child murder should not be raised."

Now, that every sentence, every word is (forgive me for using this expression here) a stinking lie—that goes without saying. But these things are fabricated now, at the present moment. They indicate that the things coming out of the spiritual stream present among us are taken seriously enough that such vicious means are considered necessary to oppose them. You can rest assured: little sectarian movements, meaning those that are supposed to have only a small number of members, are not bombarded with these sorts of things. We can only hope—I said the same thing in an article I submitted[†] for a forthcoming issue of *Dreigliederung*—that fewer and fewer people will go on believing that by arguing against such things, they somehow benefit the people who are working within the cloudy sources that we are dealing with here. Those people are exceptionally uninterested in what someone might say in response; for they have no concern for actually touching upon the truth. They are only interested in fighting in this manner against everything that is supposed to move into humanity in the form of a new spirituality. They follow the powers by which they are possessed.

I have presented this example to you so that a feeling of the serious nature of these things might be called forth—a feeling that actually must be predominant for all those who feel any serious connection with the anthroposophically-oriented spiritual science offered here. It is difficult to find the words, which are not really there in the dried-out language of today, to awaken this sense of urgency in the soul. It is so very necessary! But our souls are often lamed or paralyzed. Those things that must fill and penetrate our souls, if we are not to fall into a period of all-out decadence, by and large do not enter into them. We cannot continue to act according to ancient wisdom. We should no longer call those things that we take out of ancient streams "ideals." We should always make ourselves increasingly aware of the fact that something entirely new must be erected in human evolution.

4

THE NECESSITY FOR THE DEVELOPMENT
OF NEW SOCIAL FORMS

DORNACH, JANUARY 16, 1920

I would like to speak once again today about the law of human evolution in the post-Atlantean period. The reason is that in the next few days I have several other considerations that I would like to connect with our consideration of this law. An understanding of the very significant demands of the present and the near future will not find a footing in our times if there is not first a penetrating understanding of the way in which humanity has arrived at this current moment in civilization's evolution.

Humanity has undergone a soul evolution since the time we refer to as the great catastrophe of Atlantis, an evolution that can be grasped only from a spiritual-scientific perspective. When we examine the period of time around this great catastrophe of Atlantis, we are not looking as far back into human existence as the contemporary science of this moment in human evolution tries to look. Rather, we are looking back only to the period of time that is referred to geologically as the Ice Age, a time in which, as outward science also acknowledges, great transformations occurred in the area that we now refer to as civilized Europe. We arrive at a time somewhere around eight or nine millennia prior to the Mystery of Golgotha, and we already refer to the first great cultural age that began in post-Atlantean civilization after the great catastrophe of Atlantis as the ancient Indian epoch.

It is important that we direct our gaze toward the fact that the conditions and qualities in the human soul in that ancient period of time were fundamentally and essentially different than they were later, namely, as they are in our cultural epoch. From a spiritual-scientific perspective, it is significant to examine this soul evolution that took place in humanity. Our outward physical evolution and also the evolution of material cultural institutions and relations can only be understand once you penetrate into an understanding of soul evolution.

If we now engage in a consideration of the two-thousand-year period beginning eight or nine millennia prior to the Mystery of Golgotha and moving into the ancient Indian epoch, we encounter a humanity that developed and evolved under entirely different conditions than ones with which we are familiar. In particular, we must keep in mind, as I have often said before, that contemporary human beings undergo a development in which the physical-corporeal development parallels the soul-spiritual development, but that this active parallel development occurs only during the first few decades of an individual's life. In the first decade of life, there is the important transformation that we refer to as the changing of teeth, which occurs around the seventh year—we can draw a parallel between this transformation and important soul-spiritual developments that occur at the same time. Then, a similar moment of parallel physical-corporeal and soul-spiritual development occurs with the coming of sexual maturity in the fourteenth or fifteenth year. For modern human beings, we can still see this kind of clear, active parallel development between physical-corporeal and soul-spiritual as we move into our twenties. It is less evident, less clearly visible than it was during the period of time around year seven and year fourteen, but for a careful observer it is still very perceptible.

This parallel between physical development and spiritual development was, during the ancient Indian epoch, active in human beings into the sixth decade of life, when individuals reached their fifties. The soul-spiritual part of the human being was dependent upon the physical-corporeal development in the manner I described earlier. At a much more advanced age, people experienced the kind of transformations that we experience with the changing of teeth and the coming of sexual maturity. As such, people truly *lived* with the life of the physical body up until the time that moved into the sixth decade of their life—their fifties.

And I have drawn your attention in the past to what this actually meant for human life. Let us say that you were a person around thirty years of age; as a thirty-year-old, you would say to yourself: "Someday I will be forty, then fifty, and at that time, purely through physical development, I will be entirely different than I am right now; I will have ripened in the world in an altogether new way." People looked at the process of aging in this way much later into their lives; nowadays, we look at aging this way only in regard to our lives as children. Back then, people continued to grow, to ripen in their lives even at a more advanced age. And they had the awareness: The older you get, the more things in the world become clear to you, the more, one might say, the Being of the world moves into your soul life from the unknown depths. People experienced much later in their lives the same kind of development that we now experience with the changing of teeth and the coming of sexual maturity.

This changed insofar as this active parallel between physical and spiritual development stopped at an ever earlier age. During the next cultural epoch—the ancient Persian epoch, as I called it in my book *An Outline of Esoteric Science*—it lasted only into one's early fifties or even late forties. And in the Egypto-Chaldean epoch, it lasted only into one's early forties. During the time in which the still significant Greco-Roman culture spread itself out over the world, people were developmentally active in this way only into their early thirties. People living in ancient Greece felt like young men and women into their early thirties. And they said to themselves that something grew parallel in them as they arrived at their early thirties. Nowadays, by the time we reach our early thirties we are already dried-out mummies, at least as regards our physical-corporeal development. Nowadays, we cease to have a true connection with our physical-corporeal development at a much younger age than people did in earlier epochs.

All of this is also connected with other aspects of human evolution. The first epoch after the fall of Atlantis—the ancient Indian epoch—was populated by people who lived their lives in connection with the universe, who specifically in the experiences of their head were intimately connected with the universe. Now all that we know about the universe is what can be discovered and learned in our observatories and through our telescopes—the things that can be reckoned by the astronomers. People living in the ancient Indian epoch felt the movement of the stars in their head. They not only experienced nature on Earth in the spring, summer, fall and winter, they experienced cosmic occurrences in themselves; they might experience in themselves the age (so to speak) of a particular Sirius constellation. Things that later were imaginatively reckoned by astrologers were truly experienced by those people in the same way that we now experience fullness after eating a large meal or hunger before eating. In their head, those people truly experienced the sunrise and sunset.

It follows from this that the people living during that time period did not think of themselves merely as creatures of the Earth, but rather as members of a more-than-earthly world that simply happened to be placed on Earth. They felt like wanderers on a pilgrimage that took them for a brief stretch on Earth. They felt a strong relationship to things that were not of this Earth.

By the time of the second post-Atlantean epoch, this had already changed. The life of the entire universe was experienced less, but more experience was connected to what we might refer to as the illuminated essence, the light being of the universe. People during the ancient Persian epoch experienced the daytime and the night-time very differently. Between falling asleep and waking up again, they felt truly present in the universe. This time was filled with a meaningful content for them, whereas nowadays we experience it as a gap in our lives. A form of connection with the universe was still present then. Taking this into consideration, we can rightly say: "Just as the endpoint of active physical-corporeal development in human life diminished over time from the late 50s to the late 20s, so did the living connection between people and the universe diminish in the course of human evolution."

To be more specific, we can say: "In the first post-Atlantean epoch, the ancient Indian epoch, physical development had active parallel connection with spiritual development up to age forty-eight or forty-nine to fifty-six. In the second, in the ancient Persian epoch, people experienced developmental moments in their physical-corporeal development that were comparable to our changing of teeth and reaching sexual maturity up to age forty-two to forty-nine. In the third epoch, which we typically refer to as the Egyptian-Chaldean epoch, people experienced such developmental moments up to age thirty-five to forty-two. And in the epoch we call the Greco-Roman epoch, the fourth post-Atlantean epoch, this development lasted until age twenty-eight to thirty-five."

I	Ancient Indian	49 – 56	8167 – 5567 B.C.
II	Ancient Persian	42 – 49	5567 – 2907 B.C.
III	Egyptian-Chaldean	35 – 42	2907 – 747 B.C.
IV	Greco-Roman	28 – 35	747 B.C. – 1413 A.D.
V	Present Epoch	21 – 28	1413 A.D. – . . .

When you consider this, you will say to yourself: "The active, parallel development of the human being is diminishing over the course of time." And along with this change in the longevity of active development, the doors are slowly closing that allow human beings to have a connection with cosmic experiences in the universe. If you would note—not take notes on, but simply note—that we can say: The first epoch lasted from 8167 to 5567 before Christ; the second from 5567 to 2907, approximately; the third from 2907 to 747 before Christ; the fourth (the Greco-Roman epoch) from 747 before the Mystery of Golgotha to 1413 after the Mystery of Golgotha; and then our epoch (the fifth) began—the time in which parallel human development occurs only up to age 21 to 28. This time began in 1413, and we are still living in the midst of it. And if we want to be very exact, we must say that modern-day human beings undergo a parallel development in their spiritual and physical bodies up to age twenty-seven. At that point, the soul-spiritual part of human beings begins to free itself from the physical-corporeal part during the daytime. This separation of spiritual and physical, this emancipation of the soul-spiritual, is thereby something that, over time, occurs at an ever younger age. You can see that one day the time will come when parallel spiritual-physical development will stop once a human being reaches age fourteen, a time when the developmental moment at which one reaches sexual maturity will cease to be an important part of human development.

That time will most certainly come. The geologists still insist on projecting such long epochs for the continued evolution of humanity on Earth, for the continued evolution of the physical human being on Earth; but this physical humanity on Earth will not develop any further than the moment in which this upper boundary on active spiritual-physical development sinks to the fourteenth or thirteenth year. For beyond this point, physical human beings on Earth cannot evolve or develop any more. Women will no longer bear children. It will be the end of physical human beings on the Earth. I have said before that the predictions and analyses that the vast majority of geographers make are all based on a particular mistake. By measuring the amount of silt that a river has cast on its banks or how much mud has gone over Niagara Falls, it is possible these days to make determinations about specific geological epochs and then "prove" that such and such a flora or fauna once dominated a particular region at a time many, many, many years in the past. This would be similar to taking a look at a human stomach and the changes it has undergone in the past ten years, and then using that information to determine what that stomach could have looked like one hundred and fifty years ago. Of course one can, just as the geologists determine what the Earth will look like millions of years from now, determine what that stomach looked like three hundred years ago. Except that the Earth will not be here millions of years from now, just as the physical human being whose stomach we were considering did not exist three hundred years ago. Using the physical laws that are the basis of these scientific works, you can of course do accurate and correct experiments and figuring, but your results will be as "correct" as the determination about how a stomach would have looked three hundred years ago.

What I am presenting to you will be rejected by modern, strictly physical science. But that is precisely why what is true, what is factual, cannot be discovered by such a strict science. You can make endless predictions about the way that the Earth will look in a hundred thousand years, about what people will be like then, but by that time, human beings will no longer have an existence on Earth!

These are the things that should have made us build bridges over to spiritual-scientific reports and work. That is the only way to gain true insights into human development and into certain necessary things that must be taken up in human consciousness. Now, it should be relatively easy for you to see that people living in previous epochs experienced certain revelations simply because of the fact that they had a physical-corporeal existence, revelations that can be experienced only by people whose parallel spiritual-physical development extends beyond a certain developmental point. The ancient Persians, and even the ancient Indians, had foreheads that remained soft and malleable well into their fifties—nowadays our foreheads are only that soft when we are very young. Because they had this softer forehead, these people were able to experience revelations; it is not possible for us to receive these revelations as a child—you can receive them only if your forehead remains soft into the later years of your life. Our own mummified foreheads, which are already hardened by the time we reach thirty, cannot allow these revelations to enter us through this old, natural pathway. This makes it necessary for us to seek a different means, a purely spiritual means, of allowing our emancipated soul-spiritual aspect to receive a living content.

At the same time, this also makes it absolutely necessary for us, in our current cultural epoch, to turn ourselves toward spiritual life. For at thirty-five years of age, a person has outgrown the ascending, upward-reaching half of life; from that point on it begins to descend again. All the things that can be achieved in that first, ascending half of life are not things that modern human beings achieve naturally, relying only upon themselves. If we do nothing to achieve these things by some other means than our purely physical development, we have no chance of reaching them. Such insights should allow you to understand just how necessary it is for modern human beings to turn toward spiritual science.

The external social structures that human beings have created up to this point necessarily stem from the influence of this older, more malleable physicality. But now we have reached an age where these old structures have become rotten and flimsy, and a new structure can only be created from out of the spirit. This fact is readily apparent these days, and you need only follow current events to observe it. In order to truly understand current events, however, we must understand them in connection with the spiritual world.

I want to talk to you about something that may seem very far removed from the theme that I have just been discussing. Several times in the past I have talked about the aged generals and statesmen who are writing their memoirs these days. Among these crowds of memoir writers there is a person who (compared to the others) is one of the best and most interesting of the philistines and cynics, a man who led the Austrian troops for some time—Czernin.[†] He is one of these memoir writers. I am not praising him when I say that he is one of the best of them; for in the same breath I must also call him a philistine and a cynic, a superficial man. But all the same, his memoirs must be counted among the most interesting.

In his memoirs there is an interesting passage in which he presents arguments about things that might have been able to lessen or to bypass this catastrophe of a world war. Speaking from the perspective of an Austrian, he says: "Austria has been destroyed, has collapsed because of this World War." But if the war had not happened, it would have collapsed anyway, for it was ripe for failure. It could not stand up any longer. It was decayed and flimsy at its core. He even writes somewhat dramatically, saying: "The time had come for us to collapse; we could only choose the means of our death. No other option was open to us—only how we would die. We chose the most terrible. Well, we could see nothing better to do. Perhaps some other way would have been slower, less painful." So writes Czenin.

At its most basic level, this is an entirely correct *apercu*, for Austria's structure as a state and nation was a creation of intentions and imaginations stemming from an earlier period of history. Even if those intentions had not, shall we say, grown consciously in the minds of the Austrians, they were still present on a luciferic level. Nowadays, people are seeing how this old structure is beginning to fail and die out. People will see this failure correctly only if they come to see the inner reasons, the temporal reasons for this dying out. But they are only able to see that something is wrong when the structure strikes against something and then catastrophically collapses. For a person who stands at the forefront of the times, it simply will not do to come with an assortment of new social ideas and just take over the old state structures, as if those structures can simply be taken and used. That is not possible. We have to accept the idea that this old concept of a state has ceased to make any sense and that something different must come to take its place: the Threefold Social Order. This Threefold Social Order will create its own states and border; the old ones have lost their ability to hold together.

But people today are all sleepers. They participate in these catastrophes as they are played out. To see the inner forces driving this existence and the changes taking place in it—that is something that people simply do not have the will to do. They could only decide to do it if they learn to truly understand the spiritual-scientific underpinnings of things. Then, through a true spiritual understanding of existence, the bridges will be built between an understanding of the purely natural and the social. For in the end both areas have their own laws, which also have something to do with one another. Only when you consider the times from this perspective will you arrive at insights into what is really happening these days. We must eventually decide to say to ourselves: "If we truly want to help further human evolution, we cannot allow ourselves to be content with the things that flow into us naturally from outside, for we are able to receive these things only until we are twenty-seven years old. After that, we become mummified in our physical body; after that, our soul-spiritual elements must take their powers from the spiritual world."

A person living nowadays who undergoes only the development that is brought naturally from outside, develops actively up to the age of twenty-seven. Now, you may also take the following to be true: If nowadays most people who then move into so-called higher positions in the world experience standard primary schooling or something similar to it, this ceiling on development will be raised somewhat above twenty-seven years old, because something flows into people from this history of older cultural epochs that carries them beyond this boundary.

If, however, a man were to grow up in the modern world as a truly "self-made man" and reach twenty-seven years old without immersing his "self-made" essence into what we refer to as traditional schooling or something similar to it, he might be so far along by that point that he would be already completely in the midst of things that are true for the present moment on Earth only, things that allow no possibility of further evolution or development, things that must come to an end in this present age. For if one is to have something in one's soul that empowers future evolution, that thing must come out of the spiritual world. So if this person were to reach twenty-seven years old educated only by his own humanity, by that which came to him through natural physical-corporeal development, then at twenty-seven he could be elected to Parliament. He would understand the present world entirely, and the present world would understand him. But though he might understand the world, and though the world might understand him, it would be entirely possible that evolution could be ended the day after he was elected by a catastrophic earthquake that would wipe out everything. For his soul would contain no energy, no fuel for an ongoing Earth evolution. Such a person—a self-made man who takes in all the things that we receive naturally these days and then closes up entirely at twenty-seven and goes on to become a member of parliament, or a minister, and so on—this is the characteristic expression of the modern world.

The prototypical man of this sort is Lloyd George.[†] He is absolutely the most characteristic product of these times. If you take a look at his biography, you will find that he has everything in him that a man can take solely from his natural physical-corporeal being prior to his twenty-seventh year. But because he so soundly rejects everything that did not flow to him during this natural development, everything that might be won from a connection to something spiritual, he can never mature beyond twenty-seven years old. In terms of the number of years he has been on Earth, he is certainly much older, but in reality he is only twenty-seven. And there are many people among us in the world who also do not mature beyond twenty-seven, because they do not take up anything from the spiritual world. The fact that one's hair turns grey or that one otherwise ages physically has nothing to do with what I am talking about. It is entirely possible to be no more than twenty-seven years old, even when one is an old man who has lived seventy years on Earth and who might be the prime minister of France and be named Clémenceau.[†]

This is the secret of human evolution—that growing old has nothing to do with keeping track of the number of years one has been alive. On the contrary—if you wish to truly grow older, you must go through a process that allows the spiritual element into your soul evolution. It is therefore no accident that Lloyd George was the one who was able to speak to the modern world in a dire moment. For in such a materialistic time as this modern age, the person who could speak to the world was a man who had, in the most characteristic, natural, typical way, reached twenty-seven years old and never moved beyond it. In fact, this was exactly how old he was when he became a member of parliament and so genially aided in the development of recent events. These days, you will not come to know the world by looking only at the images that swim on the surface of so-called civilization. You will come to know the world only when you truly see it from the inside out, in the way I have indicated.

We human beings have been given two different aspects for our development—the shell and the content. People in previous ages— the first, second, and third cultural epochs—were given the content of their development, or the spiritual aspect, along with the shell, or physical aspect. The beings of the upper hierarchies still lived in the physical shell. We develop in our bodies in the following manner: in our human form are the spirits of form, in our ether body the spirit of the times, in our astral bodies the angels of the earth, and in our "I" the angels themselves. But it goes no farther than this, for we must willfully and consciously climb to those places that people of previous times reached simply by virtue of what flowed to them through their physical development.

And one cannot learn to understand the moral development of humanity without paying heed to this. The people who write histories these days are like blind people writing about color. They only write empty phrases that have no actual content. From these empty, content-less phrases stem political platforms and social programs, even so-called Ideals that inspire people to want to affect this or that kind of change in society. It is impossible to do any work in society unless you are working out of the driving forces of human evolution. It is necessary to understand the times. But you can hope to build this understanding only on a spiritual foundation.

In world events, you can see just how strangely people view these modern times. In their attempts to move beyond the everyday into something larger, people now undertake the strangest things. For example, think back to several years ago, before the world war catastrophe, before people had any idea just how insignificant they would be for civilization, to when the countries of the world participated together in "Olympic games." Now, it is true—the Greeks had Olympic games long ago. But our cultural epoch is separated by many hundreds of years from these ancient Greeks. We no longer have the same physical or soul-spiritual make-up that the ancient Greeks had. We need to find something that is appropriate to our current physical and soul-spiritual make-up. We reveal the impotence of our spirit, our complete lack of true soul content, when we continue to endlessly rehash these old traditions. Olympic games were possible for people who continued to undergo active parallel physical and soul-spiritual development into their thirty-third year. To simply reinstate a practice that people did in the past is no different than a thirty-five-year-old man suddenly deciding that he will start acting like a fifteen-year-old boy. This ideal of the Olympic games is a comparable decision.

From our present moment onward, we must seek absolutely after that inner understanding of the world based on the spiritual foundations of human evolution. For even the old connections out of which people have worked for so many years have become fragile and uncertain. A snail shell continues to last even after the snail has died. The old states nowadays hold onto their pieces of this world like old snail shells created by snails long dead, shells created by completely different imaginations. But it is necessary now for new social structures to evolve out of the renewed imaginative life of human beings. The great death of the old social structures that began in the East and has already taken hold in Central Europe will continue to spread! But this would be positive if it were properly understood, and if people were to think less about how to reinstate the old regimes and instead turn their attention to the true relationships that exist in the present, and from these true relationships to give form to the new social structures I have spoken of.

Looking at it more broadly, we must say to ourselves: "Spiritual science demands an understanding of our soul aspect that is less comfortable than the one to which we have grown accustomed." People nowadays are completely unaware of the driving forces behind the evolution and development in the midst of which they are standing. I found it interesting to see how a member of our society responded in the latest issue of *Dreigliederung*† to the style of *Kernpunkte der sozialen Frage*.† All sorts of nonsense has been written about the style of that book—that it is too difficult to understand, full of overly complicated sentences, and so on. It is a good thing that at least one person has pointed out that this book is after all a call for complete human renewal, and that it is not intended to be a sleeping aid for those who are looking for a comfortable book to read.

These days people conflate the most contradictory things, even in the moments when they believe their arguments foolproof. You can go out and talk with the so-called masses and you will find that they all demand that things be easy-to-read, accessible to all. You will find that perhaps the most demanding people in this regard are those who believe their spirits to be the most free. These people would find a more elevated style boring.

Where does this demand for accessibility, for ease of understanding come from? If these people thought about it for a moment, they might be quick to retract such judgments (which they have made so often). For the accessibility that so many free-spirited, church-hating people demand in the style of texts they read is nothing less than an aspect of that style that certain members of the clergy sought to use as a means of keeping people as dumb as possible. In their Sunday afternoon sermons, they presented only things that were "crystal clear" to the people attending church, things that were crystal clear even to the people who slept with their eyes open while they listened to the sermon. Sitting in the very back of the church there is always the little old mother who sleeps through the sermon and who, when asked about it, responds: "Well, what else is left to people in this world if we cannot have a little time to sleep at church!"

This sleepy state is closely related to the populist style that everyone demands nowadays. Both come about because of a desire to take away the ability for a certain free and living thought development in the intended audience. Precisely what people grew accustomed to hearing in the Sunday sermon is the same as what the church-hating Social democrats are demanding as a populist style. This is the connection. The people today who find the style of *Kernpunkte* difficult would roundly reject any suggestion that they were people of the church, yet the fact that they find the text so difficult can be traced back to the "crystal clear" style of Sunday afternoon church sermons. This is also something that people have to confront through spiritual science: to look directly at events and experiences in complete freedom. People tend to become the most confused when it comes to the things that govern human evolution.

Above all else, the future of human evolution will require a tremendous amount of energy in our soul lives. And this is precisely why we live in such a different time. Last Sunday, while an "Egyptian darkness"[†] descended upon us in this hall, I informed you all[†] about some of the recent attempts to attack our spiritual science. It is not uncommon, however, for someone within our circle to fixate in their thinking on such an occurrence and not be able to forgive it. We must speak out strongly against this; for these kinds of slanderous attacks[†] against anthroposophically-oriented spiritual science and the things it sees as important in society are only just beginning. Every time someone from our circle encounters one of these slanderers, we must insist the slanderer be treated as kindly as possible, whether old or young, man or woman. We must say that anyone who slanders will also be treated with the utmost kindness within our circle; when it comes to people who spread such things in the world, we must try to befriend them! This is the only thing that can be done in these times! Anyone who understands this moment in history should be able to see this clearly.

There is no reason to argue with people who spread slanderous stories everywhere. Instead, it is up to us to characterize and describe these people to the rest of the world; it is important that we not do anything harmfully or malicious to them, that we not act as though trying to compete or measure up to them, and that we make clear to other people such kinds of individuals are out there in the world. This is what is important right now! For we are standing before a crucial moment in human evolution, and all of this finger-pointing is the very worst thing that can happen in the service of humanity. It is much more comfortable to point fingers than it is to have a clear understanding of what is truly important right now, of what is truly at stake.

Above all we must be clear about the fact that a true understanding of our task in society can only be found in the spirit. But in saying that, there are naturally many other things that must be achieved along the way. On the one hand, there is our science, which is in need of a complete renewal. We can do nothing further with modern science. We must give ourselves the possibility of truly penetrating into the spiritual aspect of the natural world. We must allow ourselves the possibility of understanding natural science, medicine, and biology in general from a spiritual perspective; with the things that we would learn by opening up this possibility, we could truly develop fruitful thoughts about society and social questions. Otherwise, we will go on trying to create something new with old terms and old forms. But this is precisely what is leading us ever closer to our downfall. Humanity must ascend from these depths; but it must do so through a process of spiritual renewal. And anyone who does not resolve to look at the Old and be able to regard it truly as the Old will not be able to aid in the forward progress of humanity.

I have made this point to you in many different ways.† Today, I wanted to draw your attention to the fact (which I have also said often in the past†) that humanity is growing progressively younger in connection with the age of our lifetimes. The people of the ancient Indian epoch grew until fifty years old, then the ancient Persians aged into their forties, the Egypto-Chaldeans into their late thirties, the ancient Greeks into their early thirties. We never reach that age in the same way. We continue to trot along, but we do not truly age if we do not invigorate ourselves inwardly with the spirit. For to become older in those ancient epochs meant simultaneously to develop in your physical-corporeal form and to become wiser. Modern human beings, as they age, simply get older and do not grow wiser. They become mummies. People truly age only when they fill those mummies inwardly. The Egyptians mummified their dead. Modern day human beings have no need to be mummified, for they wander about as mummies during their lifetime and only avoid being mummies when the spirit is taken up in the living present. Then the mummies are vivified. This is absolutely necessary for humanity at present—that these mummies come to life.

Otherwise we will continue to have organizations in the world in which a wide variety of odd sounds are made by the mummies that comprise them. We call these organizations "political parties." But the sounds that come from the mummified people will gradually become purely ahrimanic voices, and it was those voices that caused the catastrophe of the last several years. This is the shadow side of the matter; this is the deadly serious part of it. If people in the present do not start to fill their mummified shells with spiritual content, they will be filled with the whispering voices of Ahriman. Then human beings will continue to walk the Earth, but the voices that speak from within them will be ahrimanic demons. We can only hinder their growing presence on the Earth by resolving to seek out a living connection to the spiritual world. Yes, this all has a very, very serious side. A striving after spiritual science in this day and age is simultaneously a striving to drive the ahrimanic spirits out of humanity, a drive to keep those ahrimanic spirits from possessing humankind.

5

INITIATION SCIENCE IN THE LIGHT
OF MODERN THINKING

DORNACH, JANUARY 17, 1920

YESTERDAY I attempted to describe to you the current moment in human evolution. I attempted to show you that the forward progress of human evolution is at present entirely dependent upon what we might call initiation science. In other words, it will be necessary first that all branches of knowledge in human culture be filled through and through with this initiation science; but secondly, it will be necessary that all of our social thoughts and feelings be also filled through and through with the feelings and empathetic thoughts that result from the consciousness of this fact: There exists a spiritual revelation, a supersensory revelation—we need only to turn ourselves toward it.

You might be persuaded by the countless number of people who come forward and say: "Yes, but history nowadays is studied quite precisely, and the things that spiritual science has to say about the character of the present moment in time and the way in which it has developed out of the prior ages is not spoken of in the mainstream study of history."

These things are not spoken of in generally accepted history because that history, uninfluenced by true spiritual knowledge, does not ask after the true impulses and forces of history. In order to know what is actually speaking through history, you must first come to understand how to ask after it in the proper manner.

Now, the important thing to understand is that the first three consecutive post-Atlantean epochs—the ancient Indian, the ancient

Persian, and the Egypto-Chaldean—were such that (using the terms that I spoke of yesterday) in each of them humanity grew ever younger than it was in the prior epoch. In other words, in the second epoch, human beings did not remain developmentally active into the same advanced age that they had in the (prior) first epoch (and it continues like this into the third, and so on). In the Greco-Roman epoch— meaning that time beginning in the eighth century before Christ and lasting until the fifteenth century—it was the case that human beings remained developmentally active into their early thirties. As this epoch drew to a close in the fifteenth century, human beings were very clearly developmentally active up to their twenty-eighth year. Nowadays, as we emphasized yesterday, the period of active development ends in our twenty-seventh year, and the end of the period is coming increasingly sooner in the life of each human being.

Now, we as human beings are only able to arrive at a relationship with the spiritual world through the medium of our physical-bodily constitution once we reach our thirties. Please do not misunderstand me here! We can, of course, by turning to spiritual science, also arrive at this relationship with the spiritual world at an earlier age; but if we as humans are to receive from the universe our own spiritual powers connected with our physical-bodily organism, this can only occur if we remain developmentally active into our thirties. Nowadays, we do not. For this reason, there is no sense in talking about the continued progress of human evolution through purely natural means. Evolution can take a step forward only when humanity is fructified by initiation science.

Now, in one of my previous lectures I have already mentioned to you[†] about the initiates in the countries of our Western civilization, especially the Anglo-American initiates. But the peculiar thing about these initiates is that from their perspective, they have it in mind to bring forth as initiation science only those things that will eventually help the English-Americans move into a position of world dominance. As strange as this sounds, it is the case. And we can accurately say: Every single claim that emerges from this side of the world will bear an imprint of this fact, which the skillful observer will perceive. More than anything else, all of these things give some indication of the variety of ways in which initiation science is handled in the Western world.

You will have noticed by now that some limited aspects of initiation truths are not being held back here. And when you look back through the things that have been presented to you in the lectures given over the course of the years, you will find in them (if you were truly awake to follow these things), a whole line of important initiation truths that are intended not just for a portion of humanity, but that are intended rather to bring the whole of humankind out of its current state of crisis and carry it toward a next step in its evolution. But, among the Western initiates in particular, you will find many people who take issue with the fact that so much of what I say here is presented to the public. This is connected with a skewed understanding of initiation science. In order to make this skewed understanding clear to you, I must present to you the following.

Initiation science always centers absolutely on the individual human beings. Even when it speaks of a group of people, it is still in reality centered on the individual. True initiation science cannot be brought forward by the same methods previously used to influence people. The Catholic Church, for example, continues to utilize this old method of influencing people at present, and not only the Catholic Church—certain political parties also make use of the same methods. This method of influence takes advantage of, if I may say it thus, the psyche of the masses; it appeals to something that inculcates a collective body of people with something in a, shall we say, hypnotizing way. You know, of course, that when you are making use of this method, it is easier, as a rule, to instill something into a group of people than into an individual to whom you yourself speak. There is some truth to this idea of mass hypnosis.

This manner of communicating, which is certainly effective, can be of no use to true initiation science. Initiation science must speak to each individual person and appeal to that individual's powers of conviction. The way of speaking that must be used by the initiation science standing at the helm of human evolution did not exist until now. This is the reason that, for example, my manner of speaking in my lectures and in my books is considered atrocious by many people, because in this speech, the rule of appealing only to an individual's own powers of conviction is strictly obeyed.

This points simultaneously to an important social principle that I have already mentioned in connection with other things in the past few days, and that you can find systematically and principally laid out in my book *The Philosophy of Freedom.*[†] If we desire to appeal to individual persons with ethical, with moral impulses, then we cannot simultaneously desire to organize our society on general abstractions; we cannot bring together groups of people like a herd of animals in order to give them some sort of general directive. Rather, we can only turn to the individual human being and wait—as every individual standing within the whole desires the Good, so will the Good come to fruition in the whole.

The social morality of the future cannot be founded on anything other than this principle of general human relations. When I published my book *The Philosophy of Freedom*, an article appeared in *The Athenaeum*[†] (for example), in which it was said that such a perspective will lead only to a kind of theoretical anarchy. It will lead to this kind of anarchy only if people do not succeed in making themselves into true human beings, if they are instead content with being sub-humans, coming together under the banner of such perspectives like a pack of animals. Lions are brought together by virtue of their physical form, as are hyenas, as are dogs; but the direction of human evolution is toward a time in the future when human beings do not organize like pack animals according to blood ties or organizational ideals, a time when the cooperation of human beings comes out of the powers of each individual.

A few days ago, I made use of a comparison[†] that may sound somewhat strange, but which I believe can illuminate this entire matter clearly. I do not know whether there are really people out there who feel somehow liberated when everywhere they see signs that read: "By decree of such and such an agency: All those who are moving forward must stand aside for those moving in the other direction." Even in highly populated cities people generally manage quite well when they encounter each other on the street—they simply pass each other by. Their human reason, those things that exist as impulses within them, keep them from simply running into one another. This is the ideal toward which humanity is striving. That we do not recognize this is our great misfortune. It is important for each of us to bear within ourselves the directives for our actions, even in regard to much more important matters, in such a way that others can rely upon us, even though no collective law regulating our actions to allow others to exist safely in our vicinity—a law that makes us all into sub-humans—be specifically addressed to each situation.

This work toward individuality—this is now connected with the most important impulses of human evolution. We will never be able to bring human individuality to this necessary place if we are able to transmit to it only the things that contemporary natural science or contemporary sociology or contemporary social motivations construct for us. Humanity will arrive at the kind of individuality that I have just described only when a collection of thoughts is awakened within it that comes out of initiation science. Through a relationship to the supersensory world humanity will be filled with such thoughts—thoughts that will make each of us into a free individual human being simultaneously able to be effective within the social order, and to do so in the greatest possible freedom. Everything depends upon human beings opening their hearts and minds to what comes out of initiation science.

Deep trust—this must become the most important social motive of the future. We must be able to build upon each other. Otherwise things will not move forward. This—what I have just said—will seem to someone who seriously takes the whole of humanity into consideration and who is sufficiently initiated in supersensory things to be self-evident enough to state: "Either this will occur or humanity will fall into the abyss. There is no third path."

You might reply that you cannot imagine a way in which a social order could be founded upon general trust. The only answer to this is: "Fine, if you are not able to imagine that, then you must instead imagine that humanity will have to fall away into oblivion. These are serious matters now, and they must be taken as such."

In a certain abstract way, the initiates of the Western countries also know this to be true. They alone say the following: "We have brought initiation science to a certain level and we can make it known to the public." But the initiation science that they will bring to the public will be one that leads toward the goals that I mentioned earlier. Now, we are touching upon an area here that is equally applicable to true initiation science as to a one-sided initiation science. Thus, the initiates of the Western nations could say: "We have knowledge of initiation science, we can bring it to the public, but this knowledge is such that it can only be directed toward the individual human being."

This is where the great concern, the terrible fear, arises for these people. They say: "Well, if we only speak to the individual human being in the future, then we will incite the War of All Against All, for then there will be no organization among human beings; then everything will be built only upon general trust, then people will find themselves in the midst of the War of All Against All." This is the fear that people experience. For that reason, these initiates desire to keep this most important of initiation truths, shall we say, locked away in a dark cellar, and allow humankind to wander toward the future in apparent illumination, though they remain asleep.

These things are important issues at present and have been ever since the middle of the nineteenth century when materialism reached its pinnacle in modern civilization and people had to begin asking: "How far will we go with initiation science?" To this day, they have not dared to bring a true initiation science out into the public from the few small circles in which it resides.

Now, a particular kind of development in education and upbringing that humanity has undergone should not be allowed to be dismantled, but thanks to an altogether ill-conceived theology this dismantling has already begun. You can follow this educational development when you study true history and not that *fable convenue* that people commonly refer to as history nowadays. Nowadays, people do not actually have any idea about the way in which something that they refer to with specific words has changed over the course of time. People talk about Catholicism, about Emperors, about aristocracy, about citizenship, and they believe that these words meant more or less the same thing in the fourteenth century, with perhaps only a few small nuances of difference in meaning. For as long as people are not clear that what was meant by "Catholicism," "Emperors," "citizenship," and "aristocracy" in the fourteenth century is not at all the same as what we mean when we says those words today, they will not truly understand history. We must be clear about the way in which the constitution of the human soul has greatly changed in the course of only a few centuries.

So what was the foundation for everything in the general upbringing and education of human beings that influenced the consciousness of the souls in the civilized world up until the fifteenth century (and in its lingering aftereffects, until much later than that)? All of it was based on the fact that human beings were in a position during those centuries to take up the supersensory world in their imaginative life; not in the manner in which we must now take it up, through spiritual science, but rather through certain atavistic conditions of human consciousness that were still present. A foundational fact filled the human soul. It was the foundational fact that was connected to the Mystery of Golgotha. People knew, in a way that befitted that time: The Christ-being came down out of the super-earthly heights, incarnated into the human being Jesus of Nazareth, and at the Mystery of Golgotha something occurred that could not have occurred according to commonly accepted, naturally verifiable laws. People had, in the concepts and mental pictures created by the Mystery of Golgotha, such ideas, such mental pictures, which they spread out over the surface of the Earth.

With these sorts of mental pictures, entirely different thought forms can be achieved than those that the everyday person now possesses. The thoughts that human beings come up with nowadays do not begin to approach the life of the supersensory world. Those human beings with a connection to the Mystery of Golgotha like the one I just described were able to call forth thought forms that had a reality in the supersensory realm. Therefore, we can also describe the present moment in the following manner: Humanity has over time lost its ability to create thought forms that have any meaning in the supersensory realm.

In this state, it is impossible to create any sort of social order that will carry the Earth forward. For that reason, all the social ideas that have been brought into humanity since roughly the sixteenth century have a character that can be described as follows: We encounter social directives in the thought forms of the modern era; such social directives exist only to be broken, meaning that they will run their course for a certain period of time and then will break down; they lack the inner strength for ongoing development.

This is precisely the secret of recent evolution. People willingly work with all sorts of social laws built upon the foundation of a worldview that emerged in the sixteenth century; all of these social directives, from the moment of their inception, bear within them the seed of death because they are not connected with thoughts that have any reality in the supersensory world. For as long as there are people in the present who do not recognize this, there can be no talk of taking a social step forward. It is not a matter of conveying social ideas in an abstract manner, perhaps out of some sort of spiritual hocus-pocus. This is not at all the point. In my *Kernpunkten der sozialen Fragen* you will not find a long chapter on spiritual science from which I then deduce social laws. Rather, I try to draw attention to things in reality that point toward what must occur. It is not a matter of deducing social life from spiritual hocus-pocus. Rather, it is a matter of each individual filling themselves with thoughts that are rooted in the supersensory. This kind of fulfillment makes it such that everything that an individual thinks has a reality in that supersensory world.

To put it paradoxically (but altogether truthfully as well), we can imagine a man—let us say a "statesman" (a word that nowadays we always say with quotation marks around it)—is saying all sorts of clever things—the sorts of things that people consider clever nowadays—but has never established any sort of connection with the supersensory world. If these things were to be brought into reality, they would always bear within them the seed of their own demise. Then another man speaks. If you did not know already that he was connected with spiritual science, then you would not necessarily notice from the things he says; he would simply speak somewhat differently about the same matters. From what he says about social questions, for example, you would not necessarily realize that he worked with spiritual science, but the fact that he does work with spiritual science gives his ideas a true impulse.

And so it is important nowadays that we not allow ourselves to be satisfied with abstract logic—we must speak realities. We are already in the midst of a period of human evolution in which (for example) a journalist might write the most beautiful things and astound people with them, and they would say: "Yes, when I read that, I see that it is incredibly pure spiritual science!" This is not what is important! It is not about the sound of the words that we say; what is important is the foundation of soul from which such words comes. It is all about what human beings carry within themselves as actual substance!

If I were to make the same comparison in an entirely different way, then I would draw upon the example that I have used often in the past:[†] There are poets today who have a relatively easy time writing poetry and compose beautiful verses that astound us. However, this is also true: Ninety-nine percent of the poetry written today is worthless. There are others whose verses sound as though they were written with a stutter; but these stammering, awkward verses might actually stream forth from a genuine fount of humanity—which is to say a genuine spiritual fount—whereas those that astound and amaze us because our language now is so developed that every door in it can open out onto something astounding and amazing, those verses might actually be collections of worthless word husks.

It is therefore necessary that we look past the words to the motive behind them. That is to say, we must not simply deal with the abstract, not simply read for the sound of the words, but rather place ourselves fully in the midst of life, and from that place within life judge the phenomena around us. And this is why it is important that spiritual science, as it is spoken of here, must come to fruition in all of the various branches of life. Otherwise, what must enter human evolution will not.

When two people talk with one another, they understand each other through language. But that language was, a relatively short time ago, something altogether different than it is today. When you understand something through language nowadays, you essentially become a slave to that language. In an earlier time, people learned a lot through the genius of language, and they actually did not think very much for themselves—they allowed language to think for them. This only lasted for so long, until the beginning of the time period that I described to you yesterday.

Now, we will move forward only when we are able to emancipate ourselves from language in our thoughts and feelings. Nowadays language essentially runs as though it were a machine in whose midst we are standing. In place of our human forces and being, Ahriman is becoming increasingly more present in the developing life of our language. It is now Ahriman who speaks when people do. As a result, we must become more and more used to taking our understanding from something other than the words themselves. We must stand deeper in the midst of life in order to understand each other now—deeper than people did during an age when the things human beings exchanged with one another were still born on the wings of language. That same exchange is no longer carried by those wings. Nowadays, it is fundamentally possible for someone to be altogether empty of any sort of true knowledge. But because language—contemporary, civilized language—has over time developed sentence structures, types of sentences, and even whole theories that lie entirely within language itself, that person would need only to slightly rearrange what is already there and will suddenly have created something seemingly new, when in actuality nothing more has been done than shuffle around the things that already existed.

You could easily conduct the following experiment, though it may sound strange. Take a look at the pronouncements of good bourgeois, materialistically-minded (in one way or another) professors, philosophers, natural scientists, and others of that kind—take a look at what these people said during the last century, in the second half of the nineteenth century, and you will find that it only requires a slight mental exercise to arrive at the following. Let us take, shall we say, some sort of paper by a particularly honest philosopher, an honest university philosopher from the second half of the nineteenth century, who expressed his opinion about one social matter or another. You could then take out certain key words and replace them with a few different key terms that appear in another sentence. You could mix the whole thing up just a little bit, and suddenly you would end up with the personal philosophy of Herr Trotsky!† If you want to come up with a personal philosophy like that of Herr Trotsky, you do not need to think for yourself—you simply need to allow language to do the thinking for you in the manner that I described earlier. But what is truly at work here are not human forces, because in a certain sense language has already emancipated itself from them—at work here are ahrimanic forces in human culture.

What I have said just now is something you can experience for yourself. You need only to open your inner soul eyes to such things. For those who do not work with words, but rather with thoughts—for them, present-day language is an altogether dreadful instrument. Nowadays, writing is not easy for those who work with thoughts. When you try to write down a sentence, it does not communicate what you want it to, because so many other people have written similar sentences. The sentence will always try to form itself from out of the collective human psyche, but you must first become the enemy of this if you want to record what rests within your soul in the form of a sentence on the page. Those who have an impact on the public and feel this enmity toward language are always in danger of surrendering their thoughts to language and coming up with beautiful programs with it.

The necessary task of forging a true place for thoughts in the world must nowadays begin in a battle with language. Nothing is more dangerous than allowing yourself always to be carried by language, meaning that you say: "And here is how you express this thing, here is how you express that one." Insofar as a stereotype for expression is present, insofar as people say, "There is only one way to express this," we cast ourselves into the common stream of language and do not work with the original thoughts lying behind it.

Our schools are terrible in this regard. Teachers in our schools who correct, according to conventional standards, every seemingly unformed but actually independent thought regularly commit gross atrocities. We should be seeking out every one of those unformed but substantially individual sentences that a school child puts down on paper. We should incorporate these thoughts into our conversations and lectures and absolutely should not swoop in with that detestable red ink and replace what comes out of youthful individuality with conventions. For nowadays the most important thing is that we look to what comes out of youthful individuality. Perhaps it will come toward us packaged in a manner that is not always comfortable, in a form that we might easily see as full of errors. If you were to read the letters that Goethe wrote as a youth with the eye of an elementary school teacher, then you would find a lot of things that needed correcting! The Austrian poet Robert Hammerling received the worst possible grade in the section on "German composition" on his final examinations! And there is still something true about what Hebbel[†] wrote in his diary—I have mentioned it often in the past: He wanted to write a drama in which a teacher of older children had a student in his class who was the reincarnated Plato.[†] The teacher would read Plato's works with his class, and the teacher would find that this "reincarnated Plato" did not understand the first thing about the texts by Plato that they were reading! Friedrich Hebbel came up with this idea for a drama, which was never brought to fruition. Nevertheless, there is some truth to the idea.

Now, we must be clear that anytime human beings are led astray by luciferic and ahrimanic forces, they are resisting the normal forward movement of humanity. Today we find ourselves at a moment when it is profoundly necessary to seek something new from the spiritual life in order to rescue humanity. It is no wonder that people are struggling very strongly with all possible forms of logical fallacies and immoralities. And because of this, I have always had to include considerations of the present moment when I speak *pro domo*, as a kind of add-on to our other considerations.

About eight days ago, I told you about the slanderous and base things that are currently making the rounds through the German newspapers[†], things whose sources are familiar, which are directed against what streams out from anthroposophically-oriented spiritual science and what it has to say about social life. But there is a particular reason that this has occurred that I would like to point out today in order to describe this matter to you more exactly. To that end, I would first like to draw your attention again to what has happened.

What has happened is that suddenly a slanderous article was published in a string of German newspapers that is well summarized in the following sentences. I have read these to you before.[†] However, let us once again place them before our souls, for it is worth it to do so in order that we might better understand the characteristics of this particular slice of our present culture:

> Rudolf Steiner as Political Informant—The famous Theosophist charlatan Dr. Rudolf Steiner, who has a following of several million people, founded a league in the spring of 1919 in support of the threefolding of the social organism, a league that was originally to be simply a religious-socialist collective before coming into contact with the Bolshevists and Communists; it now practices a form of unusual and unsavory political agitation. We have received the following reports from Dresden: According to authentic and irreproachable sources" (—please pay attention to that phrase: "according to authentic and irreproachable sources"!—) "the Society for the Threefold Social Order has found out the names of all those officials who were supposedly active in reactionary movements and is collecting material and testimonies about their actions against the rights of the people, which are then to be delivered to the Entente with the goal of extraditing these individuals. The *verity* of these accusations makes no difference whatsoever to Herr Steiner and his comrades, and that they are not afraid to make use of altogether false evidence is proven by a passage from a letter, which reads: Accusations of theft should be left out, because in those cases it is easier to prove that the accusation is false. Similarly, unbelievable accusations such as child murder should not be raised.

Now, this slanderous and altogether false article has been printed word for word in a string of German newspapers! There are many things in it that are astounding, but let me take out just one fact to start with. There is mention of letters that have supposedly been written and that are now being held up as authentic documents. In the most recent issue of *Dreigliederung*,[†] which has not yet been distributed, I have made expressly clear that I am familiar with the sources out of which these things originate. For the moment, however, I would like to read for you a little document, from which you learn the nature of the so-called authentic basis on which stand the people who disseminate such things into the world.

After this whole flood of spitefulness had run its course, after I had also received confirmation from various places about the murky sources of this vulgarity (which I would have known regardless), I received the following letter from a friend.[†] I have only just received this letter, but it was written—please take careful note of this—*before* the newspaper articles were published. In other words, the things that this letter contains were set down before those articles appeared. Please keep this fact in mind. The letter reads:

> A long-standing member of our anthroposophical society, who is apparently still an active officer, was given access to the two letters currently being circulated within the administration and quite understandably causing quite a stir. These letters bear the inscription: to IRD or R in Berlin, and are therefore probably addressed to the same place, though whether they originate from the same place or different places is unknown, for there is no signature. In the first letter, the talk is of Steiner's league and the Freemasons, and it states that in the near future, Steiner's league will be distributing pamphlets made to appear as though they came from the Monarchists, though the actual intention will be to make the Monarchists and the Anti-Semitic movement look ridiculous. In other words: Steiner's league will attempt to fight against the Monarchists by posing as them. These pamphlets are supposedly printed already, and a signature written in a different hand has been arranged for each region.

So you can see, there is a factory somewhere where they make fake letters! These letters are actually circulating out there. It goes on to say:

In the second letter, the following recommendation was made: "Since there are still a number of Monarchist-friendly officers in the armies, it will be absolutely necessary to depose them from their positions, and this should be done in the following shameless manner. Among the members of the army who served under these officers during the campaigns, people should be sought out who would swear under oath that these officers committed a large number of outrageous moral turpitudes." At the same time, it was mentioned that these transgressions must be believable, and that for this reason things such as rape and child murder should not be made as accusations. This list of sins and transgressions would then be transmitted to the Entente through a certain Herr Grelling†—this is the only name used in any of the letters—"and the Entente would then demand the immediate dismissal of the officers named."

The person mentioned in this letter saw both of these fake documents with his own eyes.

So this is the letter named in the newspaper article, the letter that was widely circulated (there were probably numerous copies) and bore the inscription: To such and such a place in Berlin! First these letters were forged, fabricated, and then a newspaper article was written about them. This is the way in which they are attacking us!

I would like to know whether more things are needed in order to make it really understandable just how necessary it is to wake up! A moral footing for humanity has emerged from everything that has happened in the last few years, though it is rooted in the impossibilities that preceded it and bear blossoms such as these.

It is important that we not continue to sleep, but rather come to recognize the mire in which we are stuck. It might be all too easy, if we do not speak strongly about these matters, for other people, even those among our own ranks, to say: "Should we not simply write to the nice men who fabricated these letters and then wrote false articles based upon them, in order to try to come to terms with them?" We need to open our eyes and see the kinds of people that live side-by-side with us in the world; you will only get yourself dirty if you try to seriously engage with them. We cannot go on being asleep to things—that must be said over and over again. We must look at the connections between them. Do you believe that it should go unpunished, that (for example) in the Jesuit journals[†] in which the false claims were made that I have mentioned to you in the past,[†] that in those journals for years the fairy tale was told that I am a failed priest,[†] simply because it was then taken back with the words: That was something we heard but "that cannot be substantiated"? Do you believe that it would be right to say to this Jesuit priest:[†] Well, now you have taken back the lies that you spread? No, the right thing to say to them is: "You have violated your duty in the most irresponsible manner by spreading a rumor in the world without proof, and your retraction is entirely meaningless." Those who still understand something about morality must take it very seriously. We have heard nothing but lies in the past five years, and we are still living in the aftereffects of those lies. It is essential that we fix our gaze upon these matters seriously.

By way of this example, you can clearly see how things stand. When karma does not bring these sorts of things so close to home for everyone and therefore the experience of an individual does not become the deciding factor for the collective, then there will always be people who would prefer to make an attempt to compromise, to treat individuals such as Ferriére[†] (for example) as human beings with whom we try to work on this or that, when in reality such individuals are among the lowest of humanity in that they unscrupulously write and publish things for which they have no proof. Such things are, for those who want to stand on a firm and healthy foundation, simply no longer permissible.

If I did not have such a ready example that proved it was true, people might not be so quick to believe that there are factories for fabricating documents these days—documents which "they" then use to publicly treat people in the way demonstrated by this newspaper article.

But this sort of thing happens constantly nowadays, and the majority of the things that you read are based on nothing more than the fruits of these moral quagmires. Anyone who possesses a healthy, serious, and honest perspective on the world will recognize this and conduct themselves accordingly. It is no longer permissible for us to compromise with people who work in such a slanderous and false manner. It does not justify it to say: "One must act benevolently toward all people." Love for all people! To have love for such people demonstrates an obvious lack of love for those who have been slandered, those who have been wronged. It is a matter of knowing where to give your love. The act of loving transgressions can never lead to health for humanity. That such things must sometimes occur—that can be foreseen. But we can only foresee the way in which certain sides will choose to work with it when it does occur. You need only to open up the Jesuit literature that has been sent out since the church's decision regarding anthroposophical texts in July of 1919.[†] You need only to look the people in the eye who have written these things and examine what sort of access to reality they truly possess. Having done that, you will recognize everything that eventually leads into these sorts of moral quagmires. I will not discuss all of these murky sources today, which are very familiar to me; because of my familiarity with them I also know how all of these things are connected with each other, and that this is just the beginning.

My only hope is that very few (as few as possible) will be naïve enough to believe that anything can be solved by responding to or opposing such things. These people are not interested in whether they are claiming this or that; they only care about making a juicy claim that debases others. The content of their claims are of no consequence to them.

But we must not only look to the fact that countless people are at work in these ways among us in the world. We must also look to the fact that for decades we, the general public, out of laziness and dormancy, have exhibited a great tolerance for these practices, a desire simply to not examine how public opinion is generated nowadays. This, however, is the most important way in which we might better ourselves. If we do not deal with men like the Jesuit Zimmermann[†] or the university professor Dessoir[†] in the manner I have described, no healing can take place. The people who do not stand over and against them and do not confront them properly are guiltier than they them-selves. For this is simply how these individuals do business, even if it is rather unseemly, like the actions of Professor Dessoir.

I described that to you a short time ago.[†] But now it is impor-tant for us to finally wake up. There is a direct path between one of Dessoir's books[†] or one of Zimmermann's critiques and those moral quagmires that I have described to you. I must mention these to you as well for no other reason but to point out the symptoms of those forces that are currently working to suppress any striving after the spirit. And to that end, I would like to mention here that I was just given an article, ostensibly intended for the *Brockhaus Conversational Encyclopedia,*[†] for which that infamous man Dessoir (infamous only to us!) was to write the entry on Anthroposophy; at the same moment in which he had me write this article through a middleman,[†] he meanwhile wrote his article for that book, that sham of a book. But now think about what could happen—this article now exists here in our in-house archive! Later, it will be found there and people might think it is an article that originated with me. And consequently, somebody might then be able to say: "Yes, this article in the archive was copied by Steiner from Dessoir's entry in the encyclopedia, and then Steiner claimed it as his own!" These are the kinds of flowers that will blossom if we do not stay awake at all times! Something can be plagiarized and then rearranged in such a way that the person who originally wrote the piece will appear to be the thief, and the one who actually plagiarized will appear to be the author!

The question of morality must be tackled from a variety of sides and perspectives, but will not be taken on in a fruitful manner by anyone who does not stand firmly on the grounding of a healthy spiritual science. This is the addendum to today's lecture that I wanted also to share with you, taken out of a consideration of this historical moment.

6

CONDITIONS FOR UNDERSTANDING SUPERSENSIBLE EXPERIENCES

DORNACH, JANUARY 18, 1920

In the Future it will be impossible for human beings to arrive at any true understanding of themselves, or even any true feeling for their true being, unless they first establish a relationship to initiation science; for all of the things that human beings are able to experience in the world without having any relationship to initiation science do not contain any of the powers from which their beings are actually formed. In order to understand the picture that I am offering, you need only to think of some things that are already familiar to you from our anthroposophical reports. You need only to think about the fact that in addition to the life that human beings experience between birth and death, every human being also experiences another kind of life between death and a new birth. Just as we have experiences here on Earth through the workings of our physical-corporeal being, we also have experiences between death and a new birth, and these experiences are absolutely not insignificant for what we are doing here as we live out our lives on Earth.

Furthermore, these experiences between death and a new birth also have a not insignificant effect on everything that happens on Earth in general. Indeed only a portion (and it is actually a rather small portion) of the things that happen on Earth are caused by those who are living in physical-corporeal bodies. The dead are constantly at work in our physical world. And the powers that people living in this materialistic age will not even mention aloud—they are indeed there.

It is not only the powers of the upper hierarchies that reach out from the spiritual world and have a hand in the physical world; rather, there are also powers integrated into all that surrounds us and affects us streaming out from dead human beings. As such, a full understanding of human life can be achieved only if you take into account both the things that can be experienced with and learned from the senses and what can be learned from history here on Earth.

In the end, these powers that stream from the spiritual world are the one and only thing that will make it possible to understand all of humanity and the entire course of human evolution on Earth. A time will come in Earth evolution—it will be sometime around the year 5700 or so—when human beings (if they have followed the proper course of their evolution) will no longer walk about on the Earth incarnated in a physical body that is a product of physical parents. I have often pointed out that at that time in history, women will no longer be able to bear children. Human children will no longer be "born" in the current sense of the word, if the course of human evolution follows its natural course on Earth.

We must not give in to any misunderstanding about such a fact. It is also possible, for example, that the following would occur. The ahrimanic forces, which have grown very strong under the influence of current human impulses, could lead Earth evolution astray; they could, in a certain sense, pervert the natural course of Earth evolution. If this were to happen, then by the late sixth millennium (to the detriment of humanity) human beings could continue to maintain the same kind of physical existence and life. They would, by that time, have become much more like animals than human beings; but they would be able to maintain the same kind of physical existence. This is one of the things that the ahrimanic forces are striving to do—to disrupt the normal course of human evolution by binding humanity to the Earth longer than it should be.

But if humanity understood the best possibilities that awaited it in the course of its development, then in the sixth millennium it would simply move into a relationship with the earthly that would continue for another two and a half millennia, a relationship in which human beings still maintained a connection with the Earth, but a connection that no longer involved giving birth to physical children. The human being would be primarily a soul-spiritual being—to describe it more vividly, human beings would become a part of the clouds, the rain, the thunder and lightning. They would resonate through and in the phenomena of the natural world; and in a still later period, their relationship to the earthly would become even more spiritual than that.

It is only possible to talk about these matters if one has some concept of what occurs between death and a new birth. Although there is not an exact parallel between the way in which modern human beings are connected to the Earth between death and a new birth and the way in which they will be connected to it when they are no longer physically incarnated, there is some similarity between the two. If we follow the true sense of human evolution, then in time we will eventually come to relate to the Earth and its phenomena in a manner that is more or less similar to the way in which we now relate to it between each death and each new birth. The only difference is that our current lives between death and rebirth are somewhat more, shall we say, spiritual than the relationship that we will eventually come to have with the Earth.

But no understanding of these things can be achieved for a long time unless one turns to initiation science. Most people these days believe that achieving some understanding of the nature of existence by means of initiation science involves collecting spiritual experiences, but not in the same manner that those experiences were once given to us through our physical body. The experiences won by purely spiritual means are valued more highly today than the insights that can be achieved through healthy human understanding. This prejudice results from the fact that this healthy human understanding is not made use of in any sort of healthy manner these days. Everything that an initiate is able to ascertain and then communicate to others could also be discovered, if you were simply to give it the proper amount of effort, through a precise application of everyday healthy human understanding. And the most important task of an initiate is, above all, to translate everything that he or she ascertains about the spiritual world into the language of healthy human understanding. Much more depends on whether this translation into the language of human understanding is done properly than on whether one is able to have experiences of the spiritual world.

Of course, it is impossible to bring anything to the attention of human understanding unless one has these experiences. But the raw, unprocessed experiences that have been won but not interpreted through the lens of healthy human understanding are worthless, and have no actual or positive meaning for human life. If people condemn the application of healthy human understanding to these supersensory experiences, then it does not matter how many of them are collected, because they will be of no use to humanity's future development. On the contrary, these experiences will do humanity considerable harm, because a supersensory experience is useful only when it has been translated into the language of healthy human experience. And the truly unhealthy thing about this period of time is not that human beings are not having supersensory experiences. People could have plenty of those experiences if they wanted to; they are out there. People are simply not using their healthy human understanding to arrive at them. The thing that is missing these days is precisely the application and use of this healthy human understanding.

This is, of course, quite uncomfortable to hear in an age when people pride themselves especially on having and using this kind of healthy human understanding. But our greatest weakness in this present moment is not connected with our ability to have supersensory experiences; our greatest weakness is actually our lack of healthy logic, of truly healthy thinking, which in the end is also the power of truth. In the moment that falsehood asserts itself in the world, supersensory experiences fade away; in that moment, people lose their ability to understand supersensory experiences. People do not want to believe this. But it is the truth. The first thing that you must do, if you hope to come to terms with the supersensory world, is to scrutinize your sensory experiences with the most meticulous honesty and truth. Anyone who does not treat sensory experiences with this kind of exactness will never arrive at a true experience of the supersensory world. You can listen to as much as you want about the supersensory world, but all that you hear will be nothing more than empty words if you do not process everything that comes toward you in the world with the meticulous eye for truth.

But, observing human beings these days and the way that they avoid the truths of the sensory world will leave you with a rather dreary picture; for most people these days do not process something that they experience in such a way that their formulation of it reflects what they actually experienced. Instead, in reflecting on and forming their own picture of their experiences, they turn them into something that they would have wanted to experience, into something that is comfortable. People have no idea that they are experiencing impulses that cause them to veer in one way or another away from a true understanding of their physical experience. If we turn away from the particulars of any one instance of this, we will come to see the many different impulses stemming from everyday human connections that cause people to manipulate the truth in one way or another. Stepping back from it even further, we will come to see that most people cannot tell the truth about certain things due to their commitment to national ties or something similar. People who are committed to the idea of nationalism in one way or another can neither tell nor think the truth, in the sense that we are speaking of truth today, when it comes to certain matters.

For this reason, almost no one has said anything true about the experiences of the last four or five years, because people everywhere have been speaking from the standpoint of this or that national interest. If one hopes to come nearer to the supersensory world, it is necessary to understand that an endless number of things are due to this fact. In an age where things such as what I characterized to you yesterday are possible—do you think that in such an age there are many open pathways to the truth? There are not. Those people who are stuck in swamps of falsehood—those people spread a smoke and fog that let nothing through, nothing that a healthy human under-standing should be able to take from supersensory truths. People are just as uninterested in understanding truly and clearly that a direct connection between human beings is necessary if these supersensory truths are to take hold in social life and society. It is not possible to twist the truth on the one hand and then intend to understand super-sensory phenomena on the other.

When you say these things out loud, they seem to be almost self-evident, but they are in fact not self-evident at all. Indeed, we all need to remind ourselves of them constantly. This is the only way that we will eventually arrive at what is needed now in connection with these things. Think about what I have been saying during our days together about the key principle of human society (something that must be taken very seriously): It must be grounded in trust, in the sense to which we have referred to it here. In many respects, this trust will also be necessary in the future, regarding our knowledge and understanding, in relation to the fact that those who are in a position to speak about initiation science are listened to neither with antipathy nor with sympathy nor through the filter of any sort of personal feelings; the things that they say must be considered only by healthy human understanding. By this means it will always be clear that the Anthroposophical Society should continue to be a genuine bearer of supersensory truths in this world. This will allow it to do an incredible amount of necessary and meaningful work in the course of human evolution.

Now we must also keep in mind that collecting experiences of the supersensory world is obviously a serious and important matter. I spoke to you some time ago about how a friend of our group, who was brought near to death by a wound he suffered during the world war, wrote down some lines[†] in which he describes that in the face of death, the air around him hardened, became like granite. When I spoke of this, I drew your attention to the fact that this was abso-lutely a true experience. If you consider the most elementary things that appear in reports about crossing the threshold into the spiritual world, you will be able to gain some sense of the seriousness of the matter.

As we go about our lives during the daytime, all of the things that are around us are illuminated by sunlight—and they are also illuminated during the nighttime, for that matter, since we have electric lights now. Things are visible to us by means of the light's illumination. In a similar fashion, our other senses also perceive the things that are around us. In the moment that one crosses the threshold into the spiritual world, one must then (if I limit myself to the example of sunlight with which I began) become inwardly united with the light. One cannot see things by way of the light, because the light must be drawn within. We can see something by way of the light only when the light remains outside of us. When we unite with the light inside ourselves, then we can no longer see the things that the light illuminates. It is in that moment, when our soul being unites itself with the light within, that we realize for the first time that actually our thinking is one with the light that weaves throughout the world.

The fact that our thinking is bound up with our physical body is true only for as long as we have a physical body. In the moment that we leave behind this body, our thinking is not without any foundation or other connection; rather, our thinking is interwoven with the light, our thinking lives in the light, is one with it. However, in the moment that this light takes on its connection with our thinking, we lose the possibility of having an "I" in the same, easy manner in which people have an "I" between birth and death. In that time between birth and death, we do not need to do anything in order to have an "I." Our bodies are formed in such a way that our being is reflected in them, and it is this reflected image of our being that we call our "I." It is an accurate reflection of our true "I," but it is a reflection all the same; it is simply an image reflected in a sort of mirror. It is an image-thought, a thought-image. And it dissipates in the moment that the threshold into oneness with the light is crossed. If we were not, in that moment, to find another framework for our "I," then we would have no "I" at all. This "I" has been worked on and prepared in our physical-corporeal body during the time between birth and death. It is lost in the moment that we leave behind our physical body, and we can continue to have an experience of our "I" only by becoming one with what we may call the planetary forces, particularly the different forms of the planets' gravitational forces. We must, in fact, become so unified with the planets, with the Earth, that we feel ourselves to be a limb or extension of the Earth, the way that one of our fingers senses that it is an extension of our organism. In this connection with the Earth, we find again the possibility of recognizing our "I."

Thus, we must say from the perspective of initiation science that human beings are alive with the forces of Earth and concern themselves with the affairs of the world, illuminated from within. For the experience of those beyond the threshold, this statement is comparable to the following statement describing our experience here: we live in our physical bodies and think about things; in our lives between birth and death it might be said that we live in our physical bodies and concern ourselves with things in our thinking. As soon as we leave behind our physical bodies, we must say: "We are alive in the forces of the Earth and concern ourselves with the affairs of the world, illuminated from within, living in the light."

When these things are spoken in this way, when they are illuminated as we have just done, then they are absolutely comprehensible for healthy human understanding, regardless of how a person might otherwise think about things. And even the initiates will gain nothing from their supersensory experiences if they do not properly develop this healthy sense of reason. When you think in such a way—please take note of what I am about to say, because it is quite a serious matter—that you are able to meet and fulfill every demand that is set before you today in school tests and exams, when you adopt patterns of thinking that allow you to pass with highest marks all of the tests that your professors give you, then your healthy human sense of reason has become so addlebrained that even if a million supersensory experiences were laid before you, you would see as little of them as you might see of the physical things in a darkened room. Those things that make us acceptable to our materialistic age are the things that darken the room in which we encounter the supersensory worlds.

People today are used to thinking in a way that is only appropriate for thinking about the physical world. They are trained to grow accustomed to this way of thinking from a very young age. But a healthy sense of reason is not something whose development is founded in the physical body. Its development is founded in a liberated spiritual state. But this liberated spiritual state is taken out of us in the earliest years of our schooling. Even in those early years, the teaching materials are such that they take away the ability to develop in this free spiritual state. What good will it do us, when these important truths about the time we live in are hidden entirely from us? People may not understand why we are undertaking the work of the Stuttgart Waldorf School. But this Waldorf school shall at the very least offer a small section of humanity the opportunity to escape the addlebrained nature of these times and to have a genuine possibility of moving freely about in their own thoughts. Unless we see these matters with an understanding of just how crucial they are, we will not be able to move forward.

The tendency today is toward the general and the unspecific, which you will see confirmed in the following. People are drawn toward Anthroposophy or something like it because they are tired of the typical, outdated forms. They want something new. But the new thing that comes along is still supposed, wherever and whenever possible, to wallow in the same swamp of all the old forms of human judgment. I have come to know many people—it is not advisable to beat around the bush when it comes to these matters—who have felt it to be true that anthroposophically-oriented spiritual science has something true to say about the Mystery of Golgotha. But in and among these people there are those who only believe this to be true because by declaring their belief in it they became less offensive to the church, people who consequently found this anthroposophical spiritual science a more opportune choice than some other form of spiritual science with a different relationship to Christianity. Now, all of these people believe in something that is the truth; but some of the people who have taken it up have not done so because it is true, but rather because they saw in it a good opportunity. Naturally it is quite uncomfortable that we must admit to ourselves that the representatives, and even more so that their followers, are taking up the truth, at least outwardly. It rubs off on the non-believers as well. This cultural-historical phenomenon must therefore be carefully considered.

If we want to draw closer to the spiritual world in the proper way, we must have an interest in all things, but must not be greedy in our curiosity about anything. It is, however, so easy for people to confuse interest with curiosity. In fact, we need not learn to think about things differently; rather we must learn to relate to them differently in our feelings. If in the end anthroposophically-oriented spiritual science receives a kind of cloak that allows it to play a role in tea parties and salons or other similar things in this day and age, it will do nothing to aid this spiritual science in the true fulfillment of its task. For its task is a genuinely serious one.

The oppositional forces that are asserting themselves in so vile a manner these days are simply products of the fact that people have noticed the following: The society here is not a sect, not a "familial society" that lots of people want to be a part of. Rather, it is something seeking to meet the impulses that our times so urgently need. But what do most people care about the impulses that our times need? If only they could feel the burning desire to have some part in a new religion! This egotism of soul that so many people impress upon anthroposophically-oriented spiritual science must be overcome. If we truly want to understand this spiritual science, we must have a genuine interest in the general affairs of humanity. We must take interest in these broader affairs. These broader concerns and connections will manifest in what appear to be the smallest phenomena of life. But the entire structure of our feeling life must be altered in a certain way if we hope to direct our healthy human reason so that it becomes a part of the correct stream of spiritual science.

Let me say that again: "It is necessary to alter the entire structure of our soul life in a particular manner if we hope to integrate our healthy sense of reason into the current that flows over humanity through anthroposophically-oriented spiritual science." But how is our sense of reason directed currently by modern culture, which is so mired in materialism?

It is oriented in a such way that we feel ourselves to be primarily physical-corporeal human beings. Here we are, standing with our knees and our muscles, with our nerves. We feel like a physical human being. And if we were to draw this, we would see that our body acts like a mirror that encounters our "I," like so:

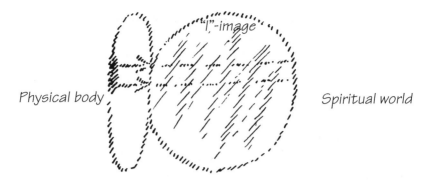

Yes—you see here that your true being exists somewhere in the spiritual regions. Over here is your physical body. Your physical body becomes a mirror and casts back a reflection of the "I." The "I" has an existence over here, but the image of that "I" is reflected back in your physical body. You are aware of this reflected "I" when you look over here [pointing to the physical body], look over here with other human beings from the place in which we all reside, even though most people nowadays are not aware of that place. And so, your "I" is reflected back to you by your physical body, as are your thoughts and feelings and will impulses. All of that is reflected back. And behind this reflected "I," there we find the physical body, and we humans call the images we see reflected before us our soul, and behind our soul we catch a glimpse of our physical body. We grasp at that physical body. But this mental picture: The physical body lying behind and the "I" emerging in front out of it—this mental picture must be drastically altered. This is an altogether passive depiction, for in it we only feel or experience thoughts because our physical bodies lie behind us.

We must learn to feel and think differently. We must learn to experience the following in our thoughts and feelings: We exist within a spiritual world; here are not plants or minerals or animals—here are angels and archangels and archai and the other beings of the hierarchies in which we live. And when an individual is filled through and through with, impregnated by these spiritual beings, the "I" then streams outward.

This "I" streams outward from the spiritual world. We must learn to feel this "I;" we must learn to feel that each of us has an "I" within us, behind which the beings of the hierarchies stand, just as the physical body composed of the three kingdoms of the natural world stands behind this "I," which is only a reflected image. We must move out of a passive experience into one that is fully active. We must learn to feel: I create my true "I" from out of the spiritual world. Then we will also learn to feel: The reflected image of my "I" is given to me through my body, which belongs to the realm of physical Being.

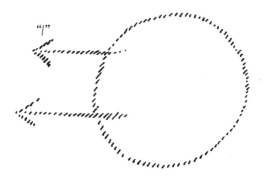

This is a reversal of what we might sense inwardly, and we must learn to settle into this reversal of that inner sense. This is what is important—not collecting data. There will be plenty of data to collect once we have first come to experience this reversal of our inner sense. Then, when we think in this active way, thoughts will come to us that will be able also to fructify our social thinking. If we experience only our reflected "I," then we will always arrive at a consideration of social thoughts originating, as I said yesterday, in a simple rearrangement of our preexisting language. Only when we desire to be active in our true "I" will we achieve truly free thinking.

This free thinking still existed in humanity in earlier centuries—not so long ago, really—due to the continued existence of certain atavistic soul conditions. Purely out of instinct, people considered it to be an ideal to achieve this kind of free thinking. We must accomplish the same thing consciously in the future. There is visible evidence of this need. Take a look at the doctoral diploma currently issued at Central European universities. People typically are not simply awarded a doctorate—rather they are promoted to the rank of "Doctor" and "Master of the Seven Liberal Arts"—arithmetic, logic, rhetoric, and so on. These titles have no meaning any longer, for nowhere in the modern university will you find these seven liberal arts. This is a carry-over, a vestige from an older time in which freeness in thinking, the development of a soul life that could raise itself up to free thinking, was what people sought in university life. People no longer have any understanding of what "liberal arts" are. The reason they are referred to as "arts," is because the striving after them took place outside of a sphere that could be perceived purely by the physical senses, in the same way that one developed the artistic life of imagination and fantasy, free and independent from sense perception. What is referred to in these university diplomas did at one time exist, just as many other things that we still find in the outward form of university life also existed. This *Magister artium liberalium*† is a very characteristic thing of this modern age.

And consequently, we must be clear about the fact that this kind of self-understanding must again be stirred to life and activity. But it is not comfortable, for people nowadays would prefer to get around on crutches, and not on their own two legs. In any case, this is what they tout as their ideals; they would prefer that all of their thoughts be taken out of physical, sense-perceptible reality. The idea that what must actually be thought must live in the free world of the spirit is something that people find uncomfortable, since it truly demands a separation from the comforts of life, a separation from everything that carries us through our soul lives as supports, as crutches. And if anyone speaks their perspective with thoughts that have absolutely nothing to do with the sensory world and were created out of totally free intuition, then people have no understanding of what is said. This is why my book *The Philosophy of Freedom*† was not understood, because it can only be grasped by a person who truly desires to develop free thinking, one who is truly a Master of Liberal Arts in an altogether new way.

These are the things that must be understood with the proper feeling and the proper sense of seriousness. In particular, I would like to say to our English friends, who are here with us only for a short time: It is important to regard the emblem of this building [the Goetheanum], built here upon this hill, as a physical symbol. This building is to stand here so that by the fact of its existence in the world, we might be able to say: "You all may prefer to think in the old ways, to which you for centuries in your sciences have been accustomed to think, and in doing so you will lead humanity to its downfall. In the manner you find comfortable, you might seek a crutch in socialism, but in doing so you will validate those things in you that contain the seeds of death and downfall." Today it is necessary to discover free thinking for the soul life—a thinking as free as the architectural, sculptural, and artistic forms out of which we have attempted to build this building. That this truth might be spoken somewhere on the Earth, not only through words, but also through forms—this is what we are trying to do here! And we should all feel that here, through these forms, something different is being spoken, something that cannot be heard anywhere else in the world; we should all feel also that what is being said here belongs to something incredibly essential in all branches of scientific and social life for the continued evolution of humanity, regarding both its knowledge and its society.

Now, I would like to say the following primarily for the benefit of our English friends (though naturally I am speaking to everyone else as well): You will see that the possibility exists—the possibility that the intent that was present at the outset of constructing this building might be lost over time, that in the future, in the very near future, this intent might no longer be present in the form that I have just described. What would happen then? This building would remain incomplete, for it still requires a great amount of sacrifice. Without that great sacrifice, it cannot be finished. This building will remain unfinished; it will stand here as a torso without limbs or head. This could be the case—that this building has to remain here as nothing more than a torso. Whether it ever becomes something more than just a torso depends on people bringing a proper understanding to the will that is to serve this building, an understanding that I have attempted to bring to expression before you in these lectures.

Do not regard it as some sort of deviation from the idealism of spirituality when I say that physical money and materials are necessary for the construction of this building, when I draw your attention to the fact that without this money or these materials, this building could not exist. You could say, "Well, this is materialism; true spirituality should have no interest in such material concerns." But if, for example, you were to go back to England, you would be presenting an incorrect perspective if you were to arrive and, in this present moment, upon which so much depends, to say only that this building will soon be finished, when in actuality there is the very real possibility that it will remain as nothing more than a torso. It would also be entirely incorrect if you were to say: "Yes, now it is just a matter of calling forth spiritual aid for its completion!"

No, when it comes to idealism and spirituality, the point is not to be miserly about material sacrifice. Being miserly when it comes to material sacrifices is not a sign of true spirituality. And when people do not properly understand the things about which I am speaking now—many people have it somewhere in the back of their minds: Since this is a spiritual matter, there is no need to bring any material sacrifice to bear upon it; and so, we can feel astounded, be amazed by spirituality, have reverence for it, hang upon it lovingly, and still keep our wallets shut tight! It will not do to serve our spirituality in this way; it will not do to keep our wallets shut so tight! On the contrary, we demonstrate our true understanding for what is to happen here when we treat our idealism and our spirituality such that we do not say: "We can be idealistic and spiritual with a closed hand and wallet,"—but rather open our hands, open our wallets. In actuality, much depends upon those open wallets: Only then, when we open our wallets, does the material truly become something insignificant, does it not?

And so, let us not consider it such a significant act, shall we say, to open up our wallets. If we consider it with the appropriate understanding of its insignificance, then we come to the heart of the matter. But to do this requires a certain strength in us, for of course we must approach other people and ask them to make a sacrifice. They will not want to do this immediately. It is also not a matter of doing this in such a way that we present the matter in a form that the people already understand. Many times, people have told us: for such and such a person, who might then open up his or her purse for us (I also do not believe that many of them really would open up their purses or wallets)—but, nevertheless, for a person who might open up his or her wallet for us, we should at least—the way that you might coat the perch in glue in order to catch a bird—we should at least do such and such a thing so that they can easily understand. But this is precisely the crux of the matter—that in doing this we are bringing a new understanding to those with whom we speak, and that they should be ignited by it, that they are opening their wallets for something that must necessarily light a fire under a lot of people! What is important is that they are to open their wallets for something altogether new, something that they do not as yet understand, and also that they are to open up their wallets for a spiritual effort.

You see, I am seemingly speaking about something that is also material. But, my dear friends, what I am saying to you today is something that I have not said for many years, and I can assure you that not speaking of it has helped matters far less than my speaking of it (I would hope) will help now. I would have gladly left it all unsaid, had not speaking actually helped anything! And this is why I have said it now—to help in the future. It is so necessary, my dear friends. But do not believe that in saying it I am trying to demand something from you: "Go to England now and tell the people there that they want money in Dornach." This is not what I mean at all. On the contrary, the important thing is that money is altogether worthless and of no real consequence if it is not used in the service of something that is most spiritual, if it is not used to work toward the goal of making what we are intending to accomplish here resonate spiritually throughout the world. If that does not come to pass, if it cannot come to pass that the spirit which is to be embodied here finds resonance throughout the world, then we have no need for this building; then it might as well remain nothing more than a torso!

And so—on the one hand, we serve with complete devotion the spirit that is desired here; and on the other hand, we make it possible for this spirit to be in the world at large. I can assure you all: I would not have made this appeal to you today if it were not absolutely necessary. Have enough trust in me to believe that I made the decision to appeal to you in this way out of a definite necessity, because I saw that it was necessary—trust enough not to merely think, after you have sailed across the English Channel: "We are spreading the spiritual teachings now; and by the way, over in Dornach they are hoping to get their building finished, but that is just a material concern." It would be more comfortable for me to be able to say this to you, but it simply will not do, for it is absolutely necessary—my dear friends, forgive me—to speak this bluntly and directly. For everything that is to happen in the near future, we are going to need a lot of money—truly, a lot. I am not saying this to you out of greed, but rather I say it for this reason—because the manner in which I have just had to speak to you is the only way of keeping what we have begun here from being left forever as a torso and nothing more. And so, I would like to direct this request in particular to our English friends: that you all, when you arrive again on your Green Island, do not forget, when you are with your friends or elsewhere, to do work also in this realm, somewhat uncomfortable to me, that I have just spoken of in a very particular tone. It is very, very important.

Next Friday at seven o'clock, we will have our next lecture. For now I would only like to add that I was, of course, speaking just now also to those who are not going across the Channel in the near future.

7

THINKING, FEELING, AND WILLING IN SOCIAL LIFE

DORNACH, JANUARY 30, 1920

In our last three meetings here,[†] I took some time to describe this building—both the process of its construction and the goal connected with it. Today I will add to these building reports something I would like to call a report on the times in the most wide-reaching sense. I must stress that this building is intended as both a representation of our anthroposophically-oriented spiritual science and a representative phenomenon of the times. In its form, its design, and its composition, it is meant as an expression of everything that is attempting to enter and must be allowed to enter this evolutionary moment, which will carry us from the present into the near future. When I speak about the great task of this time, and particularly when I indicate how important it is that the majority of people become receptive to all things spiritual, we must recognize that this task arises directly from everything that initiation science and initiation wisdom have drawn from the spiritual world.

You need not approach the demands of the spiritual world alone to understand the necessity of a spiritual intervention in these times. In one of my last lectures here,[†] I spoke to the fact that even in its outer forms, the world is visibly undergoing a vast reorganization. Nearly everyone in the world today can see that recent events have given the English-speaking people dominance over the physical Earth. We will not be discussing this shift in power today, but we will speak (and have already spoken[†]) about the fact that this shift is accompanied by a certain feeling of responsibility, a feeling that tells us clearly: There, in the moment it becomes possible to exercise power over the world, in that moment we must feel impelled to fill our every action with the spiritual impulse at present in human evolution. Not to do this, or not to desire to do this, is to bring about the downfall of human evolution.

It is not a pointless exercise in these times to consider reports about past events, and of all the various reports that could be laid out here today I would like to present this one to you. A particular confluence of events occurred in 1870: a clear-thinking man living in a German city gave a talk[†] at almost the same moment that the conflict broke out with Sudan. The people in that city had not yet heard of the conflict. This man, whom I referred to as clear-thinking, gave a talk in which he foresaw certain victories that Germany would achieve in that conflict. In this talk, the foretelling of this victory was accompanied by a demand that the victors undergo a spiritual deepening in the wake of their success. And soon after the foreseen victory had been achieved, this same man wrote an article[†] about the necessary evolution of the age itself.

In this same article, which was written almost fifty years ago, there were many noteworthy things—things that lead to two separate considerations. First of all, the article speaks to the necessity that people avoid two different imbalanced ways of looking at the world. One imbalanced worldview consists of turning toward only the abstract spiritual, and the other consists of turning toward the consideration and adoration of only the material. And then, this man demanded of his contemporaries and their successors something he referred to as "Ideal-Realism."

You can see that such a demand came at a time when people longed for a renewal of spiritual life. But if you follow everything that resulted from this longing for a renewal of spiritual life, you will discover just how incapable people were of finding a way to establish a connection between spiritual and material strivings, a way to bring into reality the concept of "Ideal-Realism." So this important demand, spoken out of a dimly felt longing, came out of a profound inability, out of the impossibility, of finding any true content in the world. It was an uncertain feeling and nothing more.

But its expression was also connected to something else. The man I am speaking of, together with several others who also felt some sort of longing for a renewal of the spiritual life, tried to draw attention to the fact that if this renewal of spiritual life did not occur, the nations of Europe would go to war and all of the culture human beings had created would be destroyed. Back then, there was also a man, who gave many lectures in Switzerland, named Johannes Scherr† (and please remember, this all was spoken about fifty years ago!) who spoke of how dangerous it was that most people were coming to self-awareness at a time when the leaders of the educational system had turned away from spiritual worldviews in favor of materialistic concepts and ideas. Even at that time, these matters were spoken of in piercing and weighty words.

What happened then? Then came a time in which a wave of materialism fell over all of Europe, a time in which people considered it acceptable to ignore the great danger that lay in not thinking about or desiring spiritual intervention. Every now and then, someone would come along and point out that despite the conscious attitudes of people in everyday life, a longing for spiritual life existed in the hidden places of the human soul more so than in any other age of earthly evolution.

But these voices were heard only on a very superficial level. Such people were not listened to seriously. And basically, we are still living in this time. The terrible occurrences of the last five years have penetrated deep into the souls of the European people, so much so that their thoughts and feelings are connected only to outer results and they are not willing to accept what we all must accept if we are to speak meaningfully about the future evolution of humanity on the Earth.

What lies before us now in Europe has been preparing itself over the course of decades. But human souls have not been preparing themselves. The majority of human souls are as unprepared as they could possibly be for a wave of intervention from the spiritual world, a wave that is pounding on the doors of life, a wave that wants to enter but that people do not want to allow into their hearts and souls. It is essential that we turn toward a spiritual consideration of the world, and it is especially important that we come to a true knowledge of the human being.

The true nature of a human being cannot be recognized unless we first recognize the spiritual world, for the human being lives with two-thirds of itself in the soul-spiritual world and only one-third in the material world. Unless we seek knowledge of spiritual life, we will remain ignorant of our true being. We must ask, in a deeper way than the one in which most questions are asked these days: Which part of our being is the area of the human soul that we encompass in the word "thinking"? Which is the part of the human soul that we encompass in the word "will"? Between the two lies our *Gemüt*, our feeling life. We will arrive naturally at knowledge of our feeling life, our *Gemüt*, when we give attention to our thinking life and the life of our conscious actions, our will life.

Follow me briefly through a consideration of exactly what is meant by "thinking." As human beings, we are aware that our thinking inwardly parallels outer life, which makes impressions upon us by one means or another. This thinking—we live in it. But at the same time, we should be aware that the majority of life is full of times when this thinking is divided by all sorts of dreams. Most people are not aware of the ways in which an un-willed element plays a role in their thought life. All of these un-willed parts of our thinking are essentially dream-like. Try to be clear in yourself about how much you control your thoughts from the very center of your will life on a daily basis. Try to be clear about how much you strive to direct these thoughts inwardly, to form them out of yourself. Try to be clear about whether most of the time your soul allows the thoughts to enter it, allows them to break through to that deeper place. They have a life of their own, these thoughts—one blurs freely into the next, and people gladly give themselves over to the games that these un-willed thoughts play with one another. There is no great difference between these daytime thought-games and the dreams that come to us while we are sleeping.

These dream-like elements intermingle with human thinking in other ways as well. People these days take part in the life of the external world. How do they participate in this life? They inform themselves about things that are happening in the world; they inform themselves in such a way that the events of life, brought about by some impulse or another, are carried over in large part into their own experience. They give themselves over to all sorts of popular agitation and excitement. You need only to investigate yourself whether this surrender to popular agitation stems from individual willing or whether it comes rather from being swept up in whatever impulses are present at a given moment! I could present many, many different things to you that come storming into thought life, that take control of our thinking without any involvement of the human will.

This was the reason I published my book *The Philosophy of Freedom*—to show that human freedom is only possible when this un-willed, dream-like thinking is removed and replaced by impulses from our fully conscious and awakened will. Now, these kinds of true thoughts—what are they like? When is it true thinking? When it comes out of the fully conscious will, when you grasp a thought such that it is truly you that grasps it. In the moment that our thoughts grasp us, we are no longer free. Only when we are able to grasp a thought with our own power, with our own being, are we truly free. Since this is the case, a thought can be nothing other than an image. Were it something other than an image, if it possessed a reality of its own, it could not allow us to be free. Everything that has a reality of its own sucks us into the whirlwind of that reality. Only an image can allow us to be free.

Think about it—all of the objects you see around you in a room have a real effect upon you. You are only completely free in relationship to the images that you see in a mirror. Those images can do nothing to you themselves; you cannot bump into those images. Were those images to have any sort of effect upon you, it would only be because you chose to undertake something in relation to them. If a fly lands on your nose (even though it is only a very small organism), you are not free; you move reflexively. This is the case with all things in reality. You are only free in relation to those things that you perceive as images, things that have no actual reality of their own, things that are simply images.

Why are our thoughts made up of nothing more than images? To answer this, we need only to recall something that you can read about in my *Outline of Esoteric Science*—namely, that human beings were once connected with a previous incarnation of the planet Earth, an incarnation that we call the Moon evolution. If you read through everything described there about Moon evolution, you will say to yourself: "During Moon evolution, humans were connected with entirely different forms of being and entirely different forces of nature than the ones we encounter now during Earth evolution." Humanity has moved through this period of Moon being. Its aftereffects are still present on Earth. Humanity evolved out of its existence on the Moon into its existence on Earth. And if you read what I have described there more exactly, you will say to yourself: "During Moon evolution humans did not yet think in the way that they now do on Earth." Back then, people lived in a realm of unconscious imagination, and this unconscious imagination was not integrated into their will, just as dreams are not integrated into our will now. Thinking was first integrated into the will after a long period of evolution, one that we are still gradually moving through in this fifth post-Atlantean epoch. What we now experience as thoughts developed out of what we experienced as pictorial images in our souls during Moon evolution.

If you consider this very carefully, you will also come to see that everything that creeps into our thinking (such as the dream-like things I just described) is a carryover of what people experienced in their soul life during Moon evolution. When we surrender to the rapid motion of our thoughts, allow our thoughts to give form to our will, allow dream-like things to play games in our thinking—in these moments the conditions of Moon evolution are, in one way or another, at play in our thinking life.

As you can see, the influence of our previous existence on the Moon extends very, very far into our everyday thinking life. You can detect it everywhere—the way your thinking, your imaginations, are intermingled with the un-willed element of those things that simply occur to you and zip through your mind. This is a carryover from Moon evolution. It is the case, therefore, that we have two different forces within our beings working directly against one another. The first impels us to control our thinking with our will, to become free in our thinking life. The second constantly tries to disrupt this free thinking with carryovers from Moon evolution: a luciferic element.

A luciferic element is part of our everyday thinking life. We cannot banish it completely. We would have to banish from ourselves everything that we were not yet able to arrive at through our free, willed thinking—and yet we must always strive for new knowledge. We must be conscious of this and clear that this is the case. It is nothing more than empty words to say that you want to escape Lucifer's influence altogether. This is nonsense, for the luciferic element always plays a role in our everyday thinking. If you want to stand and meet the present demands of human evolution, then you must have the good will to know that both forces—the true Earth forces and the luciferic forces—are constantly at play in your soul life. Only then will you achieve a real understanding of what truly lies within the human soul.

I would like to say that, in describing this, I have provided a rough sketch of one pole of the human soul. Let us now consider the other pole—the one that lies nearer to our will life. Of course, the will also plays a role in our thinking, but thus far we have only discussed thinking penetrated by will forces. Now we must consider willing penetrated by the forces of thinking.

How does our will—which then transforms into actions—play a role in our everyday life? We can come to an understanding of this by taking a look at the connection between the actions we take every day and the whole cosmic Being. Think about this for a moment: When you take a single step, when you move from this location forward to this location [steps forward], you actually alter (though in the most miniscule way) the gravitational conditions of the whole Earth. When you step here [steps backwards], you move to a different location than when you move here [steps forwards]. You influence the gravity on the Earth differently when you step here [steps forward] than when you step here [steps backwards]. But if you properly consider that you influence the gravity of the Earth just by moving across its surface, you will also come to understand a different sort of influence that you exercise upon it.

Consider for a moment something that is part of the natural world. For example, when a branch grows out of a tree trunk, this branch has a particular relationship to the Earth as a whole, just as it also has a certain relationship to that trunk from which it is growing. It has a particular gravitational relationship to all of the Earth. The Earth and the branch taken together constitute a unified whole. If you were to break that branch off the tree and lay it down somewhere nearby, you would alter the gravitational conditions of the entire Earth, if only in a very small way. The tree would sway less in the wind, and the broken branch would rustle a little on its own in some other location. You would change the gravitational conditions on the Earth differently if you were to lay the branch here as opposed to over there.

This is something that you bring into the world through the very fact of your being. So far we have only discussed the relationship between your human form and the surrounding world. But you have other influences on the world. For example, you can make something out of this tree branch. Let us say that you consciously and artfully form this branch into something that can then be put to some sort of use. To do this, you first think about what the form should be, and then you cut away everything that is not part of that form. Now you are exercising an entirely different kind of influence, one that does not involve breaking the branch off the trunk and putting it on the ground, but one that actually involves giving a different form to something nature created. Just think how much human beings do in this artistic or technical way. Think about how they form the things they take from nature, and in so doing exercise influence over the Earth!

And I ask you that when people do these things, when they alter the natural world, when they form machines and pieces of art from the things they take from nature, do they do this with their thinking? Let us consider how much of it comes from thinking. When we think about something, we create a mental image of it. For the things existing on the Earth, it makes no difference what occurs in this world of images, just as the images that appear in a mirror reflecting the objects in a room exert no influence on the objects themselves. But human beings give their mental images reality. This is the other side of the coin—when human beings, having developed out of Moon evolution, give reality to their thoughts: When we form something and place it somewhere in the world, something plays a role in all of this machinery, in all of the things we craft and form, that is not at all connected with earthly existence, just as luciferic forces bring dream-like elements into our thinking and played a role in the dream-like state of Moon evolution. So what is it that plays a role in everything that we bring into the world?

The things that we bring into the world through the actions of our liberated soul life are not products of old Moon evolution, which then gave way to our present earthly state. These things that we create will only have real significance once Earth evolution has given way to the next stage of evolution. Like a child in its mother's womb—or perhaps not yet in its mother's womb, but waiting in the spiritual world for its chance to incarnate—like a child whose existence will come sometime in the future, everything that human beings create is still in an embryonic state, waiting for its moment in the future. And we see the true nature of these things only when we see them as embryonic, when we see that their true significance lies sometime in the future. If we create something in our lives today, if we do not take nature as it is, but rather alter it somehow by giving reality to our thoughts, we are in that moment creating for the future. If instead we see what we are creating as belonging only to the present, if what we create takes up residence in our lives in such a way that we see only its momentary usefulness, then the future will come to reside unnaturally in our actions, just as the past resides unnaturally in our dream-like thinking, and ahrimanic forces will take hold of our actions.

In human life, only the child, who also creates and forms things in the world, though without the striving after usefulness, may in its unconscious state understand what it creates as existing not only for the present, but in preparation for the future. We must always be conscious that when we as human beings bring forth our machines and artistic creations, we are forming things for our next phase of existence, for Jupiter evolution. We must be conscious that our earthly existence must someday be shed, and that the true meaning of our actions will come only in some future existence.

This is the great error of modern times—people see the mechanical and artistic things they create only for their present usefulness and do not wish to become aware that we all have work to do for the future forms of our existence. In choosing to focus on the immediate usefulness of what we create, we allow Ahriman to creep into our will life.

We must ask ourselves: Was this focus on usefulness always present in human existence? It was not present as such during the times of ancient Greece, for example, and in earlier cultures. During those times, there was still awareness (even if it came from a kind of atavistic clarity) that a human being had an existence beyond an earthly form. It was in the fifteenth century that people began to strive solely after usefulness in what they created. And these days, worldwide programs are founded entirely on this desire for usefulness.

Just as it is impossible to entirely remove a dream-like element from our thinking life, it is also impossible to entirely remove this striving after usefulness. Therefore, let no one utter the empty phrase—"I want to escape from all ahrimanic influence." That is nonsense. It is impossible. Ahriman plays a role in all of our actions, with the exception of what we do as children, when we have no goal, no desire for usefulness, when we do everything simply because we want to do it. In all of our other actions we can only strive to achieve a certain kind of ideal.

How can we do this? We must be clear that there are two forces at play in our present lives as human beings. What forces? One is the force that causes us to act out of a desire for usefulness, but the other is as follows: Whenever we undertake something in life where we do not allow ourselves to be tugged and pulled about like a puppet, whenever we do something without being in this puppet-like state, then something else always accompanies our actions: We become more clever; we grow wiser; we are able to do whatever we just did *better* after we have done it. This is the other force within us. Most people, especially after they turn eighteen and believe they already know everything they need to know, do not pay attention to the fact that it is possible to grow wiser and better at the things that they do throughout the whole of their lives. The first force within is our drive for usefulness; the second is ongoing self-development, which causes us to pay attention to all that we do, that we might then observe how we can improve our human existence by doing this or that in a certain way.

The force that influences human existence in this way has a very different effect and significance than our simple sense of a thing's usefulness in a given moment. Let us examine this in light of a very, shall we say, distinguished example—let us consider the paintings of Raphael.† Raphael worked on his paintings during the span of a very brief lifetime. At some point, there will come a time in the future when nothing will be left of Raphael's paintings—there will perhaps be reproductions of them, but nothing directly connected to Raphael himself. There will someday come a time when no incarnated human being will ever be able to lay eyes on Raphael's paintings.

But Raphael will still be there, and that which Raphael became through the process of working on his paintings will still be there. Through the process of working on these paintings, Raphael was carried forward into another incarnation that was suitable to the preparation he had done. He carried that work with him during the time between his death and his next birth and then appeared in a new Earth incarnation, during which he did something else. He continued to carry that work with him throughout his life. What Raphael became through painting his pictures is what continues to live on, and would continue to exist even if the Earth were destroyed.

It is possible to refine a desire for usefulness such that one can explain why it is useful that paintings exist. If you were to think about it, you would see that there is no great difference between an unrefined desire for usefulness and a more refined one that allows someone to talk about the usefulness of Raphael's paintings. But what Raphael's individuality and soul became through the process of painting is something altogether different. That will carry over from this existence on Earth into Jupiter evolution. That is what will continue to develop in the future.

This is a very, shall we say, distinguished example of what will happen with the human soul—something which we can distinguish from actions in the external world. We must hold this differentiation up before our souls and understand how wide-reaching it is. We must understand that someday the Earth will disintegrate into the cosmos, that someday nothing will be left except human souls. When nothing remains except human souls, the results harvested from those souls' evolution will be the thing that distinguishes what our earthly existence was at the end from what it had been at the beginning. From this standpoint, we can identify what might be called the obligation that each of us has to develop ourselves during Earth evolution. We can identify the obligation each of us has to make something of ourselves so that we can be a part of the cosmos. And with this comes this thought: The Earth will end someday; the Earth will disintegrate; human souls will be all that is left!

I would like to point out that the strength needed to bear this thought, to grasp it in spite of how difficult it is—this strength is being altogether lost. And as it vanishes, Earth evolution will cease to have any meaning unless people can find the strength to bear a spiritual understanding of the Mystery of Golgotha. For at the heart of the Mystery of Golgotha, if it is understood properly, lies the seed of thoughts like this one, thoughts that arise from a true spiritual perspective. Just think about that very popular saying which the Evangelists attribute to Jesus Christ: "Heaven and Earth will pass away, but my Word shall live forever."† What Christ gives to the human soul will remain, will continue to be there even after the Earth has ended and split apart in the cosmos.

Now I ask you—and here I return to my report on these times—can the interpretations of the Mystery of Golgotha that religious teachers and theologians have made over the years still offer us the needed perspective? No, that is altogether impossible! Even the theologians and religious teachers have become materialistic. And a materialistic understanding of the Mystery of Golgotha does not hold sufficient meaning for all of our existence on Earth. Anyone who is serious about Christianity these days—I have said this from other perspectives in the past; today you hear it again from a new point of view—must seek a spiritual understanding of the Mystery of Golgotha.

In other words, true spiritual knowledge, true knowledge of the spiritual world, is absolutely necessary for humanity at present. As I mentioned at the start of this lecture, for fifty years people were powerless to imbue their "Ideal-Realism" with any true reality. This is the reason that so much misfortune has come to Europe.

But now comes the question: Do those who are able to avoid further misfortunes—living as they do in a time when people are actively speaking about spiritual science—wish to go on living as those who had not heard about spiritual science were forced to live for the last fifty years? If so, then catastrophes will befall this Earth that will make the ones we have experienced seem insignificant. There is nothing else to do but to say this directly. When people demanded a renewal of spiritual life fifty years ago, they were not able to achieve it, because its time had not yet come. Today, the time has come. Today, if you do not wish to turn toward spiritual life, then you cannot truly be serious about the continuation of human evolution! This is the responsibility that I must speak of, that must be spoken of, particularly to those who are able to take it up, building on foundations that have already been laid. We must look toward the horizon in our consideration of the world. We cannot shy away from our existence.

Imagine that a cabinet of yours has been broken into many pieces. You have the pieces in front of you; you are looking at them. Some sort of accident has broken this cabinet apart, and now the pieces of it are in front of you. What do you do? You take the pieces, you get some nails, and you fasten the pieces together to make it look like it once did. And it will. However, it will fall apart again if the pieces have become rotted, or if the nails do not hold, or if the pieces are weakened in other places.

Europe has fallen apart as if it were an old cabinet: Czechoslovakia, Hungary, Romania, Serbia, Austria-Germany, the former Germany, the former Russia, the Ukraine—these are the pieces, the remains of the cabinet. And the Western powers are trying to put these rotten pieces back together with nails that will not hold. People do not see that they are holding rotten pieces. They are gluing the old back together, thinking that in so doing they are bringing new substance into the course of human evolution. This is what they think they are doing. But that can only be accomplished through an awareness and understanding of spiritual science. And the question is: Should the world, after what Europe has gone through and what Asia and America will soon experience as well, simply glue and nail together the old rotten pieces of itself because it is the most comfortable thing to do, or should we instead seek a complete renewal of the entire being of humanity through a connection with the spiritual world? We will speak more on this tomorrow.

8

The Nature of the Threefold Social Organism

DORNACH, JANUARY 31, 1920

I would like to begin today by making you aware of something regarding the criticisms that have been brought against the connection of our anthroposophically-oriented spiritual movement with social life. You already know about the inner connection existing between the two—I have spoken of that often.[†] I have also drawn your attention[†] to just how little prepared a spiritual movement will be to fulfill the tasks of this time if it shies away from the important questions facing humanity at present, if it ignores the most crucial demands made of it in the present and the near future.

Yesterday I discussed the fact that dream-like elements creep into daily human thinking life, and I also told you about the various ways, or at least about one of the various ways, in which these dream-like elements do this. We must be especially aware of their presence in our thinking when we encounter fully-formed opinions coming to us from the outside world. It is indeed the case that we do not sufficiently examine a large portion of what we think, that we do not first live into it ourselves, and do nothing more than repeat what we have heard, treating it as though it were our own opinion. You need only look back on the countless judgments people have made in various nations during the past four or five years about the fate of the world, the worth of other nations, or the causes of the war. You will not be able to avoid the conclusion that the vast majority of these judgments—even the ones made by people whom you would have liked to think were different from the rest—are untested and unconsidered. People simply repeat them, reiterate them, treat them as though they were their own thoughts and assessments.

I might also take this opportunity to remind you that when I have spoken here about events and phenomena in the world, I have never presented fully-formed assessments to you, but rather have sought to characterize matters in such a way that they might help you arrive at your own conclusions. More and more, this mode of presentation should take hold in the world, giving people a foundation on which they can build their own opinions, rather than presenting ones to them that are already formed. But people today have the tendency, upon hearing something—particularly when it is spoken with strong self-awareness or filled with a kind of fanaticism that might be difficult to recognize—to take on fully-formed opinions as their own and repeat them in their speech and thoughts. (And since a few of our English friends are still here, I must touch on the following example, though it may also be recognizable to others from other parts of the world.)

The opinion has been expressed in certain places that anthroposophically-oriented spiritual science, which has its center here in Dornach, is getting involved in political life, and that a movement such as ours should have no such involvement. It should be noted, for one, that during its heyday the Catholic Church also was involved in affairs one would normally refer to as political.

When such an opinion is expressed, it sounds in many ways like something commonly believed. And when someone hears such an opinion expressed, it seems more or less reasonable. That person says: "Yes, there really is something to that—it is a lot of nonsense that a spiritual-scientific movement would get involved with a question like the threefolding of society."

Now, the original assessment of these matters is of the sort I have already characterized for you today—one perpetuated in a manner similar to the way that students in modern schools regurgitate countless superficial ways of thinking. This age believes it has progressed very far in the development of its thinking. And it is true that elevating our thinking to a certain level is one of the tasks we must complete if humanity is not to fall into ruin. But the call for a clear, sharp way of thinking, specifically a thinking that is inwardly true—for all unclear thinking is also treacherous—the demand for a clear, sharp, inwardly true thinking stands opposed to the impulse to think unclearly in a way that is unfinished, the impulse to simply half-think, to think something you hear as if it were your own thought and then repeat it.

I would go on to say to you that there is something fundamentally superficial about the assessment that anthroposophically-oriented spiritual science has, in considering the question of threefolding, strayed into political life, where it does not belong. This assessment is entirely abstract. It takes something that might very well be true of the Catholic Church and imposes it onto something of an entirely different nature. This would be similar to learning that it is good to put shoes on your feet, and then applying what you have learned about the proper use of shoes to determine the proper use of gloves. Such an assessment of spiritual science is equally misguided. Why? What is the most basic principle of the Threefold Social Order? Its primary intent is to clearly divide spiritual life, in order to have its own realm, from political or rights life and from economic life, which each should also be separate from the other two.

Now let us think this through objectively and clearly, not superficially like those who say that Anthroposophy should have nothing to do with politics. What are we seeking to achieve through the kind of delineation I have just described? Well, spiritual life is to stand apart from everything else; it is to develop on its own foundation and only carry out actions that come out of its own impulses. We are striving to ensure that spiritual life is no longer entwined in political and economic life, but rather free and independent in a way the Catholic Church, which was always tangled up in political and economic life, could never be. We want to ensure that we are in a position to bring all of the impulses of spiritual life into reality.

Think about how ridiculous, how superficial it is when someone says that Anthroposophy should not try to move into political life, when it is actually Anthroposophy that is demanding a social organization in which spiritual life would no longer be connected to politics at all. We should create a political system in which spiritual life can give form to itself, can have its own inner organization. And it should no longer be the case that when you want to found a school or rework a curriculum, you have to turn to individuals in the political sphere, for this is what makes us dependent upon politics. In this example you can see what truly clear thinking means in comparison to the way in which people take in what comes flying toward them and then simply stumble upon opinions about impulses that come out of the spiritual world; for the idea of the Threefold Social Order comes out of initiation science. And the person who says that anthroposophically-oriented spiritual science should have nothing to do with the Threefold Social Order does not understand anything at all and is not thinking clearly. Furthermore, that person does not understand anything about the true impulses of spiritual science, and does not see that these matters, which are connected with the great tasks of this time, are taken out of the impulses of spiritual science.

Countless assessments rife with the same sort of contradictions are publicly aired and then parroted along by a large portion of the population these days. The task that lies before us is, above all else, to attempt to arrive at a pure, clear, inwardly true thinking, free also from any attachment to nationalistic chauvinism. We will not get there unless we first recognize that right now we are very far from it; for if you do not feel how distant the judgments made today are from a place of objectivity, you will not feel the impulse to arrive at clarity, at a thinking that is inwardly true.

I would like to give you another example of how mistaken judgments move through the world, one that is unlike this misconception of the relationship between the Threefold Social Order and spiritual-scientific problems. I know well that such assessments confound many because people do not think them through. They believe that there is something to it when people say Anthroposophy should not be concerned with the Threefold Social Order, for this opinion supports those who believe that a spiritual movement can be of service in the world only when it stands apart from it. Some are striving for this sort of separation. Thus, anyone who makes judgments like this is seeing only half of the picture.

With all of this in mind, I would like to suggest that you consider that there are half-formed opinions residing deep within human beings everywhere—judgments lacking in any sort of foundation. It is especially easy (we can speak about this generally), when working out of a superficial assessment of something, to criticize this or that piece of what anthroposophically-oriented spiritual science offers. If you do not sense the depths out of which these things are drawn, it is possible to make judgments of Anthroposophy based upon the most superficial opinions of the day. This is why we so often hear from people who have actually barely even had a whiff of Anthroposophy speaking "cleverly" and saying, "Well, that I can agree with; that I do not agree with..." and so on. The task for those who have a proper feeling for these matters is always to penetrate ever deeper into them, thereby gaining some sense that initiation truths are actually drawn up from the very depths of Being; for when you truly grasp in a deeper way what I have merely touched upon so far, you will have a deeper understanding for the following.

In recent history, we have experienced an increased intermingling within the social order of spiritual life, rights life, and economic life. Modern parliaments strive, by a process of majority rules, to make decisions regarding matters about which its members may know nothing—decisions about matters that can really only be decided by someone who *does* know something about them. A single parliament is supposed to make decisions about all manner of things—about spiritual life, about political life, about economic life.

Yet, in the moment when spiritual life (let us start there) is divided from the other two—from the rights-political and from the economic spheres—it is only then that it is fully brought to human beings. Spiritual life becomes its own organism. Spiritual life should give form to itself according to the same principles by which it is constantly being drawn up from the depths. People who have something to teach should also be the ones to give form to the process by which teachers are hired or to the form that the schools take. Spiritual life should be allowed to support itself in complete freedom. This will ensure that the capabilities of each individual are always called up in service to spiritual life. This will ensure that those decisions which must be made regarding spiritual life are dependent upon the capabilities of human beings, the capacities of those human beings who are present at the time of the decision. This is the way it should be. It should not be that those who are capable of doing something or other in a particular era, at a particular time, are hindered or prevented by some sort of state or parliamentarian structure in bringing that capability forth.

This makes spiritual life entirely dependent upon human beings. But in that nothing else is allowed to affect the development of spiritual life except human beings, what I described yesterday—that ever-developing element of spiritual life—is what is actively at work in the world. I called upon Raphael as a characteristic example: If his works were to be long forgotten, then what he developed through the creation of those works would continue to exist in the world. This principle of inner development becomes the very thing that actively affects spiritual life—in other words, the separation of spiritual life from the state greatly hinders everything luciferic. And only through this division can luciferic forces be diminished. Everything in spiritual life that is dependent upon the state is imbued with luciferic impulses. When majority voting or something similar plays a role in spiritual life, marring everything coming out of human individuality, then clear thinking and definite willing (both of which come out of that human individuality) become blurred. This blurring of sharpness and definition in thinking and willing is precisely what allows the luciferic element to enter human beings. Thus, we can say, "All aspects of spiritual life bound up in political life bear a luciferic character." And in order to overcome this luciferic character, which indeed must be overcome in public spiritual life, we must free that spiritual life from the rights life. An individual human being cannot overcome it, for dream elements (I pointed this out to you yesterday) must always play a role in our spiritual life. But we withdraw from the influence of this element by participating in public spiritual life, so long as that spiritual life is held separate from the state.

Similarly, when the economic life is bound up in the state, ahrimanic elements play a role in it. The ahrimanic elements that play into economic life when the state takes part in its affairs will be defeated only when that economic life in corporations, associations, and so on (as I have often stressed here) is built upon a life of brotherhood.

You see that when we speak about the Threefold Social Order, we are dealing with truly significant principles. In the middle of this picture stands the state organization—everything relating solely to public rights.

Now, let us recall something I have talked about here before,[†] but which I will now review for those who have not heard it. Human beings live not only during their time here on Earth between birth and death, but also, we all bear within us the echoes of what we lived through between our previous death and the birth that marked the beginning of our present life. During this time between death and new birth, we experienced things in the spiritual world that continue to echo into our current lives.

How do these echoes affect life in the public sphere? Everything that human beings bring into public life in the form of their particular talents and gifts—in other words, everything that constitutes public spiritual life—all of this does not come from the Earth. Rather, these talents and gifts are echoes of the pre-earthly life. Everything that Goethe brought into the world between 1749 and 1832—all of that was influenced by what he had experienced in the spiritual world prior to 1749. He brought it all down with him. And everything here on Earth that develops in the form of art and science and religious impulses—in other words, everything that develops into earthly spiritual life—all of that is an echo of the more-than-earthly spiritual life brought by individuals through the gates of birth. If you look at literature, if you look at art—everything you find there has been sent down from the spiritual world. In these abilities we find present in our social life, we have an element that has simply been sent down to us from the spiritual worlds. Human beings bring it down by entering through the gates of birth into this world between birth and death.

On the other hand, everything done in economic life through brotherhood or non-brotherhood, everything that human beings do for one another, all of their business—as strange as it sounds, all of this does not hold any real meaning for the life between birth and death. It holds real meaning for the life that comes after death. That is where it really matters whether I spent my entire life as a miser, living with greed as my guiding principle, or whether I acted out of love for humankind. This bearing toward the world, insofar as it enters public life, insofar as it brings people into contact with one another—the significance of this bearing toward the world will be carried through the gates of death and will hold a profound meaning for the whole of our lives between the death we encounter at the end of this earthly life and the beginning of our next earthly life. We can say: "What plays out here as economic life is the cause for how we will live between death and new birth."

If, for example, an economic organization is built solely upon egotism, then human beings will be hermits, in a very extreme sense, between death and new birth. They will have great difficulty even finding other human beings. To put it briefly—the way in which people conduct themselves in economic life has a tremendous impact on the life between death and the next birth.

This leaves the rights or political life, which is the only one that is purely earthly. It holds no meaning for life either pre-birth or post-death; it only holds meaning for what happens here on Earth. If we completely separate the rights life from the two others, we also separate the earthly from all of the more-than-earthly things that are a part of our existence on Earth. Thus, there are significant principles underlying the relationships outlined in the Threefold Social Order. We divide affairs into three realms because we must hold the two vastly different areas related to the supersensory world apart from the only one related solely to the sensory life between birth and death. The things in human life that can only be decided through major-ity votes—those things can have significance here on Earth. The things we do because of talents or capacities that we are born with and develop throughout our life (as I have described to you)—these things are done out of one's human individuality. And the "Prince of this world"† (to use an old turn of phrase) rules from his throne in the moments when majority decisions somehow hinder that individual-ity. Majority rulings can be applied—it should be reiterated—only to things relating to purely earthly affairs; because for everything that holds meaning after death, the strength of human love, humanity, and good will—all things that are and can only be left to the individual—must be developed.

Along with this, let me point out something here that further strengthens the idea of the Threefold Social Order, but can only be gained through initiation science. What areas of our world does the infiltration of luciferic and ahrimanic forces affect? The infiltration of all luciferic and ahrimanic forces causes something to move into the world from out of abnormal spectrums of consciousness. When we come into the world through the gates of birth, we leave a normal spectrum of consciousness of an entirely different nature than the earthly, and enter into the earthly spectrum of consciousness. At this point, in the fifth post-Atlantean epoch, dream-consciousness—which is to say, a daytime consciousness filled with dream images—is abnormal. If we allow dreams to enter our thinking, we mix something we are only to have during our life prior to birth with all that plays out in our life between birth and death. And this intermingling is especially helpful to Lucifer in the achievement of his goal for us (which is not the normal, godly goal of Earth). Any time abnormal dream elements play into present-day consciousness, this can only lead to a greater influence of Lucifer on humanity.

It is normal to allow ourselves to develop in a dream-like state during the time in which our consciousness is itself still dream-like—namely during childhood. If we maintain the same relationship to the world that is perfectly natural for a child (for example, during the years in which we should learn to speak as though learning it in a dream) beyond the age of childhood, which a large portion of humanity does these days, then we are throwing open all of the doors and gates and windows and every other entryway that can be opened to our consciousness and allowing Lucifer to enter. If we take on public opinions as our own and do not lay a foundation for our judgments that is any deeper than the foundation laid in dreams, we are holding open the gate for Lucifer. When, for example, we are told by one side or another to consider someone a "great statesman" or a "great ruler" or "not to be blamed for the war" or a "great general" without examining it ourselves, then our reasons for having such an opinion are no different than our reasons for dreaming one thing or another.

A great number of people had, until recently, considered Woodrow Wilson[†] a great man because he brought those nonsensical "Fourteen Points" into the world. Ask yourself about the inner conviction people felt in expressing this high opinion of him, and you will find that there is no difference between the conviction they felt in thinking Woodrow Wilson a great man and the conviction they feel about something they dream. The dream comes to them with the same inner willfulness or un-willfulness as this judgment of Woodrow Wilson and his "Fourteen Points." There is no difference between dreaming while fully conscious and dreaming while sleeping. There is no difference between agreeing with the voices of the external world that Ludendorff[†] is a great general or Clémenceau[†] is a great statesmen and dreaming at night about one thing or another. But we must be aware of this. Because in noticing such things, we simultaneously arrive at an understanding of how luciferic forces take hold of us in the world. We are grasped by luciferic forces in the world in the moments when we dream while conscious. Regarding general public opinion, a large number of people in the world today have acted in a truly childish way and continue to do so to this day.

These are matters that must be taken even more seriously than most people believe. And the other important thing is that we learn lessons from life. Regarding the will, we are completely asleep—I have often said this before. I have said to you[†]: "You have mental pictures of what you do, but not of what inwardly directs your hand when you move it; people do not typically have any imagination of that." The mental picture most people have of the strange process connected with human will is as incomplete as the mental picture they have of what they do in their sleep. In most people's lives, the will exists as a kind of waking sleep.

We must work to bring this will to consciousness. In terms of Earth time, this is going to be a long process—brought to consciousness in parts, first in one area of life, then in a little while in a few others, but then particularly notably in one area—for example, in our eurythmy. In eurythmy, movements are undertaken out of fully awake consciousness. There, the will is truly integrated with full consciousness. This is why, in my introduction to eurythmy forms, I have often pointed out[†] how essential it is for the eurythmist to fight against all dormant forms of existence, and to work to achieve the opposite of dream-like things. It is a grave error to practice eurythmy in anything other than a fully conscious state, to practice it as something mystical. I mean "mystical" in the sense of the mystics of old. It is already a mistake to live mystically in everyday life and even worse when something intended to be practiced in the opposite of a dream-like state is instead practiced mystically. But we must also strive to fully integrate our will life with our fully awake consciousness in the rest of our life, outside of eurythmy, as well.

Again, we have an instance where a large number of people are working to achieve the opposite—the opposite of what should be seen as a basic task of our time. It is a basic task of our time to fill all of life with consciousness, and not merely with understanding. Understanding is very one-sided. People believe they can gain understanding of supersensory truths through mystical means, through mediums—in other words, by means that do not involve consciousness at all. There is no more luciferic-ahrimanic pathway to the spiritual world than via these pseudo-spiritual methods. On the one hand, because a medium is involved, it leads toward the luciferic. On the other hand, because people allow mediums to proclaim these "truths" to them, it leads toward the ahrimanic. And the content of such truths (or so-called truths) follows the same paths.

Everything that the medium has to say about the supersensory does not even hold as much meaning as the sensory world does. The sensory world holds significance for the whole of Earth evolution. What mediums tell us only has significance for a very brief period of time (if it touches upon truth at all). It only has meaning for certain elementary spiritual realities during a brief period of time. You will experience higher truths simply by looking at the world through healthy eyes and listening through healthy ears for a lifetime, than you do when you ask a medium to tell you something about the supersensory world.

From this and other similar matters you can see that on one hand, there is a great demand for a renewal of spiritual life at present, but that on the other hand there is also deep opposition to what has been prepared for this time in the fount of true spiritual life. People today resist the integration of the spiritual into the physical-sensory world. This resistance—it can be encountered in nearly every area of society, and it is what you should recognize behind the various objections raised against spiritual science as it is meant here. This spiritual science, as it is meant here, is clear in saying that even the things which are to enter public social life in the future must flow out of the fount of initiation. What results from that, things such as the Threefold Social Order—people do not necessarily like some of these things. There are people who say about them: I do not really like this or that part. These people should learn to understand what complete thinking is. In life, it does not matter what we like or do not like.

I once knew a woman—I have told this story often—who spent some time listening to an explanation of spiritual science. Then she said: "Yes, but this reincarnation—this repetition of lives on Earth—I do not really like that idea; I do not want to come back to Earth." Well, I tried to make it clear to her that it did not matter whether she wanted to during this lifetime, for she did not know yet what she would want between death and her next birth; by then, she would want to return. Well, she seemed to understand this and left saying that she did. That was in Berlin. Later, from Stettin, she wrote a postcard in which she said that she did not believe it; she did not like the idea of coming back to Earth.

In this case, the disruption in thinking was dynamic—it went back and forth. It can also be quite mechanical and constant. We have also experienced an instance of this close to home. The following example itself makes some sense; but the fact that it is also representative of the way that many people think—that makes a lot less sense. At a gathering, I was talking about how human beings return to Earth through reincarnation as individual human souls. Animals, I explained, have a group soul; and though each human being has an individual soul that is protected for the time between death and new birth, appearing again in that person's next life with him or her, when an animal dies it is taken back into the whole of the group soul. Each individual animal is drawn out from the group soul in birth and then retracted like a tentacle back into the group soul at death. When I said this, a woman began to argue with me: "Yes," she said—that made sense for all animals except for her dog, whom she particularly loved and whom she had raised such that he had such a very strong individual personality and would come to earth again as an individual! After that I had a conversation with another woman who said: "That woman was so silly to believe that her dog, which only has a group soul, would reincarnate as an individual. I saw right away that that could not be the case. But my parrot—he will certainly reincarnate as an individual. That is altogether different!"

To be sure, we can laugh about something like this—but in cases such as this one, we can notice the error in thinking even as it is being made. In the case of the apparent confusion about the Threefold Social Order and its relationship to spiritual science, people do *not* notice how short-sighted their thinking is! In the last five years, I have seen people favor countless assessments exactly like this example with the parrot—the people in one country make statements about what things are like everywhere else in the world, but of course their country, their home is always entirely different, just like the woman and her reincarnating parrot. We must take these matters seriously now and be able to see clearly that initiation science must also be allowed into public social life, in order to avoid any confusion about the difference between what we would like to believe and what is actually real. It may be the case that many people today are now comfortable with the Threefold Social Order. But there are two choices in the world today, and those who see things truthfully and properly have no illusions about it. They see that there are two choices: either Bolshevism spreads over the entire world, or we establish the Threefold Social Order!

Perhaps you do not like the idea of threefolding; in that case, you are choosing an old world order! Think for a moment about what is left of a large portion of Europe in the wake of these last four or five years! Consider the individual areas. For example, take a look at Austria-Germany; as it is currently—with the exception of certain individuals whom I have written about in my book *The Riddles of the Human Being*†—its general substance can be traced back to the Catholic principles of the eighth and ninth centuries A.D. Those principles are still living there, as is evidenced first by the naturally unifying presence of the so-called Hapsburg House, then by the altogether unnaturally unifying presence of the Austro-Hungarian Empire. Or consider, for example, that area once made up of the nations of the Holy Austro-Hungarian Empire—Hungary: its entire constitution is still more or less the same as it was in 1000 A.D.! And we could go through every area one by one and identify the period from which its general essence stems.

It is particularly discomfiting to say these things to people today, because they do not want to consider such matters in an unbiased way. But how are we to believe that simply by piecing together these scraps—which have grown old and rotten because they date back to the eighth or ninth century or the year 1000 A.D.—we can create well-bonded and stable structures! No—to do that, we need a true renewal of the soul life. This must be understood as fact. Thus, we must always turn toward our feeling of human responsibility to hold this soul life in view. If we are able to hold it in view, then we will also come to direct ourselves toward it.

Tomorrow, I will speak more about these matters and in particular about the relationship between what I have said today and an understanding of the Christ-impulse.

9

HISTORICAL BACKGROUNDS AND PERSONALITIES

DORNACH, FEBRUARY 1, 1920

W<small>HAT</small> I have to say today as a further development of my recent lectures will lead us to consider the deeds of individual human beings in history from a specific spiritual-scientific perspective. We are used to thinking of significant individuals in history—be they artistic, political, religious or otherwise—as people whose deeds come out of conscious impulses arising within them, and that this is the sole cause of the actions these people take in the world. And we then consider the questions that arise from this perspective, asking: What did this individual do? What did this individual say? What did this individual bring to other people? And so on.

But in the case of significant historical events, the matter is not nearly so straightforward. What is actively at work in human evolution depends upon the driving spiritual forces that stand behind history's unfolding, and individuals are simply the means and paths through which certain driving spiritual forces reach from the spiritual world into Earth's history.

This does not contradict the idea that the individuality, the subjectivity of significant persons, has an effect on the larger circles of the world. Their influence is self-evident. But you will have a true understanding of history only if you clearly see that when a so-called great individual says something or another in some place or another, the directing spiritual powers of human evolution are speaking through that person, and the individual is only a symptom of the existence of these driving forces. That individual is the doorway through which these forces enter world history.

So if, for example, someone from a particular period of history were to be quoted, and you attempted to characterize the influence of those words on the whole of that time period, then (if you were speaking from a spiritual-scientific perspective) you would not claim that this individual had only practiced such influence on the world through the force of his or her personality alone. Let me give you a specific example. Let us assume (as we do in short order) that a particular philosophical man was quoted as being especially characteristic of his time period. Someone else could come along and say: "Well, this person certainly wrote many philosophical texts, but he only had an influence on certain circles. The vast majority of people were not influenced by this person at all."

It would be entirely false to reply in such a way, because the individual mentioned, though also a philosophical figure, is simply the expression of certain forces that stand behind him, and these forces then influence and shape other forces in the world. In the individual we see only the expression of what is actively at work in that time period.

For example, the following might be the case. At some point in history, there might be some sort of spiritual stream, some sort of spiritual directive at work in the subconscious circles of human souls. This might then find expression in a particular individual, someone who is able to formulate in an uncommonly clear manner things about which larger circles of people, perhaps even entire populations, had only some small inkling. But this person might never write it down and might talk about it with only five or six other people, or might perhaps not speak about it at all. In this extreme case, it could be that centuries later, the memoirs of such a person were discovered, and in them had been written things that had never been published or distributed. Nevertheless, those memoirs might contain the characteristic ideas and forces at work in that time period.

Whenever I have attempted to describe historical figures, I have always done so from this perspective. I never intended to awaken the belief that an individual's ideas are able to have an effect only when they are administered through the normal lines of propaganda. Rather, I always wanted to demonstrate that we find expressions of the most influential ideas in individual personalities. Of course, accompanying this is the possibility that the important influence of such individuals is not felt during the time in which they are alive. It is, of course, also possible for the exact opposite to be true. Such individuals can have a very large effect on many circles of humanity. But the former point must be made expressly clear so that people do not say to themselves: "When one describes an individual as influential and significant in a particular time period, one is speaking only about something happening in some small corner of the human world; I am interested in hearing a description of what was going on for humanity as a whole." I would ask you all to consider all of what I have to say today with this perspective in mind.

I have spoken often[†] about the pronounced leap forward in the historical unfolding of humanity that occurred in the fifteenth century. Anyone who studies the soul life of civilized human beings will find that soul life in the sixteenth and seventeenth centuries was radically different than soul life in the tenth, eleventh, and twelfth centuries. I have also often indicated[†] how incorrect it is to say (though it is repeated often): "The natural world and historical events on Earth do not make any 'leaps.'" Such leaps always occur at significant moments in evolution. And one such leap in the evolution of civilized humanity occurred at the transition from the fourth post-Atlantean epoch, which ended in the fifteen century, to the fifth post-Atlantean epoch, which we are living in currently and which has only just begun. The entire way of thinking, the entire form of civilized European human thought, was different, in a certain sense, after the fifteenth century; but the changes that occurred were different for the people of each nation, for the members of each population. Certain transitional phenomena appeared in the various populations of Europe in different ways.

Now, we cannot understand the spiritual life in which we currently find ourselves if we do not have a perspective on what has developed in our spiritual life since the fifteenth century. We must have an understanding of certain characteristic aspects of this newly emerging spiritual life. As always, it is possible to describe only certain individual streams and perspectives. If you consider the time that immediately preceded this fifth post-Atlantean epoch, from the Mystery of Golgotha through to the fifteenth century, you would have to say: "During this time, a large number of people in civilized Europe were attempting to gain an understanding, a religious understanding, of Christianity." Anyone who makes the effort to study the individual perspectives on Christianity that appeared in Europe from the third and fourth centuries through the fifteenth century will find that the people of civilized Europe used all of their thinking and feeling capacities, everything they could draw up out of their souls, to understand Christianity in their own way, to gain some understanding of their own about what the world had become through the Mystery of Golgotha.

After the turn of the fifteenth century, a set of very special circumstances came about. The first of these—and for those who do not pay any regard to that tall tale typically referred to as "history," but rather pay attention to true history, all of this is entirely clear—was the emergence of what people almost everywhere refer to as scientific thinking. Before then, something altogether different was present. What is seen today as truly scientific had its beginning at the start of the fifth post-Atlantean epoch. And it was expressed with a very particular structure, and one might say it was expressed in several different ways. Actually, what was expressed was always the same, but it received a different minting in the West, in Western civilization, than it received in Central European civilization. And now, the time has come in which these matters must be considered freely, without the influence of nationalistic ideas (in the negative sense that I described yesterday).

And, should we want to consider a representative individual living at this time in which a new age was given its spiritual signature, we immediately come upon one especially characteristic of the transition from the sixteenth into the seventeenth century—the English philosopher Francis Bacon of Verulam.† Among those who consider themselves scientific, Bacon is seen as someone who revolutionized our way of thinking. But Bacon is a by-product, a symptom of something that was entering history in this new age, as I have just described. In essence, a wave of new thinking completely washed over the Western world, and Bacon is merely the individual who expressed it in the Western world most clearly. Though we are not aware of it, this wave of new thinking lives in each one of us. The way we think in the Western world, the way we express ourselves regarding the most important matters in life, is "Bacon-ian," even when people dispute Bacon's points, even when we argue against something he said. It does not have much to do with the content of what we say when offering ideas about a way of seeing the world; it has more to do first with how such ideas reach into the human heart, and then how they integrate into the impulses of the world's historical unfolding.

To make what I have just said clearer, we can cite the following paradox: In these times, one person might be a full-blown materialist and another a full-blown spiritualist, and yet both might very well speak out of the perspective of our materialistic times—there might be no great difference between the two. It does not matter nowadays whether the literal content of someone's words tends toward materialism or spiritualism; what matters is the spirit out of which one practices one perspective or the other; for what actually has an effect in the world is not the literal content of something, but the spirit out of which it comes. That is what has an impact. Only if you are an abstraction yourself will you offer anything to the world solely through the literal content of your words.

Now, we must note that Bacon—if you examine the spirit out of which his thinking comes—attempted to give a foundation to human knowledge, to science, using spiritual forces that had started to appear in the middle of the fifteenth century. The forces of knowledge placed at the disposal of human beings in this new age were to become the foundation for science. It was an important time, the beginning of the fifth post-Atlantean epoch, when Bacon came to Earth. It was, so to speak, the time in which everything was called into question, for people could no longer develop ideas about the riddles of the world by working with alchemy, astrology, and other old methods, including old religious ways of thinking. There was a drive toward renewal. In what was the presence of this drive made most evident? This drive was evidenced in the fact that this time period was a low point for all truly spiritual forces of human understanding.

Until the fifteenth century, it would have seemed impossible to try to grasp something like the Mystery of Golgotha with a purely sense-oriented understanding. It was actually held as self-evident that something like the Mystery of Golgotha had to be understood as a phenomenon of the highest sort, to be grasped with higher forces of knowing than those used to understand the natural world that is spread out around us. These higher forces of knowing still had a certain elevated place at the time of the Mystery of Golgotha. As human evolution progressed, they sank ever lower in human consciousness. And as this new age began at the turn of the fifteenth century, people no longer had any spiritual forces of understanding—they only had a sense-oriented understanding of the world.

With this sense-oriented understanding, Bacon sought to provide a foundation for scientific thinking. Consequently, he rejected all of the research methods that had been recognized as legitimate up to that point and held up experimentation as the sole means by which to build up the body of scientific knowledge. A large majority of the world is still in this place: we must experiment, we must construct devices and perform experiments, and these experiments must then provide us with our views about the nature of the world.

From a spiritual perspective, this translates to the following: Here I have a butterfly; it is too complicated for me to examine this butterfly, so I will meticulously construct a model of it out of paper maché and then examine the model. This is essentially the same as observing living nature through dead experiments, which is no different than replacing a natural living phenomenon with a corpse in the interest of observing the natural phenomenon. Even when we are working in a physics laboratory, we should be aware that we are experimenting on the corpses of natural phenomena. Of course, it is important to conduct experiments, and even to examine human corpses. But when examining a corpse you can have no illusion that it is merely a corpse lying before you. Yet when conducting experiments, we give in to the illusion that they are communicating living truths to us. If you do not already possess the spiritual intuition that allows you to pour into the experiment something of what it is about from out of the living natural world, you will not walk away from that experiment, that dead experiment, with any truths about the living natural world.

This would indicate that the way of thinking Bacon introduced was intended from the start to make death the basic principle used to explain the world's Being. Now, the peculiar thing is that in the reproductions of the living world achieved through experimentation, one does discover clues about the non-human world. But we must not delude ourselves into believing that any indications about human beings can be won through experimentation. All experimentation leads away from the Being of humankind.

Thus, it has come about that in the intervening centuries, during which that way of thinking so highly developed by Bacon was spread throughout the world, any understanding of the human being and its essential nature, of that driving, active Being that exists in the human being's inmost core, was lost.

Now, great moral and social will impulses cannot be found without turning toward that essential human nature. As a direct result of Baconian thinking, our understanding of these social and moral will impulses has disappeared during the past few centuries. Consequently, and paralleling the death of our understanding of the world as a result of Bacon's thinking, arose the morality of usefulness. It is a perfectly Baconian definition of morality: A thing is good if it is useful to human beings, either individually or collectively.

So, as a result of Bacon's thinking—and this was far more pervasive than anyone today can truly imagine—we have a scientific system of thought able to understand only the non-human world on the one hand, and a morality based on ahrimanic usefulness on the other. The latter found fuller expression in Thomas Hobbes[†]—a contemporary of Bacon—than it did in Bacon himself. But this sweeping morality of usefulness then became the basis for understanding all of the external, non-human world. It washed over all of philosophy from Locke and Hume, to Spencer, to the natural scientists from Newton to Darwin.[†] Anyone wanting to study the most characteristic parts of what came out of the Western world from its beginnings through to the development of the most recent systems of European thought must begin by studying Baconian thinking.

Now, something very important is also connected with the Baconian system of thought and morality. It only allows you to examine the non-human world, only allows you to think over morality in terms of what is useful to humans and humankind. This means that by using this system's methods of scientific and moral pursuit, you can achieve nothing in the realm of religion!

What was the consequence of this? As a result, the bearers of this system of thought strove to leave religion as it had been, to preserve and propagate it historically, not to offer it any new elements out of a new science of spirit. Bacon himself defended the most characteristic perspective—that science was not to be brought together with religion, for the connection would cause science to become fantastic; and religion was not to be brought together with science, for the connection would turn religion into heterodoxy.

And so religion was held at a comfortable distance from scientific pursuits. The new forces active in civilized humankind since the fifteenth century were directed toward scientific pursuits. None of these new forces were directed toward religion. Religion was to be preserved by the forces that had been directed toward it in the past, for people feared the new forces that might be directed toward it. They feared that it would become heterodoxy, that it would lose its true content.

What was the only thing that could have resulted from the influence of such a system of thought? What actually happened? People strove with a certain truthfulness after science and knowledge of the physical world, strove out of that same truthfulness after a morality of usefulness, but they did not want to strive after religion in the same way they strove after science. Religion was not to be touched. It was not to receive any consideration from this genuine scientific striving. At most, religion was to be studied historically.

This is what led to the difference between science and organized religion. This difference can also be explained in stronger language. It can be explained as follows (which is simply a stronger way of putting it, but this makes it more uncomfortable for those who do not like to hear the truth). It can be characterized as follows: People strive genuinely after science—namely a science that reaches out to the physical world. People also strive just as genuinely and earnestly after usefulness. But they do not turn this genuine striving toward religion, for religion must remain unsullied; science may not touch it. Genuine physical science, genuine drive for usefulness—religion as hypocrisy, religion taken from untruthfulness: this is just a stronger way of putting it, and is consequently more discomfiting for those who do not care to hear the uncensored truth about the difference between science and organized religion. But in speaking in such a strong and definite manner, one arrives at the heart of the matter. And what I have said is truly the defining character of this way of thinking, in which one recoils from the application of science to religion, in which it is not desirable for a science engaged in the study of nature and the like to play a role in religion.

For the most part, this way of thinking came naturally to Western civilization. It exists so naturally as a part of it that countless people in Western civilization do not understand that it could be any other way—one simply does not apply natural scientific principles to religion. This is characteristic of the Western world. It is entirely fitting.

But now, let us imagine the same impulse shipped over into Central Europe. I can offer you the following representative example. It does not always happen that this system of thought meets an opposition as sharp as the one Newtonian thinking encountered in Goethe. Rather, something like Darwinism, which is oriented only toward the physical body and cannot result in anything other than a morality of usefulness, is taken up by an ancient Central European, we might even say Prussian Central European man, such as Ernst Haeckel.[†] Here, things are a little different than they were in the case of Darwin. In Darwin, we see Bacon's thinking carried forward and developed. Darwin regards the natural world through his own Darwinian lens, but he continues to be a believer, just as Newton did. He quietly preserves in himself an old way of thinking in regard to purely religious matters.

Now what about Haeckel? Haeckel takes Darwinism completely into his soul. For him, there is no possibility of dividing his thinking into two parts. For him, there is no possibility of leaving religion untouched. He takes Darwinism, which one can really use to understand only the non-human world, and then, with religious fervor, he turns its gaze toward the human world and makes a religion out of it. The two parts become one. A religion results from this union.

And in this way, an impulse existing in one place has an effect all over. The impulse remains the same, but it works in different ways, specific to the various regions of the world. In the West, people effectively hold religion and Darwinism separate from one another, bearing them through the course of world evolution. Ernst Haeckel, the Central European, mixes the two together and serves up a single dish, because for him it simply does not work to hold the two next to one another, but separate. Bacon and his followers, through Spencer and Darwin, feared that religion would become heterodoxy if one were to turn science toward it. Haeckel did not have the same fear. He did the best he could with religion, for he took the same truthfulness used in pursuit of science and brought it to bear on his religious views.

The same is true in many areas. Even the Goetheanism in Goethe inwardly opposed an understanding solely of the non-human world. You need only read the prose-hymn "Nature,"† which Goethe had at least thought of in the '80s, even if he had not written it down at that time (and which has been performed here as a eurythmy piece†), and you will see that Goethe does not think of nature in the same way as Newton or Darwin. Rather, he sees it as inwardly ensouled. There is even some humor in it: "… It has thought, and is thinking still."† And throughout his life, Goethe developed ever more concrete forms of these kinds of maxims, which he wrote down in his *Fragments* on nature.

Recently, an article appeared in a paper here—a continuation of it appeared in this Sunday's paper,† I believe—that said that I, when I published the "Fragment" on nature along with a commentary in a new edition of the *Tiefurter Journal* in the papers of the Weimar Goethe Society back in the '90s†—that I emphasized too strongly that the details that Goethe was working through in the prose-hymn "Nature" went on to play a role in his work in natural science. It is strange, the objection raised in this article. It said that there are no natural philosophical ideas in this "Fragment," but rather religious ones, and that one may not connect the religious ideas in this prose-hymn with the later natural philosophical works of Goethe, as I had done. So a pedant (for what else might we call him) has the satisfaction of splitting all those seeking some understanding of humanity in two by telling them that the natural scientific ideas of Goethe are different from the religious ideas. From the very start, this conclusion was drawn in a manner that makes it clear that Baconian thinking lies behind everything this man says.

Can we now—I would like to post the question this way—also see another way in which religion and science are differentiated in modern civilization? We can indeed. Certainly, even in England, the land of Bacon, there were men such as Wycliffe† and others like him; but this did not have an influence on the actual structures of civilization. In Central Europe, on the other hand, something occurred that had a major effect upon civilization, but whose influence did not reach into the West—for example, into France. As the new era began, this fifth post-Atlantean epoch, there was no opposition in Central Europe of the sort that occurred in the West, where science was properly founded but not allowed to affect religious concerns, which were to continue in perpetuity as they had up to that point in the old forms of organized religion. In Central Europe, the opposition was instead taken up strongly in the form of the Reformation, and this resulted in that unfortunate event in Central European evolution—the inciting of the Thirty Years' War by the Jesuits—as well as everything that happened because of that war, and everything that followed after that as well. Here we see an example of how the impulse that had arisen during the fifteenth century became active in religious concerns in Central Europe.

In the smallest and in the most significant historical events, we can see that this same impulse is always there, but it is always slightly askew, drawn up out of the particularities of a certain population, of certain individuals. But again and again it is the Western world that leads the way forward, and again and again something significant occurs. The farther we look into the future development of the spiritual life in central Europe in the time since Goethe, the farther we see it moving away from Goethe. Goethe will continue to be studied by the literary historians and others, of course. After all, there is even a Goethe Institute. But Goethe is not present in any of those things. What Goethe actually intended to bring as an impulse into Central European civilization—Goethe and his followers—that impulse sickened gradually during the nineteenth century. And in the Central European world, just as Darwinism gave way to Haeckelism, all of the impulses coming out of the Western world have also gradually sickened. The Western world bears these impulses well, but the Central European world does not.

On one hand, we have Darwin, who, in his final work, using principles that are applicable only to the non-human world, gave some indications of the significance that his work might have for humans, but these indications were nowhere near as wide-reaching as the ones that Haeckel later worked on. In Darwin's case, the principles of science were applied primarily to the non-human world. In Central Europe, on the other hand, everything went the way that Haeckelism went in relation to Darwinism: People tried to fill their entire lives with impulses such as this one. They would not hold apart certain (for example religious) aspects of their lives; they attempted to push these impulses into those areas as well. And the same is true of other, similarly distinct areas of life.

Those who are older now actually experienced this when the parliamentarianism of England spread throughout all of Europe, with the exception of Prussian Germany, and was taken up just as Darwinism was taken up in Haeckelism. Parliamentarianism, as it existed in England, was a good fit for England. For the countries of Central Europe into which it has been transplanted, it is bound up with the same set of consequences that accompany Haeckel and Darwinism. The modern age arose under the influence of these things.

But we can go deeper still and characterize these historical occurrences in a deeper way. In addition to Bacon, there is another tremendous influence on the modern age in the personage of Shakespeare.[†] For those who are in a position to study spiritual life, to speak of Bacon and of Shakespeare is to allude to the same more-than-earthly source (which is then represented in the earthly: both took the same path into recent evolution, and it is known in spiritul circles that the inspiration for Bacon and for Shakespeare came from the same source. In recent times, where everything has become crude, this has even lead some to posit the well-known "Bacon-Theory," which, naturally, as it has been proposed, is complete nonsense.

But out of the very same fount from which Bacon and Shakespeare drew their inspiration—indeed, stemming from the same initiated persons—came the spiritual stream of Jacob Boehme[†] and the southern German Jacobus Baldus[†] into Central Europe. And all that came from Jacob Boehme is much more alive in Central European spiritual life than is commonly believed—here, again, we have a person who gave a form to something that worked its way as fact into the widest of circles, even if it was not expressed there in Jacob Boehme's words. We must understand clearly that a good portion of Goethe's teachings on metamorphosis can be traced back to Jacob Boehme, that a good portion of Goethe's whole organic chemistry came to him from Jacob Boehme via certain detours and circuitous routes that can also be easily traced backwards. And even though Jacobus Baldus lived in sleepy little Ingolstadt, he, too, is one of those individuals who, though he did not have a big effect on his contemporaries, gave expression in a very characteristic way to certain things that were felt and thought in the widest of circles in this newly-begun epoch.

But let us consider the strange depths of these matters: Bacon and Shakespeare, Böhme, Baldus—all came from the same source of inspiration. What came from Jacob Boehme can still be seen at the core of Central Europe's strivings, but it has grown sick. In its place, Baconian thinking, whether itself or in the form of the later Darwinism, has taken on a position of significant influence in Central Europe. Shakespeare has taken on a similar position of influence. Consider the fact that the entire second half of the eighteenth century (or at the very least the later portion of it) was influenced by Shakespeare; that nineteenth century spiritual life in Central Europe was heavily influenced by him; that Goethe, in his youth, was deeply influenced by him and only freed himself from Shakespeareanism in the '80s.

Everywhere, we can detect the same paths. Everywhere, the impulses are the same. But they work in different ways. In Central

Europe, the impulses sickened over time. The Western impulses washed over the non-human world. They made religious life into a life of hypocrisy existing next to and apart from scientific pursuits. And as these Western elements have flooded into the whole of modern civilization, we see that people even today have not arrived at a point where they can direct these spiritual powers—the spiritual science stemming from human nature itself that must take hold in modern times, just as the scientific powers directed at the non-human world have done—toward religious life. It is time for a new under-standing of Christianity—because nothing further can be done with all that has been left untouched thus far—it is time to work on a new understanding, with new spiritual powers. The old spiritual powers are used up, and those who believe today that they are at all able to understand Christianity with the old spiritual powers that have been recognized as belonging to religious life—they live in a terrible illu-sion. It must be said that a new epoch of humanity, in which the Mystery of Golgotha itself will be understood with new spiritual powers, must come. For everything that has been said about it has outlived its truth and usefulness. It has reached the point of absur-dity. It can be pieced together here and there, taken up now and again in such a way that people can treat it as something insignificant, a sort of scientific "doesn't-bother-me-any"—but humanity cannot live any longer with these things. Humanity needs the strength to draw out from within itself the new spiritual powers that will allow it to understand the Mystery of Golgotha in a new way.

This is what the people of the Western world have seen—that it is incumbent upon them to look through the lens of these new spiritual powers. For in this Western world, people have limited themselves to a simple understanding of the non-human world. This knowledge of the non-human world will never be applicable to the human world. People will have to come to an understanding of a new spiritual science, which will first offer a new outlook on the Mystery of Golgotha. What concerns only the non-human world can simply give rise to a morality of usefulness, but this morality will never bring humanity to the heights of its existence. The only thing that will help it achieve this grandeur is a morality that we know shapes us through supersensory powers at work in our souls. Such a morality, however, can never be understood by what little has been left to religious revelation in the Western world. Hence, the need for renewal.

The questions that I have touched upon here may seem to lay far, far above and beyond all aspects of everyday life, but this is not the case. These questions are the most important, world-shaping questions before us right now, and no one will be able to answer the great question, "Where do East and West stand; where do Europe, Asia, and America stand?" unless we are willing to consider these matters. For when all is said and done, what we are experiencing today are the consequences of everything that has happened in human souls throughout the course of the previous centuries.

Because people are comfortable thinking in the way they do presently, they do not want to consider these matters. And consequently, we can experience what I will call a terrible heartache, which overcomes us when we hear people nowadays speak about the great misfortunes of these times, about the various structures of contemporary politics or economic life or something of the sort, about the situation in Asia, Europe, or the Americas—it is like listening to the blind discussing color, because these people will not direct their gaze toward what lies at the very heart of these great questions.

10

The Foundations of a New Social Form

DORNACH, FEBRUARY 6, 1920

In the various lectures that have been held here recently, the topic has been what is necessary in these urgent times. Human beings must become accustomed to the idea of taking up the impulse that wants to enter the physical world. We have seen[†] that for about sixty years there has been a conflict in European life, which began sometime in the last third of the nineteenth century and in which lies all of the original causes of recent confusion. I have told you before about the fact[†] that everything happening currently is taken much too lightly, insofar as people are not willing to admit that Europe has led nothing more than a shadow existence during the twentieth century, that it is broken and cannot be pieced back together. This crisis is comparable to the crisis that occurred at the end of the Roman Empire as Christianity was gradually introduced and everything that had been in existence prior to that was swept away. Something entirely new has developed. Anyone who has an insight into life will submit to the broad perspective that everything erected since the first Christian centuries has collapsed.

Let us examine those things for a moment. The Mystery of Golgotha was there. But the existence of the Mystery of Golgotha and the understanding of the Mystery of the Golgotha are two separate things. We can make this clear by way of a comparison. Let us imagine for a moment that we are looking at a man who has this or that thing within his soul or in the impulses behind his actions. If a child were to consider this person, it would make some judgment of him; but its perspective is a childlike one. Then we could imagine that someone who was somewhat educated, who had grown up, could also develop some perspective of his own on this person. This perspective would be a more mature one. But not every person who had a more mature perspective would have a satisfactory knowledge or understanding of the person in question if that person were something of a genius. In that case, it would be necessary for others who possessed a genius of their own to develop an accurate perspective on this person.

Here we have something that exists under these conditions: a person exists, and it is possible that there are several different understandings of that person's existence. The same is true, throughout the passage of time, as regards the occurrence that brought Christianity into the world. This occurrence happened at some point in history. It stood at the moment that began our modern civilization. The understanding brought to Christianity up until now—this understanding is fundamentally rooted in the views, in the ideas, in the understandings that people were able to take up with the foundations of soul that replaced the soul foundations of the ancient Roman Empire. To substantiate this idea, you need only take a look at the now-fallen Austria, which essentially, with the exception of just a few isolated people, had a culture—meaning not only a spiritual culture, but rather a culture that stretched across all avenues of life—that at its core dated back to the first Christian centuries.

Therein lay the seed of its decline. People did not want to believe this. But everyone who was familiar with these matters could see this clearly. And the same was true of the rest of Europe as well. Europe was built on very old pictures of the world, and thereby on the basis of an older spirituality. And the Mystery of Golgotha was understood from the perspective contained in these old imaginations. But these old imaginations are now obsolete. They are no longer sufficient for providing present day human beings with an understanding of what occurred at Golgotha. Because of their conservative tendencies, people would prefer to continue seeing things from these old perspectives. In the depths of human souls, however, there is a demand for a reformation of Europe and the entire civilized world. This is the great conflict that can be noted at the base of European culture during the last sixty years or so. Something is trying to take form, but the conservative imaginations of people suppress it. Anytime a raging river is dammed up, an explosive overflow must eventually follow. This explosion has arrived in European culture. It is the years of fear and terror that have entered life now. They are nowhere near ending. They have really only just begun. The important thing now is that we build the foundations for a new understanding of life on the basis of spiritual truths. Those who are opposed to such an understanding of life—they are comparable to those who stood against Christianity during the days when Christianity spread from south to north. The waves of evolution pass such people by.

But such people can bring about much strife, and a great amount of conflict and strife is caused by such people to this day. Let us consider these matters concretely. Anyone who takes a look at those things that came into being and could be observed before 1914, and even in a certain sense during the last few years, when the catastrophe began—that person will see that on the map of Europe there were certain so-called borders between countries. Why these borders had developed in such a way over the course of centuries—that you can follow throughout history. But through a true, unbiased consideration of that history, you will come to see that these countries—from immense Russia down to the smallest nation—came from the influence of the Christ-understanding, meaning the Christ-understanding as it had been taken up in society during the time of the so-called migrations, during the time of decadence in the Roman Empire. By 1914—to name a particular year—these relationships, which were expressed in "borders" drawn onto the map of Europe to delineate countries from one another, had already become completely unnatural. There was no longer any truth in these boundaries. There was nothing in them that offered any inner stability. And if you believe it is possible that something that no longer held any truth in 1914 could be used to hold things together now—you are barking up the wrong tree. And those things, too, which are built on the basis of those relationships, are likewise far from viable.

So how do the people in Europe, along with their American brothers and sisters, intend to shape the civilized world? Let us take an unbiased look at what the European people, along with the Americans, intend to transform the civilized world into now. They intend to create something that, during the migrations in the first centuries after Christ, might have come into being from the perspectives held by the Goths, the Vandals, the Lombardians, the Heruli, the Cherusci, and so on—the perspectives held by the Romans before they were moved by Christianity. It did not come about then, although at that time people did not press back against the course of events with the same conscious strength that they do these days. But let us imagine hypothetically that Christianity was not allowed to spread as it did, that instead people had wanted to create a unified Europe, pieced together out of the worldviews of the East Goths and the West Goths, the Vandals, the Lombardians, and so on, as well as the remains of the old Roman Empire—it is an impossible imagination of Europe! The possibility of Europe as such came about only because a spiritual impulse entered it. And this spiritual impulse—it entered Europe through Christianity. Without this spiritual impulse, which changed everything, Europe would not have developed into anything from the fourth and fifth through the twentieth centuries. Think about a Europe without the impulse of Christianity during those intervening centuries: you cannot imagine it! Think for a moment about what has remained from what the Goths, the Heruli, the Lombardians, and so on brought into Europe. You will have to admit: the impulse of Christianity changed everything.

If at that time the Lombardians had suppressed that new impulse as strongly as the Czechoslovakians or the Poles or the French, for example, are suppressing the new impulses of today, then the impossible situation that I laid out hypothetically before you, would have occurred. And so, if the Lombardians had said, "We want nothing to do with Christianity. We want to stay Lombardian," they would have been acting in the same way that Czechoslovakians, the Magyars (Hungarians), or the French, the English, and so on are acting today. There is a desire not to take up the new impulse.

But without a new impulse, Europe has reached its end. Nothing will come of it. Europe is in the same position that the Vandals, Goths, and Lombardians were in at the moment when Christianity had matured enough for its impulse to enter European civilization. The vast majority of people are afraid of this idea. You are perhaps surprised to hear me say that people are "afraid" of it, because your perspective might be that actually they oppose it on the basis of this or that life principle or logical reasoning or something of the sort. This is not the case. The reason that they oppose it is unconscious fear. When you are consciously afraid of something, you cannot understand it. People invent logical reasons, they invent all sorts of observations that they imagine they have made in order to find some opposition for this thought, when in actuality, they are simply afraid of it. But they will not admit to this fear!

But the times are so urgent that it is essential for us to look unflinchingly at these matters. It is necessary these days to speak of things that may sound paradoxical to the majority of humankind. Christianity also sounded paradoxical to people when it first began to spread throughout the world. You need only to imagine how it sounded to people when a proselytizer of Christianity went some-where—let us say, for example, to Elsass in Switzerland—where people still worshipped the images of Wotan (or Woden, or Odin)† or the god Saxnot (or Saxneat),† and so on. It was an utter paradox. Today it is paradoxical for people when you say to them that anthroposophically-oriented spiritual science must speak both to a new impulse and simultaneously to a new understanding of Christianity. Except that now everything must be more conscious, now everything must be more focused than people were capable of back then.

In particular, one thing must be grasped as acutely as possible by human beings living today. We have a so-called scientific, an intellectual life. One aspect of this intellectual life I described to you in the lecture last Sunday;† I offered you a picture of the character that this intellectual life has taken on in the English-speaking world. Do not think for a moment that this intellectual life exercises no influence upon daily life. What our children learn in school, starting from the time they are six years old—this gives form to their souls, it forms the entire human being, and people walk about in the world today in the form they were given from their existence as school children, which at its core is strongly influenced—particularly now during the spread of newspapers and journals, much more than you realize— enormously influenced by what in the upper tiers of intellectual life is referred to as science. This science—it is experiencing great outward success. It has brought us to an age of telephones and airship rides; it has brought the wireless telegraph machine. In this whole area it has generated a tremendous amount of excitement.

But I have often drawn your attention in the past to a peculiarity of this science, a peculiarity of the whole of our knowledge. This lies in the fact that we can understand everything with it. We can understand machines, we can understand minerals, we can under- stand plants, we can understand animals, but with this science we can understand next to nothing about human beings. The fact that people respond to this by claiming that human beings evolved from animals—that a person is an animal at a higher stage of evolution— this claim shows that they do not understand human beings at all. It is not because human beings are actually descended from animals, but rather because people do not truly understand anything about human beings at all—because they can only express the world pictures which they possess—that they claim that human beings are descended from animals. Truly, this idea is simply a prejudice of these times, which have no science that allows people to understand the nature of human beings. At present, we are not in a position to acquire any knowledge of the human being through our education and culture. When we say "knowledge of the human being" we cannot mean the haphazard collection of various imaginations that people dream up about themselves nowadays. A true knowledge of the human being can only come out of a knowledge of what composes the true human being, the genuine human being.

When we study everything on Earth using the methods of contem- porary science, we will be able to build machines with the knowledge that we gain, we will be able to give form to mechanisms, but we will never be able to grasp any knowledge of the human being using those methods. This is precisely why anthroposophically-oriented spiritual science is there—to make the human being understandable through a relationship with the more-than-earthly. People today have a feeling, although they do not allow it to enter their imaginations of the world, that the human being can only be understood through relationships with the more-than-earthly, through supersensory means. And so it is that, for these people, no science exists to achieve this. For hundreds of years the world has struggled with this fact in many peculiar ways.

I want to give you one example—there are many that we could name—of how people have struggled with this fact over the centuries. During the beginning development of what you have known for years as anthroposophically-oriented spiritual science—at that time there were some people who encountered the foundations of this anthroposophically-oriented spiritual science that I was offering and said, "We would rather delve into the writings of the mystic Meister Eckhart† or those of the mystic Johannes Tauler.† With them, everything is much simpler. With them, we can feel good about ourselves as we muse, 'I am delving into my inmost depths. I am encountering my better half. My elevated 'I' has found the godlike person within me.'" But this is really nothing more than a refined form of egotism, nothing more than a return to an egotistical personality, a way of fleeing from collective humanity, a form of self-delusion.

In the fourteenth and fifteenth centuries, at the beginning of the time when people were losing their ability to truly understand human beings, it was clearly necessary for souls like Meister Eckhart, like Johannes Tauler, to come into the world, people who pointed to a person's inner life as a way of seeking knowledge of the human being. But now the time for this has passed. Now, this immersion and delving into the depths of your inner life no longer suffices. Now, it is crucial that we properly understand a particular aphorism spoken by Christ—this is the example that I was referring to—one of the most important and significant aphorisms that Christ spoke, which goes something like this: "When two or three people are united in my name, then I stand among them."† In other words, when someone is alone, the Christ is not there. You cannot find the Christ without first feeling a connection to collective humanity. You must seek the

Christ on a path that brings you together with all of humankind. In other words, being contented solely with one's own inner experiences leads one away from the Christ-impulse.

This is the unfortunate turn taken especially by the Protestant theology of the nineteenth century—that it takes up the impulse of having simply individual, egotistical, inner experiences of the Christ. There is one crowned head in Europe, one of the few that is still crowned, who constantly reports, at every opportunity, receiving regular spiritual knowledge—"I have personal knowledge of the Christ!" he claims. This crowned head is satisfied with this. But there are many others who say similar things. But this is precisely the great misfortune of the present moment, that people do not have any interest in collective humanity (not just individual human beings). We only come to really know ourselves when we first understand human beings as such. But we cannot understand the human being as such without seeking its origin in the more-than-earthly.

Think for a moment about how the more-than-earthly origins of the present day form of human beings are sought in my book *An Outline of Esoteric Science*. This book is so disagreeable to people for no other reason than because it turns away from all misbegotten knowledge of human beings and instead derives the human being from the whole of the cosmos, from the more-than-earthly cosmos. This understanding is crucial in these times. In this age, we must resolve to incorporate spiritual sources of knowledge into all of our current fields of study.

Here lies the, call it fault—or call it oversight, it makes no difference which word one uses because the issue is not about words—in what must be characterized as stemming from our universities and secondary schools of science, from those people who have the final word when one speaks of what people can and cannot know. The world takes up everything that comes out of European and American universities regarding the so-called wisdom of humankind, as well as everything they produce about social or technical wisdom, ignoring all those things that human beings are able to learn from within themselves. When someone today seeks out a position of leadership among human beings, even if it is a relatively low position of leadership, that person has no access to anything that would help to gain any true knowledge of the human being.

And without that human knowledge, there can be no social life. Without that human knowledge, there can be no renewal of Christianity. You can become a theologian without having the first clue about the true meaning of the Mystery of Golgotha, because most theologians today do not even know who the Christ is. You can become a judge today without having the slightest clue about the true nature of human existence. You can become a doctor without having the slightest clue about how this human existence originates in the cosmos, without knowing about the relationship between a healthy body and sick one. You can become an engineer without having the slightest clue about the effect that some sort of construction has on the entire course of Earth evolution, and you can become the brilliant inventor of the telephone without having the slightest clue about the significance of the telephone in the whole of Earth evolution. People lack a vision of human evolution. We all have a need to build a little circle around ourselves and set up a little routine in this circle, exercising it egotistically, such that we do not pay any heed to the place that the actions we are taking have within the whole Earth picture. If we were to build houses in the same way that we build the foundation for our existence these days, those houses would collapse almost immediately. If we were to shape bricks in the same way that we shape and develop our theologians, our jurists, doctors, philologists, and especially our philosophers, and if we then were to build a house with those bricks, that house would not be able to last more than a week. On a large scale, people do not notice this collapse. Things have been collapsing slowly and consistently since the last third of the nineteenth century. People do not know a thing about this. On the contrary, people are speaking nowadays about the tremendous recovery we are experiencing, and some people are even picking up the old, used bricks and claiming that we can build a new world out of them. We cannot build a new world except by allowing a new spiritual impulse to enter the very foundation of our civilized world. People will be able to slap something together, but not to truly build anything without this new spiritual impulse.

There are people—well-meaning people—who have a deep fear of the intensity of knowledge, the intensity of recognition that is sought through spiritual science. They have this fear for a very specific reason—I am not speaking to you of something that has just been imagined or reasoned out, but rather of matters of actual fact. These people say to themselves: "How boring it would be if we knew all the things about human beings that spiritual science pretends to know; then there could be no hope of any new knowledge being acquired in the future; it is hard to know whether knowledge would be of any help to us at that point." It is a bleak picture of the future, these people think, in which everything is already known!

I will not go so far as to say that this is a convenient stance to take for one who is too lazy to strive after knowledge, but I would like to point out to you that in the moment that you see through to the true nature of the human being in the manner made possible by spiritual science—only in that moment does it become possible for you to start thinking about social structures. You cannot build the foundation for any social structures without first sorting out some true knowledge of human beings. To make this clear for yourself, you need only say to yourself the following.

Take a look at everything that plays a role in our society up to this point—we do not owe the existence of these structures to the clarity of our thinking; we owe their existence to the spiritual forces that emanate from our blood itself, which were born out of the old blood ties, the blood relations that once existed. To this day, we still have in our society something that came into our world as a carryover from those old blood relations, which gave us the principle of nationalities, which found expression in that principle. The fact that one person refers to himself as English, another calls herself French, another calls himself Polish—this is rooted in all of the same things that established the connections between human beings built on direct blood ties. This principle of blood relations had a reason for existing throughout the millennia of human evolution, for it was these blood relations that brought humanity together, that formed the foundation of human society.

At the beginning of the process of Earth evolution, as you can read about in my *Outline of Esoteric Science*, human beings were not so unified. Human souls, as you are aware, had come to Earth from a wide variety of different places and honestly did not have much love for one another at first. They only learned to love one another because they were born into bodies that were related to one another by blood. In previous lectures, I have spoken† about how fiercely the anti-human powers, the luciferic-ahrimanic powers, fought against these blood relationships, this blood society of human beings. That was in ancient times. Back then, people were dependent upon blood relationships to build society with one another.

To believe that today we need only to translate these old principles of blood ties into abstract language; to believe that, by abstracting these principles into "Fourteen Points,"† we can then say, "Let everyone, even the most down-trodden, determine their own destiny!"— we must see how abstract and out of touch Woodrow Wilson is when he says such things. Today, we must see this matter clearly: things *were* that way. At one time, blood ties established the foundation for society among human beings. Now the anti-human luciferic and ahrimanic forces are fighting in a different way. They are using blood ties to lead us astray. Just as Christ did not come to the world in order to banish the law from it, but rather to take the law into himself, so must we seek not to banish the principle of blood ties from the world, but rather to manage them in the appropriate manner.

Whereas in ancient times the ahrimanic and luciferic forces sought to fight against blood ties in the human heart and sought to keep humanity divided into individual egotistical beings, nowadays it is the case that those same ahrimanic and luciferic forces are trying to lead human beings astray by making them build their society solely on the foundation of blood ties, even though the time is now ripe for us all to recognize that all human beings of body, soul, and spirit that stand before us have come down from the spiritual world, come down out of that spiritual world, having already lived through a pre-earthly life, seeking the blood into which they intend to incarnate. And a feeling for this spiritual society must be continually developed.

In pre-Christian times, the idea of reincarnation existed solely as a feeling, for a true knowledge of reincarnation only existed prior to the year 1860, before the arrival of Christianity. After 1860 B.C.E., it was known only as an instinctive feeling throughout all of Egypt, the near East, and the Greco-Roman areas. Now the time has come, however, when the understanding of a human being as a spiritual being that undergoes a development between death and a new birth will grow into a living feeling, a living knowledge—the time in which one must live fully into an imagination of the more-than-earthly significance of the human soul. For without this imagination the culture of the Earth will die. You cannot take a practical action toward developing into the future unless you are able to have some perspective on the spiritual significance of the fact that every human being is a spiritual being.

And we must add to that, as paradoxical as it may seem to people today—less paradoxical in theory, though I do not intend to make theories so much as parallels; certainly, it feels paradoxical to people these days—that we must learn not only to say: "As parents, we take joy in the birth of a new child; we take joy in the new member of our family that this new-born child is"—rather we must also learn to say: "No, we are only the means by which a spiritual individual, waiting to come into existence on Earth, finds the opportunity to do so!" The aristocratic notions of heirs and family lines, for example, must be seen as antiquated thoughts, and in their place must be brought the recognition of and feeling for the whole of humankind. Aristocrats to this day have the idea that it is their most important task to ensure the continued existence of their race, that the physical human being must have a descendent with the same name. This feeling must be turned on its head, and we must recognize that it is important to have descendents for the benefit of all of humanity, so that certain individuals who want to come down here to the Earth may have a body into which they can incarnate. The antiquated feelings continue to live on in the aristocracy, in certain aristocratic families. These people must be opposed by a feeling for that knowledge of humanity as a collective; only then will we be able to renew our understanding of the Christ. For He did not appear on the

Earth for the sake of any particular family, but rather for the sake of all humankind. He did not appear on Earth for the sake of any one nationality, but rather for the sake of all humankind. He did not appear so that those who were able to call themselves the victors in a battle could erect nations of their own design, but rather so that the collective existence of humankind could be practiced within the framework of nations.

These things lie at the root of all that is occurring in the world now. And things are such that everything which is trying to develop in earthly existence is being fought at its most fundamental level by everything that the vast majority of humanity still claims, what the majority of humanity still wants. But if people continue to live this way, they will only build things that lead society *ad absurdum*, that make their continuing existence impossible. We must either come to understand this or wallow for a long time in the chaos that has seized Europe. And the best way to perpetuate this chaos is to go on founding new nations.

For all of these reasons, we must speak openly with whomever comes to power in the near future in the physical world about the enormous responsibility that has befallen us in these times. This responsibility is a fact. The English-speaking peoples of the world bear the tremendous responsibility of no longer suppressing the spiritual and continuing to see the world from Bacon's or Newton's perspective, but rather taking up the spiritual in its new form. Try to imagine that today Newton is standing before you, presenting his worldview, about which Herman Grimm[†] rightly said:[†] "The way in which people are taking up this astronomical worldview that the Earth and the whole system of planets came from a cloud of dust, a thin fog in space that spun and spun, that from this whirlwind then emerged plants and animals and people and that one day the whole thing will collapse back into the Sun—people are approaching this the way that a hungry dog makes circles around a tender pork bone, as though this worldview were something appetizing to eat. And sometime in the future, it will take a lot of effort to understand that this Newtonian, this Kantian[†] and Laplace[†] system that people learn in school is cultural-historical nonsense." In other words, people will ask themselves: "How could it be that an entire age could be so crazy as to champion this worldview?"

Today, it is still regarded as crazy when a person takes Goethe's side and opposes Newton, when one considers the physical phenomena of the world from the Goethean perspective. But everything relating to the task of these times is connected with this. There are a few people now who are beginning to recognize this connection, and I was pleasantly surprised to see it published in the most recent issue of our journal[†] that my book *Die Kernpunkte der Sozialen Frage* has the same significance for social knowledge that the Goethean perspective once had for natural science. But just as people turned away from Goethe because he opposed the perspectives of natural science during that time period, so are people today turning away from the Threefold Social Order. Why? It opposes that which is commonly accepted, just as the Goethean perspective once did, and consequently people are refuting this Threefold Social Order.

These matters might lead you to ask: What can a person do about all of this? The first step depends upon having a proper attitude toward these matters, upon a clear and matter-of-fact discussion of them. It depends upon all of us beginning to develop a truly deep interest in the affairs of all humanity. If we look back on the last four or five years, we find that never before has there been such an opportunity to get to know someone who knew all there was to know, because actually nearly every person knew all there was to know about everything. The Germans came forward and said that they knew exactly who was to blame for the war and that, in fact, they were not at all culpable; the French came forward and said that they knew exactly how everything stood; the Italians had the long-standing *sacro egoismus*.[†] People always knew exactly what was really going on. They all had their own perspectives, they had their own thoughts, their own ideas.

It is more convenient to come up with ideas that have nothing to support them. People are French or Polish or Czechoslovakian by blood, and by this very fact, they have a particular perspective on life and on the form that it must take in Europe. They need only to do one thing or another to sense this in themselves, and all judgments that they make are simply reiterations of the judgments that they received. This is the great misfortune of our times, that without making any true effort, without having any interest in the affairs of humanity, people make completely unconscious assessments, judging this or that to be true, this or that to be essential. But the time has passed in which people can make unconscious judgments about what is or is not necessary. The time has come in which judgments can only be made out of an objective understanding of the facts, in which we must make a true effort to gain an overall understanding of the necessity of these times and of those things that the times demand from us. It tugs at your heart strings nowadays to meet people who are only interested in themselves. For this self-interest is the great misfortune of our times, and the solution will only come if people, having experienced the awful things that have occurred in the last few years, truly say to themselves: "We must take an interest in the affairs of all humankind." We cannot be satisfied with an awareness of those things that deal directly with us and the small circle of our people.

These things come as a feeling directly out of spiritual science, and I speak them to you today in order to prepare for a few closing thoughts. You see around you here this building, which is the representation of our anthroposophically-oriented spiritual science. You might have a feeling for one thing or another in the structure of this building; you would be right to do so. But only the person who has a correct feeling for this building is the one who sees in every one of its lines something demanded of us by the urgent necessity of these times, the one who sees that the building must exist as it does because our times demand one thing or another from us, because one thing or another must be felt in relation to this column or that one, in relation to this row of windows, or that row over there. Because it is necessary for humanity now to take this building—what it is intended to be—out of the entire structure of these times. And anyone who simultaneously feels—completely feels—into this entirely new style, will recognize that it has absolutely nothing to do with something specially intended for this or that. Rather, it is oriented toward the whole of humanity. There is nothing in the whole of this building that an American or an Englishman or a German or a Russian or a Japanese or Chinese person could affirm as their own. It is not formed by the feelings of any one individual. I will not (at least by those who know) be called an immodest man when I say: "I know of nothing else like this building, which is independent of individual human wills and leads toward the most universal human knowledge and understanding that currently exists."

But this must be taken up if the things that we intend to bring about for the future of humankind are to carry this future humanity toward salvation and not disaster.

11

SPIRITUAL REALITIES IN PRACTICAL LIFE

DORNACH, FEBRUARY 7, 1920

T ODAY I will introduce a few things into our considerations that will allow us to more completely examine tomorrow's theme. To discuss certain things with you, it will be necessary for me to make use of an almost aphoristic style. We have been looking at a very broad swath of the symptoms and the phenomena that have appeared in the course of history in the hopes of understanding how all of these occurrences are leading humanity to an understanding of spiritual realities. And I have also sought to make it clear that in speaking about an understanding of spiritual realities, we are not saying that people should seek to understand the spiritual world only so that they have something to fill the hours on Sundays. This is one of the most ruinous things that has developed in civilization in the last few centuries—that spiritual life has gradually become some so removed and abstract. In response to the question, "What connects the worldview—the spiritual perspective, as well as the non-spiritual—of a farmer, jurist, factory worker, salesman with the things they do on a daily basis?" (which I addressed at a public lecture† in Basel not long ago) people say: "Nothing flows from one's worldview into one's work, that is to say the carrying out of those daily tasks. An individual is a person of practical life, and that individual also has a purely abstract worldview that is colored to a greater or lesser extent by religion and science.

This has become the customary way of thinking in the course of the last centuries, and it has reached a high point now in these fateful times. And at the core of this matter lies something even more threatening, namely that people who have the good will to take up a spiritual worldview learn from its content that it has nothing to do with their practical lives. They learn that practical life is the thing that is truly real—the thing on which you must spend time on a day-to-day basis. Spirituality is there for Sundays. People remove it from their lives, feeling that those day-to-day lives are not worthy of including spirituality. I have always made every effort to make it clear that what I refer to as anthroposophically-oriented spiritual science intends to ascend to the very heights of spiritual life, but that this ascension into the spiritual world will then engender in human beings a way of thinking, a form of imagination, that will prepare them to be active and capable in nearly every sector of everyday life. People will have something from their spiritual work for the higher worlds that they can also take into their business, their practical daily lives.

This work undertaken for the spiritual world should not mislead us into saying that "the spiritual world exists apart from everything else; it must not be disturbed by the coarseness of everyday life. That the coarseness of everyday life is something separate; it should be held in contempt. The spiritual world is the higher world—the sublime world." In the past I have often and strongly pointed this out,[†] and have told you that over the years several people have come to me and said: "Ah, I have such a prosaic job! I would like to quit and dedicate myself to ideals." That is the worst maxim that one can possibly have. A person who—through destiny, through karma—is a postal worker (and a good one) does more for the world, if he or she does the job well, than being a bad poet or a bad journalist or something of that sort, which people sometimes long to be. It is important that when you draw near to spiritual realities, you take those spiritual facts into the core of your thinking and feeling in such a way that you do not remove yourself from daily life, but rather to make yourself more able to enter it.

Because this latter resolve has vanished from human life ever since the fifteenth century and because life has by and large divided into these two separate pieces—on the one hand, the practical life, looked down upon by idealists and mystic, and on the other, the mystical, religious, idealistic life, seen to be fuzzy and dreamy by practical people—we now stand in the midst of the impasse described to you yesterday.[†] This is the deeper reason for why we have reached this point. This is what has caused the current situation. In practical life, every individual stands in a little bubble, (as I described yesterday) working without a broader vision and without heartfelt participation in the whole. But, when people are idealistic enough to dedicate themselves to a spiritual worldview, they desire to take that spiritual worldview up such that it never develops into anything in practical life—for example, into a well-thought-out book or journal. There are people who actually consider it a virtue when someone does not understand and is altogether unable to grasp how a journal or a nonfiction book is composed. This is truly a great loss, and one that has become gradually more profound in the course of the last few centuries.

It is not a virtue to have no idea how to understand nonfiction books, and it is not a blessing for humankind to have people (no matter of how many of them there are) who want to be idealists by understanding nothing about practical matters and by desiring only to give themselves over to spiritual considerations. The healthy path in life is to allow these two life maxims to interpenetrate and become interdependent.

But these tremendous losses that have gradually appeared in a view of small circles during the last few centuries are also visible on a larger scale insofar as no one has actually (or truly, we might say)—no one, save for a few who have also posed the question in an utterly impractical manner—concerned themselves with the following question: How is it possible that something healthy will emerge from antiquated structures (I described to you yesterday how these appear on our maps), which were drawn up as the states of Europe prior to the war that began in 1914? Yes, people today have unfortunately not come far enough, even after the trials of the last four to five years, to really consider these matters healthily.

Think about it. If you were to have a cool head, enough to consider the far-reaching causes of the terrible catastrophes of the last four and a half or five years, you would find that they lay in the industrial and economic relationships between Central Europe and the western regions, including the Americas—relationships which had long since come into conflict with the established borders between countries. The national structures, which had been built up out of entirely different circumstances and were dependent upon relationships dating back to the Middle Ages—these national relationships were used as artistic frames placed around interests that were purely commercial and industrial. They served absolutely no purpose, but they were used in this way. And today we are so unaware of this that a long-since-hopeless (though for a short time unusually disruptive) Social Democratic movement also has absolutely no effect in the world.

Now we are experiencing the rise of Socialist theories all over, including in Asia, which are becoming particularly radical. These Socialist theories are trying to create something practical. Before the war, they had tried to make use of the frames that existed around the old states. Now they are trying to use the frames that were established after the catastrophe of the war. For example, Russia—as it has been defined since the war—is being used as a frame for Bolshevist theories. If you are able to think about reality clearly, you will see that nothing is more senseless than this attempt at framing. There is nothing more nonsensical than this structure, which was created first out of purely medieval forces and now is combined with the unnatural experiences resulting from the war and the Treaty of Versailles† (a peace accord that offers no peace at all). That this structure just east of Europe should now take up the fantasies of Lenin and Trotsky is nonsensical in the long term and so tumultuous in the present that it can only result in halting the healthy evolution of humanity in Europe.

But this understanding of reality is exactly what we might say is missing these days from the opinions of the general public. Public opinion is not built on an understanding of reality, but rather on abstractions, on abstract theories. And when something does come along that is not built on abstract theories—like the Threefold Social Order—something that is taken right out of life itself and that must be summarized in just a few words (because it is not possible to write three volumes, and people would not read them anyhow), people do not recognize the spirit of reality in it. Instead, because they are already full of other theories, people see it as simply another theory.

They no longer have any sense of what is truly taken from life itself because they have alienated themselves from reality altogether.

People today must become practical in the most eminent sense of the word, and yet they must also still be able to look into the spiritual world. For only when these two elements are able to coexist in the core of each human being will that core of humanity develop healthily into the future. When the time comes that a person will no longer be considered a fool for saying, "Over in the East there are souls that, through the particular historical relationships in Asia, have evolved in such a way that today they have little understanding of the external world and could thereby easily become the prey of materialistic Europeans; but they have also evolved such that they also are able to preserve for themselves a window to the spiritual world." When that day comes, we will actually find that there are such souls in the East. One particularly significant and representative example is the person of Rabindranath Tagore,† whom I have mentioned often before. But this Rabindranath Tagore—who is by no means an initiate, but simply an Asian intellectual—has in himself the entire spirit of Asia, one might say; and you can learn a lot about this striving spirit of Asia from his collection of lectures entitled *Nationalism*.

These souls over there in the East, however, lack the inner relationship to what impels those in Europe and America into a relationship with the external, physical world. I would like to reiterate something that I have said to you before.† It is only the last few centuries that have brought us what we might call a purely mechanistic culture. Today you will read in geography books that the world is populated by about 1.5 billion people. This, however, does not hold true when you take into consideration the amount of work that is carried out on the Earth. Let us imagine that a being from Mars were to come down to Earth and were to tally up the Earth's population. First they would ask "How much work does one human being do on Earth, when one takes into consideration his or her strengths and powers for working?" and then they would ask, "What is the total amount of work being done by everyone put together?" Even if we include all the people who were alive before the war, the numbers still will not add up—there would not be enough people. If one were to calculate how many people were on the Earth based on the amount of work being done, the answer would not be 1.5 billion, but rather more like 2 billion or 2.2 billion people.

Why? Because actually so much work is carried out by machines on this Earth that it is roughly equivalent to 700 million people. If these machines were not there and if the work that they did were instead to be carried out by human beings, there would need to be 700 million more people on Earth. I calculated that figure using the amount of coal used by the masses, and counted a work day as being eight hours long. What I have said is true according to the approximate amount of coal used in the beginning of the twentieth century and for an eight-hour work day. You could actually say, "According to the amount of work that is carried out on the Earth, there are actually 2.2 billion people on it." But the work that is carried out by purely mechanical machines and instruments—that work is done more or less entirely in Europe and America, much less in Asia. It has begun to catch on there, but it is still only in the beginning stages, for the Asian peoples do not have an understanding of the mechanization of the world. They lack entirely an understanding of the things that began in the West sometime in the last few centuries or even back in the middle of the fifteenth century.

In saying this, we must not only think about the fact that work is being done by machines; we must also realize that humanity's imaginative being turned toward this mechanization of the world. Someone today could say, "Building the Gotthard tunnel required a tremendous number of workers." But these days people cannot build something like the Gotthard tunnel without knowing about differential and integral calculations, and those originated with Leibniz[†] (the English say with Newton—but we will not concern ourselves with this quarrel). Thus, the Gotthard tunnel or the Hauenstein tunnel not from far from here could not have been built if Leibniz had not discovered differential and integral calculations in his study. The entire thinking of Europe since Copernicus[†] and Galileo[†] has been directed toward this mechanization of the world. Now read some of Rabindranath Tagore[†] and see how much he hates this mechanization of the world.

But where will this all lead? From the perspective of a spiritual worldview, it could be said, "All of these souls who are incarnated in the East—in that region we refer to as the East—they will seek to incarnate during their next lifetime in the West. The Western people will seek to incarnate during their next lifetime more toward the East. Those in the middle will need to seek a means of building a bridge between the two." But if you try to say that it is a cultural-historical demand that our educational system and other similar institutions be based on the fact that these two migrating waves of souls are crossing one another on the Earth—if you say something like that to the masses of clever people out there right now (let us take the cleverest of the bunch—those who have been elected to government positions) then you will hear them tell you that you are a fool, that what you are saying is absolutely crazy!

Nonetheless, people must recognize this reality, just as in earlier times they came to understand things we now consider anthropological truths—the intermingling of the races, and the division of the races, and so on. We must begin to consider spiritually everything that has until now been considered only from an external physiological perspective. There are good theosophists out there who, during the holidays and respites in their lives, do indeed believe that human beings live through multiple incarnations on the Earth; for them this belief is an act of faith. But nothing comes of this. If you only believe in reincarnation and karma as though they were articles of faith, it is worth nothing; it is worth about as much as writing a little blurb about something. Things like this only become worthwhile when you incorporate them into all of your thinking about the world, and also into the business, into the giving and the taking that goes on every day. These things only become worthwhile when one deals with them in a cultural-historical context. And if you do not see these matters as something that is important only on life's holidays and Sabbaths, but instead see them as something that penetrate every aspect of your life, and if you truly have such thoughts (one can play around theosophically with these thoughts a good bit, clearly), then you will have enough understanding to write a well-thought-out book or run a successful bank; and you will not feel ashamed if you find yourself in a situation where it is necessary to undertake work as a cobbler. For only those who are able to stand in the midst of practical life, who can be prepared under any circumstances to lend a hand and be involved—for those people the entire human organism is so interpenetrated with inner skillfulness and preparedness that this inner preparedness translates into thoughts that are truly full of content.

This is what must penetrate into the thinking and feeling core of human beings. It will penetrate into our culture when we familiarize ourselves with what people these days fear most of all.

We can accurately say, "There are two things that exist at present that point to two separate fears of modern-day human beings." I do not believe you will say I am wrong, if you consider the matter with an inner feeling for the truth. The first is that in nearly every circle of the civilized world there exists a deep fear of actually discovering the true causes of the war. People do not want to consider this subject. They do not want to stick their noses into it—at most they will look at their enemies, but certainly not at their own country! With very few exceptions, people avoid any consideration of the true causes of the horrible human catastrophes of recent years. They have a deep fear of it. During the war, this fear found expression in an almost idealistic fashion. At the time, there were people who took a stand and said, "From this war there will result a new way of life, a new ripening of human ideals," and so on.

People will have to study a good deal about the events of recent history in order to eventually arrive at the true causes behind this catastrophe of fear. But what they will find is that nothing positive exists within the history of this war. They will find that the old cultural and civil structures had grown rotten, that in the catastrophe of this war, they had carried themselves to the point of absurdity, that this war proves that civilization, as it had existed up to the war, had driven itself to the point of absurdity. This is one of the things of which people have such a deeply set fear—they fear an actual experience of this truth. They are so afraid these days that they have completely given up thinking about tomorrow as they live out today. The idea that the Treaty of Versailles could ever bear positive fruits in reality—no reasonable person can believe such a thing, neither on one side nor the other. And yet, because people only think about today, and not about tomorrow, this strange instrument has been put into place. That is an actual experience of the truth.

But there is also something else: people's fear of the movement toward an ever-greater consciousness in soul life. Any time that people feel justified in fleeing into unconsciousness, they are happy. When a worldview such as anthroposophically-oriented spiritual science is presented to them—a worldview that strives toward a full-fledged training of consciousness and intends, through this work with consciousness, to bring it into its full reality—then people do not want anything to do with it. It is too difficult for them. It requires activity. It requires that one have an active spiritual life. That is too difficult.

But people strive to have two things revealed to them through means that exist below the level of consciousness. Those two things are: first, what spiritual life is exactly; and second, what it is that lives in human beings. There are so many people—far more than you realize—who want nothing to do with spiritual truths arrived at through healthy soul understanding. But when through some sort of mediating force, some sort of medium, a pronouncement is made to them about this or that thing relating to the spiritual world, they fall for it immediately. They do not have to work hard to understand something this way. It comes about unconsciously, and people want to believe these unconscious things.

The other thing that follows immediately upon this is the field of psychoanalysis, which has spread itself out into the world so crassly. It is difficult to believe the incredible alacrity with which this psycho-analysis has found a place in human souls. What is it based upon? It is based upon a bunch of people in the medical field doing as they please and (it is difficult to explain briefly; I have often offered analy-ses of psychoanalysis here[†] in the past) arranging things in such a way that all that is unconsciously present in human souls is raised to the level of consciousness. The psychoanalysts listen to others talk about their dreams, discovering the disappointments and unfulfilled wishes they have experienced in the past, which have since been forgotten and which have built little islands for themselves in the individual's soul, and they seek by these means to gain clarity into what actually lives in a human soul. Particularly clever practitioners have discovered from this that an especially significant amount of what is living there amounts to unnatural experiences and unnatural feelings that have imprinted themselves deeply, only to be repressed in the unconscious. But they continue to live on within the human being. The human being becomes a slave to them. These people attribute the myth of Oedipus to the unnatural feelings that every child supposedly feels toward its mother, and so on. It is clear, from this perspective, that every girl in the tender years of her youth feels jealousy toward her mother, because the girl loves her father; and that every little boy is jealous of his father because the boy loves his mother. This then results in a whole complex of feelings, which appear in the guise of a myth in the story of Oedipus and others like it. The fact that spiritual concerns play a role in these matters, but that those spiritual considerations must be filled with the light of consciousness—people do not want to believe this. They are afraid of the idea. To bring it into the light of consciousness—people are afraid of doing that. They would like to repress everything into nebulous darkness.

I have drawn your attention in the past to the case study[†] that appears over and over again any time one speaks of psychoanalysis: A woman is invited to a get-together at the home of another woman who is sick, and there is a going-away party because the sick woman has to go to a spa. The man of the house is staying at home; the woman must go to the spa. The evening get-together has come to a close. The woman of the house has already been driven to the train station. The evening's company leaves and is on the way home. A horse-drawn carriage (not a car!) comes around the corner. The company splits, moving to the left and right out of the way. But precisely the woman about whom I am speaking moves neither to the left nor the right, but instead remains in the middle of the street and starts to run away from the horse. The driver, understandably, makes quite a racket, but the woman just keeps running, and it takes all of the driver's strength to reign in the horse, because otherwise it might have run the woman over. They arrive at a bridge. The woman—a prime subject for the psychoanalyst—throws herself into the river. The evening company, who naturally had followed close behind, rescues her. What do they do with her? Well, they bring her back to the host's house, of course. That is the next piece of important information.

Now, the psychoanalyst sits this woman down on his couch. He lets her tell him everything about what she did in her childhood. Happily, he learns from this that when she was a very little girl, she was crossing the street one day when a horse came around the corner. She was terribly frightened by this. This experience simmered under the surface in this woman's subconscious. It was waiting there. Ever since, she has been afraid of horses, and consequently, she chose to run away from the horse rather than moving to the left or the right side of the street. This is the isolated province of the woman's soul— the fear of horses housed in her subconscious.

There is indeed something hidden in this subconscious realm, but we must penetrate the subconscious with the light of nothing other than spiritual-scientific consciousness. Then we will arrive at the realization that this subconscious realm is extremely cunning under certain pathological conditions; that in the case of normal everyday human consciousness it is actually not the foundations of the Oedipus complex, nor the fear of horses, that causes one to go running along the road—it is rather a certain refinement that causes this. The woman who had been invited to the party that evening naturally desired nothing more fervently than to spend the night in that house, especially after the other woman had already been sent off to the spa, and the subconscious simply sought the first good opportunity (if it had not been a horse, it would have been something else) to orchestrate matters in such a way that the other guests had to bring her back to the house. So she accomplished her goal. Naturally, she would never have allowed herself to wound the sense of propriety that she learned through her upbringing enough to actually do something like this openly. In her conscious mind she is not so crafty; but in the subconscious reside many well-refined impulses that can be extremely cunning.

This widespread psychoanalysis has taken on such crass forms these days—so many of the hopeful intellectuals of this day and age believe in this more than you realize (I am not saying this out of insult, but rather to speak the truth). Even the theologians want to build their religion upon its foundations. This psychoanalysis is the other result of the fear that exists at present. People are afraid of consciousness. People do not want to grasp things in the clear light of consciousness, but rather want the most important things to be housed below, in their subconscious, so that they can be in control when it comes to these most important things—namely in relationship to their religious feelings. You can see this if you read William James,[†] the American. For whether it is called psychoanalysis in certain regions of Europe or whether it called by the names that William James, the American, gives to it, it is all the same. Fear of consciousness rules the day. People do not want the most important things living within human beings to be conscious. If they were, then people would have to think more when they direct their own actions with their conscious will. It is significant that people have created this justification for thinking less.

Our eurythmy is carried out entirely with, and from out of, consciousness. It is the opposite of everything dreamy. Indeed, people are afraid that by doing eurythmy they will become less artistic, because they associate artistry and dreaminess. That is nonsense. When it comes to artistry, it has nothing to with whether it comes out of one place or another; what is important is that in its forms and expressions, it is artistic. This eurythmy, which is based in supra-consciousness, the polar opposite of subconsciousness, was recently reviewed by a man whom I was told is now a doctor: he noticed a lot of the subconscious present in it. This, of course, is a good indication that this man did not understand the first thing about eurythmy.

The living core of anthroposophically-oriented spiritual science is precisely the thing that is very rarely noticed about it. And you will only notice this inner core fully when, through this spiritual science, you are able to undergo a complete training of your inner thinking, feeling, and willing that makes you more, and not less, prepared to enter and participate in life. I will not claim that every single person who has chosen anthroposophy as a system of belief is at that point. Choosing anthroposophy as a system of belief does not mean much in relation to this matter. I do not dare to claim that all anthroposophists have reached this point. But look and you will see that the things expressed in the true movement of the anthroposophical community are, by and large, the things that are brought into it from outside. Even today, very little is taken from within and brought into the outside world. And anthroposophically-oriented spiritual science will only become what it should be when it succeeds in no longer bringing in things like a predisposition toward mysticism, a remoteness from everyday life, or false idealism, and instead succeeds in carrying out into the world everything that can be taken up in anthroposophically-oriented spiritual science: an enlivening of the soul life that carries it out into one's limbs, such that it takes hold of the *entire* human being—not just their sense of faith or system of belief—and thereby influences the course of their everyday lives. This is the heart of the matter. We must seek in full earnest to achieve this.

12

TRANSFORMING SOCIAL LIFE THROUGH A
NEW UNDERSTANDING OF CHRISTIANITY

DORNACH, FEBRUARY 8, 1920

I⊤ is perhaps not very well known that not only did the entire soul makeup of human beings change over the course of time, but that the things people considered necessary for social life also went through a process of transformation. I have spoken of such matters several times in previous lectures. I have, for example, pointed out[†] that during the Roman Empire it was not a normal societal demand for children to learn the multiplication tables. On the other hand, it was very common for every child to learn the Twelve Tables of Law before they grew into adults. The perspective on what should constitute the common base of knowledge changed significantly over time. This is connected with the whole evolution of humanity. In order to gain perspective on the most important aspects of this connection, it is first necessary to direct our attention to the true form of the events of human evolution.

Before there was a society of people, the likes of which we now know, in Europe, Asia, Africa, or America, there was a broad continent in the area where the Atlantic Ocean is now. Essentially, at one time the surface of the Earth was the area of Europe between Africa on one side and America on the other, and the majority of Europe, Africa, Asia, and America was underwater.

We know that this continent of Atlantis, as we call it, sank in the wake of a tremendous and significant catastrophe. We have also spoken often in the past[†] about how a series of migrations took place away from Atlantis, as it became increasingly uninhabitable, toward the rising land masses that today make up Europe, Asia, and Africa. Basically (you can read about this in my *Outline of Esoteric Science*), the first people to populate Europe, Asia, and Africa were the descendents of the inhabitants of ancient Atlantis.

At that point in history, though, significant differences between the various populations began to appear, and the lasting effects of this differentiation are still present today. We can still understand these differences when we say to ourselves, "There were certain portions of the Atlantean population that went to the East." We will disregard America for the moment, though it, too, was populated by some descendents of Atlantis. But for now we will disregard it. So, there were certain portions of the Atlantis population that moved east. Some of them went as far as Asia, and from these populations of people that moved from west to east there developed those cultures that we refer to as the Ancient Indian culture, the Ancient Persian culture, the Egyptian-Chaldean culture, then later the Greco-Roman culture, and now in Europe the fifth post-Atalantean culture in which we are currently living, which began in the middle of the fifteenth century.

But these cultures developed in the following way: certain portions of the migrating peoples found themselves impelled by the constitution of their bodies and souls to migrate the farthest into Asia. Others stayed back in Europe. Of course, later there was another migration, which is even spoken of in public histories, during which certain portions of the Asian population moved toward Europe again. But the population of Europe today is not solely (though it is in part) made up of the descendents of those people who migrated from Asia into Europe; rather, the population of Europe today is also made up of the descendents of those who remained in Europe during the eastern migrations away from the continent of Atlantis. And much of what is still living today in European people can be attributed to the constitution of their bodies and souls, and its presence there can be explained by the fact that even those people who remained in Europe, and did not migrate all the way from Atlantis to Asia were afflicted with the same things in their bodies and souls.

In Europe, we are consequently dealing with a convergence of the most diverse elements of different populations. The fact that a certain portion of the population went to Asia while another remained in Europe—this created a significant difference, a significant differentiation between the European and Asian populations. Those people who by the eighth, seventh, and sixth millennia had already made it into Asia had evolved in such a way that they had already taken into their souls the culture of human spirituality as it could develop on the Earth. Even today, you can still notice in the people of Asia, which has in some respects lost its way, that they have cultivated this spiritual and intellectual element in the very being of their souls. We can say (and we are not speaking figuratively; this is the whole truth), "This Eastern population, which is the most preeminent branch of the Asian peoples, has not allowed the body to take on a large role in their evolution and development." Everything that is conceived and experienced, and even to a certain extent lived in the decadence of the Asian culture, is not dependent upon the bodily characteristics of a human being. It is all extremely dependent upon the characteristics of the soul. This is why in Asia today, it is not possible for the spiritual culture—which does not exist in the same way it once did, but also is not as highly valued because historical documents do not say much about it—to develop any further. It is a spiritual culture that can only be marveled at by anyone who looks into the enormous spiritual depths that the Asian people of several thousand years ago were able to plumb.

The information that has been passed down through history, what can be learned from historical documents—these things do not offer a picture of what existed in Asia as a kind of primary human wisdom. All that can be extracted today from historical documents or the works of ancient thinkers about Chaldean astronomy, the wisdom of Indian Brahmins, the wisdom of the ancient Egyptians—all of these are later products of this wisdom. All of these things are evidence of a great, wonderful, profound insight into the spiritual world. They point to a great and profound scientific connection that people back then were able to see between the Earth and the whole of the cosmos, the entire heavens above them. The people in Europe today are simply not structured in such a way that they are able to understand, even in retrospect, what was known in these ancient times; and they do not value it because they do not know how to begin to understand it. They have no possibility of directing their understanding toward these matters.

But everything that was experienced through this incredible wisdom that once existed over in the East was experienced in such a way that everything these people learned spiritually, they took up purely in their souls—their bodies had little or no part in the experience. Then, as you already are aware—and you will find the details of this in my book *Christianity as Mystical Fact*†—the view of Christianity that people were able to achieve emerged from everything that was taken from this incredible wisdom of the ancient East. Essentially, this view of Christianity is a direct offshoot of the ancient East. And partly through its connection with the Greeks, and partly through the transformation it underwent through the Mystery of Golgotha, the ancient wisdom itself came to Europe.

Now direct your attention to something that is of particular importance: Those things, which in the East were developed in the soul without the participation of any bodily organization—those traveled through southern Europe and Africa into the rest of Europe, encountering the populations of people who, with the exception of those who had migrated back to Europe from Asia, were otherwise the descendents of the people who had chosen not to go all the way to the East during the migrations away from Atlantis. And so the question arises: What was different about the constitution of those people who stayed behind, that made them decide not to travel to Asia, but remain in Europe?

This brings us to something of incredible significance. We have arrived at a point where we must see clearly that these people who remained behind in Europe during the eastward migrations from Atlantis experienced all that they knew both outwardly and inwardly; every insight into the spiritual world or about the social and economic and commercial ordering of the world—they experienced all of this through the functions of their physical bodies. In the foundation of the European population lies the fundamental fact that the vast majority of Europeans primarily take up everything they experience through the structure of their physical bodies. The people who journeyed farther to the East were so constituted that they took up more within their souls; because it was not naturally given to them, they neglected the development of their physical functions and everything that was to be taken up through the physical directly from the world and from human organizations. In building the foundations of their culture, the Europeans made use of the physical mechanism of their brains, the physical mechanism of their whole bodies.

And consequently, we now have a very strange phenomenon before us—what developed in Asia from an incredible primary wisdom, and has ultimately given us a view of Christianity, has now found its way to Europe and been taken up there under entirely different circumstances and conditions than the ones under which it was developed in Asia. In Asia it was developed purely in the soul; in Europe it is taken up through the body. How is it possible that it could be taken up through the body? It could be taken up through the body because actually the bodies of Europeans evolved such that they are able to become the proper vehicles of the spiritual. The physical form, the bodies of Asians, were not structured in this way. The populations of Europe remained behind so that in the climate and other cultural conditions of ancient Europe they could make their bodies receptive and prepared to take up experiences of knowledge, impulses of the will, and so on.

In the context of the entire world structure, it is necessary to have one perspective on one thing and an entirely different perspective on some other thing; but truly everything has a place in the world and brings something good to it. Some people are not able to understand this. It is true that we make attempts to point out the detriments of materialism, but on the other hand, we must also recognize that materialism had to come into the world until the nineteenth century. Only now must we move beyond it. Some people, in regard to such questions, find it much more comfortable to say: "The human body is simply the machine in which the soul resides; the soul is heavenly, the body earthly—let us abide in the realm of soul." This is a comfortable understanding of life. But this is the service that materialism has performed in the world. It has taught people that the body also participates in the spiritual realm, that among certain elements of the human races, the body was structured such that it could take up the spirit.

And the most distinguished people were those impacted by Christianity. In the very beginning of the time when Christianity spread throughout Europe, the bodies of the European people were good receptive instruments for the taking up of Christianity; because they had been formed in a particular way by the spiritual world, the physical brains of the European people were excellent receiving instruments for Christianity. And while in Asia, Christianity entered a culture that, after a centuries-long, millennia-long evolution, was a culture meant only for souls in Europe—though Christianity in Asia encountered a decadent and dying culture, a soul culture well-suited to ancient times but no longer good for the age in which Christianity came into the world—this Christianity encountered receptive people who had a physical body structured such that they grew into this Christianity, making their bodies into receiving instruments for it.

For in these bodies, there still lived much spirit—cosmic spirit, nature spirit. This is precisely what is significant about the first population of European people after Atlantis—that in their bodies, there was spirit, and that Christianity was taken up in this spirit present in their bodies. But this spirit gradually disappeared. This spirit ceased to exist. This spirit did not remain in the bodies of Europeans. And this is at the core of the transition that occurred in the middle of the fifteenth century C.E.—that essentially, the nature spirit present in the bodies of Europeans began to disappear; that their bodies began to lose their ability to understand through their physicality what they had at once taken up with a vigorous strength (vigorous because it was bodily) as Christianity.

Consequently, a true understanding of Christianity dissipated gradually after the fifteenth century. Only the traditions of it remained. The relationships that lie at its core are actually misunderstood. In everyday physical science, they are misunderstood completely. It is believed that it is possible to study a human being by taking a corpse into a laboratory and anatomizing it. In doing this, one learns only the littlest bit about human beings, for the intricate structure of this human being changes almost from one century to the next. Human beings from one century are, as regards the intricate details of their physical constitution, entirely different from the human beings of previous centuries. Because this does not appear on a large scale and cannot be detected with crude scientific methods, people do not want to hear about it. But a human being is a very intricate and complex structure, and something that evolves after something else in the course of time continues to exist next to what came before.

In the field of crude physical anatomy, there is a belief (though it is only a belief) that if you were to take blood from a Western individual and then to take blood from an Eastern individual, you would be drawing the same blood. Blood is blood. But this perspective that blood is blood is totally nonsensical when seen from a true and deeper knowledge of the human being. I can explain these matters only with the aid of a schematic and can also offer to you today only the results of far-reaching research. But the results are of extreme importance. If I were to depict something in a drawing to you—understanding that if it were not a drawing, but actual, it would appear somewhat differently—I would draw it something like this. If I were to draw a blood clot in the veins of a Western individual's living body, I would draw it like this (see drawing a). If I were to draw a blood clot in the veins of a Russian individual, I would have to draw it like this (see drawing b).

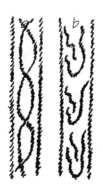

The way in which one set of these lines relates to the other set is the way in which the inner, physical character of the blood in an Eastern individual relates to the blood in a Western individual. But the development of blood is connected with what I described earlier as physical receptivity. This physical, bodily receptivity, as I said, has disappeared. Today, at least for the people in western Europe and America, the bodily offers nothing spiritual. The spiritual must be sought through other pathways, the pathways offered by anthropo-sophically-oriented spiritual science. We can say (to put it bluntly): "The spiritual elements taken in through the physical body, which served to provide an understanding of Christianity until the middle of the fifteenth century—those spiritual elements have petrified. In the Western world today, people are living in petrified bodies; and everything practiced in the West is part of a purely mechanistic culture, which comes from the dead, petrified structures of the physi-cal body. So this change is not as simple as the way in which current, abstract historians depict it; rather it is a change that deeply affects the inner being of our human bodies.

Most people close themselves off to what I have said to you just now. But just as the Romans learned the Twelve Tables of Law, just as it was later customary to think that everyone had to learn their multi-plication tables, at some point in the not-too-distant future, (a future toward which we must always be working) we will have to consider such elementary concepts about human evolution a necessary part of basic education. Otherwise, every fifteen years a catastrophe will befall human evolution like the one we have experienced in the last five or six years. The real cause of the confusion that has befallen us in the last five or six years is that people have closed themselves off to the new form of education that wants to enter civilized human-ity. And if people want to continue living and working out of the fossilized material structure of their bodies, then they will continue to concoct things that will lead, every fifteen to twenty years, to the kind of entanglement we experienced in Europe in 1914. There are only two possibilities before us: Either we become comfortable with the entrance into humanity of a new form of education, so that we might also allow in an influx of a new understanding of Christianity supported by spiritual science; or we face the fact that destructive elements are entering into human social life with terrible force.

Our English friends will be returning to England soon (hopefully not too soon), and when they do they will probably encounter that man whom I have described as a very particular kind of representative individual of the modern age,[†] because in his entire life—though he is much older now—he has not developed beyond his twenty-seventh year. They will encounter the trend-setting (he is probably still a trend-setter, even now) Lloyd George[†]—that man who is able to be a trend-setter precisely because he remained developmentally active into his twenty-seventh year, and then was elected to Parliament (of course), and since then ceased to be developmentally active. Even as an old man he still thinks like a twenty-seven year old, which is to say: immaturely. You will find unusual ideas coming out of such minds, for example: Up to now, we have sided with the counter-revolution in Russia. But that revolution has been put down. It is no longer profitable to side with the counter-revolution, so let us try to make arrangements with the Bolshevists. Let us try to make some sort of tolerable peace with them.

Today, this is typical thinking for a man who stands far removed from any insight into the true laws of life, one who has no idea about reality in the world. And this is how other so-called "statesmen" think—I notice that I always write "statesman" in quotes these days. We must not forget about the most excellent of these "statesmen"— Woodrow Wilson—who far outshone the rest and whom the entire world, at a certain moment in European evolution, allowed to greatly mislead them. When it came to these matters, you truly had to be "the voice of one crying in the wilderness," particularly at certain moments. During the times when the whole world was bowing down before Woodrow Wilson, I always said the same thing here in Switzerland about him[†]—the same thing that I say to you now today. Now the world is beginning to see—now that it is too late—how out-of-touch with reality everything is that comes from Woodrow Wilson. And people who sat with him at the Versailles conference were astounded by how little instinct about reality this man brought with him from America to Europe.

The affairs in the midst of which we are currently living must be considered with a broad perspective if we are to even begin to speak about them. And you will not be able to consider them at all if you do not make it a principle in your life that a certain revelation about the human being must in the very near future enter our general practice of education, just as the multiplication table became a part of that general education at a certain point in history.

Whether social demands will appear or not is not a matter for discussion, just as you cannot discuss whether an earthquake will occur in a certain area or not. But what we can discuss is how we relate to these demands when they do enter the world. No one will be able to take an appropriate stance toward these occurrences without true human knowledge, as it is described here. We must all fill ourselves deeply with an awareness of this. And whether the life of civilized Europe will be able to continue into the future or not will depend on whether there is a large enough number of people who can see the impossibility of an ongoing world regime that is heavily influenced by such out-of-touch individuals as Lloyd George.

You all know that I am not speaking from any sort of chauvinistic perspective or from any particular side. Rather, I am speaking from a purely factual perspective, one that flows naturally out of an observation of the objective facts. I certainly have never, as a German (or a so-called German), had anything against Woodrow Wilson or Lloyd George. Compared to other people living today, Lloyd George is a good fellow. But he is also a man who has never developed beyond his twenty-seventh year as a human being, one who is not in a position to take up in himself what can really only be taken up after you reach a certain stage of development—after moving beyond the thirtieth year. Because our petrified European bodies, which do not actively work toward taking up something spiritual, lose the possibility of development when we reach our thirties. An individual can become a member of Parliament at that point—even a very accomplished, unusually good parliamentarian like Lloyd George, who (as we all know) pushed through several very notable reforms once he was made a minister. It is true, is it not, that one deals with people who have opposing views by taking them out of Parliament, where they might get restless, and putting them into the ministry. At the appropriate moment, they made Lloyd George a minister in England, primarily because they did not want to have him as a part of the opposition. But they made him a minister and also said: "Give him the department that he does not know anything about." This is the typical way to deal with dangerous parliamentarians. And see—when Lloyd George was appointed to the department about which he knew nothing, he displayed a feverish work ethic, introduced reforms that are truly noteworthy, and the others looked on in disbelief.

We must be able to assess all of these occurrences with a perspective on the laws of human evolution. In general, there is nothing comfortable about judging humanity in its particularities, and it is especially unusual for people these days to be actually responsive to others around them. People prefer to simply label others and leave it at that. We are not curious enough to go through the uncomfortable process of truly meeting another person and learning whether he or she is capable of something, whether there is something in his or her soul that has the possibility of accomplishing something in the world. We do not want to get involved in the business of making assessments of people based on the true impressions that we get of them in life. We require other ways of making assessments.

Here is a man who has graduated from school, one who possesses a doctoral diploma—he must be a wise man. We do not have to get to know him first; we simply need to know: he took some tests, or he is (I do not know whether I should actually say "he was") a councilor in the government. Excellent—then he is already someone to be respected. We do not need to bother ourselves any more about whether he possesses any strength of soul that would allow him to accomplish something reality by another means. The government appointed him a councilor ["Rat"], with a "t," and not the fifth wheel ["Rad"] of the wagon, with a "d." We need to have an external assessment of an individual's potential.

In the future, we will need to have, instead, a true and direct relationship between one human being and another. We will achieve this kind of relationship if we develop our human spiritual forces in the way spoken of here. That way comes through spiritual science. If, for example, you were to look at my *Outline of Esoteric Science*, you could simply read what you find there; you could take up the content that appears on those pages. If you take up the content of that book in such a way that you are able to repeat everything in it from memory, then I would find it far more useful if you were to read a cookbook instead—or, if you did not happen to be a woman, then some sort of treatise on tariff agreements. That would be more useful than read-ing my *Outline of Esoteric Science*. The true meaning of this *Outline of Esoteric Science* only comes through when the particular form of the thoughts therein—which annoys people enough that they have dismissed it as "poorly written"—when the particular manner of writing and thinking in the book works instructively on the whole constitution of your soul; when the "how" and not the "what" gives form to the soul. If you read *An Outline of Esoteric Science* (it could also be another book) and allow it to affect you in this way, you will find that your inner sight actually grows much stronger, such that it eventually develops into true knowledge of the human being. Something entirely different than a simple memorization of the information in a book results when you read it in this way. Today, people imagine that when they read a book, they have done the most important task when they have taken up the content enough to pass an exam on it. Spiritual-scientific books are never intended to be read in this fashion. The most essential task has not been completed if you are simply able to list all the major points on your fingers. Rather, the truly essential task has only been completed when the things in the book have crossed over into the whole of your soul constitution, into the whole of your soul make-up—when you have used the book to develop soul forces intended for use in life itself.

For decades, I have been saying this in a wide variety of ways. But still, in a large number of circles, people consider it to be the most important thing to know: The human being is composed of this and that; we live through multiple incarnations on the Earth; and so on. This is not the most important thing. Rather, the most important thing is that, by means of this whole way of thinking I have just described, human beings grasp something that cannot be grasped by any other means. And this thing that our will comes to grips with—it must be there. If it is not, then all of the well-intentioned people who say, for example: "Christianity must always be present in the world"—they will achieve nothing. For just as you could never draw magnetic attraction out of an un-magnetized piece of iron, so can you never (should nothing else come into human life) get true Christianity out of what has become of Europeans. It might be able to live on in a traditional form for a time, but people will be taking up that tradition out of a place of untruthfulness.

This is why it is essential that something be grasped in the human soul that will lead to a new understanding of the Mystery of Golgotha, and thereby to a new understanding of the whole of Christianity. In the ancient, pre-Christian times (as I have indicated before), there was a wide-spread, magnificent, noteworthy primary wisdom, and those who marvel at this pagan wisdom are right to do so; and those who marvel at this pagan wisdom in the time when it was already beginning to resemble Christian wisdom are even more right to do so. The first Christian Church Fathers were actually wiser, much wiser, than their contemporary followers. Their current followers have forbidden the reading of anthroposophical texts. As you are aware, it has been forbidden for Catholics to read them by decree of the Congregation of Holy Offices in Rome since July 18, 1919. But the first Christian Church Fathers once said: "What we now call Christianity has always been here, but it existed in other forms, and Heraclitus and Socrates and Plato[†] were all, in their own way, Christians before the Mystery of Golgotha." Naturally, for contemporary members of Catholic congregations, even though it comes from genuine Fathers of the Church, this statement is heretical—very heretical! But you must admit: It just goes to show you. This decree of the Roman Catholic Church forbidding that Catholics read anthroposophical books is actually the proper result of the evolution of the Roman Catholic Church, and therefore, we must recognize that a new spiritual stream must enter the world that allows for a new understanding of Christianity.

As I said, the pre-Christian worldview is, in a certain sense, admirable. But it did not extend to certain things such as earthly nature.

And in saying that, I touch upon something that is particularly important to recognize about Earth evolution. In regard to everything that comprises the human as a physical being, human evolution was actually a given. Sometime in the fifteenth pre-Christian century, still during the time of ancient Atlantis, human beings had, to a certain, more or less completed extent, already developed for themselves all of the details of their physical forms, which have slowly hardened (to a greater or lesser degree) over time. But in regard to the main portion of evolution, the evolution of human cognition, this was not the case. There, something was withheld as a great human epiphany, a knowledge of the human being, disseminated through the leaders of the mystery cults until the time of the occurrence at Golgotha. What the ancient pagan sages possessed was essentially a reflection of a much older wisdom, one that was still able to observe things spiritually; but it was all merely a reflection. Then the Mystery of Golgotha entered the world—which is to say that nothing less than something more-than-earthly entered: the Christ Being. Something from spheres that are necessarily more-than-earthly descended to Earth and bound itself to a physical human body—the body of Jesus of Nazareth. Thereby, something happened in earthly human evolution that had never happened in all of the preceding Earth evolution: something cosmic entered humanity. Since the fifteenth century before Christ up until the time of the Mystery of Golgotha, human beings had essentially been living out an inheritance from an earlier time in their soul and head beings, but with new physical bodies. Then, something entered human evolution that bound Heaven and Earth together in a certain sense. A more-than-earthly Being bound itself to a human body.

It was still possible for the human beings who had remained the furthest behind in Europe to understand such a mystery, the ones who still had certain nature-spiritual aspects in their physical bodies. It was not possible for those who went the farthest into Asia to understand it. It was, in a manner of speaking, a gift from God for these Europeans to have bodies that, through their physical make-up, were receptive to Christianity. In the fifteenth century, that receptivity ceased, and therefore spiritual knowledge must now come into the world in order to give us a new understanding of the

Mystery of Golgotha. Unless we are able to see into this sequence of human evolution, humanity will cease to progress and will meet its downfall, because what entered Earth evolution through the Mystery of Golgotha will simply vanish. Unless we arrive at a spiritual under-standing of the connection between Earth and the more-than-earthly world, the Mystery of Golgotha cannot continue to live in the world.

Because this fact exists, those who would prefer to uphold the old and traditional ways—and you know how many of them there are in the world, because I have always shared with you the hateful attacks that come in from every side from time to time[†]—have turned venomously against the truth proclaimed by spiritual science that we are dealing with a cosmic Christ Being—one that is not merely earthly, but rather cosmic. It is certainly peculiar, but it is nonethe-less true that, for example, the Roman-Catholic clergy and the Jesuits are particularly bothered by the fact that spiritual science speaks of a cosmic Christ. Something occurred once that has led to a division of the spirits today. And we must not close our eyes to this fact; indeed, we must open our eyes to it. In order to participate in establishing everything that can be established for humankind down to the most specific conditions one finds oneself in, we must have insight into the larger relationships of life.

Do not say to yourself: "There is not time." You will sometimes hear it said: "A person has so much to do these days, so very much to do, that there is no time to glimpse spiritual truths." I would like to tally up with you the amount spent chitchatting at "five o'clock teas" and "snacks" and "afternoon teas" and "morning drinks" and, in certain areas, "evening drinks" (there are such things) and also just in "shooting the breeze" and things of the sort, and you will see that there is a considerable amount of time in which people would have the opportunity (if they wanted to) of familiarizing themselves with things of tremendous import to the future of human evolution. It has nothing to do with time; it has to do with people's nonchalance, with their dormancy.

The disease *Enchephalitis lethargica*[†] has begun to be physically evident in some individuals now; it has already afflicted many others in all avenues of life in their soul life. Sleeping sickness of the soul is a very widespread epidemic. Because in the end, what really matters is having the will to actuate one's spiritual forces. When you go to study at a university these days (with only a handful of exceptions—one could count them on two hands), you don't have to exercise your thinking. A certain mass of information (mostly about the results of experiments that have been done) is disseminated—you can simply absorb that kind of information. There is no need to engage your thinking powers to do so. But this kind of education must be replaced by something that sets thinking in motion, something that activates all of the soul powers within people and causes zeal to replace nonchalance and dormancy in our inner soul lives. It is possible to be very active in your outer life and fast asleep in your soul. But this must cease to be in human evolution. Stopping this is an absolute and profound necessity.

People today say: "We must have bread to eat, first and foremost." Certainly this is true. But if we do not start thinking about encountering the structures of the spiritual world so that our bread can also be made tomorrow, then we will find ourselves only able to eat what the Earth offers up, and tomorrow and the next day, we will have no bread. The old systems of thought will provide us with bread for a little while yet. But the day after tomorrow—metaphorically speaking, of course—we will find ourselves with no bread if we do not drive our earthly institutions out of the directives of a new spirituality.

Think about these things, for they are matters of great importance.

13

MEMORY, INTELLIGENCE, AND THE SENSES
IN RELATION TO THE SPIRITUAL WORLD

DORNACH, FEBRUARY 13, 1920

I have often drawn your attention in the past[†] to the primary wisdom that human beings once possessed, which can be described as a wisdom that made them conscious of being citizens of the entire cosmos, not merely of the Earth. Cast your soul's gaze over what exists in the consciousness of a present-day thinking person, and what exists in the consciousness of someone who thinks about the relationship between human beings and the world on the basis of certain scientific foundations. The two are one and the same. Just as the majority of people during Earth's antiquity experienced in their thinking and feeling lives the things that were taught in the Mysteries—the mysteries that were the center-point of the surrounding culture and civilization—so do present-day people in all walks of life take up the things taught and researched in today's modern mysteries—the universities and secondary schools. The relationship between the mysteries of old and the things that the majority of the population once believed is the same as the relationship between the present-day population and universities. What the old Mystery teachers understood to be the relationship between a human being and the Sun, the relationship between a human being and the animal world—this was naturally also believed by the population at large. What today's university and college professors say (and also do not say) about the relationship between the human being and the Sun, the relationship between the human being and the Moon—this is all believed by the majority of people.

The idea that everything there is to know about the human being is exhausted by the theory human beings evolved physically from animal predecessors is an incredibly one-sided truth; it does not offer a complete picture of the facts. But human beings in modern times relate to their initiates—their university professors—as ancient peoples once related to those initiated into the Mysteries. Psychologically, there is no real difference between these two relationships. Except that the people in ancient times were aware that everything in the human being is connected not only with the things that develop on Earth, but also with everything that the eye can see when it turns toward the heavens. All of the processes that occur in human beings (including the physical ones) are processes that are connected with what happens on the Sun, with what happens on the other planets in the solar system.

If you read my *Outline of Esoteric Science,* you will see that this awareness, that the human being has a relationship not only to the Earth, but also to the more-than-earthly world, is to be reestablished through anthroposophical spiritual science (which the *Outline of Esoteric Science* is meant to serve). There, it is indicated that our Earth itself is only a temporary incarnation of that Being which previously had existed as Moon, Sun, and Saturn, and it is also indicated that the human being will continue to evolve, and these later evolutionary forms of the human being will be connected with future evolutionary forms of Earth—with Jupiter, Venus, and Vulcan. In this, all that belongs to the human being is lifted above the merely earthly. The human gaze will again turn toward the cosmos. This is one of the things that must enter our awareness, if we are not to degenerate on Earth: that the human being belongs to the cosmos, that the human is connected in its inner Being to more-than-earthly spheres.

Why must we become conscious of this? We must become conscious of it because self-knowledge is necessary; not the self-knowledge that exists in the incubator of one's own beloved "I," but the knowledge of the human as a universal Being. This self-knowledge must spread throughout the world. It must become increasingly common knowledge. Unless human beings come to an understanding of themselves, there will be no place for them—in particular, no place for them in the future of human evolution. But achieving this understanding is not simply a matter of incubating this secondary, chaotic, inner human being a little so that it grows; it is rather a matter of considering this concrete, inner human being in all its aspects, just as you would not simply describe the natural world by pointing and saying "Nature! Nature! Nature!" but would rather indicate different aspects and say, "Here are plants, here are animals," and then go on to sort the plants into their respective genus and species. In the same way, we must identify the same sorts of divisions within human soul life, particularly the various metamorphoses of that soul life.

Now let us describe these individual metamorphoses of the soul life from one angle, so to speak. First is the metamorphosis of our soul life that is the most connected with our physical bodies, that is the most the dependent upon our physical bodies. This is the soul capacity that we refer to as memory or the ability to recollect. Through memory, we are able to renew the experiences of our individual lifetime. Through our ability to recollect, we are able to follow a thread from a particular moment—from around two, three, four, or more years after our birth—up the things happening in the present moment. A person would become inwardly sick if this thread were broken. I have spoken about this often in the past.[†] If ever we would look back on some part of our life in such a way that we lose our memory of certain things that preceded it, then the connection with our experience is gone. And this would cause us to grow sick in our sense of ourselves. On the other hand, we can easily recognize how deeply memory is connected with our physical bodies. We need only to recall a fact that I have often hinted at[†] and that is widely known— that when we suffer from insomnia, or when other experiences in our life make us unable to sleep well, our memory suffers as a result. This alone (as well as many other things) proves how dependent memory is upon the physical body.

Less dependent on our physical bodies, which is to say more independent from our physical constitution, is what we refer to as intelligence. But this intelligence is still strongly dependent upon our physical constitution. Memory has relationship only to an individual. Intelligence is something we share with other human beings, at least at a high level. Certainly one person might be more or less intelligent than another (usually every person considers himself or herself the most intelligent of all). In general, you could say that it is certainly a fact that one person is more intelligent and another person less so, but there is a general uniformity spread out over the spectrum of human intelligence. Whereas the content of each person's memory is his or her own and cannot be seen by another—whereas the content of memory is therefore something very individual, the content of intelligence is similar for all of humanity. It is thereby less bound to the physical constitution of a human being. The physical constitution of a human being is actually like a mirror to unfolding processes of intelligence. Anyone who claims that the processes of the human nervous system and brain create thoughts is as foolish as the person standing before a mirror in which Fräulein Scholl, Fräulein Laval, and Herr Grosheintz[†] appear, claiming: "The mirror has created Fräulein Scholl, Fräulein Laval and Herr Dr. Grosheintz." Just as the mirror is related to the three people I named, and just as those three people have an existence outside of that mirror and actually have nothing further to do with it, so does intelligence merely allow itself to be reflected through the brain to appear in our consciousness. The processes of intelligence exist outside of the brain. We would know nothing of our intelligence if we did not have a brain. The processes of intelligence would not be reflected there. But these intelligence processes have an existence outside of the brain as well—processes that are merely reflected in it.

And then we come to the third capacity of the human soul, which is, by and large, the least dependent upon our physical constitution. People have a hard time believing this, because they consider this faculty to be the most dependent upon on physical constitution. This is the capacity of sense activity. Take the eye. The eye itself has nothing to do with the processes of sight. The process of seeing is much less dependent upon the eye than the process of intelligence is dependent upon the brain. What the eye has to do with seeing is altogether different. The processes that occur in our consciousness as the content of sight—these processes have nothing to do with the eye. What occurs in the eye has an effect only because our consciousness, our "I," is present for the process of seeing. Please, pay close attention to this fundamental, but not easily understood difference.

Take, for example, a man who, through some sort of illness, has lost both of his eyes. Because of this, he has not lost the process of sight as such. Rather, he has lost the ability to perceive the process of sight in his "I." His "I" is not aware of this. It is simply his "I" as it was before, but with the process of sight turned off. What occurs in this example can be compared with the following.

Imagine you have three telegraph stations: A, B, and C. At each telegraph station, you have stationed a telegraph operator. If the operator in A sends a telegraph to the operator in C, then the man stationed in C will be able to read the message sent from A to C. There is no need to discuss whether the Morse code machine in A created the content of the message or not. The machine is simply the transmitter. Similarly, the Morse code machine in C cannot read—it is simply the receiver. If then, on the path between A and C, we were to insert station B, then the operator in station B could sit there and hear or read along; he would simply need to let the strokes appear on the page in front of him, and then he could read along. So B has been inserted in the message stream along which the content of the telegraph is transmitted. But the content that travels from A to C has absolutely nothing to do with the processes that play out in the Morse code device in station B. Because the device in that station is turned on, the content is simply perceived.

Naturally, if the device were not turned on, then that content would not be perceived. The same is true of the human eye. The processes of the eye have nothing to do with the inner truth of sight. The eye is simply turned on in the processes of seeing. And because the eye is turned on, the "I" is able to see through the process of sight. But the eye is absolutely not the thing that transmits or affects or does anything with the content in the process of seeing. It is simply the receiving device for the "I." Paradoxically, we could say (if we do not expose ourselves to the danger that those big-headed, misguided people today would find to be a paradox) that our eye, as a sense organ, has nothing to do with sight, but everything to do with what our "I" has knowledge of sight. Sense organs such as the ones we currently possess

—which is to say, the higher sense organs—are not there for seeing; they are there so that the "I" can know sight. I would like to write this sentence on the board: *Higher sense organs are not there to transmit sense processes; they are there so that the "I" can know of sense processes.*

There we have the three so-called "higher" soul faculties: memory, intelligence, and sense activity. The "I" is integrated into them. It is most strongly integrated into the physical body in memory, less so in intelligence, and least of all in sense activity.

What I have just outlined for you comes from the following truths. Memory did not always exist in human beings as it does now. It evolved into its present form. And what lies at the root of this evolution into memory was a primary fact of human existence during the last incarnation of the planet that is now our Earth—during Moon evolution. Back then, memory existed as a form of unconscious, dreamlike Imagination. Memory was once dreamlike Imagination. Because our physical bodies developed into the form that they currently possess, this lively, dreamlike Imagination, which once filled human soul life completely during Moon evolution, was able to develop into what we now call our memory.

During Sun evolution, when we did not have a physical form like the one we currently possess, when we were beings of the sort I describe in my *Outline of Esoteric Science*, our intelligence was dormant Inspiration. This dormant Inspiration went on to develop into our modern-day intelligence. Sense activity, on the other hand, was once a form of very dull Intuition during Saturn evolution. Again, you can read more exact descriptions of all of this in my *Outline of Esoteric Science*. And this dull Intuition went on to develop into our present-day sense activities.

	Moon Evolution	Sun Evolution	Saturn Evolution
Sense activity			Dull Intuition
Intelligence		Dormant Inspiration	
Memory	Dreamlike Imagination		

Now, you might ask: "Why is it so difficult for people to arrive at truths of such import?" And once these truths are communicated to them, you might ask: "Why are they so resistant to this?" Well, you see, the answer is in the nature of the things themselves. We had a dull Intuition during Saturn evolution. Over time, it evolved into our sense activities. But actually, we can only prove that one of our present-day senses developed directly out of the structures of the ancient senses present on Saturn—our hearing. Hearing most clearly has its origins in Saturn evolution. Sight came about later on—you can also read about all of this in my *Outline of Esoteric Science*—mostly during Sun evolution. But already, you can see that though the origins lie on ancient Saturn in the form of dull Intuition, new senses were added on later. During Sun evolution, new senses came about that were not yet as highly developed as the ones that originated on Saturn. During Moon evolution, more new senses came into being, and during Earth evolution as well. On Earth, we developed our sense of taste, which is actually the least developed of the senses. Taste, if we considered it by itself, apart from our other senses, could be described as a kind of dull Intuition in our physical form, an undeveloped and dull Intuition.

It is similar in regard to the sense of smell. In that case, something particularly unusual is evident. I would recommend the following to anyone who is interested: Take a look at physiology or psychology (and by that I mean psychology—soul science—as it is written about currently)—you will see that much is written in those fields about the senses. What is written in those fields about the senses—anyone who considers it impartially will recognize that it is only true of the sense of touch. You will perhaps remember what I wrote in my book *Theosophy* about the relationship between the higher senses and the sense of touch[†]—something that Goethe had already noted as well.[†] Educated men and women in our society want to describe the senses, but they only describe that aspect of the senses that developed entirely on Earth, that aspect that made its first appearance on Earth. In the case of sight, this kind of description hits upon the truth just like (and you can say this literally) a fist hits an eye. For what is described in psychology texts is not actually sight; what is described in those texts will only come about if you hit yourself in the eye with your fist. This is the origin of that quaint doctrine based in the so-called specific sense energies[†] of the eye, energies that did not come from sight, but were rather evidenced by the fact that when a blow was delivered to the eye, one saw a whole variety of colors and shapes. These learned gentlemen are actually describing quite accurately something that happens when you hit your eye with your fist. And with that description, they are attempting to understand sight.

You can understand the senses only when you consider them in connection to things that are not here any longer: Saturn evolution, Sun evolution, Moon evolution. You can understand intelligence only when you consider it in connection with things that are no longer here: Sun evolution, Moon evolution. You can understand memory only when you understand it in connection to something that is no longer here: Moon evolution. And from Earth evolution, you can only understand what the "I" takes from the senses, from memory, and from intelligence; for it is during Earth evolution that the "I" was first incorporated into the physical body. And the organs that developed in human beings during Earth evolution are absolutely not there to disseminate the higher soul faculties, but rather to allow these higher soul faculties to be revealed through an "I." We have eyes for our "I," ears for our "I," a nose for our "I," not a nose for smelling—which might otherwise be correct, since it was first developed during Earth evolution; but it is no longer altogether correct in that it will also continue to evolve through Earth evolution. But we do not have eyes for seeing or ears for hearing either—we have ears so that our "I" can know something about the things that come in through our ears, just as a telegraph machine is turned on so that a telegraph operator (and not the machine itself) can know of the communications passing between stations A and C. Insofar as we continue to say that we have eyes for seeing, ears for hearing, and insofar as everything is clothed in this mode of expression, we speak something that has no truth and no reality. We speak in illusions. We speak in falsehoods. We are not aware of the true reason that we have physical bodies. We do not have them for the purposes of disseminating our higher soul faculties; we have bodies so that our "I" can have some experience of these higher soul faculties. Our whole physical form is a depiction of our "I." And we are constituted in the way that we are constituted because we each have an I. In our physical bodies, we are to become aware of the physical depiction of our I. For our physical body, in the form that we currently bear, we first received from the Earth. And it does no good to take up things that were not given to us by the Earth, things that were not derived from what has occurred on the Earth, and then to look for the causes and origins of those things in what has occurred on the Earth.

Just as we are able to say that Moon evolution gave the most to our memory because our memory's origin lies in that evolutionary phase; just as we can say that Sun evolution gave the most to our intelligence because its origin lies in that evolutionary phase (and so on back to Saturn evolution and sense activity), so must we also recognize that these higher soul capacities also have something to do with the beings of the upper hierarchies—namely, that our memory has a connection to the angels, our intelligence to the archangels, and our senses to the archai.

	Moon Evolution	Sun Evolution	Saturn Evolution
Sense activity			Dull Intuition Archai
Intelligence		Dormant Inspiration Archangels	
Memory	Dreamlike Imagination Angels		

And here I come to an important chapter of spiritual knowledge. Imagine for a moment that in human self-knowledge, you are reflecting on memory, on our ability to recollect. You say: "I am turning my inner organ, my soul organ toward the activity of memory." But when you consider this act from a fully conscious place, then you must also go on to say to yourself: "In this act, in this process of recollection, there are angels living and moving throughout that inner organ." Take a moment now and try to remember something that you experienced yesterday, some sort of experience that you had. In doing this, you have carried out an inner soul process. In the process that occurred, during which a thought from yesterday again appeared within you, an experience from yesterday revealed itself anew in your memory—an angel is active in all of that activity. And when you think about something intelligently—and it must actually be thinking intelligently, not merely brooding, not merely doing what most people call intelligent thinking, which is really nothing more than cooking one's memory more thoroughly, than allowing the body to stew upon memories. Thinking begins truly when you actively and inwardly take up your thoughts. So, when one develops this sort of inner activity, an archangel is present for that. And when you so much as listen to or look at what is around you, then you must say to yourself: "In my ears and in my eyes are the thrones of the archai— the spirits of time." Whenever you find yourself asking: "Where are the spirits of time, the archai, who rule over each age of the world as it follows on the next?"—then you should not go looking for them in distant or unfamiliar regions; you need only to look in the sense organs of human beings. There is where they sit. A decadent time (in regard to sense perceptions) has already sought the gods up above in the heavens, where they are not to be found—and the spirits of time in the heavens as well, where they are not to be found. When a person asks: "Then where are the spirits of time?"—they are sitting in his eyes, in her ears. Their thrones are there.

From another perspective, this helps to illuminate something that I once described to you when I spoke of the places within human beings that provide guidance to the events of nature. In certain esoteric circles, when you allow yourself to hear the right sayings and be pointed in the correct directions, you will find that the truths that I have laid out for you are also hinted at in these sayings, which come from ancient times; that the human being is a temple for the gods that stand above him, meaning for the beings of the upper hierarchies. This is meant in the most literal sense. For when you ask: "Where does one find the angels, archangels, and archai?"—then I must respond by saying: "In the organs of human memory, human intelligence, and human sense perceptions." You have to say (if you speak truly) that the human being is truly filled with spirit, meaning that it is filled with spiritual beings. The Catholic Church did not want human beings to be aware of this, which is why in 869 C.E. at the Eighth Ecumenical Council,† they forbade people to have any knowledge of or belief about spiritual things, establishing the dogma that human beings are comprised only of body and soul.

This human is a vastly complex being, and if you, let us say for example, were to place yourself on a distant star and were to observe the happenings on Earth from that perspective, the mineral world would immediately vanish and would only appear outwardly as a shining light. The plant kingdom and the animal kingdom would also be barely perceptible. You would not be able to perceive individual human beings either, but the thrones would be there in the space around the Earth, occupied by angels, archangels, and archai. And a being who had the necessary capacities of sight and perception to see things as such from that distant star would say: "The Earth is a body in space that is the home of the archai, archangels, and angels." In the words of the gods, it would be said that the Earth is the home of the spirits of time, the archangels, and the angels. In the everyday speech of human beings, this translates to: The human being has sense organs, instruments of intelligence, and a constitution for memory. But humanity is called upon to truly come to know the human being, to seek the true relationship between this human being and the spiritual world.

Before now, the pendulum of civilization had swung in a different direction. People investigated the chemical properties of foodstuffs in order to understand which parts of food human beings absorbed into their bodies. Our physicality was understood to be the same as what we took from our food, and so on—people sought out these sorts of relationships. They said: "The things that are out there in the world in the various plants and animals find their way into human beings; one moment it is out there in the form of cabbage and cow, the next moment it is taken into the form of the human being and actually constitutes that form." They see a steer; they look at it. Then, they see a person who has eaten the meat that came from that steer; and they follow the trail of the meat that this person ate—which until a few days before had been a part of the steer—attempting to determine how it has been integrated into that person's inner workings. Here we have the relationship between the physical and the natural world. Here we have traced the way in which the meat, which was once a part of the steer's haunches, afterwards becomes a part of the human being's inner workings.

We have spent enough time tracing this relationship. We have concocted a worldview out of it, resulting from the pendulum swinging far to one particular side of the spectrum of human worldviews. Now it is time for the pendulum to swing in the other direction. Now we must come to know that the soul element of human beings also has a relationship to the spiritual world, to spiritual substance. And what comprise spiritual substance—archangels, archai, angels—they are in human beings just as the steer is in a human being after a person eats a piece of meat; they are in human bodies. Contemporary science admits the latter point, but still ridicules the former. But for the future evolution of humankind, it is just as necessary for people to know what relationship they have to angels as it is for them to know what relationship they have to steers or cabbage (I mean physical cabbage)!

We are at a critical juncture in time—the necessity is before us to turn toward the way in which the spiritual world plays into our soul lives, having spent long enough considering very one-sidedly the way in which the physical world plays into the physical aspects of human beings. For the human being's further development, now it is not enough to hear certain abstract religious truths dogmatically proclaimed by devotees of a church. We all have to busy ourselves with thinking about what relationship our earthly form has to the spiritual world. First of all, this spiritual world has a relationship to the "I." We will learn about other relationships tomorrow. But that which appears in our earthly form as a constitution for the capacity of memory has a relationship to the hierarchy of angels. That which is embedded into our constitution for our capacity of intelligence has a relationship to the world of the archangels. That which announces itself to us in our higher senses, namely the things that unfold in our high arts—this has a relationship to the world of the archai, the spirits of time.

We must become able as human beings not only to chat with one another about the fact that a spiritual world exists; we must become able to feel the concrete relationships between human beings and the spiritual world. We must become able to feel that what echoes in us as the sense of hearing is actually a product of a long developing fact that is now intermingled with our world, something in which the archai are active. We must become able to understand that when we are thinking, we are existing in a world that is filled with archangels; whenever we recollect things, we exist in a world that is filled with angels; and when we become conscious of our "I," for which we always require our physical bodies most of all, then it is a revelation of our "I." At that moment, we are for the first time in the world in which the human being moves and weaves. Even in the Greek Mysteries, it was said: "When you meet the Guardian of the Threshold, then you learn to recognize in a higher way the things that exist in human beings." On this side of the Threshold, we only come to know thoughts that hearken back to a prior experience. On the other side of the Threshold, the angels flit and scurry about us. On this side of the Threshold, we come to know the intelligent Being. On the other side of the Threshold, we experience the way in which the archangels flit and scurry about us. On this side of the Threshold, we perceive the sensory world. On the other side of the Threshold, we come to know the way in the archai, the spirits of time, move in and out through our eyes, through our ears.

We must therefore see to it that conscious awareness is awakened in each individual human being—the awareness that we each stand in a relationship to the spiritual world by the very fact of our physical constitution. This must, however, be awakened concretely in each of the individual organs. We must learn to feel ourselves a part of a spiritual world, whereas the worldview which has presently reached its zenith only allows us to feel as though we live in the physical world. This feeling—that we are living only in a physical world—will forever be the dominant feeling, unless the occurrence at Golgotha is allowed to enter in. The fact that we have the ability to develop again a conscious awareness of our relationship to the spiritual is owed to the Mystery of Golgotha. But what we owe to the Mystery of Golgotha must be sought freely out of our own inner impulses. Christianity requires freedom.

What we are able to know through this about our relationship to the spiritual world—this can actually gain true efficacy in humanity. And the efficacy which we have tried to lay as the pedagogical foundation in the Stuttgart Waldorf School—this is born out of this conscious awareness, that the human being is something more than a synthesis of external natural phenomena. There, the teachers are to teach and lecture in such a way that they are not only aware of the baby that grows up physically—the being that, once it has been weaned off of milk, will over time take in cabbage and beef— but also aware of the soul being, in which the beings of the higher spiritual world actively participate. And insofar as we are educating in our classes, we are leading the activity of the beings of these higher hierarchies into the being of the developing child. People should not simply learn to kneel at the altar and pray for their own egotism; they should learn to make all that they do in the world into acts of worship. Nowadays, what people need to learn is that everything that a human being does in the world must be done as an act of worship, as the completion of an urgent task. But this is opposed by those who do not want to allow human beings to take part in these higher tasks of humanity.

When I was trying yesterday in St. Gallen† to discuss the effectiveness, the productiveness of the things that can flow out of spiritual knowledge into the field of education, I was told that we have now reached a point at which the clerical newspapers in St. Gallen contained no advertisements about the lecture I was giving that day, meaning they had refused even to give notice about it. This kind of opposition will become ever better organized. Organization is understood by all sides. I only say this to you so that you are aware of the opposition to the inclusion of truth in the world, which has become ever more present and effective. I will tell you of these things again and again. I also would like you to be not unfamiliar with these little

facts so that you truly feel that it is not a task for dormant souls—
advocating for the truth of Christ. On the contrary, it is increasingly
a task for those souls that are awake. We also need organizations
in order to counteract the organization forming on the other side.
Tomorrow we will speak of this further.

14

THE METAMORPHOSIS OF FEELING, DESIRING, AND WANTING

DORNACH, FEBRUARY 14, 1920

I would like briefly, in the interest of review, to draw your attention to what I presented to you in the lecture yesterday, because today I am going to add to this further things relating to the Being of human-kind. What I had to say to you yesterday consisted of the following: We turned our gaze first of all toward the three faculties of the human soul dedicated primarily to knowledge. We drew our attention to the fact that there are three cognitive faculties in the human soul—first the capacity of recollection or memory, then the capacity we refer to as intelligence, and finally the capacity of sense perception.

Then I pointed out to you that these three soul faculties could be understood only when you took into consideration their development. In order to understand memory (which, in comparison to the other two, is the youngest of the human capacities), you must turn your gaze back toward a time when the Earth did not yet have the form that it possesses currently, a time when the Earth was going through Moon evolution, the phase immediately prior to its current phase as Earth evolution. The origin of what has now become memory in us can be found in this Moon evolution and appeared there not as memory, but as a dreamlike Imagination that filled the human being completely (which I have often described in the past in connection with other things[†]). What was once dreamlike Imagination during Moon evolution for the beings that would later develop into Earth human beings—this became the capacity of memory during Earth evolution.

Of all the cognitive soul capacities, this memory, as I have told you,[†] is the one most bound up with human physicality. Intelligence is less bound up with our physical bodies. It is more independent of them, in the sense that I described to you yesterday. But in order to discover its origins, you must look back in time further, beyond Moon evolution—you have to go back to Sun evolution. There, you will find the beginnings of the faculty that exists in us today as intelligence in the form of dormant Inspiration. You must look the farthest back in time in order to find the origins of what (as I explained yesterday) is the most independent from our physical bodies, although people today believe this least of all because they are coming out of a materialistic worldview: To discover the origins of sense perceptions, you have to go back to Saturn evolution. And in the beings that would eventually become Earth human beings, you find the origin of these sense perceptions in the form of a dull Intuition.

We went on yesterday to see that insofar as we bear these three soul capacities within us, we also harbor the Beings of the upper hierarchies in us in the structures underlying these soul capacities. In the structures of our sense perceptions, we harbor the archai, the spirits of time. They reside in our humanity. Through what we possess as intelligence, insofar as this intelligence is connected to the mirroring structure in us that reflects our concepts and ideas (which actually come out of the spiritual world), bringing them to our consciousness, we harbor the archangels. And through what works in our physical being and disseminates memory, we harbor the angels. In this way, we are connected by our cognitive faculties to the past; in this way, we are connected by our cognitive faculties to the upper hierarchies.

According to an old custom, these three human faculties are referred to as the higher faculties. And if I were to sketch out a depiction of the human being for you, if I were to visually depict a sort of schematic of the human being, I would draw something like this (See p. 203). First, I would sketch out the capacity of sense activity. I would attempt to do that by drawing a white background. First of all, I would depict in our schematic the sense activity in the physical structure of the human being itself, and must therefore draw it something like this, so that I end up with the right relationship between things later (blue). The bulk of sense activity takes place in our head, after all. Of course, the whole of the human being is filled with sense activity, but for now I would like to draw the sense activity here in the head (blue).

If I then wanted to draw in the intelligence, I would have to do so in the following manner in order to make it clear: sense activity is directed outwards (blue); intelligence (green) has its reflecting structure more in the brain itself. Deeper still is the structure underlying memory—already very connected with the physical structure itself. In reality, memory (red) is connected with the lowest part of the nervous system structure and with the limbs and torso. I could then make transitions between sense activity and intelligence by drawing in this section here (indigo) as a point of transition between the two. You know that some of our concepts and ideas have a particularly vivid or graphic nature. Though I drew sense activity as such here with blue, I would draw-in this section of indigo as a point of transition to intelligence. For more abstract concepts, I have drawn this area of green; and for those concepts that are intimately connected with memory, I have drawn them as the transition from green to red through orange toward this section of yellow. In this way, I have moved from outer to inner in drawing the structure of the human being as it relates to the cognitive faculties of the soul. If you think of the physical structures, particularly of the eyes and ears, shaded blue, moving through indigo into green as sense activity fades to intelligence, brightening through yellow to red as it moves into memory—you can take from this sequence of colors a kind of schematic that closely shadows the reality of the human soul or cognitive capacities.

Now, in the nature of human beings, everything is connected and interacts with everything else. This is what makes the work of materialistically-minded people so difficult—the fact that everything is connected in human nature. You cannot draw neat and clean boxes separating one part from another. Things are not that distinctly separated in human nature, but you can learn all kinds of things about the relationship between different aspects by drawing a schematic like this. In fact, you can see that the way in which the color red relates to the color green is the same way that the capacity for memory and

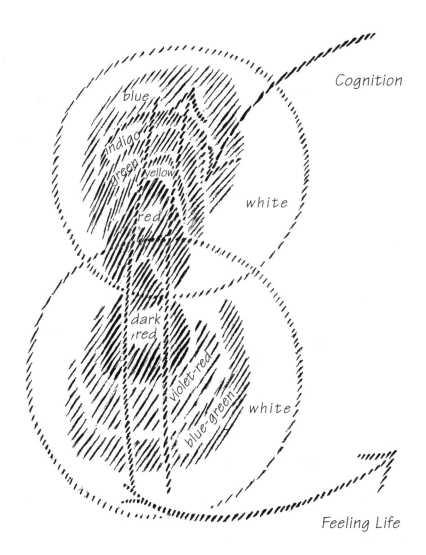

the capacity for intelligence relate to one another through their inner properties; and the way in which green relates to blue is the same ways in which intelligence relates to sense activity.

Now, we also have other capacities in the human soul—capacities are the most bound up with our physical bodies (to a greater or lesser extent) as human beings on Earth. The first of these is our feeling life. Whereas memory, intelligence, and sense activity are progressively connected to our awakened consciousness, feeling is something that is still very dreamlike in human beings. I have spoken of this often. Whereas memory is something that, in the distant past, developed originally as a faculty during Moon evolution—intelligence during Sun evolution, sense activity during Saturn evolution—the feeling life as it exists for us today (though the beginnings of it came earlier during Moon evolution, they are less important in these considerations) belongs to human beings on Earth. What we received in our organism as human beings on Earth actually made us, for the first time, into feeling beings.

But just as memory is something that has moved beyond its initial stage as a faculty of soul and arrived on the Earth at a higher stage of development, and one can (if one possesses enough supersensory insight to do so) recognize that memory is in many ways an older capacity for human beings; you can also recognize that the feeling life is only in its first stage as a human capacity. If you have the proper understanding to do so, you can look at what we currently refer to as our feeling life and see that in the future it will become something altogether different. Just as, had you been an observer of Moon evolution and examined the dreamlike Imagination that existed then, you would have said: "Later, that will become the capacity of human memory"—so must you consider the feeling life today and say: "When Earth is no longer here, when it has become something different, when the Earth has evolved in the coming Jupiter evolution, only then will the feeling life become what it is meant to develop into." Feeling life today is in an embryonic stage in human beings. It exists as a seed. Something will arise later out of feeling—the thing that it is to become in the future. In our feelings, we bear something within us that is related to what it will become during Jupiter evolution, in the same way that a child in its mother's womb is related to the human being who has already been born. Our feeling life is something embryonic, and later, during Jupiter evolution, it will blossom into fully developed, fully conscious Imagination.

Another soul capacity that is connected with our physical organism is our appetites, our desires. These desires are even more embryonic than our feeling life. Everything in the life of desires will only develop into what it is meant to be during Venus evolution. Our desires are today very tightly bound to our physical structure. They will eventually free themselves of this. Just as our intelligence was tightly bound to the bodily structures of our being during Sun evolution, as I described in my *Outline of Esoteric Science*, so is the life of desires bound to the bodily structures of human beings today. It will appear during the future Venus evolution, free from the bodily structures of the beings of that time, and it will come into being then as fully conscious Inspiration.

The most embryonic of all of our soul capacities is the will life. The will is called upon to become something vast and cosmic in the future, something through which the human being can come to belong to the entire cosmos—the human being shall be individualized, and yet shall live out its individual impulses as actualities in the world. This, however, is only to come about during Vulcan evolution, when the will-life develops into fully conscious Intuition.

So, in our feelings, desires, and willing, we belong in a way to future stages of evolution. These capacities reside in us so that the human being can be prepared for its future existence through them. But we also are brought into a relationship with the world through them, in that these human capacities have a connection to the world around us. Just as memory, intelligence, and sense activity connect us with the surrounding spiritual world through their relationship with angels, archangels, and archai, so do our feelings, desires, and will connect us with the surrounding physical world, but in such a way that the relationship between our feelings and the surrounding world is one in which our feelings constantly draw-in the mineral kingdom during Earth evolution. Everything that makes up the mineral kingdom around us will disappear at the end of Earth evolution, and the forces that human beings shall then draw into themselves from the mineral kingdom are the forces of feeling. Consequently, we must accept a special relationship between the feeling life and the mineral kingdom (see schematic below). We must also accept a special relationship between the life of desires and the plant kingdom. Just as on Jupiter (which will be the next incarnation of the planet Earth) there will be no mineral kingdom because during Earth evolution the feeling life will have drawn it up into itself, so will there be no plant kingdom during Venus evolution, and the human will-life will draw the animal kingdom into itself during Venus evolution. And when we glimpse ahead into Vulcan evolution, the future Vulcan incarnation of our planet Earth will not have these three kingdoms on it; rather, it will have only the beings that make up the current human kingdom, in the form that they will have evolved into at that time.

Higher Faculties

Sense activity	Saturn (dull Intuition)	Archai
Intelligence	Sun (dormant Inspiration)	Archangels
Memory	Moon (dreamlike Imagination)	Angels

Lower Faculties: Social World

Feeling	Jupiter (fully conscious Imagination)	Mineral Kingdom
Desires	Venus (fully conscious Inspiration)	Plant Kingdom
Willing	Vulcan (fully conscious Intuition)	Animal Kingdom

In response to everything that I have just said, some people nowadays might come forward and say: "I am not really interested in what I once was and what form my memory, intelligence, and sense perceptions had on Saturn or the Sun or the Moon; I am just happy with my existence now as a citizen of the Earth. What do I care about things that I know nothing about anymore, which happened on earlier incarnations of our planet? I am not interested in such things! And by the same token, I am not interested in what my feelings (which are of great interest to me now) will become on Jupiter or what my desires will develop into on the far-distant Venus. These desires are what drive me now; but this lady Venus—she does not interest me yet because she is not here right now, and I am only interested in ladies who are around now. And the same goes for the will and what it might become in some distant, distant future!"

Certainly, many people feel this way, and the culture nowadays would very much prefer to remain asleep in relation to everything that is trying to assert itself in regard to this knowledge—people do not want to awaken to it. But human evolution will not continue into the future unless we have this knowledge. For it is deeply true that everything is intermingled and interwoven in the human organism—the physical, soul, and spiritual structures of the human being; but one must also be able to distinguish things from one another. Just as the higher faculties can be drawn schematically from sense activity down to memory, so can I now also draw-in the lower faculties, which have been developed especially here on Earth (see drawing on page 203).

I have to do this in the following manner: a somewhat deeper shade of red (unfortunately, I do not have a different shade of chalk here) will represent our feeling life. But these feelings stretch all throughout our intelligence, our sense activity, and our memory as well. Then, when I have to draw the activity of our desires, I actually use a shade of violet-red. And if I were to draw the will life as it currently exists, I would have to draw it with a blue-green. As such, the human being has a dual existence—a higher human being (upper circle) that is essentially a cognitive being, and a lower human being (lower circle) that is essentially a being of desires and appetites, with feeling and willing as the two poles of these desires.

Now, as it happens, those things that compose the lower human being on Earth play into the upper being of the human, meaning that the willing, as well as the desires, as well as the feelings play a role in the upper being of the human (arrow pointing upwards). In other words, our sense activity is such that in it, we have everything that has developed out of the dull Intuition of Saturn evolution. But if in our eyes and in our ears we only carried those things that come from the dull Intuition of Saturn, then we would be truly dry and barren beings. We would perceive the outer world with senses that worked mechanically and automatically. We would think clinically and dryly about this physical world, and we would remember the things that we experienced without warmth. The fact that we experience what we have experienced as our own concerns, that for the most part we do not consider our experiences with indifference or remember our personal life as a collection of individual stones in a kaleidoscope, this makes our feelings, desires, and will ascend up into our memories, our intelligence, our sense activities. In looking on things in the outer physical world, we find that they bring us pleasure. They please us through the integration of desires, our feelings, or our will life. When we think about something, we do not think clinically or dryly, but rather we bring a certain enthusiasm into our ideas. We would not do this if we possessed only the things that had been given to us as the powers of intelligence from Sun evolution. We do this because the Earth has filled us with a will life, with desires, with feelings, even if these things are still in an embryonic state. The same is true of our capacity to recollect things. In our higher faculties, the things that, according to an old custom, are referred to as our lower faculties, because they are more connected to our physical bodies, always play some role. We must hold tight to this first and foremost. Our higher soul faculties, which would be nothing more than dried-out bowels in this world if they were nothing more than what had developed out of the faculties from Saturn, Sun, and Moon evolution, are illuminated and warmed by the lower soul faculties—the willing, desiring, and feeling—and we become warm, feeling human beings, even when we think.

All the same, there are a tremendous number of people nowadays who strive for objectivity in such a way that they want to rid their intelligence of feelings and desires; but this is either nothing more than an illusion, if people believe that they can actually rid their sense activity, their intelligence, and their memory of the lower soul faculties; or, if one actually casts them out—and this is only possible to certain extent—then what! It is possible to cast the lower soul faculties out of the higher ones only to a certain extent. For example, you can cast them out when you step up to the lectern and present on various fields of science to freshmen or upperclassmen. In that instance, it is possible to cast the lower, the actual earthly soul faculties, out of one's intelligence. But you cannot cast them out entirely. After you leave behind your philosophizing and go back home, then real desires and feeling fill your intelligence as, for instance, you complain about what your housekeeper has fixed for your dinner, not to mention your sense activities of tasting and smelling and so on. And thus, one's existence is composed of a confusing mixture of being the desiccated philistine who has cast the lower soul faculties out of the higher and then is all-too capable of passionate emotions when served something that has too much salt or pepper, or is burned or otherwise not cooked properly!

Our lower soul faculties must play some role in the high soul faculties. But as a matter of fact, since the middle of the fifteenth century, there has been a movement in human evolution to make our sense activities, our intelligence, ever more pure, and someday in the future it will extend to our memory as well. As of now, it has not reached that point. People want to liberate these attributes. Indeed, they want not only to become like the desiccated philistine that I described earlier (only because this desiccated philistine is actually more connected with what human nature generally forms us to be), they actually want the entire physical body of the human being to become dried-out and desiccated, as I described in an earlier lecture,[†] so that the higher soul faculties will be less and less illuminated and warmed by the lower. People will actually become these sorts of dried-out shells when they are not filled with the things that can come out of spiritual revelation.

In fact, we must fructify sense activity, intelligence, and memory in the coming period of evolution with what is revealed to us from the spiritual world, because the earthly gifts that have been coming to our higher faculties in the form of willing, desires, and feelings are gradually drying up. We cannot just snidely criticize these starchy philistines, as we have just done; rather, we must simultaneously recognize that this philistine is a kind of pioneer into the future drying-up of our higher soul faculties, who is already experiencing in the body what will befall

all of humanity in the near future. The problem is that the philistine does not also feel how necessary it is that this desiccated being also be filled with spiritual revelation. This drying-up must be replaced by spiritual revelation. Just as human beings were, until now, used to experiencing the upward-streaming (arrow upward) of the will life, desires, and feelings into their memory, intelligence, and sense activities, so must they now experience the streaming downwards of the revelations of the spiritual world through spiritual knowledge (arrow downward, upper right), so that their sense activities, intelligence, and memory can be filled with the things with which they are no longer being filled—because our physical bodies are becoming ever more dried-out and desiccated by earthly decadence.

First and foremost, we must come to grips with the fact that we are facing a time in which everything operating in human sense activity, intelligence, and memory must welcome spiritual revelation into its inner being in order for human culture to make any progress forward. Let us turn now to these lower human faculties, which only exist at present in an embryonic form. These lower human faculties are what primarily bring us into a relationship with our surrounding world. Even inwardly, they stand in relationship to the surrounding world through a connection to the mineral kingdom, the plant kingdom, and the animal kingdom, which together compose the world around us. When we feel, we experience feeling in regard to the things in the world around us; when we desire something, we desire something in the surrounding world; when we engage in an act of will, we take an a direct role in the active Being of our surrounding world. In all of this, we stand in the midst of the world around us. And what, if we were to ask, will happen as these things continue to develop; what will become of the feelings, desires, and will of the human beings that live together on the Earth?

When you consider everything we call the social world with a spiritual eye, you see that it is entirely the result of the willing, desires, and feelings of coexisting human beings. And everything we experience as human beings as feelings, everything that we want from one another and from the natural world, and everything that occurs between people as the result of willing—all of this is actually the outer world. When we desire something, we are a part of the social order, far more than we believe is the case. We are made into a being that desires something through our place in the social world, and our will engages the social will everywhere, such that the things occurring in the social world occur because of our will. Thus, an independent life exists within the thing that we refer to as our social order—a life of human feelings, desires, and will. The current Social Democratic Party claims that everything that exists in the world is a result of economics, of economic forces as they develop over time. No. The things that exist in the external world are an objectification of the feelings, desires, and will-forces of the human beings living together in society. Things that appear first within human beings as feelings go on to create conditions that bring about something in human social life. The same is also true of human desires, and especially true of human will. But in human nature, everything is interconnected. Here below I have drawn in the colors that represent our feelings, desires, and will. The cognitive faculties—sense activity, actual intelligence, memory—work their way downwards and then have an effect on the social world through our will (lower arrow, pointing to the right).

In the future, if human beings continue to harden in their physical bodies, then little will be able to flow out of them into the social world. The experiences of our senses, our intelligence, and our individual human memories and the thoughts associated with them will all flow out into the social world without first making their way through our feelings, desires, and wills. In other words: If we rely only on the physical earthly structures of our bodies and things continue develop accordingly, then our bodies will harden and we will be left only with sense perceptions, intelligence, and memory that are not fructified by the spiritual world; and then desiccated intelligence, purely physical sense activity, and egotistical memories of individual human beings will be the rule of the day in social life.

The things that are beginning to happen now in Russia will spread ever farther into the rest of the world. In Russia, the seed has been planted in Leninism and Trotskyism, preparing a social order that stems solely from sense experiences, intelligence, and a few egotistical memories of individual human beings. People do not realize yet that this eastern European society is striving to be a purely rationalistic society, one that is to be formed purely out of the cognitive faculties of earthly human beings resulting from the evolution out of Saturn, Sun, and Moon evolution, and that they are seeking to consciously eliminate everything that might be taken out of the spiritual world.

This feeling that teaches us how solidified human civilization is becoming, such that human beings are turning into nothing more than ambulatory machines; this feeling that teaches us what will become of the world when we continue to entrust it to dictators like Lenin and Trosky; this feeling must come out of knowledge of the Being of human nature that we have placed before our souls in the past two days. A knowledge such as this shows us that it is a simple necessity in human nature that illumination and warmth ascend into the higher soul faculties through spiritual revelation, so that the things that are to come from intelligence and sense perception and memory do not flow out into social life without being first fructified by the spiritual world. Human beings must learn to feel what connects them with the whole of Earth's existence, and they must learn to feel out of spiritual knowledge the things that are beginning to brew in the East, threatening to consume all of Asia in an ever-accelerating pace of life. Human beings must learn to feel this as the great and terrible sickness of modern civilization—a sickness that must be healed. And it can only be healed properly when it is diagnosed correctly.

To pursue spiritual science today means to seek a process for healing our sickened society. This must be felt by a sufficiently large portion of the population on Earth, and it must be felt deeply and fundamentally. Without spiritual science, this kind of feeling will not fill us. And nowadays, all of the major actions in the world are carried out without any feeling for what is actually being done. The actions taken at Versailles† were nothing less and are nothing less than an inculcation of poison into society—a poison that is bound to make humanity sicker than it was before. For everything that is done without a knowledge of the future requirements of life on Earth is a harmful and sickening action for humanity's ongoing evolution.

People nowadays typically hear statements like these as being spoken out of emotion and passion. Here, I am not speaking them to you from that place. Here, they are derived from a knowledge of the Being of human nature. And here it can be shown that the spiritual life of human beings, which is born in memory, intelligence, and sense activity, cannot exist long into the future unless it is fructified by the spiritual world.

People today will not admit this. But why will they not admit it? They will not admit it for historical reasons. Since the middle of the fifteenth century, we have been working endlessly on the structures that we now consider the bearers of civilization—the modern states and countries. But in the future, these modern-day countries can be of relevance to the things related to human life between birth and death (I have spoken of this here in connection with other things[†]). They may not be involved at all in things that establish a connection between human beings and the spiritual world. Human beings must, in the future, become able to receive the spiritual world into their memory, intelligence, and sense activity as individuals. Only the individual human being can do this; only each of us individually can do this. In the future, the individual must become the mediator between heaven and Earth, between the spiritual world and the physical world. And people nowadays rightly feel—though the way in which they arrive at these feelings is actually backward—but nevertheless, they feel that it is somehow improper when streams that should flow only into individuals, instead flow into so-called official state business. When the Russian czar and his wife used the inner experience of Rasputin[†] to guide their leadership of the country, people were rightly afraid, for revelations that come from the spiritual world should play only into spiritual life and not into the rights life. In the case of the latter, we should allow only healthy reason that has been developed out of spiritual revelation to play a role. Well, Rapustin never got to healthy reason—he simply stuck with the revelations.

On the other hand, in external social life, the only thing that should find a place is what is connected with the lower faculties of human beings, with the faculties developing here on Earth, with desires, feelings, and will. These things develop in the interaction of one human with another; and they do not develop through interchange with the abstract whole of humanity, only within circles of people who share a common interest, within circles connected through their particular common desires, their particular feelings about one thing or another, or through the will that they must develop together.

This lays the groundwork for the necessity of a threefolding of public life. In the future, the state, which may not allow spiritual life to enter into its affairs directly, also may not stretch its influence into that spiritual life. Spiritual life must be allowed to have its own independent place, because it cannot progress unless it is allowed to receive the revelations of the spirit. The state, when it is healthy, will dispense with spiritual revelations. If it steers itself toward the things that it thinks are good for it—spiritual life—then it will make that spiritual life into something terrible. Spiritual life must be divided from the state—an independent limb. By the same token, economic life may not be connected with the rights life, with the state, for this economic life must root itself firmly in feelings, desires, and wills of societies of individuals who are brought together by common interests as it emerges and develops in their associations and companies.

To put it briefly, just as the physicist comes to understand the complex phenomena of physical nature through performing simple research, so must we come to understand through a knowledge of human nature, with its higher faculties (memory, intelligence, and sense activity) and lower faculties (will, desires, and feelings) what is to occur in the evolution of humankind. The person who comes forward and discusses social ideas with a social will derived from a strong but altogether empty self-consciousness and the tone now commonly recognized as *the* persuasive human tone of voice is like a person who sits down before a telegraph machine without the slightest clue about electricity and magnetism (these very simple concepts) and presumes to explain the telegraph machine out of his total lack of knowledge. The people who talk about sociology nowadays are in most cases speaking out with the same awareness of their subject (even though it sounds very learned to most people) that a person who has never even heard of electricity has when he sees a Morse code machine in a telegraph station and says: "Inside of that device are a bunch of little knights (you cannot see them) who go riding over to the other station with the message (you cannot see that when it happens either)." And with that, he had described it all quite properly. Marxism's explanation of social reality is no different; our university sociologists' explanations of social reality are no different.

Reality presents itself truly only when we have first come to know human nature. But you come to know human nature only through a relationship to the entire cosmic order. For memory is connected with the more-than-earthly; intelligence is connected with the more-than-earthly; sense activity is connected with the more-than-earthly. The feeling life will become what it is truly to become only after the Earth is no longer here—the life of appetites and of the will becoming what they are truly to become sometime in the more distant future. Just as you must be conversant with simple concepts like the thermal properties of organisms and the properties of acoustics in order to be a physicist, so must people (and as many people as possible) become conversant with the basic connections between human beings and the world in order to speak about social matters. For what is to be brought about in social life is born into that social order by human beings. But the human being also bears the whole of the cosmos within itself.

Of course, there are those chinwags who speak out of some left-over and outdated perspective, saying that the human being is a microcosm, a little world in and of itself within the macrocosm. But they do not understand it, because they speak only in abstractions. The only person who has a right to speak about microcosms and macrocosms is the one who knows that before there were human beings on Earth, there were human beings on the Moon that possessed a dreamlike Imagination. Moon evolution ended and the Earth came into being. Out of that which was there no longer, but which once had been, human memory developed. Memory did not originate on the Earth. The only thing original to the Earth was the human "I" and its contact with and shaping of the present physical form of the human body. We must come to understand the human being concretely, or otherwise, we have no business referring to it as a microcosm.

My friends, we can only aid in the healing of this decadent civilization when we finally come to see that the human being must be spoken of as a cosmic being in those institutions and establishments in which philosophy is currently taught as if it were a collection of dog-eared abstractions. The consequences of this abstract, this purely abstract humanity appear in such philosophers as the American William James,[†] the Englishman Spencer,[†] the Frenchman Bergson,[†] or the German Kant[†] from Königsberg. These abstractions hide from humanity what it truly is. But the living knowledge of the spiritual world, which we must strive after through the pursuit of spiritual science, can bring human beings true self-knowledge.

More on this tomorrow.

15

A SPIRITUAL CONTEMPLATION OF
THREEFOLDING

DORNACH, FEBRUARY 15, 1920

YESTERDAY and the day before, I attempted to present to you how necessary it is for the future evolution of humanity that human beings arrive at true self-knowledge, meaning a knowledge of humanity's Being itself; and also that it is altogether impossible to arrive at a knowledge of humanity's Being without first discovering the connection between that Being and the more-than-earthly worlds. The physical body of the human being is only a small part of what it bears through the journey of its life. But this physical body alone, in the form in which it currently exists, is essentially a product of the Earth. Everything else that is a part of the human being is not a product of the Earth as I discussed with you in the two previous lectures.

Now, the current physical structure of the human body already hints at the fact that the human being as such is a being with an existence that extends beyond the immediate present. To be sure, the physical structure of the body points directly toward the earthly; but within its earthly context, the physical structure of the human body directs us to look beyond this immediate historical moment into the past and into the future. We named several cognitive faculties of the human soul in the previous lectures: sense activity, intelligence, the ability to recollect things; and we also named feelings, desires, and will activity as faculties of a more appetitive nature.

Now, if we ask ourselves: "What must human beings have within their physical bodies that allows them to develop these cognitive faculties?"—we must direct our gaze toward the structure of the human head and everything that is connected with it. The physical structure of the human head is necessary, though only in the sense that I discussed yesterday (and really only in that sense), in order for the "I," for earthly human consciousness, to develop these cognitive faculties. It is not correct to believe, as a result, that the eye must necessarily be what brings about our sense of sight; but it is correct to say that the eye is the transmitter of sight experiences to the ego and to consciousness. And the same goes for the other, specifically the higher senses.

In this way (and with many variations on what I have just said), the physical human body points directly toward the earthly; but at the same time, it hints at something beyond the present moment, such that we can say: "The physical body of a person that we see standing before us points backward toward that person's previous incarnation in the physical structure of the head." Just as our intelligence points backward toward the far distant past, toward Sun evolution, so do our present physical bodies with their earthly arrangement of cognitive soul faculties (meaning the directing of those cognitive faculties toward the ego-consciousness) point backward toward our previous lifetimes.

I have already drawn your attention in the past[†] to what the human head actually is. Schematically, you could depict it as follows (see drawing): The human being consists of a head, and then of the rest of the body. Let us say that this is our current lifetime (middle), this is our previous lifetime (left) and this is our next lifetime (right). We can say: "The head we possess now in our current lifetime came about through a metamorphosis of the limbs and torso of the physical body that we possessed in our previous lifetime, and we have lost the head we had during that previous lifetime." Of course, I do not mean that the actually physical organism of our limbs and torso (that is self-evident). Rather, I mean the forces, the shaping powers that the physical structure possessed. Everything that we currently bear as part of our bodies, excluding the head, which is the bearer of our cognitive faculties on behalf of our ego—our limbs and torso—these will become the physical structure of our head in our next incarnation.

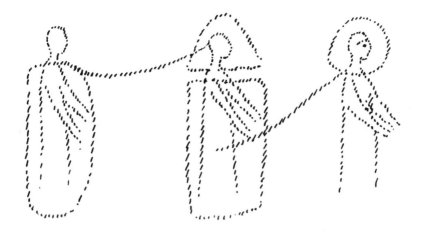

You all bear within you now the forces that will be concentrated into your heads during your next earthly life. The actions that you take with your arms, the actions you perform with your legs—all of this will go into the inner structure of your head in your next incarnation. And the forces that stream outward from your head during your next earthly life—that becomes your karma, your destiny for the incarnation to come. But everything that is to become your destiny in that coming incarnation travels into those future lifetimes first through the limbs and torso that you have now.

If, let us say, you have an intimate relationship with another person during one lifetime, this is something that involves actions taken by your physical body. This will then become a force within the structure of your head in your next incarnation, which will in turn affect your destiny. And so, our head and the capacities within it are always connected with our previous incarnations, namely with the torsos and limbs we had during that prior lifetime. The human being lies at the root of these great transformations. The head is a transformed physical structure stemming from a prior incarnation; and the physical structure of the current body, and particularly its limbs, lays the foundation for the structure of the head in the next earthly life.

In a certain sense, this has a definite practical significance for human society. For when people come to know that they are integrated into human evolution in this manner, then they begin to feel

their way into this life on Earth properly and will be able to understand certain things that would be otherwise incomprehensible. We
are currently living (as I have said before) in the fifth post-Atlantean
epoch. This epoch began in the middle of the fifteenth century—in
other words, in the middle of the fifteenth century, European civilization and its American counterpart (as it later developed) received a
different set of conditions for its existence. But as of now, the results
of these new conditions have not truly come into the world. Human
beings in civilized nations are living mostly on the basis of habits
(including habits of thinking) that are more appropriate to the prior,
fourth post-Atlantean epoch. We have not steeped our intelligence
in things that belong to the present—we have continued to teach
ourselves Greek, and Latin, and so on. An ancient Greek would have
had a different perspective on these matters. He would have been
confused if, in the time of ancient Greek culture, a teacher had not
taught his child Greek, but rather Egyptian or Persian or something
of the sort. The time has now passed in which we can allow ourselves
to linger on the remnants of the Greco-Roman era.

All of the people who were born after the middle of the fifteenth
century were by and large reincarnations of those who had lived as
physical beings on the Earth during the Greco-Roman period. What
did they bring with them—these reincarnated souls? The heads that
came from the bodies they had during the Greco-Roman period. So if
someone was born in, let us say the sixteenth or seventeenth century,
that person came to Earth with a head—one could also say, with
cognitive soul faculties, insofar as the head transmits those faculties
for our ego-consciousness—that stemmed from the body that he or
she had in the Greco-Roman era, and, consequently, with predispositions that also stemmed from that Greco-Roman era. But this period
is now coming to an end, if it has not ended already. Soon, there will
no longer be people being born whose head stems from that epoch;
instead, there are an increasing number of people being born who
lived their previous incarnation in the fifth post-Atlantean epoch, or
at the very least toward the end of the fourth post-Atlantean epoch,
when they led their lives in an entirely different way than those who
lived in the thick of the forth post-Atlantean epoch. This is not

yet true of everyone, but it is true of many, particularly the leading figures of the world.

If you want to live into human evolution with a fully-awakened consciousness, then you must take this into consideration: Your head stems from your previous incarnation on the Earth, and in your body, you are preparing the things that will become your head in your next incarnation on the Earth. And a time must come when an insufficient awareness of this connection in human beings between past and future incarnations becomes as clear an indication of stupidity as not knowing your own age, or believing that you were born only a few weeks ago even though you are an adult, or believing as a ten-year-old that you will always be ten and never grow into an elderly person. Nowadays, people live very egotistically during their life on Earth. At most, people believe that we all experience multiple lives on Earth, but it is merely a belief and not the kind of practical everyday wisdom that this feeling of being in between incarnations must become, just as it is common knowledge that a forty year old man was at one time a child and then a young adult and will go on to become an older man. We must expand the boundaries around the things that human consciousness grasps.

This expansion will not occur in a living way unless it is fructified by knowledge that comes from spiritual science. Otherwise, it will be nothing more than an abstract belief. Otherwise, we will never get beyond people saying: "Oh yes, I know that I have already lived on Earth countless times before and I will live here on Earth countless times in the future." But this kind of belief is meaningless. The only feeling of true integration with human evolution is the feeling that as far as your head is concerned, you are an older person because your head is the grown-up body of your prior incarnation; as far as the rest of your body goes, you are a baby because that body will grow up into only a head in your next incarnation—this feeling for the human as a being with two distinct parts that has been placed at this moment in time must become an integral part of our living consciousness.

And just as people are trying to determine the differences between individuals and populations and races of people by measuring their skulls and doing other similar and interesting things, so will they come to understand the differentiation between individuals living on the Earth based upon soul-spiritual knowledge that cannot be achieved without the kinds of basic foundation that we have been developing in recent days. People will have to question the soul-spiritual characteristics of the human beings spread across the world. And salvation will not come until the science practiced at our universities is completely filled with and integrated into the kind of thinking and perceptions that we have learned in recent days. Our universities will lead humanity to its downfall unless they are fructified in all aspects of their work by that cosmic knowledge that nowadays can only be won through the pursuit of spiritual science. At the same time, the religious feelings of people in the future must be born up by the knowledge that people can achieve of the soul-spiritual world. There is no other way forward. Because if we simply cast our gaze toward the soul-spiritual world, we will grow used to characterizing the groups of people living on the Earth according to their particular soul-spiritual characteristics, instead of merely discussing their physical characteristics, as contemporary anthropology does. But this matter has a very serious and practical side. Certain things that play out in the present moment, things that lie at the root of the serious events of this time cannot be looked at properly if one lacks the possibility of directing one's gaze toward the spiritual qualities of various segments of humanity. And in that regard, I would like to draw your attention to something that seems to me to be of particular importance.

During this terrible war and its aftermath, well-intentioned people have often called for a unified Europe. Actually, this cry for a unified Europe was already voiced in 1870 by Ernest Renan,[†] the French biographer of the life of Jesus and the Apostles. During the recent war, it was reiterated often. Renan said that if Europe is to be saved, it is absolutely necessary for a partnership to be established, a peaceful partnership between France, Great Britain, and Germany. In particular, the people who were not beguiled by public opinion or by the assessments disseminated by others who were particularly focused on one issue or another supported this view during the war; the call came from many well-intentioned and impartial people. Now, you can say on the other hand: "Europe's evolution during the last few decades was such that it actually counteracted those things that a reasonable person would have to recognize as necessary if European civilization is to continue into the future. Without this peaceful partnership"—said these impartial people—"Europe is finished." But in the past few years, we have never arrived at this peaceful partnership; at most, we have the illusion of such a partnership.

Now, if we turn our eyes toward the outward relationships between European nations (but looking at the outer world in the interest of testing soul-spiritual truths), we can clearly see what differentiates the three aspects of human existence. We must not forget here that since the beginning of the fifth post-Atlantean epoch and then during the end of that initial period (which has now ended completely), Europe developed and France progressively organized into an ever more unified nation whose various sections felt that they were part of a unified whole. We might say: "The soul life of every French man and woman moved toward the feeling of being part of a unified nation, bearing within its consciousness some part of the words: 'I am a Frenchman.'" You can study all that these four words came to mean over the course of centuries: "I am a Frenchman."

If we draw our attention to the development of that phrase: "I am a Frenchman!"—then we must also take a look at the simultaneous events occurring in German development. Nothing developed within the now fallen German Empire that can be attached or ever could be attached to the phrase: "I am a German!" To say loudly and passion-ately: "I am a German!" before the year 1848 would have gotten you locked up; you would have been thrown in jail. It was the worst political crime you could commit. People have forgotten this. It was the worst of political crimes to feel like a German. For in Germany, local principalities had completely taken over the land, and it was forbidden, inwardly forbidden, to understand the whole of the terri-tory occupied by the German peoples as a unity. For the first time in 1848, some people came up with the idea that you could actually consider all of the territory that belonged to the Germans as some sort of unified whole. But even then, this idea was considered heretical; it was treated as heresy.

Only those people who were historically bound up in the evolution of the German people felt this unity as something that was part of their inner experience; they saw it as something extremely personal. Read the way in which such people, who thought and spoke truthfully about these matters, like Herman Grimm[†] for example, looked back at their own youth (which still had taken place sometime before the 1850s); read about how they describe having no possibility of expressing the judgments residing in their feelings, their felt conclusion: "I am a German." There is a tremendous difference here. But consider this huge difference inwardly. Consider the fact that even though it was a political crime, that the police would punish you for calling yourself a German, even in the first half of the nineteenth century, nevertheless the unified spiritual culture of Germany had already long been in existence. Gotheanism and everything that was a part of it was already there; nobody read Goethe, but he had had his effect; nobody understood Goethe, but he had said things of tremendous importance for all German people. But the "German people" were never allowed to express in the public sphere that they belonged together. At the very least, it was allowed to exist as a thought with no claim on reality; in other words, it lived within the German people as though it were something buried in the foundations of their consciousness with no outward political reality. In its historical development, France took everything that was felt inwardly, everything that composed its unity, and made it into outward political reality. In Germany, everything that existed in external society contradicted what lived within these Germans as inner spiritual truth. This is a very significant different between Central Europe and Western Europe. When you take this up and when you can paint a picture of it in detail for yourself, only then will you understand the history of the nineteenth century. And when these things and all of the details about them live in the thought-feeling core [Gemüt] of all Europeans (though right now they are counting on partnership and commonality of feeling), then very soon all of these feelings of fear that have lead to the present downward spiral will cease.

But we will not be able to develop these kind of international feelings unless we are able to consider the totality of the human being and begin to understand each person in regard to his or her intelligence and capacity for wanting and desiring; for in turning our consciousness toward these secrets of the human being, we become aware of the need to engage such considerations. These considerations, which we have just gone about engaging, are what teach us the truth about what all of this depends upon. Why is it the case that the French consolidated into such a compact collective of people in which each individual felt he was a Frenchman, which was a feeling forbidden to the German people until the arrival of Bismarck's German Empire? What was the cause of that?

The reason is that in France, a continuation of the old Greco-Roman Being was founded—a Being that I have described to you here for weeks[†] as predominantly a political-judicial Being. This political-judicial Being came into Latin culture from the Egyptians via the Romans. The French people took it over. There is no population on Earth that has a better feeling for judicial and political life than the French. If on the other hand, you were to find the proper way to penetrate through those, shall we say, oppressive aspects of German evolution in the nineteenth century—the things that counteracted any outward political developments, that made it necessary to lock people up if they felt that they were German rather than Prussian or Bavarian or Austrian—then you will see clearly into those things with which everything else is connection. And if you study the details concretely of what German spiritual life became at the turn of the nineteenth century—if you do not study this in the way that unprincipled schools drill it into people, if you study the way in which Goetheanism flowed into the great spirits (who are all but forgotten—those who were celebrated as great during the spiritual antipode), if you study the way in which Goetheanism flowed into men like Troxler[†] and Schubert[†] and so on—then you will discover that the utter lack of talent for political life, the dormant nature of the German people when it came to political life, the danger of being locked up if you desired to be a statesman for the whole of Germany—all of this actually predestined the German people to develop a great understanding for the spiritual, for spiritual life. This has been beaten back by the industrial, commercial developments in

Germany since the 1870s. These developments effectively did away with the German spirit; they came as invaders from without and took away everything that was connected with spiritual life. Goetheanism has been forgotten. The fact that a spirit like Leibniz[†] (for example) once lived among the Germans is more important for our school teachers to know than the writings of Cicero.[†] But nowadays, they hardly know that Leibniz ever lived.

These are things that come into our considerations and are more deeply seated than all of the other things that people nowadays name as the differences between Central Europe and Western Europe. And when people today talk about the need for peace accords between Central Europe and Western Europe, they must understand clearly that the whole spiritual evolution of Europe proves that such a peace can only come into existence when the German people come to feel about themselves: "We are not destined for the outward legal-political life; we are called upon to practice spiritual life." But they must be enabled to do this; presently it has been made impossible for them. Presently they also have no accountability for it. We must come to recognize that the truly political people are the French people, because it is that population that best understands how the individual human being feels as a member of a political state. In this way, we have divided the spiritual life from the rights or political life in the big picture of European civilization. These things are simultaneously distributed within a given population in the form of individual gifts and proclivities. And the economic life, the actual area of new human evolution, is given to the English-American people. Everything related to the understanding of the economic life has found its most thorough thought in England and America. The French do not understand anything about economics; they are better bankers. The Germans have never understood the first thing about economics, and they have absolutely no talent for it. And when they have attempted to practice economics in recent decades, insofar as they spoke about an economic boom and having their own "place under the sun,"[†] or something along those lines, the real meaning of all of this talk was that they were speaking about something for which they had no talent, and in speaking about, they knocked the true German

Being to the floor. For even everything that popped up in the form of economic parliamentarianism in the second half of the nineteenth century came over from England. All the way into Hungary, the people who are considered good parliamentarians when it comes to economics are students of English thought. If you take a look at which people in the parliaments were the most effective in bringing forward parliamentarianism, as has been the case for some time in the Austrian parliament and for an especially long period of time in the Hungarian parliament, and if you then take a look at where these people studied, you will find: It was in England that they learned this economic parliamentarianism. And when you ask: "Where did the German Social Democratic Party come from?"—then you will find: Marx[†] and Engels[†] had to go to England and study English economic relationships in order to cook up the theories that were then taken up in German spiritual life and worked through to their ultimate consequences. And where are Leninism and Trotskyism initially rooted? The roots begin in English economic thought; except that the English are wary of thinking through the ultimate consequences of their economic ideas.

So here we have the three areas about which I have often spoken; I have said that they must establish a threefold relationship with one another—German: spiritual; French: political-judicial; English: economic. How will we be able to discover the possibility of international cooperation? Through an outpouring of the principle of threefolding over these areas. For only in this way will it be possible for those that have a particular talent for one area to engage in an exchange with the others. This will not be possible otherwise. This is the spiritual impulse. For this reason, more than any other, we must study the history of the nineteenth century.

You cannot study history if you have only been taught the things that are taught nowadays in school. This history is only there to be forgotten, because you cannot do anything with this history in your life. A history lesson is meaningful only when you can do something in your life with what you have learned. But you can develop such a history lesson only when you are able to see through the whole of a human being. And the same is true of the other branches of our current higher education. The way in which things are currently taught in our universities will lead to our downfall. Ascending to some new beginning for our education can only result through fructification of knowledge in spiritual science. All of the things that are supposed to occur nowadays have already been prepared in our history. But do not think for a moment that the correct historical relationships can be properly seen by anyone who is not familiar enough with Anthroposophy to understand, for example, these three "spiritual" figures (see earlier drawing, p. 219) and their relationship to one another, or understand the things that we were speaking about yesterday and the day before. For only by ascending to such thoughts is one able to regard others in the full depth of their Being. Otherwise, one has no interest for the other; otherwise, one is contented with the things that were given by schoolroom science, and is compelled to spend one's free time doing those things that people nowadays spend their free time doing.

Such things should be spoken of far and wide so that there might be a sufficiently large number of people who have an understanding of them. Everything nowadays is dependent on there being a sufficiently large number of people who have some understanding of such things. Until there is this sufficiently large number of people who have such an understanding, we can do nothing with these things in the world. We cannot simply turn to institutions, we cannot simply establish new organizational practices; rather, it is necessary that there be as many people as possible who have knowledge of these things in their cognitive soul faculties, that we might then establish new institutions with these people. Then, the oppositional forces will not be able to stand against us anymore.

Nowadays, you will discover something strange if you examine the thoughts that people have about European life, about the way in which European life should play out between one person and the next. I must tell you here a little about the specific details regarding what occurs. Today I would like to include just a small probe into all of the important concerns that we have before us to consider. Monsieur Ferriére[†]—who, as I told you, perpetuated the slanderous rumor that I had been an advisor to the former German Emperor,

that I have been in essence the "Rasputin"† to the German Emperor,†
and so on†—he was told off by Dr. Boos† in an "open letter,"† and in
a postscript to that letter I also mentioned what I have explained here
in the past about my relationship—or should I say lack thereof—to
the German Emperor. Now, the man had to admit that he had lied.†
But he admitted it in a very particular way, a way that is also characteristic of the times. I will attempt as clearly as possible to offer to
you in German the French sentences that he wrote. I am actually very
glad to present them to you in German, for in German they take on
a certain character which I would like to lend to them. So, after the
letter from Dr. Boos comes the following:

"We [the editors] have given the above letter from Dr. Roman
Boos to our correspondent"—this is referring to the Herr Ferriére—
"who sent us the following reply: 'The above document is typical for
a psychologist. Here we see what Latin irony becomes when seen by
German eyes. Most likely, these people"—he means those who have
German eyes—"take everything seriously. But my readers, they did
not allow themselves to be misled! My article contains comedy—
de la plaisanterie—but no ill will—*méchancetés*. And I was poorly
educated—I identify this as my fault in the hopes that my partner in
conversation will not hold it against me." Elegant. He assumes that
"he will not hold it against me—*ne m'en voudra pas*"! "By partner in
conversation I mean the sociologist, whom I referred to as a sociologist [Dr. Steiner], and not the signer of the above letter, to whom I
made no mention in my article [Dr. Boos]. Indeed—*au fait*—what
is one to make of this affair?"

And so, a man is able to excuse himself with such useless words
after not only lying, but committing a most base and vile slander. But
you run the risk of being called "stupid" and "unrefined" if you take
these things so "seriously," if you claim that the defamation is not a
plaisanterie but rather a *méchanceté*.

Then it goes on, and now we come to something particularly
noteworthy:

"At the time I wrote my article, I knew Rudolf Steiner only from
his printed works. Since that time I have come to know him through
people who are close to him. My opinion of him has changed entirely

and I had prepared an article in which I presented my respect for the moral significance of his personal work. I admit that the letter from M. R. Boos has left me somewhat cold."

That is just wonderful, is it not? Quite wonderful! He would have written the most beautiful article, full of accolades, if only someone had not told him off! Still, I cannot be persuaded by the idea that this is simply a characteristic of the Latin race (as opposed to the Germanic race mentioned earlier), for it would be rather offensive if one were to regard all lies and slander in the Latin race as something elegantly laudatory, as merely *plaisanterie*. This cannot be only a peculiar characteristic of the Latin race... now, the gentleman continues:

"I could provide answers to many different things in this letter, but what would be the use?—*à quoi bon?*—One of the qualities of Latin speech is brevity. I was wrong, I see plainly, to abandon the realm of verifiable facts. I take back my erroneous claims, and I conclude from this experience that the rumors which circulate about, even if they come from a variety of sources and from people whom one has every right to consider well-informed, can nevertheless be false. I will take careful note of this."[†]

So, first of all, this man is so naïve as to believe that he must take all rumors which circulate to be true, since he is only now taking note of the fact that they might not be; and secondly (yes, here we again run the risk of being considered "unrefined," or, as Ferriére would put it, "German"): Just try to think through "elegant" thoughts like these—it is impossible, is it not, for apparently you are not permitted to do so without belonging to that group of people about whom Ferriére says: *"Vraiment, ces gens-là prennent tout au sérieux."* But you cannot help but do so, you have to ask yourself: "So, he takes careful note of the fact that not all rumors that circulate are to be believed; but if you are a person like Ferriére, then would you not be precisely the kind of person most like to bring those rumors out into a wide variety of circles?" Well, there is no use in seeking any true thoughts behind the words of such people.

From a document such as this, you can clearly see that it is not a matter of bringing such people to reason. We can only hope to make the rest of the public aware of the fact that shameful people like this are running about in the world, writing articles and spreading falsehoods. It is not a matter of repudiating these people, but rather a matter of rendering them harmless, for the fact that these people exist—this is what is truly harmful.

When nothing happens in the world out of spiritual wisdom, we rapidly move ever farther away from the time in which such a sensibility can truly spread throughout the world. For in the end, materialists of all stripes and from all sides will continue increasingly to speak in this way about those who take things up spiritually: "Ah, these people, they take everything so seriously!" Soon enough, it will be considered serious to speak at all about spirit. And indeed, it is serious; but then we are not supposed to be serious! For as long as this kind of sensibility spreads—and it is spreading now—there will be no solid ground on which to better the state of things in Europe. These are the people who have brought Europe to this point. But we must work to ensure that a sufficient number of people gain an understanding of the fact, so that it will be different. This should already be evident now to those who have in some manner encountered true spiritual-scientific striving.

Next Friday, I will speak particularly about the development of imperialism in the world, which means that it will be an episodic lecture, a brief overview of the historical development of imperialism from the most ancient times, from Egyptian imperialism, through to present-day imperialism.

16

THE DEVELOPMENT OF IMPERIALISM: I

DORNACH, FEBRUARY 20, 1920

My lecture will be episodic today, an interpolation of sorts into our other considerations. The reason is that our English friends will soon be returning to their home country, and I would like them to have a lot to take back from their time here. To that end, I will deliver my considerations today such that one aspect or another might serve to support the necessary effectiveness of these words. Also to that end, I want to address a few things about imperialism today, specifically looking at it historically—from a spiritual-scientific historical perspective—rather than examining imperialism in the present (that can perhaps come tomorrow).

Imperialism is a phenomenon that has been spoken of often nowadays, and there is a more or less clear awareness in those who speak about it of its connection with the collective phenomena of contemporary social life. But when people do speak about these sorts of things, they do not consider (at least not sufficiently) that we all are living in the stream of humanity's history, that we are standing in the midst of a very particular evolutionary epoch and that we can understand this evolutionary epoch only when we know from whence come the phenomena that currently surround us, in whose midst we are currently living. The effective imperialism of today (and it will be effective into the future), which is practiced by the English-American peoples and is essentially ringing in a new age for humankind, manifests itself at its most basic level as primarily economic imperialism.

But the essential thing about this is that everything said about these matters, everything that is connected to this economic imperialism, is essentially untrue—it is, in fact, altogether false; it is full of hot air, shall we say, and in being full of hot air it more or less consciously leads us toward non-truthfulness. But in order to see that in these times reality is altogether different than the things that are said about reality, it is necessary to peer deeply into the historical stream of these matters.

To demonstrate the public's powers of discernment in regard to the facts of the contemporary world, I need only to point out to you one example. We all experienced the way in which Woodrow Wilson was glorified all over Europe and even in Germany itself. Our friends in Switzerland know well that during this period of glorifying Woodrow Wilson I consistently spoke out against him;† for it goes without saying that during the time when everyone was glorifying Woodrow Wilson, he was what he still is today. Already reports are coming in—and in saying this, I do not mean to suggest that it is necessarily true—that people in America are now saying that Woodrow Wilson is unfit for the presidency, that they are questioning his ability to make good decisions. Public opinion, as it winds its way confusedly through the world these days, shows its true nature sufficiently in such instances as this—such examples demonstrate its true worth.

And let us not forget a second example of this. In the last four or five years, there has been an extraordinary amount of talk about any number of beautiful and wonderful ideas: self-determination for all people, and the like. These words were untrue; for all that lay behind them was of an entirely different nature—it all had to do with questions of power. And anyone who truly seeks an understanding must always return to the reality of what is said, thought, and judged. That person must pay particularly close attention when a word such as "imperialism" ("Imperial Federation"† is the official word for it since the beginning of the twentieth century in England) is used—in these words, we find the most recent derivatives of a long progression of evolution and development, and these words lead backward into distant and diverse times. Their meaning can be found only through a true study of history.

We will not go as far back into history as one could go back through spiritual-scientific study; but we will at least go back to several millennia before the Christian calendar. There we find first and foremost several imperialistic empires in Asia and a slight variation on such imperialistic empires in Egypt. Very characteristic of the Eastern impulse is the Persian Empire, which is somewhat known to history; but particularly characteristic is the Assyrian Empire. Now, it would be wrong to identify the first phase of imperialism solely in the final periods (described in our histories) of the Assyrian Empire, because you simply cannot understand the dominant impulses of the Assyrian Empire unless you are able to go back to earlier conditions in the East. Even China, whose entire structure dates back to the far distant past, has changed enough that you cannot recognize in that structure (which existed until recently) the actual character of Eastern imperialism. We can, however, still peer through the relationships that are historically known and see what actually underlies them.

Now, we will not understand the whole of the ancient Eastern imperialism if we are not familiar with the general understanding of the relationship between the people of a particular area (let us say a particular empire) and those whom we would now refer to as the rulers or the ruling class of that empire. It goes without saying that words we use such as "ruler" or "king" or something of the sort do not express what was felt about the rulers or the ruling class at that time. Only with great difficulty can we form a mental picture of the feeling world that existed in human beings three or four millennia before the beginning of the Christian calendar system, because it is so difficult for us to look back on the way in which human beings understood the relationship of the spiritual world to the physical world in that ancient time. Nowadays when most people think about a spiritual world (if they think about the spiritual world at all), they imagine it in some distant nether-world. And if people talk about the spiritual world—we must all talk about the spiritual world again in the future as something that exists around us, just as the sensory world does—then everything said has something of the quality of what, for example, lead us to Protestant thinking. In ancient times, the essence of the matter is namely that no differentiation was made between the physical world and the spiritual world.

This is so much the case that when we speak about things relating to those ancient times, we can barely form any sort of organized mental picture of it, so different was the mental and imaginative life of those ancient peoples from the mental and imaginative life of modern day human beings. Everything that had a physical existence—rulers, the ruled, a ruling class, enslaved people—all of this was reality. It was not something that could be called physical reality, but rather it was *the* reality. It was simultaneously the physical and the spiritual reality. And the rulers of the Eastern empires—who or what were they then? The ruler of an Eastern empire was its god. And all across that empire, the people did not see a god somewhere above the clouds in those ancient times—I am always speaking of ancient times here. For these people, there was no choir of spiritual beings surrounding an almighty god. This is a perspective from a later period of human history. Rather, those whom we would call ministers or courtiers (whether out of disrespect or respect) were beings with a godly nature. Everyone clearly understood that by going through the Mystery schools these individuals had become something greater than normal human beings. People looked to them as Protestant individuals look to their god or as somewhat more liberal circles look to their unseen angels or something of the sort. For unseen angels or an unseen god existing in a supersensory world above and beyond reality simply did not exist for the peoples of the East. Everything that was spiritual lived within individuals. In normal human beings lived a human soul. In those we would call rulers lived a divine soul—a god.

We can no longer form any imagination or understanding of this mental picture of a true godly realm that exists simultaneously a physical realm. That, let us say, the king truly possessed the power and dignity of a god is self-evidently absurd in this day and age, but it was once the reality during the time of Eastern imperialism. People simply did not speak about anything that could be understood as purely spiritual.

A slight variation, as I said, was present in Egypt, for in that area we find a transition into a later period. So if we go all the way back to the oldest forms of imperialism, we find that this imperialism stems from the fact that the king, the ruler, who is a god—a god, a son of heaven with a true physical existence on the Earth—is in fact the Father of heaven. This is so paradoxical for modern-day human beings that it hardly seems believable, but it is true. But this fact is intimately connected with what we can observe in Assyrian documents about the way in which imperialistic conquests were justified: Conquests were simply undertaken. The right to make such conquests was simply derived from the fact that one had always to expand the realm of one's god. If an area was conquered and the conquered people became the subjects of another realm, then they had to honor the conqueror as their god. People were not thinking about this as an expansion of a religious worldview. Why would they have needed to? After all, everything was actualized in the physical world. When the people of the conquered territory paid outward tribute to their conquerors, when they followed them, then everything was as it should be. They could believe what they wanted. Beliefs—which is to say one's personal opinions—were left altogether untouched in ancient times. People did not concern themselves with them.

This was the first form in which imperialism appeared. The second form was one in which the ruling class—those who were to take on a dominant, leading role—were not themselves gods but rather sent by God or inspired by God and filled by the divine. In the first stage of imperialism we were dealing with a reality. This is an essential fact. First phase of imperialism: we were dealing with reality.

When such a ruler of the ancient East appeared among his people, he always wore his regalia, for he was entitled, as a god, to wear such clothing. Those were the clothes of a god. That was how a god was to look. This simply means that the way in which the ruler appeared was the style among the gods. And those who were his paladins were not simply clerks or simple functionaries but were rather higher beings who surrounded him and did what they did by virtue of their existence as higher beings.

Then came the time, as I said before, in which people saw rulers and those who were their paladins as sent by God, as individuals filled by the divine, as those commissioned by God. This was the prevailing idea even at the time of Dionysius the Areopagite.† Read his letters, in which he describes the entire hierarchy of deacons, archdeacons, bishops, and archbishops—the whole hierarchy of the church. How does he describe this hierarchy? Dionysius the Areopagite describes it all as though in this earthly, churchly hierarchy one finds a reflection of what exists in the supersensory world with God and his elementary powers, archangels, and angels. Thus, there exists a heavenly hierarchy above, and beneath is its reflection: the earthly hierarchy. The members of the earthly hierarchy—the deacons and archdeacons—don their robes and carry out their rituals because these things are symbols. In the first phase of imperialism we were dealing with reality, in the second phase we are dealing with symbols. Naturally, this has all been more or less forgotten, for in the general consciousness of human beings nowadays, even among those who are Catholic, there is little awareness that the deacons, priests, deans, bishops, and archbishops are the representatives, the proxy agents, of the heavenly hierarchies. But this fact has merely been lost to memory.

With these steps forward, imperialism reached what I would like to call a point of division—a true fork in the road. On one side, that which held leadership and command tended more toward those sent by God, toward a priesthood in which the priests were kings. On the other side, there was a greater movement toward the earthly—but the position of ruler came always with the grace of God; it was always directed and commissioned by God. Fundamentally, these are simply two slight variations of the same thing. And we find both variations in the course of human history: in church society and in political society.

During the first period of imperialism, when everything was present in physical reality, such a division would have been unthinkable. But in the second phase of imperialism this separation occurred. There we find some individuals who tended more toward earthly leadership, though always as a ruler sent by God, as well as other individuals also sent by God who tended toward leadership in the church. This lasted well into the Middle Ages; and I would like to point out that the life of the God-sent kings and priests in a physical empire, in the outer reality, lasted up to the year 1806 in one characteristic historical phenomenon. Of course, the Roman Church continued to exist and spread in the physical world after that point; that existence was more on the side of the priestly. But the thing that really held the Middle Ages together, the thing that strictly maintained the principle of the God-sent ruler here on the physical Earth was the Holy Roman Empire of the German Nation, which (as I mentioned) came to an end only in 1806. This was the name of what existed in Central Europe as a sort of Empire: the Holy Roman Empire of the German Nation. In the word "Holy," you find a trace of the godly element that existed on the Earth in ancient times. "Roman" points back to the empire's origins. "German Nation" indicates the thing over which this empire was lain —the more earthly element upon which it was imposed.

And so in the second phase of imperialism, we no longer find the anointed imperialism of the church. Instead we have the intermingling of both godly and earthly anointed individuals within the empire. This began back in the old Roman empire in pre-Christian times and lasted into the later years of the Middle Ages. The new imperialism that developed possessed a double nature: the Holy Roman Empire of the German Nation. Think about it for a moment—it all goes back to Charlemagne.[†] Charlemagne was crowned by the pope in Rome. Thereby, the position of the king was publicly made into a symbol, and consequently that which exists here on the physical Earth is not all of reality. The people of the Middle Ages did not honor Charlemagne or Otto I[†] as gods as the people in ancient times would have done, but they saw them as individuals sent by God. And that idea had to be constantly reinforced. Over time, it naturally weakened in human consciousness. But when it was made somehow visible, then as a symbolic act it took on a reality as a symbol at the very least. The emperors of the Holy Roman Empire of the German Nation went to Rome so that they could be crowned by the pope. Istwan I,[†] the Hungarian, also went to Rome from Hungary in the year 1000 C.E. to be made king by the pope. The spiritual powers imparted a blessing upon the individuals who ruled in the physical world, and thereby awarded them power.

But this led to the entrance of something new into human consciousness, causing them to believe that they had the authority and right to incorporate all others into this empire, whose leader had been anointed by God. Dante himself was of the opinion that the emperor of the Holy Roman Empire of the German Nation was fundamentally entitled to rule the entire world. In this opinion of Dante's we find the formulation of imperialism.[†]

In the legends and lore that have crystallized in human consciousness throughout the course of our history, things are expressed that, as a general rule, can be considered from a wide variety of perspectives, and do not have just one interpretation. We could say: In the eleventh and twelfth centuries there must still have been a strong awareness in Europe—even if it were a bit unclear, more of a feeling awareness, but one that was felt very strongly—that back in ancient times over in the East there had been people on Earth, people who lived a physical existence on Earth, who had actually been gods. This was simply not a superstition, oh no—on the contrary, people thought: "Nowadays such gods cannot live on the Earth anymore because the Earth has become so evil. That thing which once made human beings into gods has been lost—the 'Holy Grail' has been lost, and now, in the Middle Ages, you can only reach it in the way that Parzival did: You seek the path to finding the God within, whereas once God had a physical reality within an empire. Now that empire is just a collection of symbols and signs, and one must find God in those symbols, in those signs."

From all things that ever existed, vestiges remain. Reality becomes diluted. Vestiges remain in a wide variety of forms. As a general rule, when something, for as long as it has a reality in the world, is clear and singular, it becomes ambiguous and multifaceted as time passes. And consequently, a wide variety of things in Europe have sprung up from the clarity and singularity of old. For as long as the Holy Roman Empire of the German Nation held any meaning for human consciousness, the leader of that Holy Roman Empire of the German Nation was powerful, able to tame the individual angel-symbols that were the princes of the various territories; for people still had it in their consciousness that it was his right to do this. But his right was based more or less in something ideal. Over time, that gradually lost its meaning. As a result, this left the princes of the territories on their own. And speaking generally, in the Holy Roman Empire of the German Nation, we have something that gradually pushed out its true inner substance, leaving only the external shell. That earthly human beings were sent by God to be leaders was gradually lost to consciousness. And the expression of that fact, that people were no longer able to think of earthly human beings as sent by God, is Protestantism. Protestantism is the protest against the true meaning of the individual "sent by God."

If the principle of Protestantism were truly to penetrate into our consciousness, then no crowned head or knighted individual could ever say that this was "by the Grace of God." But these things remain as vestiges of the past. These vestiges remained in the world through 1918, and then they disappeared. These vestiges, which had lost all of their inner meaning, still remained as outward phenomena in the world. These German territorial princes were still there as outward phenomena; but they only had any true meaning back in older times when they were symbols of an inspirited heavenly Empire.

There are still other vestiges of the past that exist in the world in a way that makes it difficult to know from which period they are a carryover. It was not so long ago that a Central European bishop— or perhaps it might have been an archbishop—published a pastoral letter† in which he basically proclaimed that a Catholic priest is more powerful than Jesus Christ, as proven by the simple fact that when a Catholic priest carries out the ritual of transubstantiation at the altar, Jesus Christ is obligated to be present in the host. The ritual of transubstantiation can only be completed through the powers of the priest. In other words, the action that the priest carries out compels the Christ Jesus to be present at the altar. Thus, the more powerful being is not the Christ Jesus, but rather the one who carries out the ritual of transubstantiation at the altar!

When we want to understand such a thing, which (as I mentioned) was published only a few years ago in a pastoral letter, we must look back not to the second phase of imperialism, but rather to the first phase of imperialism, and how completely the Catholic Church and its subsidiaries preserved many aspects of this first phase of imperialism. In that, we find a vestige of the consciousness that those who rule on the Earth are gods, whereas Jesus Christ is only the son of God. The content of this pastoral letter is, for someone with a Protestant consciousness, as impossible to believe as the idea that thousands of years ago people saw their rulers as gods is for a person nowadays to believe. But actually all of these things are historical facts, are truths that in the historical Being, in historical reality have played a role. The vestiges of these truths are still present in the world to this day.

And so it is that early realities play into the later phenomena of the world. This is not to say that the worldviews remain the same; but the practices that emerge from these worldviews do remain the same. Take a look at the way in which the teachings of Muhammad† have spread across the world. Muhammad himself certainly never said: "Muhammad is your God"—as a priest-leader of the ancient world might have said several thousand years earlier. He limited himself to a declaration that was already more fitting to his time period, saying: "There is a God and Muhammad is his prophet." Thus, in human consciousness he took on the position of a "God-sent" individual, the second phase of imperialism. In terms of the manner in which Muhammad's thought and teachings spread across the world, however, the first phase of imperialism is more fitting. The Muslims were never intolerant of people who held other beliefs, so long as they paid tribute to the God of Muhammad. The Muslims were content to conquer others and make them their subjects just as it was done in ancient times, where there was also little concern for a person's beliefs; for in the end, it made no difference what a person believed as long as he simply recognized the power of the ruling god. The manner in which the Muslims spread across the world is a practice dating back to the first phase of imperialism.

And in Russian despotism, in the czars of Russia, something also remained from the first phase of imperialism, strongly colored by its movement through the second phase. In the whole way in which the people of Russia think of the czar, or at the very least in the mood that exists in their feeling core, there is something that can be traced back to the first phase of imperialism. As a result, there has been so little interest in bringing together what actually exists in the consciousness of the Russian people with the things that stream out from the czars; for actually the czar's position of rule in Russia is based in German and Mongolian elements and not actually the elements of the Russian peasants. Thus, the vestiges of earlier times continue to exist in the present. Even in the recent historical periods, we can find these vestiges of the past.

This brings us to the third phase of imperialism. Though it has been fully formed only since the beginning of the twentieth century, when Chamberlain[†] and his people came up with the concept of the "Imperial Federation," its origins lie farther into the past, sometime in the second half of the seventeenth century. At that time, there was that great revolution in England, which for all of the Anglo-American peoples living in Western territories effectively turned the personage of the king, who had once been a god and then had been God-sent, into a mere shadow, a mere... we cannot say "decoration," but into a position merely tolerated. After the seventeenth century, the laws and acts of a population came out of what was desired by the people (of course, this was at first divided along class lines).

Then, the Anglo-American peoples brought different prior experiences and preconditions to this, shall we say, "will of the people" idea, this system of popular voting, than did others, such as the French, the descendents of the Romans, the Latins. The Latin peoples, particularly the French, underwent a revolution of their own in the eighteenth century. But due to the influence of things that I described to you here not long ago,[†] the French as a people are actually more "kingly" than any other people of the world. You do not need to have a king as your leader in order to be kingly. To be sure, a person cannot continue to act as the ruler of a people after his head has been chopped off. But the French people are kingly—imperialistic—without having a king at the helm. It has to do with the condition of the French soul. This collective feeling of oneness as a people, this collective folk consciousness, is actually a very real vestige of the consciousness at the time of Louis XIV.[†]

But the English-speaking peoples brought other preconditions and prior experiences to the idea we can call the "will of the people." And gradually, out of the assessments that effectively became public opinion, out of the things that streamed out into society from the elected officials in Parliament, the third form of imperialism emerged and developed, formulated first by individuals such as Chamberlain and others like him. But we will try to consider it on the soul level today—this third form of imperialism.

The first imperialism had reality: A person was a god in the consciousness of the other people. His paladins were gods surrounding him—lesser gods. Second imperialism: All things on the Earth are symbols and signs. God was simply at work within individuals. Third form of imperialism: Everything on Earth that originates and streams outward from the human soul is divested of its status as a symbol or sign. Just as we moved from realities to symbols and signs, so do we now move from symbols and signs to phrases.

This is said without any stirrings of feeling—*sine ira*. It is a purely objective description of a fact resulting from the necessary process of earthly Becoming. Since the seventeenth century, it is truly the case that everything occurring in the public life of the Anglo-American peoples—everything spoken or written in books of law—is the "will of the people" (divided along class lines, of course). Perhaps tomorrow or the next day we will come to a description of this "will of the people." But it is a phrase; the relationship that exists between what is spoken and reality is not the same as the one between a symbol and reality. This is the course things follow in the human soul, it moves in this progression: from reality to symbol and then to phrase—to dried-out, empty words. And what results from out of these dried-out and empty words becomes the principal reality of the time. No person would ever imagine that the resulting reality was once godly in its origin.

For let us think for a moment about the foundation of that imperialism whose dominant element is the phrase: in the first imperialism, the king; in the second imperialism, the anointed; in the third imperialism, the phrase. It goes without saying that nothing real will ever result from the principle of majority rules—only dominant phrases will come of it. And these realities drift about below and are consequently never perceived to be somehow godly or divine.

Let us take a look at one of the important foundations for the things that occur as reality: colonization. Colonization plays a major role in the development of the third imperialism. For the whole colonial system, the spread of the empire into the colonies, the "Imperial Federation" is the final form, the means of centralizing this effort. But how did these colonies originally take form as limbs of the empire? Think about what actually occurred: Adventurers—individuals for whom no one had any real use within the empire, people who were a little rough around the edges—moved out into the colonies, got rich, and then went home and spent all of their money. This, however, did not do anything to turn them into distinguished people, so they continued to be adventurers—bohemians. And thus, the colonial empire was brought together. This is the reality that existed under the influence of the phrase.

But vestiges of the past remain. Just as symbols and phrases or territorial princes and czars remained from the original realities of the world, realities continue to exist from the adventurous undertakings of the somewhat notorious, odious colonists—realities that we now find ourselves left with. Is it not the case that at some point these adventurers were (shall we say) "adopted?" Their sons—well, they were perhaps not quite so notorious and odious; they smelled a little better than their fathers. Their grandsons smelled much better than their grandfathers, and then, you see—then comes a time where everything smells lovely. In this case the phrase usurps something, and already the odious act begins to smell altogether good. The state stretches broad its wings and becomes the protector, and suddenly everything is above board.

It is necessary, however, that we grasp the true point of these things—it is perhaps impossible to call them by their true name, for the names we use seldom give an indication of the reality of the things. It is necessary because only by doing that can we begin to understand the tasks given to us by this time and the responsibility that this time has placed before us. Only by doing that can we come to see that so-called history, meaning the history taught and studied in schools and universities, in a fable convenu. This history does not call the things by their true names. On the contrary, it has the effect of gradually attaching these names to untruths.

It is a terrible thing, is it not—what I have just described? But you see, now it is the time to channel this sense, this feeling of responsibility, even if only a little bit. Let us consider now the other side of this matter. Let us look back for a moment at an ancient empire. It was all real, real on Earth in human perception; the priest-kings arose from the Mystery schools. The second was no longer on Earth—rather, the second was symbolic. There is a wide gap separating the ancient rulers and the paladins who hung upon them like godly jewels and the "red or black eagles" denoting the third, fourth, or first rank that were then hung upon individuals. But nevertheless, this is the path of history. Things went from reality to nothingness and finally they became no longer a symbol, but fundamentally nothing more than the expression of a phrase. Is it not the case that now the superficiality of the general phrase-system that spread from the West out into the rest of the world has penetrated even into public affairs? I have even heard now of "titular heads of state"! Now, the rulers and advisors had unusually little to rule or advise anyway—or in some cases knew little about how to rule or advise—but "titular heads of state"! And still, everything can be traced back to that old practice of which I spoke.

In the first phase I talked about, everything that existed in the physical world, everything that was real on Earth, was also thought to be altogether spiritual; in the second phase, it was thought to be simply filled with spiritual substance. And the third phase must grow beyond its current form, which I have just described to you—it must grow beyond the empire of the phrase and all the realities associated with it that we have just talked about. The third phase must bring into reality the spiritual empire here on Earth.

Whereas in the first phase, physical reality was thought to be spiritual, we may not allow ourselves to think of physical reality as spiritual only in the future, but therefore spiritual reality must be present here in the physical world. In other words, spiritual reality must live and exist beside physical reality. We must all move about and through the physical world while simultaneously recognizing a spiritual reality and being able to speak about a truly extant supersensory world that, though invisible, is nevertheless there and must be supported by us.

I spoke before of something very negative—the phrase. But if the outer world had not moved so completely into empty phrases, there would be no space into which the spiritual empire could enter. It is because everything old has now become nothing more than an empty phrase that an empty space now exists for the spiritual empire to fill. Especially in the West, in the Anglo-American world, everything is managed in such a way that a lot of people continue to speak in, shall we say, old familiar idioms about any number of things that come from days of old. As I have said, this will continue to roll along like a ball rolling down a hill. In people's words, this will continue to roll along. You can find countless sayings and phrases in the West that have lost all meaning but continue to be regularly used. But the actual idea of a phrase containing no reality, a phrase out of which all true reality has already been squeezed—that lives not only in these old sayings and phrase, but actually in everything identified by old words. In those empty phrases is the space wherein the spiritual, where something that is not in accord with any of the things of old, can take hold. It was necessary for the old to become nothing more than a phrase. We must throw out everything old that continues to fester within our language and bring in something altogether new, which can stream out toward us only from the spiritual world.

Only then can a Christ-empire come to be on the Earth. For the following must be accepted as a reality in that empire: "My kingdom is not of this world."† In the empire of this world in which the Christ-empire first appeared, there was still much that existed in this world that had not yet become an empty phrase. But everything that came from an older time in the Western world was foreordained to become an empty phrase. Yes, in the West, in the Anglo-American world, all human traditions and practices will become empty phrases. Consequently, the responsibility lies there to place a spirit in the empty receptacle left behind, a spirit of whom it can be said: "His kingdom is not of this world!" This is the great responsibility of our time. It is not about the form into which things have developed. What is important is what we do now that they have so developed. And thus, these things become part of a continuity.

Our discussion tomorrow might further actualize this continuity—we will talk about the secret societies that are active beneath the surface in the Western world. These societies traditionally move from the second phase of imperialism toward the third, for in the Anglo-American peoples we find two different imperialisms intermingled with one another: the economic imperialism of Chamberlain and the symbolic imperialism of the secret societies, which are very actively and effectively integrated but necessarily kept secret from the population at large.

17

THE DEVELOPMENT OF IMPERIALISM: II

DORNACH, FEBRUARY 21, 1920

I have been speaking to you about the historical origins of what we can nowadays call imperialism, and you will already have noted from what I said yesterday that these considerations of imperialism are dependent upon being able to recognize that phenomena of the present, which were at one time real elements of life, are in reality nothing more than vestiges of an older time. In that older time, these practices, rituals, and institutions all had their own genuine meaning. They were, by and large, realities. That reality was lost over time. They developed through a period of existence as symbols and finally became nothing more than empty phrases.

We are living now entirely in the age of the empty phrase. We need simply to come to see that the empty phrases of the present are necessarily rooted in a past out of which they have grown, and that on the other hand these empty phrases are a preparatory stage for what must enter now into human evolution. If reality had not transformed into phrases—meaning into something that is essentially an extant illusion—it would not be possible for something altogether new to come into being. New things could not come into the world if, for example, the visible, perceptible gods in human form still towered over the human race, as was the case during the Roman Empire when the last descendents of these gods lived. For the Roman emperors were—even if it was not felt as fully as it had once been during more ancient times—they were nonetheless gods in their pretensions. Nero was a god in human form, at least if we follow the assumptions and hypotheses made about him. Over the course of time, these things lost their true meaning. They traveled through the age of symbols and allegories and then became nothing more than phrases.

Now, it is the case that the more completely these things transform into empty phrases, the more the ground is prepared for the entrance into a new reality, a spiritual life that is not taken out of the sensory world but rather the supersensory world; a spiritual life that does not find godly spiritual beings in the forms of human beings but rather finds true and genuine spiritual beings existing in and among the visible, physical human beings on the Earth. The empire of the empty phrase must exist first and must then also be recognized for what it is. Then it will be possible for a new spiritual life to develop. If you want to understand the present based on such, shall we say, uncomfortable premises, then you must be able to gaze upon the birth of a new spiritual life occurring alongside the dissolution into illusion of everything that once had reality in human evolution.

It is all too natural that we desire to cling to the old realities, even after they have become nothing more than empty phrases; for, to see clearly that things have become these empty phrases engenders an uncertainty in our feeling core. When we are forced to admit that these old things have become mere phrases, we believe that we no longer have a secure floor beneath our feet. People love to delude themselves, because they believe that in the moment they accept that the delusion is a delusion, they will suddenly drift up into the air. But you would no longer believe that you will drift off aimlessly like this if you were able to feel truly the solidity of the new spiritual life. We are living currently in an age in which we must be a participant both in the life of the dying phrase and in the burgeoning spiritual life. This will be made possible especially by the continuing emergence of the English-speaking peoples of the world and the things which they have traditionally maintained since an earlier time and about which they still speak, the way in which those things have necessarily become empty phrases, and the way in which economic life continues to exist as a reality amidst those phrases (just as I described to you yesterday: economic life is the only thing that can be truly real in a world of empty phrases).

But a time will come—a moment of particular importance. In the moment when we feel that we are dealing only with that economic life—which, in the third and fourth generation, will of course become "fair and square," as I described to you yesterday—and otherwise with nothing more than phrases... in this moment, we will have a feeling of the nothingness of humankind, the base existence within a physical life that composes the whole of reality. This knowledge must be born in the peoples of the Western world especially. The moment must come in which this conviction takes hold in our souls: We can no longer grab hold of anything about which we speak. The only reality that surrounds us is the acquisition and preparation of things for our stomachs and digestion. As long we do not see that the empty phrases in the world are phrases, as long as we do not know that economics is the only true reality in the world, we will not arrive at the necessary understanding. When we do arrive at the necessary understanding, however, then human nature can do nothing other than say to itself: "In order to be a human being, we must bring a spiritual reality to this physical reality consisting solely of economic life."

The dawning moment of this knowledge must come soon. Without it, human evolution can go no farther. For the same reason that we are moving in the direction of a new spiritual life, we must also immerse ourselves at present in the element of the empty phrase.

Now, the strongest gift, the greatest talent for this knowledge exists in the people of the West. In the West, the right preconditions exist for a dawning of this knowledge, whereas the rest of the peoples of Europe, for example, are in less of a position to have such knowledge dawn for them with the necessary intensity. For in those regions, other relationships dominate, which hinder the possibility of seeing through the illusions as fundamentally or radically as can occur in the West. You need only to turn your gaze again toward the historical relationships to understand this.

Think for a moment about the fact that the various populations of German origin have been united since the time of the descendents of Charlemagne, since the Sachsen and Staufen leaders of the Holy

Roman Empire of the German Nation, as I said yesterday. This Holy Roman Empire of the German Nation was essentially an entire network of various symbols. Everything within it had the character of signs and symbols. In everything that you came across, it was necessary to trace back the signs and symbols until you found some form of reality. But this penetration of the signs and symbols did not lead to a fully spiritual reality. The church prevented this from occurring. By and large, you would arrive at some nebulous place, drifting about in a spiritual reality. Consequently, everything that the Middle Ages and the descendents of the European church communities had to say about such a spiritual reality had the quality of something only half-grasped, something not-completely-understood. It had the quality of a light shining through the colored panes of glass in a medieval church. People shrank away from the spiritual world when they arrived at it through the symbols and signs of the Middle Ages. They shrank back from a clear, direct understanding. On the contrary, people preferred to describe the matter such that it continued to exist as something half-unknown that could not be penetrated by knowledge.

And the same was actually true in the case of outward social relationships. Anyone who studies with an inner sense the history of the Holy Roman Empire of the German Nation—and the history of Switzerland is also inwardly connected with this history of the Holy Roman Empire of the German Nation—will see that one nonsensical thing was always built upon the last nonsensical thing from one age to the next. People tried to use these nonsensical things to take up the matter of societal organization, seeking to live within it and understand it on the basis of these things possessing no clarity—until in 1806, people finally noticed (even the Hapsburgs noticed it at the time) that the whole Holy Roman Empire of the German Nation no longer made any sense. And the especially gifted—and by that I mean gifted in a negative sense—Emperor Franz I, resigned the German imperial crown after completing a personal, or as they call it in this case, "in-house" switch, of the Austrian crown not two years before. The whole thing lost any possibility of continuing to exist, because in the end, people could no longer find any meaning behind these symbols. And for the people of Central Europe, nothing was left except for a sense of striving, a desire that reached out toward all possible things, but contained within it little sense or meaning.

This resulted in the founding of the empire in 1870/71, complete with its own inner contradiction. A German emperor was named, but the position did not result from any relationships that existed in reality. The title was simply invented. In France, if something similar had occurred, an *empereur* reinstated, then the people might perhaps have understood, at least partially, because they still had within them some actual substance for such a thing. But within the Being of the German people there was just a name, which might have proven that they had some talent for creating names that had no meaning, that they had some talent for acting in service of the empty phrase, on the one hand, and of the neighboring reality of an economic life that otherwise had nothing to do with phrases, on the other. But there was no such talent in Central Europe. In order to understand what came about in Central Europe, we must be clear about the fact that history should not be studied through abstract concepts, but rather through realities! We can throw out a question and aim at reality: What is it actually that came into being in the German Empire between 1871 and 1914? Everything that existed there, everything that people saw around them was only an illusion. What was the reality? Well, you see, when it comes to historical phenomena, it is the case that something occurs, but something altogether different is contained below the surface. When the first phenomena, the illusion, disappears, then the second will appear on its heels in reality.

We should not try to analyze this, but rather we must look to the reality, the concrete things. What developed in the German Empire between 1871 and 1914 does not manifest during this time period, for everything happening then was all illusion; the reality follows on its heels. The reality is everything that has occurred since November of 1918. This is what truly holds power at present. The archetypical character of the Wilhelmine period is Noske.† The true nature of everything that had been developing for decades only emerged when the current individuals in power took their posts. The ex-emperor of the German Empire is defined by the so-called revolutionary figures in power at present. The conditions that lay beneath the surface decades ago, during a time when people abandoned themselves to the illusions that existed—those are the conditions that now exist in reality.

And in this way, we can truly study history, insofar as we seek the involution within the evolution, insofar as we seek to discover what is developing beneath the surface. What then is the true nature of eighteenth-century czarism? The former Russian czarism (when its reality truly appears) now takes the form of Lenin and Trotsky—Bolshevism.[†] This is the concrete reality of what was once mere illusion. Czarism was simply the lie that swam over the surface; the truth of czarism appeared as soon as it had faded away. Lenin is nothing else if not a former Czar; once you strip away his surface layer, you are left only with his true reality, and in this case, that reality is named Lenin or Trotsky. Or, continuing with this same idea, if you strip away the surface layer from people like Caprivi or Hohenlohe or Bethmann Hollweg,[†] you are left with Noske, Scheidemann,[†] and others like them. These are the true figures, and the others were simply illusions superimposed upon them.

What is important is that we not illustrate a historical phenomena using abstract concepts and ideas, but that we instead use those things that really were there in history. The definition of one thing in history will always be another fact or event, and never an abstract concept. This is what it means to truly study reality. And it follows from this that we must always be careful to direct our gaze onto the true realities of any situation; for nowadays we live in an age in which many realities must be seen through, in which realities must be constantly laid bare by stripping away the outer layer.

This phenomenon can be seen especially when you study the makeup, the content, of those secret societies that have a particularly strong influence within the English-speaking people, an influence that goes unsuspected by the public. These are societies that work together under particular sympathetic outward rules, societies that in the fifth post-Atlantean epoch have achieved an ever-increasing influence in the world.

If you look back to the year 1720, you will find that in England there were a few members in such societies. These members were simply the implements by and large, with those who had actual influence standing somewhere behind them; but back then, there were also only a few people who were members of these societies. If we look at the statistics nowadays, we find that in the society of Freemasons (the kind of society which is a useful implement in the hands of the secret societies), there are 488 lodges in London, 1,354 lodges in all of Great Britain, 486 English-speaking lodges in the colonies and abroad; and associated with those we also have the so-called Royal Arch Masons, who hold the outward practices of freemasonry a bit more secretly than the others—there are 836 lodges of that society in the world.

Now it is important first of all to cast our gaze on the fact that the substantial content of what exists in these lodges is an implement for these individuals who are truly empowered behind the scenes. And then it is a matter of finding the reasons why these powers have continued to have an unusually large significance to this day. The actual substantial content goes back to the distant past. And those who are always insisting that the content of Freemasonry dates back to the distant past are not altogether wrong, even if their descriptions of the things are often nebulous or perhaps even intentionally false. But looking back toward the distant past touches upon a background that is certainly true. Indeed, it goes so far back into the past that we can accurately say: "The time out of which these things come is that of the first ancient phase of imperialism, when gods walked among us in human form."

At that time, everything that was said in these lodges (and particularly everything that they practiced) made sense. Then it all became symbols. The true sense of these things has been there for ages. We can accurately say that within the lodges that exist currently, there is barely any awareness or content in the things that are said and done. But the symbols remained. The symbols have propagated themselves within the realm of the empty phrase. Consequently, in English-speaking areas and those areas connected with them, we have two layers of cultural ferment existing beside one another: the altogether exoteric, outward phrase that dominates public life, and the symbols protected purely out of a sense of tradition within the secret societies. No one makes any effort to trace them back to their true origins, but they are protected and maintained as symbols. And so, the symbol becomes a phrase in the form of a symbol, or a symbol that has undergone the development into a phrase but appeared in the world in a different form. Thus, we have the outward exoteric phrases of public life, which find expression in everyday human speech and carry on an existence in the parliament, for example, and then we also have in secret societies the ongoing existence of symbols that are by and large not understood by those who have inherited these symbols. They are things with the quality of an empty phrase but the form of a symbol.

This is an important fact—that next to the purely verbal phrase of external life we also have the cultural phrase, the ceremonial phrase. For these ceremonial phrases always hide a spiritual element within. And in secret societies, which have genuine ceremonial forms, meaning ones that date back to genuine practices of old, it can happen that individuals who are particularly gifted due to their karma can arrive at an understanding of the true meaning of these symbols. After all, sometimes even a blind chicken can find a kernel of corn. So it can sometimes happen that especially gifted individuals can arrive at the meaning behind these ceremonies; afterwards they are removed from the secret society. This prevents them from causing any more harm to that secret society. For the thing that is important for these societies is not insight and understanding—it is power. Therefore, it is only about maintaining and protecting the secret rituals in their traditional form. And in practicing these traditional forms, they have a certain power. Why?

I have already spoken of the character of the content of these traditional forms. But this content is, of course, connected to the people who band together in these secret societies. Think about how many people belong to the various lodges of these societies around the world. But they were won over to the idea of joining these lodges by certain factors. And one of the most important factors that originally won these people over to the lodges—even though this particular factor is transgressed against in a variety of ways by nearly all of the lodges, especially nowadays, though this does not dissipate their effectiveness... one of the most important perspectives under which people have bound together in these lodges is the fact that religious beliefs were not discussed or questioned. Certainly, these days this principle has been violated. There are lodges of Freemasons in the world who, for example, will not allow any Jews to join. It goes without saying that such lodges exist; but these lodges do not understand the foundational principle. The foundational principle is to take in people of all religions. This is one of the main foundational principles—to pay no heed to the content of an individual's beliefs. The other is to pay no attention to a person's class or other differences in the world outside of the lodge. People who are members of a true lodge are all brothers, regardless of whether they are lords or working-class citizens, but this principle has also been violated. Most lodges will not accept any working-class citizens and will only take in lords and others who are amenable to them. But this has nothing to do with the foundational principles as such. Everyone within a lodge is nevertheless united under the slogan: "All are brothers." There are ranks within the society, but these have nothing to do with the class divisions, the social divisions in human interaction outside of the lodge. Thus, the members of the lodge are united under principles that have nothing to do with the outside world, nothing to do with our external society, for in our external society we have divided people first and foremost according to their religious beliefs, which play a large role there (religious beliefs do not play any role in a true lodge), and furthermore no one could claim that people in external society are all brothers. In the lodges, those who are members, at least, are brothers.

But such things have real significance. The principles under which a group of people are brought together is not inconsequential. When a group of people are brought together under a unified religious belief, then in actual life this society is, in its principles, only built upon external power, upon a form of power that is now dead. When a group of people is united by the perspective that a person's religious beliefs make no difference, then a society will result that possesses a strong spiritual power. This is the reason the Catholic Church always had to support its power through political means—because they wanted to unite people under a certain more or less unified religious belief. The church grew more powerful the less people depended upon religious beliefs, the less the hierarchy of the church, the less Rome itself depended upon religious beliefs. For in external life, in the social order of the physical world, to hold religious convictions in the position of authority within a society was to render that society powerless. A society can only step forward as a powerful presence when it pays no attention to religious beliefs.

This is of particular importance in this age of the empty phrase. For next to the external phrase stands the esoteric phrase, the phrase of the ceremony, the phrase of the cult. And actually out of this backdrop the social confusion of the present arose in our reality. We can cite some very peculiar evidence of the phrase-like quality of this age. You all know that until the middle of the nineteenth century, there were two opposing parties in the English parliament—the liberal party, the Whigs, and the conservative party, the Tories. Whigs and Tories were opposed to one another. But what kind of names were these actually? In the first half of the nineteenth century people took them very seriously. You referred to a liberal as a Whig and did not need to feel embarrassed about it; you referred to the others as Tories and did not need to feel embarrassed about that either. But when these names first arrived on the scene during the early days of the English parliament, what were those two names at that time? The term "Whig" had formerly been an insult. It came to parliament as an insult. As an alliance formed in Scotland against the particularly stringent English regulations that had been instated there, a group of Scottish individuals banded together and were then referred to insultingly as Whigs in England. So you see, a phrase travelled so far as to go from being an insult to an official name for a political party. Think about how this all played out in reality. The reality is that the members of this Scottish alliance were referred to as Whigs in England. Then it was the highly honorable liberals who were not insulted, but rather defined by the term "Whig." And the "Tories"— that was a name that came from Ireland. It was the term used to refer to followers of the popery. Then this name, which had been an insulting name for members of the Irish popery, became the official name for English conservatives. All of this played itself out in the realm of names, the domain of terms, the empire of phrases. True reality has nothing to do with any of it. This is an example that, shall we say, is taken from the surface layer. For you could find other examples exactly like this one, first and foremost in the English-speaking world, but also in the rest of the world, insofar as it was and is afflicted by the empty phrase.

But why is it then that so many people band together under principles that are absolutely admirable, such as those who come together in the lodges? It does not really matter that some small amount of truly dubious existence is also present in these lodges. What matters is the underlying principle. It is extremely significant that people come together under very powerful perspectives and that they come together in ceremonial phrases, in a phrase-like cult, which then for its part gives the group cohesion out of a true spiritual basis.

Of course, it is also the case that when someone is, let us say, a powerful minister and needs an undersecretary, it goes without saying that he would prefer to appoint his Freemason Brother than to appoint just anyone off the street. This preference is even justifiable, for he knows his Brother better and can work with him more effectively. A mob can be established by the same justifiable means, which is never negative for the relationships that it builds, but which must nevertheless cease to work in this manner in the world.

But what is it then that will take its place? It is noteworthy that precisely in this age in which empty phrases are dominant in public life—that in this age of the empty phrase a spiritual stream has entered the world, a spiritual society with decidedly effective principles! This spiritual society has been very secretive, not so much about its existence, but about the actual inner impulse that drives it. Why is that exactly? Because we live in the age of the empty phrase, and the phrase has allowed realities to be falsified. For what is it that is actually taking form? What already more or less exists? First there is the independent economic life, which is no longer in accord with the empty phrase; the spiritual life, which has been pushed underground; and the rights life, which paces the world as a phrase in a toga with more or less the same meaning for the physical world as jurisprudence and the English judges who sit on the bench in their legal regalia. The relationship between this legal regalia and the reality that exists in the world is the same as the relationship between jurisprudence and the underlying reality of the world. A threefold structure in the empire of the empty phrase, a threefold structure in falsehood—but proof for the necessity of the Threefold Social Order.

You see, to instate the Threefold Social Order is in essence to replace lies and empty phrases with truth, but specifically with truth as reality, whereas currently we are living in an age in which reality is not truth but rather empty phrases and everything connected with them. It is just as possible to carry on with empty phrases in the spiritual life as it is in the rights or political life; only in the economic life is this not possible. For in that case, we must take into consideration some larger issues that people continue to argue against in many of my public lectures (the same arguments come up again and again). After I have described the way in which a human being moves through the course that I spoke of in my book *How to Know Higher Worlds*† and arrive at the idea of developing an inner sight into the spiritual world, into spiritual reality, then someone at every third lecture stands up during the discussion and says: "Yes, but how can a person know that what he is seeing inwardly is reality? There is such a thing as autosuggestion, after all. This entire spiritual world could simply be a product of autosuggestion! There is even the suggestion that when a person just thinks of lemonade, he can taste the lemonade in his mouth; the person suggests the taste of lemonade to himself. There is no actual taste of lemonade there, but a person has simply to think of it and then can taste it in his mouth." In response to this, I always say: "It all depends upon standing fully in reality. It is certainly true that a person can suggest to himself the taste of lemonade, but he cannot quench his thirst by suggesting it to himself in his thoughts. The quenching of thirst is missing." So if you step far enough away from it, you are easily led back to reality. We can have phrases in the realm of the spirit, we can even have empty phrases in the realm of politics and state affairs, but we cannot easily have phrases in the realm of economic life because we cannot eat them, or at the very least cannot be made full by them.

And consequently, in the age of the empty phrase, economic reality is left in the most characteristic position of all realities. And in the moment—I have to say this again—in which we recognize that the illusion is an illusion, that an empty phrase is an empty phrase, a tremendous feeling of shame will emerge: Despite the fact that we human beings possess reason, we do nothing with this reason except tend to the basic economic needs of physical life, though even animals manage to tend to their own physical needs without possessing reason. When we human beings do nothing else with our reason except tend to the basic economic concerns of life such as providing food for ourselves and getting the other basic things essential to physical life, then we are prostituting out our reason, we are using our reason to provide something that animals are perfectly capable of providing for themselves without the luxury of reason. In the moment this self-awareness dawns upon us—the moment when we recognize the empty phrase as an empty phrase—in this moment a great feeling of shame will emerge, followed by the turnabout. Then will emerge an insight into the necessity for a renewal of the spiritual world.

This must, however, be prepared for adequately, and that will occur only when a sufficiently large number of people are able to see through the relationships existing at present. For what good does it do when people fool themselves about what is real at the moment? What good does it do to believe in Lloyd George[†] when you can see that everything that comes out of his mouth is nothing more than an empty phrase? What good does it do that the whole world bows down before Woodrow Wilson, even though you can clearly see that his politics are nothing but empty phrases? What good does it do to think about European relations on the basis of principles that have been inbred and inherited from a time centuries ago, principles that can have no power in the relationships of the contemporary world?

We should also see symbols in the phenomena of history. We should be clear about the fact that already in the phenomena of the external world, peculiar and noteworthy things are happening. The Hapsburgs—they have left Elsass, moving through Switzerland toward the East, ever onward toward the East. They arrived at their easternmost point when they became apostolic kings of Hungary. But in this journey from West to East lies the singular fact that Western realities are fading and disappearing into the East.

The House of Hohenzollern did not go nearly as far—just from Nuremberg to Berlin—but also travelled from West to East. This historical sign is indeed a real symbol that we would do well to pay attention to. And we must also cast our gaze upon what is truly reality among all the empty phrases. For that reason, it is impossible for anyone to gain an understanding of reality from the things that live in public opinion. Anyone nowadays who has any sense of actuality will arrive at very strange conclusions trying to analyze those things that appear in public life, all of the reproductions and emulations found throughout the world, such as the Whigs and the Tories. One eventually finds their origins—they once were terms of insult and then people found it necessary to take them seriously, because it was not easy to find any good serious names for the realities that existed in the world. This is how it goes with a lot of things these days; with an incredible number of things, this is how it goes. In public life nowadays, we try to enshroud words in a very particular kind of mystical darkness, and we do not notice. We do not notice that we are living in the age of empty phrases.

For example, I know of one very interesting codex full of boldly composed phrases. When you open up this codex, you find sentences of a very peculiar nature, sentences like: "What is the law?—The law is the will of the people"—and it goes on from there. Yes, my dear friends: "The law is the will of the people...!" People—for human beings nowadays, this is nothing more than a collection of individuals. But this collection is supposed to have a will of its own! All of the assertions made in the codex of phrases are of the same nature as this one. You have the feeling when you read it that somebody enjoyed the luxury of having enough time to transcribe everything that existed in public life, in the language of the empty phrase, and publish it as a codex. And do you know what this codex of phrases is called? *The State*,[†] and Woodrow Wilson is its author. And this codex of phrases first appeared in the 1890s. In the 1980s, Woodrow Wilson did not intend to have the luxury of time, enough to gather together all of the phrases existing in the public sphere—but as it happens, he did. This is how little the things that people in their phrase-like existence think and say have to do with what really comes out of it. Woodrow

Wilson thought that he had published the collected political wisdom of the day, but in reality he had written a codex full of empty phrases. Several years ago, a German individual longed so strongly to eat the oats of empty phrases that he has now translated this thick book into German,[†] so that you can now read it in German as well. I imagine that it will also be translated into other languages, but I do not know for sure.

Unless we see through to the truth of these things, unless we fix our eyes on the realities of these matters, we will not move forward. Nowadays, a person will go nowhere with lesser thinking. We have to incite our feeling cores to greater thinking. Tomorrow we will speak further about that.

18

THE DEVELOPMENT OF IMPERIALISM: III

DORNACH, FEBRUARY 22, 1920

IF you think back over what we considered yesterday and the day before, you will see that the nature of imperialism is such that in a society of people represented by the word "imperialism," something that was at one time a sort of duty—a clear, if not always justified task—is carried on, as time passes, almost automatically. When it comes to historical events in human evolution, it is the case that due to a kind of inertia we hold onto certain things that were at one time justifiable or at least explicable, things that once had reasons for existing even though the impulses behind them have now been lost. When at some point in history a society of people found it necessary to defend itself, this was certainly justifiable. In the interest of defense, certain jobs were created—police officers and military positions. But after the danger against which the people had to defend themselves has passed, those positions that were created continue to exist; the society must continue to have people filling them. The people who fill those positions want to continue doing their jobs, and consequently something is created which, when you consider true relationships in the world, has no explicable reason for continuing to exist. It might even be the case that something which had once been created for defense actually becomes something aggressive. And indeed, this is actually true in the case of all the imperialists, with the exception of the original imperialism of the first phase of humanity, which I spoke about two days ago. In that case, the justification for spreading the empire of the ruler as far and wide as possible can be derived from the fact that in the consciousness of the people at that time, a ruler was actually a god. In all of the ensuing forms of imperialism, it is fundamentally the case that the inner impulse to expand the influence of a particular empire cannot exist.

Let us consider once more from a very particular perspective what actually occurred in the historical development of humanity. We find that in the most ancient times, which we cannot fully trace in our history, but in which certain facts that can be historically traced continue to shine forth—that in these times the will of those who were looked to as godly figures was the indisputable element of power. In this stage of imperialism, there was fundamentally nothing to discuss in public life; but the reason that no discussion was possible is based on the fact that the ruler was a god strolling about the Earth in human form. This provided, if I can be permitted to say so, a sure and firm grounding for the ordering of public and social affairs.

Now, gradually all of those things founded upon on the basis of a firm, genuine, godly-human will faded into the second phase. In the second phase, everything that can be observed in physical life, whether it be people, insignias, the actions of rulers or upper-class individuals—all of that was a symbol, a sign. Whereas in the first phase of imperialism, the spirit was thought of as existing completely within the physical world, in the second phase everything that exists in the physical world was thought to be a reflection, an image, a symbol of things that do not exist in the physical world but can only be depicted through the people, actions, and other things that are part of the physical world.

This time in which this second phase played itself out is the first period in which discussion actually became possible in the world of human thought, at least as far as public affairs are concerned. In the first phase of imperialism, we actually cannot talk at all about what we now refer to as "rights." We cannot talk about any sort of state institutions or structures. We can only talk about the appearance of godly figures in the form of physical human beings. We can only talk about the fact that in social affairs the concrete and true will of physical human beings was at work. At that time, the question of whether that will was justified or not made no sense. It simply was. It was to be followed. To discuss whether the god in human form should or should not do what was done was nonsensical. In those very ancient times in which the conditions existed that I have just described to you as being characteristic of them, this also did not occur.

But when people began to see in the physical world around them only the image of the spiritual world, when people began to talk about what St. Augustine† called "the City of God," meaning a city that exists here on Earth but is a reflection of heavenly structures and heavenly personalities, then it was possible for one person to believe that what these individuals who were reflecting the divine did was correct, that it was indeed an accurate reflection, whereas another person might take issue with this and could say: "That is not an accurate reflection of the divine." In that, we find the first possibility of a discussion. Contemporary people believe that criticism and discussion have always been present throughout the course of human evolution because they are so used to criticizing and discussing everything. This is not the case. Discussion and criticism first appeared in the second phase of imperialism that I described to you. During that phase, it also became possible for the first time for an individual to make assessments and judgments inwardly, meaning it became possible to attach a predicate to a subject. In the most ancient forms of human expression, personal assessment simply did not exist when it came to public affairs. In the second phase of imperialism, preparations could for the first time begin for things such as what we now refer to as parliament; for the idea of a parliament only makes sense when one is able to have discussions about public affairs. So even the most primitive form of public discussion appears first as a characteristic of the second phase of imperialism.

Insofar as the characteristically Western form of imperialism has spread more or less across the entire world, we are living nowadays in the third phase, in that third phase which I have described to you, insofar as the soul life enters into our considerations, as the age of the empty phrase. This phrase "imperialism," as I described it yesterday, is one in which the inner substance has vanished from discussion and in which anyone can be right, or at least you can believe that you are right, and in which no one can prove you wrong either, because within the world of empty phrases basically any claim can be made. But early phases always continue to exist in the ones that follow upon them. This is fundamentally why the inner impulses of the imperialists continue to emerge and develop in the present. People only look at things on a very superficial level. When the early German Emperor wrote his ethos in a book[†]: "the King's will is the supreme law"—as he did, what does that mean? It means that in the age of the empty phrase, the Emperor spoke words that would have had meaning only during the first phase of imperialism. During that first phase, it was in fact the case that the will of the ruler was the most supreme law.

The idea of rights, which is always implicit in any discussion and has a string of lawyers and advocates in tow, is fundamentally a characteristic of the second phase of imperialism, and it can be understood within the context of its reality in that second phase. Anyone who has followed the many discussions about the origin and nature of rights can gather from these discussions that there is something enigmatic and opalescent in the nature of the concept itself, because when considering rights you are dealing with something that comes from the second age of imperialism, in which spiritual reality illuminated, shimmered behind, shone through the material world, such that when we have before us only the outer shell of the symbol, which can also be present in words and the practice of law, then it is possible to argue about the nature of rights, to take sides in a discussion in public life about rights and law.

In this age of the empty phrase, we lose all understanding of how necessary it is in our social relations, if we are to find an anchor for the concept of rights, for this perspective to take hold: The spiritual realm is shining here into the physical realm. And when this understanding is lost, then people start to define rights in the way that I presented to you yesterday in the example of Woodrow Wilson. Today I want to read to you word-for-word a definition that Woodrow Wilson offered of rights, and you will see that this definition proves itself to be nothing more than a bunch of empty words. I cited this definition yesterday, and today I want to cite it again more exactly. He writes: "Law is the will of the state concerning its own organization and conduct and the civic conduct of those under its authority."†

So, the state has a will! We should imagine a man standing totally within abstract idealism, to say nothing of materialism (for the two are much the same, abstract idealism and materialism), and from that place saying: "Law is the will of the state." The state supposedly has a will. You would have to be forsaken by all spirits of a more concrete perspective in order to even attempt to say or write something like this statement. But it is nonetheless found in that work that I told you about yesterday, in that codex of phraseology: *The State: Elements of Historical and Practical Politics* by Woodrow Wilson.

In that same book there are other interesting things as well. As an aside, I would like to draw your attention to one passage in which Woodrow Wilson writes about the German Empire, after saying that the efforts to found this German Empire had been going on for some time before aspiring to its present form in 1870/71. He concludes this section with the following sentences: "The final impulse was given to the new processes of union by the Franco-Prussian War of 1870-71. Prussia's successes in that contest, won, as it seemed, in the interest of German patriotism, broke the coldness of the middle states toward their great northern neighbor; they joined the rest of Germany, and the German Empire was formed (Palace of Versailles, January 18, 1871)."†

This was written by the same man who, sometime later, united in Versailles with those who had, in their "impertinence," given the inducement for the formation of the German Empire back then. Many things in modern-day public opinion originate precisely in something like this, that humanity is so appallingly superficial and does not take care with anything. If you resolve to make judgments on the basis of objective considerations, then things always come out differently than what swims about in the contemporary public sphere and is repeated over and over again by thousands upon thousands of people.

And so, in the second stadium, we are dealing with something that leads to the possibility of discussion, something that actually makes possible, for the first time, the concept of public rights. In the third stadium, we are dealing, as we have seen, with the economic life as an actual reality. And yesterday, we showed how in the course of historical evolution, this age of the phrase is absolutely necessary, so that the phrase, no longer full of any content, can then open the eyes of human beings to the necessity of bringing spirituality, new spirituality, into the wider world.

For the moment, people have only a meager imagination of this new spirituality. And for that reason, it is understandable that this new spirituality faces the grossest of misunderstandings. For this new spirituality must take hold in the deepest underground places of human life. And for as much as the secret societies of the world, as regards their substance, their content, are merely traditionally preserving the old ways in their substance, in their content, the outward practice of being "brothers" without bringing considerations of class in the outer world into the lodge and without paying attention to individual, subjective beliefs is something that in a certain sense (though also something else, which I will describe to you momentarily) is preparing the future in the proper manner.

Let us examine something altogether banal, entirely ordinary, that we might say nowadays (and I ask you to pay particular attention to this): "The tree is green." This is a sentence that belongs entirely to the second stadium of human evolution: "The tree is green." Perhaps you will understand this best if I ask you to imagine that you are to paint that which is expressed by the assessment: "The tree is green." You cannot paint this! It is impossible to paint: "The tree is green." You might have a big white (or some other color) piece of paper and then put green color onto it, but you will be painting nothing of a tree! And if you were first to paint something of a tree without putting any green there, then you would end up with something that only addresses the object.

If you wanted to paint: "The tree is green"—you would actually have to paint a dead thing. The manner in which we join subject to predicate in our language is fundamentally useful only for our worldview of dead things, of the unliving world. Because we do not still possess an imagination of how everything in the world is living and of how we are to express ourselves over and against a world in which all is living and moving, we construct statements such as: "The tree is green"—which actually says that a relationship exists between something and the color green, whereas in actuality the *color green* is the creative element, the thing with living and effective power in this circumstance. The transformation of human thinking and feeling must take place all the way into the depths of the soul life—which will a long time from now be called forth—and this transformation will then carry into outward social relationships, into the interactions between people.

In regard to all of this, we are now standing just at the very beginning stage. But we must be able to see which of the paths forward leads us toward the light. I said before: "There is something significant about people coming together in such a way that the subjective beliefs of each individual play no role." And from this perspective, follow for a moment—but do it truly in your own thoughts—the way in which things are laid out in Anthroposophy. Never are things described in such a way as to offer definitions or general judgments. We try—though we must deal with the fact that people do not always take it up in this manner—but nevertheless, the fundamental attempt is made to offer pictures, to describe things from the greatest variety of angles, and as such it is actually entirely senseless when people try nail down something truly spoken as a spiritual-scientific truth to a judgment of either yes or no. There are certainly people at present who are always wanting to do this, but it is impossible.

Because we are moving from out of the second stadium of imperialism into the third stadium, it happens over and over that somebody poses the question: "What would be good for me to do, since I am struggling with this or that difficulty in my life?" Advice is given. "Aha," says the asker, "so when I find myself in this position in life, I should do this or that." We generalize! But each situation has only a very limited meaning, for judgments that fall out of the spiritual world always have only an individual meaning, are applicable only to the particular matter at hand. This practice of generalizing, to which we are accustomed because of the experience of the second stadium of human evolution, may not be carried forward into the future. People nowadays are just so very used to taking things from the past and continuing them into the future. We can overcome the things that continue to live on perniciously in our souls by stepping back and seeing these matters with full clarity.

Yesterday, I indicated to you that in many ways, the Catholic Church hearkens back to the first stadium of imperialism. It contains, in large part, something like a trace or shadow of the first stadium of human evolution, a trace or shadow that was during certain periods condensed into a form of soul imperialism, for example during the eleventh century, during which time the monks from Cluny† actually had much more control in Europe than people realize. From that group came the Pope Gregory VII,† the powerful, imperialistic Pope. The fact that actually, according to the Roman Catholic dogma, the priests consider themselves to be more than the Christ, because they are able to demand that the Christ be present at the altar—this fact clearly demonstrate that the institution of the Catholic Church is in fact the shadow of what once existed during the first stadium of human evolution in the most ancient form of imperialism.

Now, you know that there is a great enmity between the Catholic Church and all of the societies that served as the instruments of the Freemasons (or at least a certain sect of the Freemasons) in the Western areas of the world. Nowadays, this enmity is spreading far and wide, and in this lecture today I can do no more to demonstrate in any specific details how this enmity has recently expanded. But one thing can be said, that in these secret societies one fact lives very strongly—namely, the insight that the Catholic Church is merely the shadow of the now defunct imperialism of the first stadium. This is actually one of the most basic teachings of these secret societies, that the Catholic Church is the shadow, the last remnant of the first stadium of imperialism. The Holy Roman Empire of the German Nation continued to use this frame; Charlemagne and the Ottos were crowned by the Pope, used the imperialism of the soul as a means of anointing themselves for the imperialism of the external world. They took what was already there, what had remained from ancient times, and used that mold to cast something new. In this way, the imperialism of the second stadium was cast in the frame of the first stadium of imperialism.

Now we have arrived at the third stadium, which has shown itself particularly in the Western regions of the world; we have arrived at economic imperialism. This economic imperialism has as its foundation and backdrop (as I have already said) a spiritual world of secret societies that sate themselves with phrase-like symbols. But if we can see clearly that the outward constitution, the social make-up, of the church is only a shadow of something that was formerly present and now holds no meaning, then we still are not seeing through the second stadium of imperialism, and in this we find the great state of illusion in which the present-day statesmen in particular find themselves. It is always so telling that Woodrow Wilson is able to speak of the "will of the state." He would no longer be able to speak of the "will of the church," but he speaks of the "will of the state" as if it were something altogether self-evident.

Now, the state as a carrier of the rights life, taken as a totality, as a whole, only had the meaning ascribed to it at present during the second stadium of human evolution. Whereas in the most ancient times, the church was everything, or rather that thing from which the church resulted was everything; in the second stadium that thing from which the state has now resulted was everything. When it comes to the church, this has been noticed, particularly within the secret societies; when it comes to the state, it has not yet been noticed. For the time being, we continue to pour everything into the mold of the state, just as in the Middle Ages, all new things were poured into the mold of the church; into the state we pour everything that has been united under the banner of a certain concept of freedom. The whole economic imperialism of Great Britain has been cast in the frame of the state. And all those who have been well-educated in Great Britain see something self-evident in the state, something to which they can readily ascribe a will.

This must also be seen clearly, however, so that this understanding of the state can go the same way as the understanding of the church went. We must recognize: When, for the collective social organism, we hold to a concept of the state as merely an institution of the rights life and then jam everything else into this rights institution, we are perpetuating a shadow just as the church perpetuated a shadow (as is

now known to the secret societies). But there is still little consciousness of this. Think just a moment about the way in which everything
that gets people worked up in outward affairs is nowadays jammed
into the concept of the state. There are people who are nationalists,
chauvinists, and so on—everything that people refer to as a nation,
national, chauvinist, all of this is incorporated into the frame of the
state! We press nationalism into that frame and build the concept of
a nationalist state. Or let us say that someone has certain perspectives
on, say, socialism, even totally radical socialism: again we take up the
frame of the state! Instead of pressing nationalism into it, now we are
forcing socialism into the frame. But people have no understanding
of the fact that this frame is now only a shadowy construction just as
the make-up of the church has become a shadowy concept.[†]

In certain Protestant churches, one is given to understand that
the church is just an outward institution, that the Being of religion
must take root in the heart of each person. This stadium of human
evolution has not yet arrived as regards our understanding of the
state; otherwise, people would not have tried to press all possible
nationalities into the drawing-up of European borders, of national
borders, after the latest military encounters. But no one is reckoning with these matters. They are not reckoning with the fact that
what happens in the historical evolution of humanity is life and not
mechanics. And coming into being and dying out both belong to life.

But something different belongs to an imperialistic understanding.
What belongs to that understanding is that one does not think at all
about the future. It belongs to the whole understanding of the outward
affairs of humanity at present, that people do not have any living
thoughts about the future, only dead thoughts. They think: "Today
we are building something; it is good, and it will stay here forever."
The feminist movement, socialism, nationalism—they all think in this
manner: "We are founding something now; it begins with us. People
have been waiting for us, waiting for the moment when we would be
this clever. But now we have come up with the cleverest thing that ever
will be; it will last for all eternity." This would be more or less the same
thought that I would have to have if I had raised a child until he was
eighteen years old and then said to myself: "Now I have raised him

properly and he will stay just like he is now." He will, however, grow older, and he will also die, and it is the same way with everything that comes into being in human evolution.

I have come now to what I was hinting at earlier—to what must be brought to the principle of having no concern for subjective beliefs or to human brotherhood. What must be brought to this is the living perspective that in this earthly life we must also reckon with death; what must be brought to it is the conscious awareness: We are creating institutions in the present that must necessarily also die out, for they bear within them the principle of Death, institutions that have no desire to exist eternally, that do not think for a moment about being something ever-present.

But how can such a thing be realized? Well, under the influence of the thinking that comes out of the second stadium it never will be realized. But if that feeling of shame about which I spoke yesterday enters, if we come to recognize: We are living in the Kingdom of the Phrase, in which only economic life, only economic imperialism, holds any sway—then there will be a call for the spirit that moves, though unseen, all throughout reality. There will be a call for recognition of the spirit that speaks of the spiritual world as an invisible kingdom, as a kingdom that is not of this world and in which consequently the Christ-impulse will truly be able to take hold. There will be a call for the recognition of just such a kingdom.

This can only be so when the social organism is threefolded: the economic life managing itself; the rights life serving no longer as the absolute, all-compassing understanding of the state, and the state functioning only as the frame for that which truly lies within the rights life; and the spiritual life existing in true freedom, meaning in such a way that it can truly take form in reality as spiritual life. Spirit can move among people only when it is dependent upon nothing but itself, and when all institutions that serve the spirit are dependent upon nothing other than themselves.

What do we have then when we have this threefolded organism, this social organism? We then have an economic life. Its nature is exactly the same as the nature of the original form of imperialism. Everything that moves within it is also present entirely within life on the physical

Earth. In this economic branch, the managing forces must truly come out of the economic life itself. I do not believe that anyone would be of the opinion, were this economic organism to be organized in the manner described in my *Kernpunkte*,[†] that anything supersensory is connected with the economic life. When we eat, when we prepare our food, when we make our clothes, this is all reality; the aesthetics of them might be symbolic, but the clothing itself is just reality.

When we then examine the second branch of the social organism, we find that we do not have for the future the same kind of symbolism that existed in the second stadium of human evolution, wherein the state, the embodied rights life, was a totality, but in everything that emerges from one human being we have a picture of that which lives in all other human beings. We have constructed the symbols anew from out of the present moment. What one human being does will always be a guide for the entire form of the social rights constitution that is constructed.

And the third will not be a symbol and not a phrase; rather, it will become spiritual reality. The spirit will have the possibility of truly living among human beings.

And so, the inner social order can only be built if we truly move toward inner truthfulness. During the era of the empty phrase, however, this is particularly difficult. For in the age of the empty phrase, people are used to a certain refined cleverness, but this refined cleverness is, in actuality, fundamentally nothing more than a game with the word representations of old concepts. Think for a moment of that characteristic example—that suddenly it emerges from out of the imperialism of the phrase that it would be good for the king or queen of England[†] to also hold the title "Emperor of India." Absolutely nothing has actually changed. Of course, many excellent reasons can be found for awarding this title "Empress of India" or "Emperor of India." But think about what would have happened if this were not done—nothing would have gone differently! The emperor of Austria, who is now among those who has been chased out of his throne, bore until the time of his ousting, among his other titles, one particularly peculiar title. It was (if I can remember them all) Franz Joseph I,[†] Emperor of Austria, apostolic King of Hungary, King of Bohemia,

Dalmatia, Croatia, Slovenia, Galicia, Lodomeria, Illyria, and so on. Among these other titles, there was the title "King of Jerusalem"! The Austrian emperor—until he was no longer emperor—had the title King of Jerusalem. This dated back to the Crusades. There is no better way to prove the role that meaninglessness plays at present. And meaninglessness actually plays a much larger role than you might believe.

What is important is that we ascend to this recognition of what is phrase-like at present. And this is made more difficult by the fact that those who are living within the phrases are simply rolling around the word representations of old concepts in their brains and believe that they are thinking. But we can return truly to thinking only when we infuse our inner soul lives with substance, and this can only come out of a recognition of the spiritual world, of spiritual life. Only by infusing ourselves with spiritual life can we again become human beings full of content after having become an intestine of the empty phrase, a phrase-bowel that is altogether empty, satisfied only by word husks.

Out of the feeling of shame I already hinted at yesterday will emerge a call for the spirit. And the possibility for this spirit to spread throughout the world will come about only if the spiritual life develops independently. Otherwise we will always have to work within little holes, as we have been forced to do with the Waldorf School,[†] because the school regulations in Württemberg had just such a hole that made it possible to establish a Waldorf school according to purely spiritual laws, spiritual principles, something which would have been possible in almost no other place in the world nowadays. But we can truly build those things connected with spiritual life from the spiritual world only when the other two branches of the social organism do not exert their influence in it, when these things are truly taken purely out of the spiritual world.

At the moment, the tendency of this age is to do just the opposite. But this tendency of the current age will never reckon with the fact that a new spiritual life will appear more and more on the Earth with each new generation. It makes no difference whether an absolutist state or a Soviet republic is established now: If people move forward with the establishment of such things without a conscious awareness that everything created is subject to life and must therefore change with time and ultimately die out, must go through new forms and metamorphoses, then the only thing that they are truly preparing is that each new generation will become revolutionaries, for they will only incorporate into the social life of the present what is considered good for the immediate present. What must come toward our foundational laws, which in the Western regions of the world are still firmly secluded within the empty phrase, is the ability to see the social organism as something living. It can only be seen as something living when its threefold nature is understood. For this reason, a great, terrible, and intense responsibility lies with those who, through economic privilege, are expanding an imperialism over almost the entire world—the responsibility to become aware that the practice of a true spiritual life must be poured into this imperialism. It must be experienced as outright mockery and scorn that in the British Isles an economic empire has been founded that rules the entire world and that then, when particularly deep, mystical spirituality is desired, they turn to what has been economically conquered, economically exploited, and take their spirituality from that. We have the obligation to allow spiritual substance to flow freely from itself into the outward form of the social organism.

This is the conscious awareness that I believe our British friends must take away from here—the conscious awareness that in this historical moment, all of those who belong to world organisms in which the English language is spoken have an obligation to bring true spirituality into the outward economic empire. For when it comes to this matter, it is a situation of either-or: Either our strivings remain purely within the scope of the economic empire, in which case the downfall of earthly civilization is the only possible result—or spirit will be poured into this economic empire, in which case the intended results of Earth evolution will actually be achieved. I would like to say here: Every morning, you should hold this truth before yourself and regard it solemnly, and each individual action you take should be taken with this impulse in mind. The world clock is tolling solemnly now. We have by and large reached the zenith of the empty phrase. When all content has been squeezed out of the phrase, a content that once entered it in a different form and no longer has any meaning, we must take up what can once again bring a truly substantial content to our social life and our soul life. We must be clear that the outcome of this either-or scenario is up to each individual to decide and that each and every person must take part in this decision with his or her inner powers of soul. Otherwise, we are not actually living out true human affairs.

But the longing for illusions is incredibly great, particularly now in this age of the empty phrase. People would so prefer to push away the seriousness of life. People do not want to gaze upon the truth that moves through our evolution. Would people have allowed themselves to be deceived by Wilsonism if they truly possessed the inner desire to be clarified by the truth? This desire must come. The longing for truth must be awoken in humanity. Above all, the longing for the freedom of spiritual life must be awakened in humanity, along with the knowledge that one has not a right to call oneself a Christian if one does not understand what is meant by the saying: "My kingdom is not of this world."

This means that the Kingdom of Christ must become an invisible kingdom, a truly invisible kingdom, a kingdom that we speak about in the way we speak about things we cannot see. Only once spiritual science has begun to move amongst us will we be able to speak of such a kingdom. An outward-oriented church or state cannot bring this kingdom into reality, nor can an economic empire. Only the will of individual human beings living within a liberated spiritual life can realize this kingdom.

People can scarcely believe that in those areas in which they live, the areas that are populated, much can be done for the liberation of the spiritual life. Therefore, action must be taken precisely in those areas that are not already a part of the political realm, the economic realm, or obviously the soon-to-be spiritual realm. Above all, we must be infused with the knowledge that we have not yet arrived at the time when we can say: "Things have been going downhill, now everything is looking up again!" No, if people do not take actions from out of the spiritual world, then things will not turn upward, but rather will continue to go downhill. Humanity does not currently live on something that it produces—for in order to produce something we must again act under the impulses of the spiritual—humanity is living nowadays off of reserves, of old reserves that will someday be used up. And it is childish and naïve to believe that someday we will hit bottom and then suddenly everything will start to get better even if we just sit on our hands. This is not at all the case. And the hope would be that saying something like what I have just spoken would light a fire in each person's soul that would direct them toward the anthroposophical movement. We would also hope that the spirit that so greatly haunted those who have perhaps found their way to the anthroposophical movement will be conquered by the spirit that is spoken of here. Certainly it is often true that the individuals who come toward such a movement want something for themselves, for their own souls. They can have this as well, but only when they are also able to place their souls in service to the whole. They should move further down their own paths, to be sure, but do so in such a way that the whole of humanity might also move further down its path. This cannot be said often enough. This should also be added to the other thought that I earlier said you should hold up before yourself and consider every morning.

If the deepest inner impulse of this movement had been taken completely seriously, we would have been father along in our path today. But much of what is done in our circles currently is not an advancement toward the future but a hindrance. We must take council with ourselves about this fact. This is very important. And above all, we should not believe that the most potent oppositional forces are not looming over us from all sides, ready to fight against any striving toward the salvation of humanity.

Several times, I have pointed out to you here the things that are being done to combat this movement in the world, the animosity that has been directed toward this movement. I feel it is my responsibility to familiarize you with these things so that you might see that you should never say to yourself: "Now we have successfully disproved this or that." We have disproved nothing, because when it comes to this kind of opposition it is not a matter of somehow representing the truth. They make as little contact with the actual affair as possible but then deliver defamations from as many different angles as they can.

I would like to read to you a passage from a letter that arrived recently in Stuttgart from Kristiania.† I would just like to read one section: "Several of our anthroposophical friends are working together at a so-called 'adult education center' in Kristania with one Schirmer. This Herr Schirmer is in one sense a very capable teacher, but is also a fanatical racist and a sworn Anti-Semite. At a recent gathering at which three of us gave lectures on the Threefold Social Order, he sought to argue against us, or rather against the *Kernpunkte* from Dr. Steiner, though without any particular success. The chap holds some sway among circles of teachers, and he is working on his own in a manner not dissimilar to the Threefold Social Order, insofar as he represents freedom and lively objectiveness to the children he teachers, but still he is working against the Threefold Social Order and Dr. Steiner for the simple reason that he harbors a suspicion that Dr. Steiner is a Jew. This is probably not actually so terrible. No doubt we must expect and overcome far more and greater oppositions than this. But now he has received confirmation of his suspicion: He turned to an "authority," namely to the editor of the political-anthropological monthly *Berlin-Steglitz*. This monthly, which is outright anti-Semitic, wrote to him that Dr. Steiner is a Jew through and through. He has connections with the Zionists, actually is tied to them directly. And the editor added that they, the anti-Semites, have had their eye on you for quite some time. Herr Schirmer went on to explain that an outright persecution of the Jews is now beginning in Germany, and that all Jews currently on the black lists of the anti-Semites should simply be gunned down or, as they say, rendered harmless," and so on.

You see, the crux of the matter here has nothing to do with something that is in any way anti-Semitic; that is simply the surface layer. In connection with situations like these, people use insults with which they are able to communicate as much as possible to those who somehow hear those insults. But such things also point to something that most people nowadays do not want to see, something about which they would rather continue to deceive themselves. It is much more serious today than you would like to think. And what is important is that we not misjudge the gravity of this time, but rather become clear about the fact that when it comes to such things—things that work against everything that we mean when we speak of the forward progress of humanity—we are seeing only the beginning, and that we may never, without doing harm to our obligations, turn our gaze away from everything now appearing in the form of a radical evil within humanity, everything now being realized as radical evil within humanity. The worst thing that can happen now is to believe, having listened to insults and empty phrases, that everything that verbalization gives to old concepts and understanding, that all of that still is somehow rooted in human reality, and that we do not draw forth a new reality from the fonts of the spiritual world itself.

This, my dear friends, was something of what I wanted still to say to you today, what I wanted to say first and foremost for all of you, but particularly for those whose visit we have so heartily enjoyed, particularly for our English friends, that after their return they might direct their behavior and actions there, where it will be important for them to do so, out of a certain knowledge and awareness. You will have noticed that here I have not spoken well or ill of anyone. I have not spoken to flatter anyone. Here I have spoken simply to communicate the truth. I have also come to know Theosophists: When they have spoken to people from a foreign country, they began their talk about what an honor it is to be able to spread the teachings of spiritual life within the borders of that great nation that had gained so much glory for itself. I could not speak to you here in such a manner. But I think that you all came to hear the truth, and I believe that in this manner I have served you as best I can, in that I attempted to speak the unadorned truth. You will have seen from these lectures that to speak the truth nowadays is not a comfortable thing, for the truth calls up more opposition now than ever before. Do not shy away from this opposition, for in this time, the two are one and the same: having enemies and speaking the truth. These things must be seen for what they are. And we will understand them best when we also have as a foundation of this oppositional understanding the desire always to hear the truth.

This is what I wanted to say today, both to the group at large and in particular to our English friends, in my last lecture to you before my trip to Germany.[†]

REFERENCE NOTES

Page 1, "the remarks I made … last December"
See the lectures from December 12, 13, and 14, 1919, in *Die Sendung Michaels.*
*Die Offenbarung der eigentlichen Geheimnisse des Menschenwesens [The mission of
the archangel Michael. The revelation of the actual mysteries of the human being],*
(12 lectures, Dornach, 1919), GA 194.

Page 1, "the public lectures"
Here Steiner is referring to the three lectures given in Basel on January 5, 6, and
7, 1920, in *Vom Einheitsstaat zum dreigliedrigen sozialen Organismus [From the
unified state to the threefold social organism],* (11 lectures given in various locations, 1920), GA 334.

Page 4, "Rabindranath Tagore"
(1881-1941), Indian poet, philosopher, pedagogue and freedom fighter.
Descendent of a Bengalese family that traces its lineage back to Bhatta-Narajana,
a Sanskrit playwright of the eighth century. Became internationally famous after
the publication of his work *Gitanjali*, an English-language prose edition of a
selection of his religious poetry. In 1913, he received the Nobel Peace Prize for
Literature for this work.

Page 4, "what will come of Leninism"
Vladimir Ilyich Lenin, born Ulyanov (1870-1924), leader of Bolshevism,
founder of the USSR.

Page 6, "Spencer"
Herbert Spencer (1820-1903), English philosopher, proponent of the material-
istic/mechanistic understanding of evolution.

Page 6, "Darwin"
Charles Darwin (1809-1882), English natural scientist, founder of Darwinism—
the materialistic understanding of evolution..

Page 6, "such great spirits …"
Johann Wolfgang von Goethe (1749-1832); Johann Gottlieb Fichte (1762-
1814); Friedrich Wilhelm Joseph von Schelling (1775-1854); Georg Wilhelm
Friedrich Hegel (1770-1831); Johann Gottfried Herder (1744-1903)—the
great German philosophers of the eighteenth and nineteenth centuries. See also
Rudolf Steiner's book *Die Rätsel der Philosophie in ihrer Geschichte alse Umriss
dargestellt [The Riddles of Philosophy, CW 18]* (1914), GA 18, and (except as
regards Herder) *Vom Menschrätsel. Ausgesprochenes und Unausgesprochenes im*

Denken, Schauen, Sinnen einer Reihe deutscher und österreichischer Persönlichkeiten [The Riddles of the Human Being] (1916), GA 20.

Page 6, "the Cotta family"
The famous book publishing family from Stuttgart, originally from Sachsen before moving to Tübingen. The Cottas were the sole publishers of Goethe's work until the copyright term at last expired.

Page 9, "a certain report"
See the lecture "Die sittlichen und religiösen Kräfte im Sinner der Geisteswissenschaft," given on January 7, 1920, and appearing in GA 334 (see also the notes from the beginning of this lecture).

Page 9, "the sorts of things I said recently in Basel"
This is the same report that led to the passage of a law on August 10, 1842, forbidding children under ten years old from working a full day. That law was eventually made more stringent by the passage of further regulations based on other reports similar to this one.

Page 9, "'spirit' was abolished in 869"
At the Eighth Catholic Ecumenical Council in Constantinople in 869, organized to oppose and depose Photius, the Patriarch of Constantinople, it was established in the eleventh section of the *Canones contra Photium* that the human being is to be seen as a creature of body and soul, and that the soul had "certain spiritual characteristics" ("unam animam rationabilem et intelletualem"). The Catholic philosopher Otto Willmann, who was highly esteemed by Rudolf Steiner, wrote in his three-volume work: *The History of Idealism* (*Geschichte des Idealismus*, first edition, Braunschweig 1894): *Christian idealism as the fulfillment of the ancient* (second volume, p. 111): "The abuse carried out by the Gnostics in their Pauline differentiation between the pneumatic and the physical human being, which they disbursed as proof of their perfection as the ambassadors of the Christ (now beholden to church law), was affirmed by the church in their express *disavowal of the Trinity*.

Page 10, "Newton"
Isaac Newton (1642-1727), English natural scientist, mathematician, and astronomer. Founder of classical theoretical physics and a mechanistic understanding of the universe.

Page 11, "You would not believe with what little understanding the world is ruled"
This saying can be traced back to Pope Julius III (1550-1555), but is also sometimes (apparently incorrectly) attributed to the Swedish Chancellor Axel Oxenstjerna (1583-1654). See also: *Geflügelte Word. Der Zitatenschatz des deutschen Volkes*, collected by Georg Büchmann, 26th edition, Berlin,

1919, p. 455. (Translator's note: Modern English readers might imagine *Bartlett's Book of Familiar Quotations* as an equivalent of the cited volume from Büchmann).

Page 11, "An Outline of Esoteric Science"
An Outline of Esoteric Science (1910), CW 13.

Page 11, "Karl Kautsky"
(1854-1938), Socialist and orthodox Marxist. *Wie der Weltkrieg entstand. Dargestellt nach aktenmaterial des Deutschen Auswärtigen Amts*, Bern, 1919.

Page 12, "on the first page of his book"
Ibid. p. 14.

Page 14, "Now, I have in the past ... two facts of life "
See, for example, the lecture given on December 13, 1919 in *Die Sendung Michaels. Die Offenbarung der eigentlichen Geheimnisse des Menschenwesens {The mission of the archangel Michael]* (12 lectures given in Dornach, 1919), GA 194; and the lectures from given on November 18, 19 and 25, 1917 in *Individuelle Giestwesen und ihr Wirken in der Seele des Menschen [Individual spiritual beings and their influence in the soul of the human being],* (9 lectures given in various locations, 1917), GA 178.

Page 16, "We have also spoken in the past ..."
See, for example, the lecture from May 23, 1915, in *Kunst- und Lebensfragen im Lichte der Geisteswissenschaft [Questions of art and life in the light of spiritual science],* (13 lectures, Dornach, 1915), GA 162. See also the lectures from November 15, 1917, (St. Gallen) in *Individuelle Geistwesen und ihr Wirken in der Seele des Menschen* (9 lectures given in various locations, 1917), GA 178, and those from October 18 and November 1917 (Basel) in *Geisteswissenschaftliche Ergebnisse über das Wesen des Menschen* (10 lectures given in Basel and Bern, 1917/18), GA 72.

Page 20, "Copernican-ism"
Nicholas Copernicus (1473-1543), Polish astronomer, canon, jurist, humanist; founder of the heliocentric theory of the solar system.

Page 20, "Galileo-ism"
Galileo Galilei (1564-1642), Italian natural scientist, physicist; developed the foundations of mechanics and discovered the laws of free fall, the pendulum, and inertia.

Page 23, "the poet was right when he said ... "
The poet is Goethe and the poem is *On The Divine*: "The Sun sheds its light / Over evil and good," referencing Matthew, 5:45.

Page 23, "so does the Earth desire ..."
Translator's note: A pun is lost here: "so möchte sich die Erde 'drücken'" means both that the Earth wants to "make itself scarce" and also that the Earth wants to "weigh or press down" (*drücken*). Steiner is subtly pointing out that the familiar actions of the Earth's forces, namely that they give things weight and press down upon them (*drücken*), also point toward the esoteric desires of those same forces, namely to make themselves scarce from this planetary system (*sich drücken*).

Page 26, "the Moon *nimmt ab* ..."
Translator's note: nimmt zu... nimmt ab – That is to say: "waxes" and "wanes," respectively. Steiner's point here is that the two German verbs for "to wax" and "to wane" are *zunehmen* and *abnehmen*, respectively. The shape of the initial letters of these two verbs — *z* and *a* — can, with a little imagination, be derived from the shape of the crescent Moon at the two extremes of the stages of waxing and waning.

Page 26, "it says the opposite"
Translator's note: The French equivalent of our verbs "to wax" and "to wane" are *croître* and *décroître*, respectively. Though he does not make it explicit, Steiner clearly sees the shape of a waning crescent as the shape of a "c," which would point to the verb *croître*—that is, "to wax." Thus, the Moon's physical shape is telling us that it is waxing (*croître*) rather than telling the truth and saying that it is waning (*décroître*).

Page 26, "The Moon is a liar"
"Luna mendax." This Latin proverb cannot be traced.

Page 28, "I read an article today..."
"Englands russische Politik" (England's Russian Policy), *National-Zeitung*, Basel, seventy-ninth Annual 1920 (January 6), Number 9, evening edition.

Page 31, "The Apollonian percept: 'Know thyself'"
Inscription of the Temple to Apollo at Delphi, credited to one of the seven wise men (Thales or Chilon).

Page 33, "Galileo ..."
See note p. 20.

Page 33, "Giordano Bruno"
(1548-1600), Italian philosopher, co-founder of modern worldviews. According to his teachings, there are countless "Minima" or "Monads," up to the "Monad of all Monads"—God. Bruno was forced to leave the Dominican order in 1576, and his life ended on the pyre of the Inquisition.

Page 33, "Copernicus"
See note p. 20.

Page 35, "the one who can assert "
See, for example, the German philosopher Friedrich Albert Lange (1828-1875) in his work *Geschichte des Materialismus und Kritik seiner Bedeutung in der Gegenwart* (Leipzi o. J.—1866). For more on Lange, see Rudolf Steiner: *Die Rätsel der Philosophie in ihrer Geschichte als Umriss dargestellt [The Riddles of Philosophy]*, (1914), CW 18, entry on Lange.

Page 36, "a conversation with a man in Vienna..."
The person who is mentioned here is Heinrich Friedjung (1851-1920), an Austrian historian and political author. He founded the *Deutsche Wochenschrift* along with several others, which Rudolf Steiner edited from January to July 1888.

Page 37, "Georg Gottfried Gervinus"
(1805-1871), a history writer and literary historian. His book, *Geschichte der poetischen National-Literartur der Deutschen*, 5 volumes, Leipzig 1835-1842 (editions that appeared later were published under the title *Geschichte der deutschen Dichtung*).

Page 37, "Hammerling"
Robert Hammerling (1830-1889), Austrian poet. *Homunculus. Modernes Epos in zehn Gesängen*, Hamburg 1888.

Page 38, "One of the leading minds of contemporary Central Europe..."
It is not known to whom Steiner was referring here.

Page 39, "*The Philosophy of Freedom*"
Die Philosophie der Freiheit. Grundzüge einer modernen Weltanschauung – Seelische Beobachtungsresultate nach naturwissenschaftlicher Methode (1894), GA 4.

Page 39, "Whatever your do for another human being, you do for me"
Matthew 25:40.

Page 40, "Jesus of Nazareth – the 'simple man'"
See for example Heinrich Weinel: *Jesus im neunzehnten Jahrhundert*, Tübingen and Leipzig, 1903, Introduction, p. 6: "To be sure, it is not the Christ of the past, the God of the Old Testament, but rather Jesus of Nazareth to whom the people of this time turn, once again seeking answers to questions about their concerns. For a long, long time was this simple and courageous man hidden in the streaming glories of the Heavenly Father..."

Page 41, "in the idea of threefolding"
Rudolf Steiner's call for a reformation of the social life during and after the First World War transcended high above the ideological and politically-motivated debates that raged on during that time period. Beginning with a critique of parliamentarianism and a centralized governmental system, he developed his "Threefold Social Order" based upon precise observations of the human and the social organism. It called for independent branches within society, drawing upon the French Revolution ideals of Freedom, Equality, and Brotherhood: a political/rights life based upon the principles of equality and justice, existing in between a free and independent spiritual life and an economic life directed toward the ideal of brotherhood. – See Steiner's book *Die Kernpunkte der sozialen Frage in den Lebensnotwendigkeiten der Gegenwart und Zukunft* (1919), GA 23; his *Aufsätze über die Dreigliederung des sozialen Organismus und zur Zeitlage 1915-1921*, GA 24; and his lecture cycles GA 328 to GA 341. See also the *Beiträge zur Rudolf Steiner Gesamtausgabe*, Dornach, volumes 25/25/, 27/28/, 88 and 103.

Page 43, "Recently I read you a letter..."
This occurred during the lecture given on December 14, 1919, which appears in *Die Sendung Michaels. Die Offenbarung der eigentlichen Geheimnisse des Menschenwesens [The Mission of the Archangel Michael].* (12 lectures given in Dornach in 1919), GA 194. Rudolf Steiner read the following passage from this letter that Stein wrote to his wife: "Yesterday I was in Reutlingen, where Professor Traub spoke against Steiner. I approached him to discuss this. It was a battle of life and death. I accused Traub of being an ignorant man totally unqualified to talk about the material that he was dealing with. His response came haltingly. He was broken. The town priest spoke up then, and I had backed him so much into a corner through my citation of passages from the Bible that he, regarding the passage in which Christ speaks about reincarnation, said desperately: Christ is *wrong* here—the town priest of Reutlingen said this. I stood up then and cried: Listen! This is what religion has come to—a God who errs!. —The crowd was in an uproar. People tried first to interrupt me, silence me, crying: "Get to the point!" shuffling and stamping their feet. I, however, spoke very calmly, pointed my hand toward Professor Traub and said: This is the authority! I was applauded and was victorious. The man is finished. To this day, I am still half-dead myself." Based on this passage from the letter, the people meant by the "churchman" and his "helper" are Professor Traub (born 1860, Professor of Theology in Tübingen) and the town priest of Reutlingen. See also the lecture given on December 21, 1919, in *Weltsilvester und Neujahrsgedanken [Cosmic New Year]* (5 lectures given in Stuttgart in 1919/20), GA 195.

Page 43, "Dr. Stein"
Walter Johannes Stein (1891-1957), mathematician, author and lecturer, teacher at the Waldorf school in Stuttgart.

Page 43, "the dim light in this hall..."
There was a power outage that day.

Page 43, "this 'unenlightened' publication"
This newspaper article is from the *Breisgauer Zeitung*, 72nd Annual, 1920, No. 4 (January 5th). Rudolf Steiner mentions this article again in Lecture Five of this volume.

Page 44, "the Society for the Threefold Social Order"
The Society for the Threefold Social Order was founded on April 22, 1919, in Stuttgart. Rudolf Steiner had published a pamphlet entitled "A General Call to the German People and to the Cultural World" ("Aufruf an das deutsche Volk und an die Kulturwelt") and also had this article published in the German press (it is reprinted in *Die Kernpunkte der sozialen Frage in den Lebensnotwendigkeiten der Gegenwart und Zukunft* [1919], GA 23, beginning on p. 157). A committee comprised of W. von Blume, E. Molt, and C. Unger, who also co-signed the "General Call" and saw to its distribution, was then expanded into a working group of seven individuals (they were joined by H. Kühn, E. Leinhas, M. Benzinger, and T. Binder). The members of the society became those who were in agreement with the "General Call." See also Hella Wiesberger: "Rudolf Steiners öffentliches Wirken für die Dreigliederung des sozialen Organismus – Die Gründung der Waldorfschule" in *Beiträge zur Rudolf Steiner Gesamtausgabe* (formerly *Nachrichten der Rudolf Steiner-Nachlassverwaltung*), No. 27/28, Michaeli/Weihnachten 1969.

Page 44, "an article I submitted..."
Rudolf Steiner: "Ideenabwege und Publizistenmoral" in *Dreigliederung des Sozialen Organismus*, Stuttgart, 1st Annual, 1919/20, No. 28 (Jan. 1920); can be found in *Aufsätze über die Dreigliederung des sozialen Organismus und zur Zeitlage 1915-1921*, GA 24.

Page 53, "Ottokar Czernin"
(1872-1932), Austro-Hungarian Minister for Foreign Affairs from 1916 to 1918. *Im Weltkriege*, Berlin and Vienna, 1919, p. 38: "The downfall of the monarchy was, [...] altogether unavoidable... Austria-Hungary's final hour had come... The flash of the shot in Sarajevo came to us like a bolt of lightning that illuminates the surrounding area for a split second in the nighttime. It became clear that the bell announcing the downfall of the monarchy had sounded. The bells in Sarajevo, which began to ring half an hour after the murder, were the monarchy's death knell... The form that this downfall would have taken, had the war been somehow avoided, we naturally cannot say. Certainly it would have been less terrible than this war has been. More gradual, most likely, and probably without dragging the rest of the world into hot water with it. We had to die. We could choose the means by which that death would come, and we have chosen the most terrible."

Page 55, "Lloyd George"
David Lloyd George (1863-1945); English statesman; became a liberal [Abgeordneter] in 1890; served as prime minister from 1916-1922; during World War I he was one of the highest ranked advisors in the Entente. When Steiner suggests that we "take a look at his biography," he is referring generally to the course of the man's life.

Page 56, "Clémenceau"
Georges Clémenceau (1841-1929); French statesman; served as prime minister from 1906-1909 and again from 1917-1920, during which time he also served as the defense minister.

Page 58, "in the latest issue of *Dreigliederung*"
See the article written by Friedrich Doldinger entitled "Zur Sprache der *Kernpunkte*" in *Dreigliderung des Sozialen Organismus*, Stuttgart, first Annual 1919/20, No. 27 (January 1920).See also Wilhelm von Heydbrand's article "Über die Gedankenformen in dem Buche Dr. R. Steiners *Die Kernpunkte der sozialen Frage*" ibid., No. 21 (November 1919).

Page 58, "*Kernpunkte der sozialen Frage*"
Kernpunkte der sozialen Frage in den Lebensnotwendigkeiten der Gegenwart und Zukunft (1919), GA 23.

Page 59, "while and "Egyptian darkness"..."
A common expression referring to one of the "plagues of Egypt" spoken of in Exodus 10:21 and the following verses.

Page 59, "Last Sunday... I informed you all"
Steiner is referring to the previous lecture in this volume, given on January 11, 1920.

Page 59, "these kinds of slanderous attacks"
Referring to Prof. Dessoir; Prof. Traub; the "Breisgauer Zeitung" (anonymous); "Stimmen der Zeit" (Otto Zimmermann S. J.); "Suisse-Belique-Outremer" (Dr. Adolphe Ferriére); and others.

Page 60, "I have made this point to you in many different ways."
See the lecture given on January 11, 1920, in this volume. For other examples, see also the lecture given on December 28, 1918, in *Wie kann die Menschheit den Christus wiederfinden? Das dreifache Schattendasein unserer Zeit und das neue Christus-Licht* (8 lectures given in Basel and Dornach 1918/19), GA 187; and the lecture given on October 3, 1919 in *Soziales Verständnis aus geisteswissenschaftlicher Erkenntnis* (15 lectures given in Dornach, 1919), GA 191.

Page 60, "which I have also said often in the past..."
See for example the lecture given on January 11, 1918, in *Mysterienwahrheiten und Weihnachtsimpulse. Alte Mythen und ihre Bedeutung* (16 lectures given in Basel and Dornach 1917/18), GA 180, the lecture given on December 25, 1918, in GA 187 (see full citation above), or the lectures given on May 29 and July 17, 1917, in *Menschliche und menschheitliche Entwicklungswahrheiten, Das Karma des Materialismus* (17 lectures given in Berlin, 1917), GA 176.

Page 63, "in one of my previous lectures I have already mentioned to you"
Steiner is referring to the lecture given on January 9, 1920, also appearing in this volume.

Page 65, "*The Philosophy of Freedom*"
Die Philosophie der Freiheit (1894), GA 4.

Page 65, "an article appeared in *The Athenaeum*"
The Athenaeum: Journal of English and Foreign Literature, Science, the Fine Arts, Music, and the Drama, London. In No. 3480, published on July 7, 1894, on page 17, Robert Zimmerman writes: "...Rudolf Steiner in his book entitled *Philosophie der Freiheit* and Bruno Wille in his *Philosophie der Befreiung* start from Nietzsche's standpoint, but go far beyond him, and end in a theoretical anarchy, which, even in the domain of practice, allows of no moral prescriptions."

Page 65, "A few days ago, I made use of a comparison..."
On January 11th, 1920, Lecture Three in this volume.

Page 70, "If I were to make the same comparison... used often in the past"
See for example the lecture given on March 29, 1919, collected in *Vergangenheits- und Zukunftsimpulse im sozialen Geschehen* (12 lectures given in Dornach, 1919), GA 190. In regard to this matter, also see the statements made about Roman rhetoric in the lecture given on October 13, 1918 in *Die Polarität von Dauer und Entwickleung im Menschenleben. Die kosmische Vorgeschichte der Menschheit* (15 lectures given in Dornach, 1918), GA 184.

Page 72, "Herr Trotsky"
Leo Davidovich Trotsky (born Bronstein) (1879-1940), a close colleague of Lenin, founder of the Red Army.

Page 73, "Hebbel"
Friedrich Hebbel (1813-1863), German poet. *Tagebücher* (Diaries) in *Sämtliche Werke in zehn Teilen* (Collected Works in Ten Volumes), Berlin etc. (o.J.), Volume 9, Neues Tagebuch No. 1336, p. 202: "Nach der Seelenwanderung ist es möglich, dass Plato jetzt wieder auf einer Schulbank Prügel beommt, weil er den Plato

versteht." (After the transmigration of the soul, it is possible that Plato would later be bent over a school bench and chided for not understanding his own texts.)

Page 73, "who was the reincarnated Plato"
(427-347 B.C.), Greek philosopher.

Page 73, "About eight days ago, I told you..."
On January 11, 1920, Lecture Three in this volume.

Page 74, "slanderous article... I have read these to you before."
The sentences appeared in the *Mannheimer General-Anzeiger*, No. 2, Evening edition (January 2, 1920). This is one of the versions of the main article (though with a few alterations), which originated in the office of a Berlin newspaper. Rudolf Steiner had read a slightly different version of this article on January 11; see Lecture Three in this volume.

Page 74, "the most recent issue of *Dreigliederung*"
"Ideenabwege und Publizistenmoral" See note for p. 44. The "sources" (that is to say, the authors of the original article) are not identified any more specifically in that article.

Page 75, "I received the following letter from a friend."
Could not be found or verified.

Page 76, "Herr Grelling"
This is probably the journalist and LL.D. Richard Grelling, the author of "J'accuse! von einem Duetschen," Lausanne, 1915, and not Kurt Grelling, the author of "Anti-J'accuse. Eine deutsche Antwort," Zurich, 1916.

Page 77, "Jesuit journals"
Stimmen aus Maria-Laach, Catholic Papers, Freiburg im Breisgau, the primary Jesuit publication in Germany, founded in 1869. (The Benedictine monastery Maria-Laach was controlled by the Jesuits from 1863-1873.) After 1914, the journal appeared under the name *Stimmen der Zeit.*

Page 77, "the false claims that I have mentioned to you in the past"
Rudolf Steiner spoke in a variety of his lectures about the many various attacks that Otto Zimmermann and others at the journal *Stimmen aus Maria-Laach / Stimmen der Zeit* directed against him, the most extensive examples being in the lecture given in Dornach on December 3, 1919 (not reprinted in any volume). In regard to the specific claim that he is a failed priest (see also the following note), Rudolf Steiner spoke about this many times, for example in the lecture "Geist-Erkenntnis als Tatengrundlage" given on December 30, 1919, collected in *Gedankenfreiheit und soziale Kräfte. Die sozialen Forderungen der Gengenwart*

und ihre praktische Verwirklichung (6 lectures given in 1919), GA 333, or in the lecture given on November 21, 1919 in *Die Sendung Michaels. Die Offenbarung der eigentlichen Geheimnisse des Menschenwesens* (12 lectures given in Dornach, 1919), GA 194.

Page 77, "fairy tale was told that I am a failed priest"
This defamation was first brought to the world by the Theosophist Annie Besant and was then taken up by the Jesuit Giovanni Busnelli. In his work *Manuale di Teosofia* (*Handbook of Theosophy*, 4 volumes, Rome 1911-1915, Volume 3, p. 17), Busnelli describes Rudolf Steiner as a "former Catholic Priest." In his talk, Zimmermann latched onto this lie from Busnelli's work and spoke about "the (from what I hear) fallen Priest" (in: "Stimmen aus Maria-Laach" [see above note], 1912, Volume 83(1), Issue 6). Zimmermann finally took back this claim six years later with this superficial explanation: "Frau Besant had said of Steiner that most terrible of all terrible things — that he was a Jesuit pupil — but this could not be upheld, and the judgment of a foreign writer (Giovanni Busnelli) that he was a failed priest, even less so…" (in *Stimmen der Zeit* [see above note], 48th Annual, July 1918, Volume 95, Issue 10).

Page 77, "Do you believe that it would be right to say to this Jesuit priest"
Otto Zimmermann. See notes for pp. 77 and 78.

Page 77, "Ferriére"
(1879-1960), Swiss sociologist and pedagogue. For more on Ferriére's slander-ous statements see Lecture Fifteen in this volume and notes to p. 229.

Page 78, "the Jesuit literature… July of 1919."
Steiner is referring to the decree given by the Congregation of Holy Officials in Rome on July 18, 1919, which answered the question, "whether the teachings that are referred to nowadays as theosophical, can be appropri-ately blended with the teachings of the Catholic church, and whether it is thereby permissible to be associated with the Theosophical society, to attend their gatherings, to read their books, journals, pamphlets, or letters (libros ephemrides, diaria, scripta)." The answer was: "Negative in omnibus,"— "No to all points" (Acta Apostolica sedis 11, 1919, 317). Otto Zimmermann and other Catholic spiritual leaders expanded the scope of this decision to include anthroposophical texts as well. The "Jesuit literature" refers, among other things, to Zimmermann's article: "Die kirchliche Verurteilung der Theosophie," in "Stimmen der Zeit" (see notes for p. 77), 50th Annual, November 1919, Volume 98, Issue 2.

Page 78, "like the Jesuit Zimmermann"
Otto Zimmermann. See notes for pp. 77 and 78.

Page 78, "university professor Dessoir"
Max Dessoir (1867-1947), psychologists and aesthetician. For more of Steiner's words on Dessoir, see *Von Seelenrätseln* (1917), GA 21.

Page 79, "I described that to you a short time ago."
On December 3, 1919, in a lecture not reprinted in any collected volume.

Page 79, "one of Dessoir's books"
Max Dessoir: *Vom Jenseit der Seele. Die Geheimwissenschaft in kritischer Beleuchtung*, Stuttgart, 1917. 2nd edition printed in Stuttgart in 1918 with a trivial response to Rudolf Steiner's *Von Seelenrätseln* (see note above) in the forward. In this regard, see also (among other things) Rudolf Steiner's lecture "Wissenschaftliche Zeiterscheinungen" given on June 26, 1917, collected in *Menschliche und menschheitliche Entwicklungswahrheiten. Das Karma des Materialismus.* (17 lectures given in Berlin, 1917), GA 176; and Friedrich Rittelmeyer's article "Max Dessoir und Rudolf Steiner" in the *Süddeutschen Monatsheften,* 1917, Annual, Issue 1.

Page 79, "*Brockhaus Conversational Encyclopedia*"
At issue here are several articles for the 15th edition of *Der grosse Brockhaus. Handbuch des Wissens,* Leipzig, 1919, of which only two—on "The Etheric Body" and "Franz Hartmann" (1838-1912), doctor and theosophist—appear to have been submitted by Rudolf Steiner. While the latter article was simply not included at all, the former appeared in a version edited and shortened to one-seventh of its former length by Dessoir. For more on this matter, see the descriptions of it by Walter Johannes Stein and Alfred Meebold in *Die Drei,* a monthly publication, Stuttgart 1922, 2nd Annual, Volume 7 and 8, pages 626 and 627 respectively.

What follows is a reprinting of the original text as written by Rudolf Steiner (1) and then the version as edited by Dessoir (2):

> (1) Ether Bodies – A subtle body underlying the crude (perceptible by the physical senses) human body (and the physical bodies of other organisms). Recent theosophists have described it as a system of forces that take their orderly content from the world's spiritual foundation and find their figuration (objectification) in the organic forms of the physical-sensible bodies. When the ancient vitalists spoke of the speculative-mystical "life force," they were not referring to the ether body. However, the ether body does coincide well with the "schema" referred to as the "inner human being" by the early philosophers, and it also appears in the world pictures offered by Origenes and Augustine. In more recent times, it has found support in philosophers such as Troxler, J. H. Fichte, and others. It can also be found in Kant, though it has there been overturned by skepticism into the dreams of a spiritual seer as the soul's inner being, one that carries all aspects of the physical human's abilities with it into the inner life. For recent theosophy, the ether body is a reality that can become

perceptible when the "inner senses" of the observer are awakened and actualized through a prescribed method of spiritual education from the latent condition in which they find themselves in normal human life. Then the ether body shows itself to be a subtle figuration of a fluid (never taking on a specific form) system of forces that flow through the physical body and in the area in front of the physical body (like a kind of mirror image of the back) transitions into the indefinite (into the forces of the cosmos). It forms a bridge between the physical body and the higher forms of human existence—the soul and the spirit. While a human being sleeps, the ether body remains fully connected to the physical body while the soul and the spirit absent themselves from the regions of the physical sense organs and the central nervous system (though not from the other organs and the auxiliary nervous system). When a human being dreams, the spirit has left the physical sense organs and the central nervous system, but the soul most likely has not. (This departure should not be thought of spatially but rather dynamically). In death, the ether body, soul and spirit (the soul is also known as the astral body, the spirit as the human "I" or ego body) leave the physical-sensible corpse (both spatially and dynamically); these three aspects of the human being remain connected for a brief period of time (several days), then the ether body leaves the soul and the spirit. By natural law, it then crosses over into the realm of general cosmic forces: one part of it into the etheric sphere of the Earth, another part into the ether world that does not belong to the Earth. This dissolution of the ether body is entirely different and specific to each individual, according to the age and the character of that individual's life. An observation of the laws governing this dissolution is among the most difficult problems of spiritual science. This form of dissolution is connected to the character of the physical Earth and forms a portion of the destiny that the soul and spirit encounter after they have crossed over into the spiritual world following their separation from the ether body.

(2) Ether body – According to the teachings of recent theosophy, the ether body is a subtle body underlying the crude (perceptible by the physical senses) body of human beings and other living forms of life. It is said to become perceptible when the "inner senses" of the observer are awakened through a prescribed method of spiritual education and is said then to show itself to be a system of forces that constantly changes and never takes on a definite form.

Page 79, "he had me write this article through a middleman"
This is a reference to Alfred Meebold.

Page 85, "I spoke to you some time ago... wrote down some lines"
Steiner is referring here to the poem *Narkose* by Karl Thylmann (1888-1916). The lines to which he is referring are as follows: "Cotton my flesh, the air granite, / The air delicate star shimmering granite... / Such is death! The air turns to star-granite / The air is celestial shimmering granite..." These lines appear

in: *Karl Thylmann – Briefe*, edited by Joanna Thylmann, o. J., p. 165. – Rudolf Steiner also spoke about these lines and their meaning in the lecture given on November 15, 1919, in Dornach: "Such an impression must be understood... For in the circles that form around the wisdom of the future, precisely this is one of the most common experiences, that the world presses in around a person as though the air suddenly solidified (*translator's note:* in German: *erstarren* – note the "star" here, though the actual German for star is *Stern*) into granite. It is possible to know when these things happen this way. You need only to consider that the ahrimanic forces are striving to make the whole Earth solidify in this way." This lecture appears in: *Soziales Verständnis aus geisteswissenschaftlicher Erkenntnis* (15 lectures given in Dornach, 1919), GA 191.

Page 92, "*Magister artium liberalium*"
At German universities, this is simply a less commonly used version of the title Doctor of Philosophy. In England, it has continued to exist in the title "Master of Arts."

Page 92, "*The Philosophy of Freedom*"
See note for p. 39.

Page 97, "In our last three meetings here..."
Steiner is referring to the three slide lectures given on January 23, 24, and 25, 1920. They appear under the title *Architektur, Plastik und Malerei des Ersten Goetheanum*, (Dornach, 1982).

Page 97, "In one of my last lectures here"
Steiner is referring to the lecture given on January 17, 1920.

Page 97, "and have already spoken"
See especially the lecture given on December 14, 1919, collected in GA 194 (see note for p. 1).

Page 98, "a clear-thinking man living in a German city gave a talk"
This refers to Moriz Carrière. See *Die sittliche Weltordnung*, Leipzig 1877, pp. 1-13. From the opening: "The moral world order (sittliche Weltordnung) is the sign and the task of our time." The talk was given on September 3, 1870, at an assembly in Munich.

(In the first German edition of this book (1966) the speaker was erroneously identified as Johannes Scherr, since Rudolf Steiner speaks of Scherr a short time later in this passage).

Page 98, "this same man wrote an article..."
"Die Idee des Vollkommenen und das Seinsollende" chapter 4 in *Die sittliche Weltordnung* (see above), pp. 149-176.

Page 99, "Johannes Scherr"
Johannes Scherr (1817-1886), author, cultural and literary historian; eventually became a professor at the Polytechnikum in Zurich.

Page 107, "Raphael"
Raphael Sanzio (1483-1520), Italian painter. Along with Michelangelo and Leonardo, one of the most important masters of the Italian Renaissance.

Page 108, "Heaven and Earth will pass away, but my Word shall live forever."
Matthew 24:35; Mark 13:31; Luke 21:33.

Page 111, "You already know... I have spoken of that often"
For more on the relationship between Anthroposophy and the Threefold Social Order see the lecture given on October 3, 1919, collected in *Soziales Verständnis aus geisteswissenschaftlicher Erkenntnis* (15 lectures given in Dornach, 1919), GA 191.

Page 111, "I have also drawn your attention"
Compare with the beginning of this lecture cycle in the lecture given on January 9. For further comparison, see also the lecture cycle *Die soziale Frage als Bewusstseinsfrage* (8 lectures given in Dornach, 1919), GA 189; or the lectures given on December 12, 1919 in *Die Sendung Michaels. Die Offenbarung der eigentlichen Geheimnisse des Menschenwesens* (12 lectures given in Dornach, 1919), GA 194 and on November 30, 1918 in *Die soziale Grundforderung unserer Zeit – In geänderter Zeitlage* (12 lectures given in Dornach and Bern, 1918), GA 186.

Page 117, "something that I have talked about here before"
See the lecture given on October 23, 1919 in *Soziales Verständnis aus geisteswissenschaftlicher Erkenntnis* (15 lectures given in Dornach, 1919) GA 191.

Page 118, "'Prince of this world'"
John 12:31; 14:30; 16:11. This expression was made common by Martin Luther's song "Ein' Feste Burg ist unser Gott" ("A solid castle is our God").

Page 120, "Woodrow Wilson"
(1836-1924), President of the USA from 1912 to 1920. As the head of the Entente in 1918, he announced the "Fourteen Points," for the reformation and reorganization of the world after World War I, founded upon the principle of a people's right to self-determination. Wilson presented the "Fourteen Points" in his speech, "A Program for World Peace: Speeches to the U.S. Congress" on January 8, 1918. See "The Speeches of Woodrow Wilson," printed in Bern in 1919 both in English and in German.

Page 120, "Ludendorff"
Erich Ludendorff (1865-1937), served as Hindenburg's chief of staff.

Page 120, "Clémenceau"
See note for p. 56.

Page 120, "I have often said this before. I have said to you"
See especially the following lectures: October 18 and 19, and November 9, 1919 in GA 191; December 28, 1917 in GA 187.

Page 121, "in my introduction to eurythmy forms, I have often pointed out"
See the introductions to the forms given on January 25 and 31, 1920 (the latter was given immediately prior to this lecture), reprinted in *Eurythmie: Die Offenbarung der sprechenden Seele. Eine Fortbildung der Goetheschen Metamorphosenanschauungim Bereich der menschlichen Bewegung* (speeches from 1918-1924), GA 227. (The introduction from January 31 is reprinted there in an abbreviated form).

Page 123, "*The Riddles of the Human Being*"
Vom Menschenrätsel: Ausgesprochenes und Unausgesprochenes im Denken, Schauen und Sinnen einer Reihe deutscher und österreichischer Persönlichkeiten (1916), GA 20.

Page 127, "I have spoken often"
See for example the lectures from November 28 and 29 as well as December 6, 7, 12 and 13, 1919, all reprinted in *Die Sendung Michaels. Die Offenabrung der eigntlichen Geheimnisse des Menschenwesens* (12 lectures given in Dornach, 1919), GA 194; the lecture from October 18, 1918, reprinted in *Geschichtliche Symptomatologie* (9 lectures given in Dornach in 1918), GA 185; and from November 6, 1919, reprinted in *Die Befreigung des Menschenwesens als Grundlage für eine soziale Neugestaltung. Altes Denken und neues soziales Wollen* (9 lectures given in various locations, 1919), GA 329. See also the cycle of lectures from 1922/23 *Die Entstehungsmoment der Naturwissenschaft in der Weltgeschichte und ihre seitherige Entwickelung* (9 lectures given in Dornach, 1922/23), GA 326.

Page 127, "I have also often indicated..."
See for example the lecture from December 12, 1919.

Page 128, "Francis Bacon von Verulam"
(1561-1679), English statesman, advocate, philosopher, humanist, essayist and doctor. The founder of empiricism. He saw the pursuit of natural scientific research as the sole source of certain knowledge and said that it would bring on an era of complete renewal for both the spiritual and the economic life. His system of thought is expressed characteristically in his utopia *Nova Atlantis* (German edition: *Neu-Atlantis. Eine utopische Erzählung*, Leipzig, Reclam, o. J., 1926).

Page 131, "Thomas Hobbes"
(1588-1679), English philosopher.

Page 131, "from Locke and Hume, to Spencer ..."
John Locke (1632-1704), English philosopher, student of medicine, and theologian. David Hume (1711-1776), English philosopher and historian. Herbert Spencer (1820-1903), English philosopher. Isaac Newton, see note for p. 10. Charles Darwin, see note for p. 6.

Page 133, "Ernst Haeckel"
(1834-1919), zoologist and natural scientist.

Page 134, "You need only read the prose-hymn 'Nature'"
This essay by Goethe was composed in 1780 and appeared in *Tiefurter Journal* No. 32, 1782, under the title "Fragment" and without any indication of the author. Later, it bore the title "Die Natur. Aphoristisch" ("Nature: Aphoristic"). It was then reprinted in the volume *Goethes Naturwissenschaftliche Schriften* (*Goethe's Natural Scientific Writings*), edited and with an introduction and notes by Rudolf Steiner; photomechanical reprint of the first edition in Kürschner's *Deutsche National-Litteratur* (*German National Literature*), Dornach, 5 volumes, GA 1 a-e, Vol. 2, GA 1b, p. 5.

Page 134, "performed here as a eurythmy piece"
Goethe's prose-hymn "Nature" was first performed on January 15, 1919. The eurythmy forms are printed in *Rudolf Steiner – Eurythmieformen*, Volume 3: Eurythmy forms to the poetry of Johann Wolfgang von Goethe, GA K 23, pp. 26-35.

Page 134, "... It has thought, and is thinking still."
Translator's note: (It has thought, and is thinking still. – *gedacht hat sie, und sinnt beständigt.*) The "humor" that Steiner refers to here is a sadly untranslatable pun on the word "sinnt" (to think) and "sind" (to be), which are near homophones in German. Therefore, this line—"It has thought and is thinking still"—might also read (if you hear it as "sind" and not "sinnt"): "It has thought and is existing still." In the context of the whole "Fragment," in which Goethe writes about the tension between the constancy and mutability of Nature's existence, this pun takes on greater meaning, but even in German it is not exactly laugh-out-loud humor. Rather, Steiner sees in this very subtle and meaningful turn of phrase something that he calls "humor," but that modern readers might more readily recognize as "playful intelligence" or "wit." I have preserved Steiner's word choice here, aware of the possible risk that this might make it seem as though he has no sense of humor whatsoever, because Steiner's point is that this pun proves that Goethe saw Nature as "ensouled," and words such as "intelligence" or "wit" are sometimes understood as lacking that crucial soul element.

Page 134, "an article appeared… in this Sunday's paper"
Rudolf Steiner's essay "On the 'Fragment' on Nature" appeared in volume 7 of the *Schriften der Goethe-Gesellschaft* (*Writings of the Goethe Society*), 1892 and is reprinted in *Methodische Grundlagen der Anthroposophie 1884-1901. Gesammelte Aufsätze zur Philosophie, Naturwissenschaft, Äesthetik und Seelenkunde*, GA 30. In this piece of writing, Rudolf Steiner deals, among other things, with the question of whether the "Fragment" can best be attributed to Goethe or to his friend Georg Christoph Tobler. On this topic, see also the comments that Rudolf Steiner made at a eurythmy performance of April 17, 1920. In *Eurythmie. Die Offenbarung der sprechenden Seele* (speeches from 1918-1924), GA 227 and in the third volume of the *Eurythmieformen* (see above), p. XIX. In both volumes, the comments are given in an abbreviated form.

Page 134, "when I published the "Fragment" on nature… back in the '90s"
One article appeared in the Sunday edition of the "Basler Nachrichten" No. 2 on January 11, 1920 by Paul Wernle: "Der Verfasser des Fragments 'Natur' im Journal von Tiefurt" ("The Author of the Fragment 'Nature' in the Journal from Tiefurt"). A further elaboration appeared in No. 5 (February 1, 1920) by H. Trog: "Zur Verfasserschaft des Fragments über die 'Natur'" ("On The Identity of the Author of the Fragment on 'Nature'"). Quoting Wernle: "… From the explanations that Rudolf Steiner, one among those working at the Goethe Archive, offers on the Fragment 'Nature' at the end of the new edition of the Journal from Tiefurt, one can see that none other than Goethe himself turned the attention of his closest circle of friends onto Tobler as the author… But among those who research Goethe there are some brilliant minds who know this better than Goethe himself… for when Rudolf Steiner wrote his comments he was in possession of all of the necessary materials that point to Tobler and away from Goethe as regards the question of authorship. Nevertheless, he clung tight to Goethe's spiritual authorship, allowing Tobler to play the roll only of a reporter, copying down the words he hears as exactly as possible; he describes what Tobler wrote or did as a "more or less word-for-word report from memory." The reasons that Steiner offers as justification lie in the inner connection between the Goethe's later natural scientific ideas and the stated life program that appears in this fragment and that underlies all of Goethe's thought on nature… It seems to me that Rudolf Steiner has interpreted this fragment incorrectly, if he claims to find the seeds of all of Goethe's later natural philosophical ideas within it. To me, it seems that this fragment has no relationship to ensuing later natural research, no matter how much a natural researcher might try to wring from it a series of subsequent ideas. It would be more accurate for us to call it a system of beliefs; religion is present there, though the opposite of what is meant by 'religion' within the fragment…"

Page 135, "Wycliffe"
John Wycliffe—roughly 1325-1384, English Reformer (Doctor evangelicus). He viciously attacked the whole system of the medieval church and translated

the Bible into English. In 1415, he was declared a heretic at the Council of Constance.

Page 136, "Shakespeare"
William Shakespeare (1564-1616).

Page 137, "Boehme"
Jacob Boehme (1575-1624), German mystic and philosopher. See also the lecture on Jacob Boehme given on May 3, 1906 in *Die Welträtsel und die Anthroposophie* (22 lectures given in Berlin, 1905/06), GA 54.

Page 137, "Jacobus Baldus"
(1604-1668), Jesuit poet.

Page 140, "We have seen…"
Steiner has described the events that started in the last third of the nineteenth century and led to the first World War as ones that occurred on a wide variety of levels:

> In 1879, after a battle in Heaven, the spirits of darkness were cast down to Earth by Michael and continued to affect and act upon the world afterward. See, for example, the lectures from October 26, 1917, in *Die spirituellen Hintergründe der äussern Welt. Der Struz der Geister der Finsternis* (14 lectures given in Dornach, 1917), GA 177; and from November 6, 11, and 13, 1917, in *Individuelle Geistwesen und ihr Wirken in der Seele des Menschen* (9 lectures given in various locations, 1918), GA 178.

> Certain initiates who spoke of the necessity of a world war that would change the face of southern and eastern Europe also had an effect upon the world. See, among others, the lecture given of January 9, 1920, also collected in this volume.

> The fact that a spiritual world was not allowed to enter into human life was a cause of the war. See, for example, the lectures from January 1, 1919, in *Wie kann die Menschheit den Christus wiederfinden? Das dreifache Schattendasein unserer Zeit und das neue Christus-Licht* (8 lectures given in Basel and Dornach, 1918/19); and from December 20, 1918, in *Die soziale Grundforderung unserer Zeit – In geänderter Zeitlage* (12 lectures given in Dornach and Bern, 1918), GA 186. See also the lecture from January 30, 1920, also collected in this volume.

> A further cause of the war was the fact that materialistic individuals died in the last decade of the nineteenth century without being able to take spiritual concepts along with them. This is described in the lecture from September 29, 1917, in *Die spirituellen Hintergründe…* (see above for full citation).

The political circumstances are described at length in the lecture from November 9, 1918, in *Entwichlungsgeschichtliche Unterlagen zur Bildung eines sozialen Urteils* (8 lectures given in Dornach, 1918), GA 185a.

For further information on similar topics, see also the lecture cycle *Zeitgeschichtliche Betrachtungen. Das Karma der Unwahrhaftigkeit. Erster Teil* (13 lectures given in Dornach and Basel, 1916), GA 173.

Page 140, "I have told you before about the fact"
In the lectures from January 30 and 31, 1920, also collected in this volume.

Page 144, "Wotan (or Woden, or Odin)"
In German mythology, Wotan is the ruler of the Norse gods.

Page 144, "Saxnot (or Saxneat)"
The old Saxon name of a god who was also known as Ziu or Tyr. For more on Saxnot/Saxneat, see Ludwig Laistner in *Württembergische Vierteljahresheft für Landesgeschichte* (*Württemberg Quarterly of Regional History*), Stuttgart, 1892.

Page 144, "I described to you in the lecture last Sunday"
Referring to the lecture given on February 1, 1920, also collected in this volume.

Page 146, "Meister Eckhart"
Around 1260-1327, German mystic, Dominican, and master of theology. He taught in Paris, Strassbourg, and Cologne and served in leading posts both in the Dominican Order and the Church. His major work was based in scholasticism and the writings of Dionysius the Areopagite. Copies of his sermons, lectures and treatises, written in a creative and formative Middle High German, circulated at least in part without any oversight by Meister Eckhart himself. After being decried as a heretic, Meister Eckhart died in the course of the trial.

Page 146, "Johannes Tauler"
Around 1300-1361, German mystic, Dominican and preacher. He was a student of Meister Eckhart. He worked as a confessor and preached primarily in his hometown of Strassbourg, though sometimes also in Basel.

Page 146, "When two or three people are united in my name, then I stand among them."
Matthew 18:20.

Page 150, "In previous lectures, I have spoken"
See, for example, the lecture from October 26, 1917, in *Die spirituellen Hintergründe der äussern Welt. Der Sturz der Geister der Finsternis* (14 lectures given in Dornach, 1917), GA 177. See also the lecture from March 30, April

4, and April 29, 1906, in *Das christliche Mysterium* (31 lectures given in various locations, 1906/07), GA 97.

Page 150, "Fourteen points"
See note for p. 120.

Page 152, "Herman Grimm"
(1828-1901), art and literature historian. (*Translator's note:* English readers who are most familiar with "The Brothers Grimm" should take note that Herman Grimm is *not* one of those two, far more famous Grimm's, who were named Jakob and Wilhelm).

Page 152, "about which Herman Grimm rightly said"
The Life and Times of Goethe (German title: *Goethe: Vorlesungen gehalten an der Kgl. Universität zu Berlin*), English translation by Sarah Holland Adams, 1893, published by Little, Brown and Company in Boston (4th edition). The passage to which Steiner is referring reads literally (in Holland's translation):

> "Long since... the Laplace-Kantian hypothesis of the origin and the future destruction of this earth had gained ground. Out of the rotating nebulae (children learn this in school nowadays) is formed the central gas drop, which afterward becomes the Earth, and which as a congealing ball passes through all its phases, including the episode of its tenantry by the human race, until finally, as a burned-out slag, it falls back into the Sun—a long, but to most people perfectly conceivable, process, for whose accomplishment no other agency is needed than some outside power to sustain an equal degree of heat in the Sun.
>
> No more hopeless perspective for the future can be thought of than this which is forced upon us today as a scientific necessity. A carcass which even a hungry dog would hesitate to approach is a refreshingly appetizing morsel compare with this last excrement of creation as which our earth is to be restored to the Sun; and the scientific eagerness with which this generation accepts and believes such views is the sign of a morbid imagination, which learned men of the future will exert much ingenuity in explaining as a historical phenomenon."

Page 152, "Kantian"
Immanuel Kant (1724-1804), philosopher, mathematician, natural scientist. For more on the Kant-Laplace Theory see Kant's *Allegemeine Naturgeshichte und Theorie des Himmels oder Versuch von der Verfassung und dem mechanischen Ursprunge des ganzen Weltgebäudes nach Newtonschen Grundsatzen abgehandelt* (originally published 1755, English title: *Universal Natural History and the Theory of the Heavens*).

Page 152, "Laplace"
Pierre Simon Laplace (1749-1827), French mathematician and astronomer.

Traité de Mécanique céleste (5 volumes, originally published in 1799. English title: *Celestial Mechanics*).

Page 153, "in the most recent issue of our journal..."
Steiner is referring to the weekly journal *Dreigliederung des sozialen Organismus* (*Threefolding the Social Organism*), published by the Society for the Threefold Social Order (see note 54). The chief editor was Ernst Uehli. It was published from July 1919 to June 1922 before it was renamed *Anthroposophie. Wochenschift für freies Geistesleben* (*Anthroposophy: A Weekly Journal for Free Spiritual Life*). In 1931, this journal was united with *Die Drei* and published as a monthly journal. (Source: Hans Erhard Lauer: *Deutschlands Wiedergeburt aus dem Geiste Goethes*, 1st annual, 1919/20, No. 30, Jan. 1920).

Page 153, "*sacro egoismus*"
"Sacro egoismo per l'Italia": Words of the Italian Prime Minister Antonio Salandra, spoken on October 18, 1914 to his ministers and sometimes translated into English as "egocentric nationalism."

Page 156, "I addressed at a public lecture"
Given in Basel on October 20, 1919: "Geisteswissenschaft (Anthroposophie) und die Bedingungen der Kultur in Gegenwart und Zukunft" ("Spiritual Science [Anthroposophy] and the Cultural Needs of the Present and Future"):

> ... Spiritual life has gradually taken on an altogether abstract character. Think for a moment about form that the religious, the aesthetic, the artistic worldview-convictions of a (shall we say) merchant or a manufacturer or a clerk have taken. These convictions are things that he experiences in his soul; they do not extend into the bank-book or the things that he does in his office. The result is that the place where these convictions originate is not the same place that the ideas and impulses expressed in his bank-book come from. The highest place of origin is, "With God!" but this is also everything whereby the actions that are brought to expression are connected with that which he carries through the world as an abstract spiritual life and soul life...

In *Die Befreiung des Menschenwesen als Grundlage für eine soziale Neugestaltung. Altes Denken und neues soziales Wollen* (9 lectures given in various locations, 1919), GA 329.

Page 157, "In the past I have often and strongly pointed this out"
See for example the lecture from November 12, 1916 in *Das Karma des Berufes des Menschen in Anknüpfung an Goethes Leben* (10 lectures given in Dornach, 1916), GA 172.

Page 158, "described to you yesterday."
In the lecture from February 6, 1920, in this volume.

Page 159, "Treaty of Versailles"
The peace treaty between Germany and 26 enemy powers at the end of World War One; signed on June 28, 1919, and ratified on January 10, 1920. The United States did not ratify the Treaty of Versailles.

Page 160, "Rabindranath Tagore"
See note for p. 4. *Nationalism*, translated into German by H. Meyer. Franck, Leipzig, 1918.

Page 160, "something that I have said to you before."
See the lectures from August 19, 1918 in *Die Wissenschaft vom Werden des Menschen* (9 lectures given in Dornach, 1918), GA 183; and from December 1 and 20, 1918, in *Die soziale Grundforderung unserer Zeit – In geänderter Zeitlage* (12 lectures given in Dornach and Berne, 1918), GA 186.

Page 161, "Leibniz"
Gottfried Wilhelm Freiherr von Leibniz (1646-171), German philosopher, teacher and statesman, jurist, physicist, mathematician, doctor, theologist and philologist. Differential calculus made possible calculations with differentials (that is to calculations with infinite minor differentiations) and, together with integral calculus, was very significant for a wide variety of natural scientific and mechanical problems. Differential and integral calculus (together called infinitesimal calculus) was discovered toward the end of the 1700s by Newton and Leibniz, independent of one another.

Page 161, "Copernicus"
See note for p. 20.

Page 161, "Galileo"
See note for p. 20.

Page 161, "Now read some of Rabindranath Tagore..."
In the collection of lectures, *Nationalism*, mentioned above.

Page 164, "I have often offered analyses of psychoanalysis here..."
See for example the lecture from September 13-16, 1915, in *Probleme des Zusammenlebens in der Anthroposophischen Gesellschaft. Zur Dornacher Krise vom Jahre 1915.* (7 lectures given in Dornach, 1915), GA 253; from November 13, 1916, in *Das Karma des Berufes*; and from November 10 and 11, 1917, in *Individuelle Geistwesen und ihr Wirken in der Seele des Menschen* (9 lectures given in various locations, 1917), GA 178.

Page 165, "I have drawn your attention in the past to a case study..."
This case study from psychoanalysis was described by Rudolf Steiner in the

lectures from November 10 and 11, 1917 (see above). See also the lectures given in Berlin from January 22 and March 12, 1918, in *Erdensterben und Weltenleben. Anthroposophische Lebensgaben. Bewusstseinsnotwendigkeiten fur Gegenwart und Zukunft* (21 lectures given in Berlin, 1918), GA 181.

Page 167, "William James"
(1842-1910), the most significant American practitioner of introspective psychology and also of the philosophical school of pragmatism. Professor of Philosophy at Harvard University. Author of countless philosophical and psychological works.

Page 169, "I have, for example, pointed out..."
See, for example, the lecture from December 6, 1919 in *Die Sendung Michaels. Die Offenbarung der eigentlichen Geheimnisse des Menschenwesens* (12 lectures given in Dornach, 1919), GA 194.

Page 169, "Twelve Tables of Law"
(Latin: *Lex duodecim tabularum*). The Roman law was set down on 12 iron tablets in the year 450 B.C.E. and held to be the source of all further Roman law. Only fragments of these tablets remain.

Page 169, "We have also spoken often in the past..."
The migrations out of the sinking continent of Atlantis were often mentioned and described by Rudolf Steiner in his lectures. See also the chapter on "World Evolution and the Human Being" in *An Outline of Esoteric Science* (1910), CW 13.

Page 172, "in my book *Christianity as Mystical Fact*"
Das Christentum als mystische Tatsache und die Mysterien des Altertums (1902), CW 8.

Page 177, "I have described as a representative individual of the modern age"
I have described as a representative individual of the modern age. In the lecture from September 30, 1917, in *Die spirituellen Hintergründe...*, GA 177.

Page 177, "Lloyd George"
David Lloyd George (1863-1945), English prime minister from 1916-1922. From more on his achievements in Parliament, see the "Basler Nachrichten," 76th Annual, 1920 (February, 8), daily edition (February 7). The Swiss press-telegraph had, just a few days before this lecture, received a special report from London that defined Lloyd George's stance on the Russian question as follows: "It is a definite fact that the anti-Bolshevist movement in the Russian civil war collapsed. For as long as the anti-Bolshevist were able to fight, England was compelled to support them, just as the Russian had in their time aided

England in its fight against Germany while the Bolshevists had supported Germany... The collapse of the anti-Bolshevist movement cannot be attributed to a breakdown in England's support of it... The best thing that can now be done— should it even be the case that it can be done—*is to secure an amenable peace agreement with the Bolshevists.*" Also see note for p. 55.

Page 177, "I have always said the same thing here in Switzerland about him"
See, for example, the lecture from October 1, 1917 in *Die spirituellen Hinergründe*; or the lecture given in Basel from October 20, 1919 in *Die Befreiung des Menschenwesens*, GA 329.

Page 181, "Heraclitus and Socrates and Plato"
Heraclitus (540-480 B.C.E.), Socrates (469-399 B.C.E.), Plato (427-347 B.C.E.).

Page 183, "attacks that come in from every side from time to time"
For example in the lecture of August 19, 1918, in *Die Wissenschaft vom Werden des Menschen* (9 lectures, Dornach, 1918), GA 183; and in the lecture of December 6, 1919 (see also November 30) in *Die Sendung Michaels. Die Offenbarung der eigentlichen Geheimnisse des Menschenwesens* (12 lectures, Dornach, 1919), GA 194.

Page 183, "*Encephalitis lethargica*"
At the time, this was an epidemic strain of encephalitis that caused sluggishness and partial palsy or paralysis.

Page 185, "I have often drawn your attention in the past"
See the lecture from January 11, 1920, in this volume and also the lectures from October 10 and 17, 1919, in *Soziales Verständnis aus geisteswissenschaftlicher Erkenntnis* (15 lectures, Dornach, 1919), GA 191.

Page 187, "I have spoken about this often in the past."
See, for example, the lecture from July 17, 1915 in *Kunst- und Lebensfragen im Lichte der Geisteswissenschaft* (13 lectures, Dornach, 1915), GA 162; from December 7, 1919, in *Die Sendung Michaels. Die Offenbarung der eigentlichen Geheimnisse des Menschenwesens* (12 lectures, Dornach, 1919), GA 194; or the lecture given in Vienna from April 6, 1914, in *Inneres Wesen des Menschen und Leben zeischen Tod und neuer Geburt* (8 lectures, Vienna, 1914), GA 153.

Page 187, "a fact that I have often hinted at..."
See the lectures from August 28 and 29, 1919, in *Allgemeine Menschenkunde als Grundlage der Pädagogik (I)* (14 lectures, Stuttgart, 1919), GA 293.

Page 188, "Fräulein Scholl, Fräulein Laval, Herrn Dr. Grosheintz"
Rudolf Steiner is naming three members of the audience here.

Page 191, "the higher senses and the sense of touch"
See *Theosophy* (1904), CW 9, in the first section ("The Soul World") of the chapter entitled "The Three Worlds."

Page 191, "something that Goethe had already noted as well"
This refers to the passage: "Der Chirurg muss mit Geistesaugen, oft nicht einmal vom Tastsinn unterstützt, die innere verletzte Stelle zu finden wissen…" ("The surgeon must know to use his spiritual eyes, supported often by his sense of touch, in order to find the damaged place within…") (Sophien-Ausgabe, II. Abt., Volume 8: *Zur Morphologie*, Part III, "Versuch einer allgemeinen Knochenlehre. Tibia und Fibula," p. 218.

Page 192, "doctrine based in the so-called specific sense energies"
Founded by the physiologist Johannes Müller (1801-1858).

Page 195, "869 C.E. at the Eighth Ecumenical Council"
See note for p. 9.

Page 198, "yesterday in St. Gallen"
This refers to the as-yet-unpublished lecture given to the members of the society, "Die erzieherischen Kräfte in der Volksgemeinschaft" ("The educative forces in the society of a people [Volk]"), from February 12, 1920.

Page 200, "often described in the past in connection with other things"
The dreamlike Imagination of the ancient Moon evolution was often described by Rudolf Steiner. A lengthy description can be found, for example, in his books *Aus der Akasha-Chronik* [English edition is *Cosmic Memory*] (1904-1908), GA 11, and *An Outline of Esoteric Science* (1910), CW 13 (Chapter: "World Evolution and the Human Being"). For more on the connection between present-day memory and this old form of consciousness, see also the lectures from August 26 and 27, 1916, in *Das Rätsel des Menschen. Die geistigen Hintergründe der menschlichen Geschichte* (15 lectures, Dornach, 1916), GA 170.

Page 201, "as I have told you"
In the lecture from February 13, 1920, also in this volume.

Page 209, "as I described in an earlier lecture"
See, for example, the lecture from February 8, 1920, also in this volume.

Page 212, "The actions taken at Versailles"
See note for p. 159.

Page 213, "I have spoken of this here in connection with other things"
See the lecture from February 16, 1919, in *Die soziale Frage als Bewusstseinsfrage*

(8 lectures, Dornach, 1919), GA 189 (on spiritual life, political life, and economic life and their relationship to pre-birth, earthly, and post-death life).

Page 213, "Grigori Yefimovich Rasputin"
(1871-1916), Russian monk and alleged performer of miracles. Influential advisor to Czar Nicolas II and particularly the Czarina. Murdered in 1916 by a group of higher-up Russian individuals.

Page 216, "William James"
See note for p. 167.

Page 216, "Spencer"
See note for p. 6.

Page 216, "Henri Bergson"
(1859-1941), French philosopher.

Page 216, "Kant"
See note for p. 152. (Kant was born, lived and died in Königsberg).

Page 218, "I have already drawn your attention in the past..."
Rudolf Steiner has often described this process of metamorphosis. See, for example, the cycle *Das Rätsel des Menschen. Die geistigen Hintergründe der menschlichen Geschichte* (15 lectures, Dornach, 1916), GA 170, and also the lectures from August 18, 25, and 26, and from September 2, 1918, in *Die Wissenschaft vom Werden des Menschen* (9 lectures, Dornach, 1918), GA 183, and from December 27 and 29, 1918, in *Wie kann die Menschheit den Christus wiederfinden? Das dreifache Schattendasein unserer Zeit und das neue Christus-Licht* (8 lectures, Basel and Dornach 1918/19), GA 187.

Page 222, "Ernst Renan"
(1823-1892), French scholar and philosopher. Professor of Hebrew, Chaldean, and Syrian languages at the Collège de France. He was first a clergyman. The article to which Steiner is referring is "La guerre entre la France et l'Allemagne" appearing in *Revue des deux Mondes*, 40th Annual, Volume 89, Paris, 1870 (September 15): "La grandeur intellectuelle et morale de l'Europe repose sur une triple alliance, don't la rupture est un deuil pour le progès, l'alliance entre la France, l'Allemagne, et l'Angelterre. Unies, ces trios grandes forces conduiraient le monde et le conduiraient bien, entraînant nécessairement après ells les autres elements, considérables encore, don't se compose le réseau enropéen."

Page 224, "Herman Grimm"
Fragments, Volume 1, Berlin and Stuttgart, 1900, p. 212: (translated here from

the German) "For those of us today (1891), the War of Independence against Napoleon is no longer the most significant event of recent memory, as it was when I was a child (born 1828); instead we look back on the more recent Wars of Independence against Austria and France. We were, at one time, a people in whose laps our children learned that they were never willingly to take part in anything that would benefit the fate of our country. Now, the German people are ordered to do just that. Fifty years ago, it would have been an unheard of beginning to make it clear to children in their education that one day they would all be citizens of a great German Empire, and that among each child's obligations to God, the Emperor, and the Country, he would also have the responsibility of electing, on the basis of his own assessments of the country's needs, an individual to represent his opinions in the German Parliament. Even suggesting such a thing would have sounded like high treason, and would perhaps have ruined the life of the man who suggested it."

Page 225, "a Being that I have described to you here for weeks"
Probably refers to the lecture from December 15, 1919, in *Die Sendung Michaels. Die Offenbarung der eigentlichen Geheimnisse des Menschenwesens* (12 lectures, Dornach, 1919), GA 194.

Page 225, "Troxler"
Ignaz Paul Vital Troxler (1780-1866), doctor, philosopher and pedagogue. Professor in Basel and Bern.

Page 225, "Schubert"
Gotthilf Heinrich von Schubert (1780-1860), doctor and natural philosopher.

Page 226, "Leibniz"
See note for p. 161.

Page 226, "Cicero"
Marcus Tullius Cicero (106-43 B.C.E.), Roman statesman, speaker and author.

Page 226, "place under the Sun"
The words of the Imperial Chancellor, Bernhard Fürst von Bülow, in the Reichtags session on December 6, 1897, referring to the capture of Kiao-Chau. The phrase probably can be traced back to the famous conversation that supposedly took place between Alexander the Great and Diogenes of Sinope.

Page 227, "Marx"
Karl Marx (1818-1883), founder of economic socialism and historical materialism. He spent the second half of his life in England.

Page 227, "Engels"
Friedrich Engels (1820-1895), Marxist sociologist, founder of Communist

theory. Friend of Karl Marx. Early on, he took over a branch of his father's textile company in Manchester and, from the impressions of his time in England, wrote the book *Die Lage der arbeitenden Klassen in England* (English title: *The Conditions of the Working Class in England in 1844*) (Leipzig, 1845).

Page 228, "Monsieur Ferriére"
Adolphe Ferriére (1879-1960), Swiss sociologist and pedagogue.

Page 229, "Rasputin"
See lecture 14 and note for p. 213.

Page 229, "German Emperor"
Wilhelm II (French: Guillaume II), 1859-1941, Emperor from 1888-1918.

Page 229, "... and so on"
In the newspaper "Suisse-Belgique-Outremer" (1st annual, No. 3-4, July/ August, 1919, p. 19), Ferrière published an article entitled "La loi du progrès économique et la justice sociale. II. L'organisme social," and made the following claim: "Quel abîme, si nous passons d'un Emile Waxweiler à un Rudolf Steiner! L'un est, au premier abord, obscure dans sa terminologie, mais sa pensée est d'une claret aiguë. L'autre développe ses pensées en une langue que ses intimes pourront trouver Claire; mais sa pensée nous paraît éminemment obscure! L'écrivian allemande est théosophe. On affirme qu'il fut le conseiller intime, le confident et l'inspirateur de Guillaume II; par déférence nous ne répéterons point l'expression de 'Rapoutine' de Guillaume II, par laquelle nous l'avons entendu designer." Rudolf Steiner offered a translation of this text in his lecture from December 21, 1919: "What a path it is from the clear thoughts of Waxweiler to the obscure thoughts of Rudolf Steiner! But this man has also become the confidante of Wilhelm II, and it has been said that in recent years he has given important pieces of advice to Wilhelm II, so that have called this man the "Rasputin" of Wilhelm II. We do not want to make ourselves the perpetuators of such a rumor..." This lecture appears in *Weltsilvester und Neujahrsgedanken* (5 lectures given in Stuttgart, 1919/20), GA 195. Rudolf Steiner also spoke at length about this slander and the perspectives connected with it in his lecture from December 7, 1919, in *Die Sendung Michaels. Die Offenbarung der eigentlichen Geheimnisse des Menschenwesens* (12 lectures, Dornach, 1919), GA 194, appendix.

Page 229, "Dr. Boos"
Roman Boos (1889-1952), anthroposophical speaker and social scientific author, pioneer of the movement for the Threefold Social Order.

Page 229, "in an 'open letter'"
Dr. Boos' answer to Dr. Ferrière appeared in the newspaper "Suisse-Belgique Outremer," 1920, No. 5, p. 15 ff. The "postscript" that Rudolf Steiner refers to comes from a letter that he wrote to Boos on December 16, 1919, which Boos

then included in his "open letter." This letter from Dr. Steiner was not kept in its original form, and in the aforementioned newspaper it appeared in a French translation; therefore, the original words of Dr. Steiner are not known. What follows is a translation from the French version of that letter:

"Dear Dr. Boos,

In regard to your letter responding to the attack by Dr. Ferrière, my answer is as follows: I have never, in all my life, had the slightest opportunity to exchange even one word with Wilhelm II. I belong to that group of people who have seldom seen the Emperor, and then only from a *great distance*. The first time was in Weimar at the funeral of the Grand Duchess Sophie as he stepped away from the casket. The second time was in the theater in Berlin, where he was sitting in the Emperor's box. And the third time was on the Friedrichsstrasse in Berlin—he passed by on his way back from a military exercise, surrounded by his generals. If it seems that I have a particularly clear memory of these times, it is because they are the only times I have ever seen him. In addition, I have never exerted any effort either to come into direct contact with this person or to reach him indirectly.

Dr. Ferrière is therefore spreading a very bold piece of slander, which he is embellishing with rhetoric whose grotesque logic would be humorous, were it not also so morally objectionable.

Until now, I had heard nothing of this attack. But I must decline to enter into any sort of substantive discussion about an article by an author who, from the very first line, has Dr. Ferrière's attitude toward what is true—an author who stomps on the most elementary rules of morality in such a way.

With best wishes, Dr. Rudolf Steiner

Page 229, "The man had to admit that he had lied"
The editors of the paper printed Dr. Ferrière's answer to the "open letter" from Dr. Boos in the same issue: "Nous avons communiqué la letter ouvert de m. Roman Boos à notre correspondant, qui nous répond ce qui suit: 'Le document cridessus est typique, pour le psychologue. Voilà ci que deviant l'ironie latine sous des yeux germaniques. Vraiment, ces gens-la prennent tout au sérieux. Mais mes lecterus, eux, ne s'y étaint pas trompé. Mon article contenait de la plaisanterie, mais aucune méchanceté. Et si j'ai été mal renseigné, j'en fais mon mea culpa avec la conviction que mon interlocuteur ne m'en voudra pas. Par interlocuteur, j'entends le sociologue auquel l'ai parlé en sociologue et non signataire de la letter ci-dessus don't je n'ai pas fait mention dans mon article. Au fait, que vient-il faire en cetter affaire?'"

Page 230, "I will take careful note of this."
The rest of the letter in French, which Steiner does not read during his lecture, is as follows: A l'époque où j'ai écrit mon article, je ne connaissais Mr. Rudolf Steiner que par ses imprimés. Depuis lors, j'ai appris à le connaître par des personnes qui le connaissent de près. Mon opinion s'est transformée du tout

au tout et j'avais préparé un article où je marquais mon respect pour la portée morale de son oeuvre personelle. J'aoue que la letter de M. R. Boos refroidit quelque peu mon ardeur." From Ferrière: "Je pourrais répondre une foule de choses à cette letter. A quoi bon? Une des qualities latines est d'être bref. J'ai eu tort, je le reconnais, de quitter le terrain des faits contrôlables. Je retire mes affirmations erronées et j'en conclus qe les bruits qui courent, meme s'ils eminent de plusiers milieux différents et de gens qu'on a leiu de croire bien informé, peuvent être faux. Dont acte."

Page 233, "I consistently spoke out against him"
In the public lecture "Anthroposophie und Sozialwissenschaft. Geisteswissenschaftliche Ergebnisse über Recht, Moral, und soziale Lebensformen," from November 14, 1917 in Zurich, collected in *Die Ergänzung heutiger Wissenschaften durch Anthroposophie* (8 lectures given in Zurich, 1917/18), GA 73, Rudolf Steiner speaks out against Wilson, who was attempting to understand social structures using natural-scientific imaginations. The final result of the difficulties that Wilson encountered upon returning to America, which Steiner alludes to here, was that the United States refused to ratify the Treaty of Versailles, which Wilson had worked on so fiercely in cooperation with the other Allies. In the fall of 1920, Wilson lost the presidency in a decisive vote to the Republican Harding.

Page 233, "The 'Imperial Federation League'"
Founded in England in 1884. The power of this imperialism of "greater Britain" was visible around the turn of the century in the activities of Joseph Chamberlain (1836-1906).

Page 237, "Dionysius the Areopagite"
A member of the Areopagus court in Athens, and was converted to Christianity by Paul (see Acts 17:34). His writings were first mentioned in the sixth century. The works that have been ascribed to him include the essays *Divine Names, Mystical Theology, Celestial Hierarchy and Ecclesiastical Hierarchy*.

Page 238, "Charlemagne"
(742-814), from 768 on the King of the Franks, from 800 on the Roman Emperor. Was crowned the first German Emperor in Rome by Pope Leo III.

Page 238, "Otto I"
"The Great," (912-973), son of Heinrich II, Emperor from 936-973.

Page 238, "Istwan I'"
Istwan (Stephan) "the Holy" (969-1038). From 1000 until his death, Istwan with the King of Hungary. After coming to terms with a reactionary pagan insurgency, Istwan continued the Christianization of Hungary (which had

recently been beaten back to its own territory after a defeat on the battlefield in 955) that had been started by his father, despite the continued resistance of the pagan tribes In the process, he consolidated state and church and was canonized in 1087.

Page 239, "the formulation of imperialism"

This "formulation" appears in *De Monarchia*, Book 1, Chapter VIII. An English translation can be found online at "The Online Library of Liberty" (oll.liberty-fund.org) from which is taken the following selection: "The human race, there-fore, is ordered well, nay, is ordered for the best, when according to the utmost of its power it becomes like unto God. But the human race is most like unto God when it is most one, for the principle of unity dwells in Him alone… But the human race is most one when all are united together, a state which is mani-festly impossible unless humanity as a whole becomes subject to one Prince…"

Page 240, "an archbishop published a pastoral letter"

This refers to the archbishop of Salzburg, Johannes Baptist Katschthaler, 1832-1914. His pastoral letter from February 2, 1905, "The honor befitting a Catholic priest," is published in Carl Mirbt's *Sources of Papal and Roman Catholic History* (4th edition, Tübingen, 1924), Chapter 645, pp. 497-499. What follows is the passage relating the consecration powers of a priest: "Honor the priests, for they have the power to consecrate. Powers of sanctification belong to the priest—to him alone, and not to the Protestant pastors, is given this wondrous power. The power to consecrate, to make the body of the Lord and his precious blood, with all of his humanity and all of his divinity, present in the form of the bread and the wine; to transform bread and wine into the genuine body and precious blood of our Lord—what a lofty, august, and wondrous power! Where in heaven is such a power to be found, as that which is possessed by the Catholic priest? The angels? The Holy Mother? Mary bore Christ, the son of God, in her womb and birthed Him in a stall in Bethlehem. Yes. But consider what occurs at a holy Mass! Does not the same thing occur beneath the sanctified hands of the priest during that moment of holy transformation? In the bread and the wine, Christ is made real, is made really and truly present, and is thus reborn. There in Bethlehem, Mary bore her holy child and wrapped it in swaddling clothes, and the priest performs the same deed and lays the Host upon the cloth. *Mary brought the Holy Child to Earth once.* And see—*the priest performs this deed not once, but hundreds and thousands of times, every time he performs a Mass.*

There in the stall was the Holy Child that was brought into the world through Mary, *small, fragile, and mortal.* Here upon the alter, *under the hands of the priest, Christ exists in his full glory, strong and immortal,* as he is when he sits in Heaven at the right hand of God, gloriously triumphant, complete in every way. Do they only bring forth the body, the blood of the Lord? No. Rather they *sacrifice*—they make a sacrifice to the Holy Father. It is the same thing that Christ did, both violently at Calvary and peacefully at the Last Supper. There, the everlasting High Priest Jesus Christ sacrificed his flesh, blood and life to the heavenly Father, and here in the holy Mass, His deputies, the Catholic priests, perform the same deed. The priests have stepped forward to take His place so that they might carry on the same rites of sacrifice that He once performed. He has vested in them the right to His holy humanity, and simultaneously given them the power over His body. The priest is capable not only of calling forth His body to the altar, of sealing Him in the tabernacle, of offering Him up to the congregation; the priest is also given the power to offer Him, the son of God become flesh and blood, as a peaceful sacrifice for both living and dead. Christ, the Son of God the Father, created both by Heaven and by Earth, who bears the whole of the cosmos within him, is beholden to the will of the Catholic Priest." (emphasis from taken Mirbt's reprinting).

Page 241, "Muhammad"
(570-632), prophet and founder of Islam.

Page 242, "Chamberlain"
Joseph Chamberlain (1836-1914), British statesman. See also note for p. 233.

Page 242, "the things that I described to you here not long ago"
In the lecture from February 15, 1920, also collected in this volume.

Page 242, "Louis XIV"
(1638-1715), King of France, called the "Sun King." The phrase "L'état c'est moi," has been attributed to him.

Page 246, "My kingdom is not of this world"
John 18:36.

Page 252, "Noske"
Gustav Noske (1868-1946), lumberjack, later editor of Social Democratic newspapers, quelled the Wilhelmshaven Mutiny in Kiel in November 1918, named Supreme Commander of the German troupes in Berlin on January 6, 1919, and defense minister of Germany on February 13, 1919. In February 1920, when Rudolf Steiner gave this lecture, he still held that post, and would hold it until March 30, 1920.

Page 253, "now takes the form of Lenin and Trotsky—Bolshevism."
Rudolf Steiner spoke at various times about the connection between these two ambassadors of Bolshevism and Russian czarism. For example, look in *Die Befreiung des Menschenwesens als Grundlage für eine soziale Neugestaltung. Altes Denken und neues soziales Wollen* (9 lectures, 1919), GA 329, at the discussion following the lecture given on March 11, 1919; or the question and answer session for the lecture from October 25, 1919, in *Sozial Zukunft* (6 lectures, Zurich, 1919), GA 332a.

Page 253, "people like Caprivi or Hohenlohe or Bethmann Hollweg"
Chancellors of the German Republic: Caprivi (1890-1894), Hohenlohe (1894-1900), Bülow (1900-1909), Bethmann Hollweg (1909-1917).

Page 253, "Scheidemann"
Philipp Scheidemann (1863-1839), publisher, journalist, editor, Social Democratic member of the Reichtag (since 1903), secretary of state under Chancellor Max von Baden (Oct. 1918), member of the new Worker's Republic (November 9, 1918).

Page 259, "*How to Know Higher Worlds*"
Written 1904/05, CW 10.

Page 260, "Lloyd George"
See notes for pp. 55 and 177.

Page 261, "*The State*"
Woodrow Wilson, 1889.

Page 262, "a German individual... has translated this book into German"
Der Staat. Elemnte historischer und praktischer Politik, authorized translation by Günther Thomas, Berlin and Leipzig, 1913.

Page 265, "St. Augustine"
Aurelius Augustine (354-430), church teacher and significant philosopher of Christian antiquity. *De civitae dei* (*The City of God*), author of 22 books.

Page 266, "When the early German emperor wrote his ethos in a book"
Wilhelm II wrote, in 1891, in the Golden Book of the City of Munich: "Regis voluntas suprema lex." See also J. von Kürenburg's *War alles falsch? Das Leben Kaiser Wilhelms II. (Was everything false? The Life of Wilhelm II)* Basel/Olten, 1940, p. 190.

Page 267, "Law is the will of the state"
Wilson, Woodrow. *The State: Elements of Historical and Practical Politics.* D. C. Heath & Co. Publishers: New York, 1918. 69.

Page 267, "and the German Empire was formed..."
Ibid. 446.

Page 270, "monks from Cluny"
A town in the French region of Saône-et-Loire, which was the center of the Benedictine Order "The Congregation of Cluny," or the "Cluniac Order," an affiliation of various cloisters with the abbot of Cluny as leader. Pope Gregory

II, a member of the Cluniac Order, was able to start a Cluniac Reformation and unseat the leadership in both the state and the church. The abbots were seen by Rome as equal in stature to bishops and they were furnished with the appropriate privileges. The increase in wealth led to a secularization of the order.

Page 270, "Pope Gregory VII"
Pope from 1073-1085; see above note.

Page 272, "the Church has become a shadowy concept"
Rudolf Steiner drew two diagonally-hatched circles on the board, but their direction connection to the text is not known. The marginalia for this drawing has therefore been left out of this left. The board appears reprinted in a separate volume — *Rudolf Steiner, Wandtafelzeichnungen zum Vortragswerk* — as No. 18.

Page 274, "in my *Kernpunkte*"
Die Kernpunkte der sozialen Frage in den Lebensnotwendigkeiten der Gegenwart und Zukunft (1919), GA 23.

Page 274, "queen of England"
Victoria (1818-1901), Queen of England from 1837-1901.

Page 274, "Franz Joseph I"
(1830-1916), Emperor of Austria from 1848-1916. "Chased off" by Emperor Karl I, 1887-1992, Emperor of Austria from 1916-1918.

Page 275, "Waldorf School"
This refers to the Free Waldorf School in Stuttgart, which opened on September 7, 1919 and was approved by the standing administration in Würtemmberg on March 8, 1920. The "hole" in the Württemberg school codes was that there was the possibility for freedom in the appointment of teachers. This possibility was crucial to the school's existence at the beginning, since there were not enough certified teachers suitable for the job who were willing to take on the risk of this appointment. This "hole" was closed a short time later. Furthermore, there was the possibility of taking an unlimited number of children into the first class. This freedom was also limited later on.

Page 279, "a letter that arrived recently in Stuttgart from Kristiania"
There is no known copy of this letter. The identity of the people and the monthly publication mentioned in it cannot be ascertained.

Page 280, "in my last lecture to you before my trip to Germany"
Rudolf Steiner went a few days later to Stuttgart for two weeks (the second natural science course (CW 321), founding of the organization "Der Kommende Tag" ["The Coming Day"], etc.).

RUDOLF STEINER'S COLLECTED WORKS

The German Edition of Rudolf Steiner's Collected Works (the Gesamtausgabe [GA] published by Rudolf Steiner Verlag, Dornach, Switzerland) presently runs to over 354 titles, organized either by type of work (written or spoken), chronology, audience (public or other), or subject (education, art, etc.). For ease of comparison, the Collected Works in English [CW] follows the German organization exactly. A complete listing of the CWs follows with literal translations of the German titles. Other than in the case of the books published in his lifetime, titles were rarely given by Rudolf Steiner himself, and were often provided by the editors of the German editions. The titles in English are not necessarily the same as the German; and, indeed, over the past seventy-five years have frequently been different, with the same book sometimes appearing under different titles.

For ease of identification and to avoid confusion, we suggest that readers looking for a title should do so by CW number. Because the work of creating the Collected Works of Rudolf Steiner is an ongoing process, with new titles being published every year, we have not indicated in this listing which books are presently available. To find out what titles in the Collected Works are currently in print, please check our website at www.steinerbooks.org, or write to SteinerBooks 610 Main Street, Great Barrington, MA 01230:

Written Work

CW 1	Goethe: Natural-Scientific Writings, Introduction, with Footnotes and Explanations in the text by Rudolf Steiner
CW 2	Outlines of an Epistemology of the Goethean World View, with Special Consideration of Schiller
CW 3	Truth and Science
CW 4	The Philosophy of Freedom
CW 4a	Documents to "The Philosophy of Freedom"
CW 5	Friedrich Nietzsche, A Fighter against His Own Time
CW 6	Goethe's Worldview
CW 6a	Now in CW 30
CW 7	Mysticism at the Dawn of Modern Spiritual Life and Its Relationship with Modern Worldviews
CW 8	Christianity as Mystical Fact and the Mysteries of Antiquity
CW 9	Theosophy: An Introduction into Supersensible World Knowledge and Human Purpose
CW 10	How Does One Attain Knowledge of Higher Worlds?
CW 11	From the Akasha-Chronicle
CW 12	Levels of Higher Knowledge

Lectures to the Members of the Anthroposophical Society

SIGNIFICANT EVENTS
IN THE LIFE OF RUDOLF STEINER

1829: June 23: birth of Johann Steiner (1829-1910)—Rudolf Steiner's father—in Geras, Lower Austria.

1834: May 8: birth of Franciska Blie (1834-1918)—Rudolf Steiner's mother—in Horn, Lower Austria. "My father and mother were both children of the glorious Lower Austrian forest district north of the Danube."

1860: May 16: marriage of Johann Steiner and Franciska Blie.

1861: February 25: birth of *Rudolf Joseph Lorenz Steiner* in Kraljevec, Croatia, near the border with Hungary, where Johann Steiner works as a telegrapher for the South Austria Railroad. Rudolf Steiner is baptized two days later, February 27, the date usually given as his birthday.

1862: Summer: the family moves to Mödling, Lower Austria.

1863: The family moves to Pottschach, Lower Austria, near the Styrian border, where Johann Steiner becomes stationmaster. "The view stretched to the mountains...majestic peaks in the distance and the sweet charm of nature in the immediate surroundings."

1864: November 15: birth of Rudolf Steiner's sister, Leopoldine (d. November 1, 1927). She will become a seamstress and live with her parents for the rest of her life.

1866: July 28: birth of Rudolf Steiner's deaf-mute brother, Gustav (d. May 1, 1941).

1867: Rudolf Steiner enters the village school. Following a disagreement between his father and the schoolmaster, whose wife falsely accused the boy of causing a commotion, Rudolf Steiner is taken out of school and taught at home.

1868: A critical experience. Unknown to the family, an aunt dies in a distant town. Sitting in the station waiting room, Rudolf Steiner sees her "form," which speaks to him, asking for help. "Beginning with this experience, a new soul life began in the boy, one in which not only the outer trees and mountains spoke to him, but also the worlds that lay behind them. From this moment on, the boy began to live with the spirits of nature...."

1869: The family moves to the peaceful, rural village of Neudorfl, near Wiener-Neustadt in present-day Hungary. Rudolf Steiner attends the village school. Because of the "unorthodoxy" of his writing and spelling, he has to do "extra lessons."

1870: Through a book lent to him by his tutor, he discovers geometry: "To grasp something purely in the spirit brought me inner happiness. I know that I first learned happiness through geometry." The same tutor allows him to draw, while other students still struggle with their reading and writing. "An artistic element" thus enters his education.

1871:   Though his parents are not religious, Rudolf Steiner becomes a "church child," a favorite of the priest, who was "an exceptional character." "Up to the age of ten or eleven, among those I came to know, he was far and away the most significant." Among other things, he introduces Steiner to Copernican, heliocentric cosmology. As an altar boy, Rudolf Steiner serves at Masses, funerals, and Corpus Christi processions. At year's end, after an incident in which he escapes a thrashing, his father forbids him to go to church.

1872:   Rudolf Steiner transfers to grammar school in Wiener-Neustadt, a five-mile walk from home, which must be done in all weathers.

1873-75: Through his teachers and on his own, Rudolf Steiner has many wonderful experiences with science and mathematics. Outside school, he teaches himself analytic geometry, trigonometry, differential equations, and calculus.

1876:   Rudolf Steiner begins tutoring other students. He learns bookbinding from his father. He also teaches himself stenography.

1877:   Rudolf Steiner discovers Kant's *Critique of Pure Reason*, which he reads and rereads. He also discovers and reads von Rotteck's *World History*.

1878:   He studies extensively in contemporary psychology and philosophy.

1879:   Rudolf Steiner graduates from high school with honors. His father is transferred to Inzersdorf, near Vienna. He uses his first visit to Vienna "to purchase a great number of philosophy books"—Kant, Fichte, Schelling, and Hegel, as well as numerous histories of philosophy. His aim: to find a path from the "I" to nature.

October 1879-1883: Rudolf Steiner attends the Technical College in Vienna—to study mathematics, chemistry, physics, mineralogy, botany, zoology, biology, geology, and mechanics—with a scholarship. He also attends lectures in history and literature, while avidly reading philosophy on his own. His two favorite professors are Karl Julius Schröer (German language and literature) and Edmund Reitlinger (physics). He also audits lectures by Robert Zimmerman on aesthetics and Franz Brentano on philosophy. During this year he begins his friendship with Moritz Zitter (1861-1921), who will help support him financially when he is in Berlin.

1880:   Rudolf Steiner attends lectures on Schiller and Goethe by Karl Julius Schröer, who becomes his mentor. Also "through a remarkable combination of circumstances," he meets Felix Koguzki, an "herb gatherer" and healer, who could "see deeply into the secrets of nature." Rudolf Steiner will meet and study with this "emissary of the Master" throughout his time in Vienna.

1881:   January: "… I didn't sleep a wink. I was busy with philosophical problems until about 12:30 a.m. Then, finally, I threw myself down on my couch. All my striving during the previous year had been to research whether the following statement by Schelling was true or not: *Within everyone dwells a secret, marvelous capacity to draw back from the stream of time—out of the self clothed in all that comes to us from outside—into our innermost being and there, in the immutable form of the Eternal, to look into ourselves.* I believe, and I am still quite certain of it, that I discovered this capacity in myself; I had long had an inkling of it. Now the whole of idealist philosophy stood before me in modified form. What's a sleepless night compared to that!"

Rudolf Steiner begins communicating with leading thinkers of the day, who send him books in return, which he reads eagerly.

July: "I am not one of those who dives into the day like an animal in human form. I pursue a quite specific goal, an idealistic aim—knowledge of the truth! This cannot be done offhandedly. It requires the greatest striving in the world, free of all egotism, and equally of all resignation."

August: Steiner puts down on paper for the first time thoughts for a "Philosophy of Freedom." "The striving for the absolute: this human yearning is freedom." He also seeks to outline a "peasant philosophy," describing what the worldview of a "peasant"—one who lives close to the earth and the old ways—really is.

1881-1882: Felix Koguzki, the herb gatherer, reveals himself to be the envoy of another, higher initiatory personality, who instructs Rudolf Steiner to penetrate Fichte's philosophy and to master modern scientific thinking as a preparation for right entry into the spirit. This "Master" also teaches him the double (evolutionary and involutionary) nature of time.

1882:   Through the offices of Karl Julius Schröer, Rudolf Steiner is asked by Joseph Kurschner to edit Goethe's scientific works for the *Deutschen National-Literatur* edition. He writes "A Possible Critique of Atomistic Concepts" and sends it to Friedrich Theodore Vischer.

1883:   Rudolf Steiner completes his college studies and begins work on the Goethe project.

1884:   First volume of Goethe's *Scientific Writings* (CW 1) appears (March). He lectures on Goethe and Lessing, and Goethe's approach to science. In July, he enters the household of Ladislaus and Pauline Specht as tutor to the four Specht boys. He will live there until 1890. At this time, he meets Josef Breuer (1842-1925), the coauthor with Sigmund Freud of *Studies in Hysteria*, who is the Specht family doctor.

1885:   While continuing to edit Goethe's writings, Rudolf Steiner reads deeply in contemporary philosophy (Edouard von Hartmann, Johannes Volkelt, and Richard Wahle, among others).

1886:   May: Rudolf Steiner sends Kurschner the manuscript of *Outlines of Goethe's Theory of Knowledge* (CW 2), which appears in October, and which he sends out widely. He also meets the poet Marie Eugenie Delle Grazie and writes "Nature and Our Ideals" for her. He attends her salon, where he meets many priests, theologians, and philosophers, who will become his friends. Meanwhile, the director of the Goethe Archive in Weimar requests his collaboration with the *Sophien* edition of Goethe's works, particularly the writings on color.

1887:   At the beginning of the year, Rudolf Steiner is very sick. As the year progresses and his health improves, he becomes increasingly "a man of letters," lecturing, writing essays, and taking part in Austrian cultural life. In August-September, the second volume of Goethe's *Scientific Writings* appears.

1888:   January-July: Rudolf Steiner assumes editorship of the "German Weekly" (*Deutsche Wochenschrift*). He begins lecturing more intensively, giving, for example, a lecture titled "Goethe as Father of a New Aesthetics." He meets and becomes soul friends with Friedrich Eckstein (1861-1939), a vegetarian, philosopher of symbolism, alchemist, and musician, who will introduce him to various spiritual currents (including Theosophy) and with whom he will meditate and interpret esoteric and alchemical texts.

1889:   Rudolf Steiner first reads Nietzsche (*Beyond Good and Evil*). He encounters Theosophy again and learns of Madame Blavatsky in the Theosophical circle around Marie Lang (1858-1934). Here he also meets well-known figures of Austrian life, as well as esoteric figures like the occultist Franz Hartman and Karl Leinigen-Billigen (translator of C.G. Harrison's *The Transcendental Universe*.) During this period, Steiner first reads A.P. Sinnett's *Esoteric Buddhism* and Mabel Collins's *Light on the Path*. He also begins traveling, visiting Budapest, Weimar, and Berlin (where he meets philosopher Edouard von Hartman).

1890:   Rudolf Steiner finishes volume 3 of Goethe's scientific writings. He begins his doctoral dissertation, which will become *Truth and Science* (CW 3). He also meets the poet and feminist Rosa Mayreder (1858-1938), with whom he can exchange his most intimate thoughts. In September, Rudolf Steiner moves to Weimar to work in the Goethe-Schiller Archive.

1891:   Volume 3 of the Kurschner edition of Goethe appears. Meanwhile, Rudolf Steiner edits Goethe's studies in mineralogy and scientific writings for the *Sophien* edition. He meets Ludwig Laistner of the Cotta Publishing Company, who asks for a book on the basic question of metaphysics. From this will result, ultimately, *The Philosophy of Freedom* (CW 4), which will be published not by Cotta but by Emil Felber. In October, Rudolf Steiner takes the oral exam for a doctorate in philosophy, mathematics, and mechanics at Rostock University, receiving his doctorate on the twenty-sixth. In November, he gives his first lecture on Goethe's "Fairy Tale" in Vienna.

1892:   Rudolf Steiner continues work at the Goethe-Schiller Archive and on his *Philosophy of Freedom*. *Truth and Science*, his doctoral dissertation, is published. Steiner undertakes to write introductions to books on Schopenhauer and Jean Paul for Cotta. At year's end, he finds lodging with Anna Eunike, née Schulz (1853-1911), a widow with four daughters and a son. He also develops a friendship with Otto Erich Hartleben (1864-1905) with whom he shares literary interests.

1893: Rudolf Steiner begins his habit of producing many reviews and articles. In March, he gives a lecture titled "Hypnotism, with Reference to Spiritism." In September, volume 4 of the Kurschner edition is completed. In November, *The Philosophy of Freedom* appears. This year, too, he meets John Henry Mackay (1864-1933), the anarchist, and Max Stirner, a scholar and biographer.

1894: Rudolf Steiner meets Elisabeth Förster Nietzsche, the philosopher's sister, and begins to read Nietzsche in earnest, beginning with the as yet unpublished *Antichrist*. He also meets Ernst Haeckel (1834-1919). In the fall, he begins to write *Nietzsche, A Fighter against His Time* (CW 5).

1895: May, *Nietzsche, A Fighter against His Time* appears.

1896: January 22: Rudolf Steiner sees Friedrich Nietzsche for the first and only time. Moves between the Nietzsche and the Goethe-Schiller Archives, where he completes his work before year's end. He falls out with Elisabeth Förster Nietzsche, thus ending his association with the Nietzsche Archive.

1897: Rudolf Steiner finishes the manuscript of *Goethe's Worldview* (CW 6). He moves to Berlin with Anna Eunike and begins editorship of the *Magazin fur Literatur*. From now on, Steiner will write countless reviews, literary and philosophical articles, and so on. He begins lecturing at the "Free Literary Society." In September, he attends the Zionist Congress in Basel. He sides with Dreyfus in the Dreyfus affair.

1898: Rudolf Steiner is very active as an editor in the political, artistic, and theatrical life of Berlin. He becomes friendly with John Henry Mackay and poet Ludwig Jacobowski (1868-1900). He joins Jacobowski's circle of writers, artists, and scientists—"The Coming Ones" (*Die Kommenden*)—and contributes lectures to the group until 1903. He also lectures at the "League for College Pedagogy." He writes an article for Goethe's sesquicentennial, "Goethe's Secret Revelation," on the "Fairy Tale of the Green Snake and the Beautiful Lily."

1888-89: "This was a trying time for my soul as I looked at Christianity. . . . I was able to progress only by contemplating, by means of spiritual perception, the evolution of Christianity . . . . Conscious knowledge of real Christianity began to dawn in me around the turn of the century. This seed continued to develop. My soul trial occurred shortly before the beginning of the twentieth century. It was decisive for my soul's development that I stood spiritually before the Mystery of Golgotha in a deep and solemn celebration of knowledge."

1899: Rudolf Steiner begins teaching and giving lectures and lecture cycles at the Workers' College, founded by Wilhelm Liebknecht (1826-1900). He will continue to do so until 1904. Writes: *Literature and Spiritual Life in the Nineteenth Century; Individualism in Philosophy; Haeckel and His Opponents; Poetry in the Present;* and begins what will become (fifteen years later). *The Riddles of Philosophy* (CW 18). He also meets many artists and writers, including Käthe Kollwitz, Stefan

Zweig, and Rainer Maria Rilke. On October 31, he marries Anna Eunike.

1900: "I thought that the turn of the century must bring humanity a new light. It seemed to me that the separation of human thinking and willing from the spirit had peaked. A turn or reversal of direction in human evolution seemed to me a necessity." Rudolf Steiner finishes *World and Life Views in the Nineteenth Century* (the second part of what will become *The Riddles of Philosophy*) and dedicates it to Ernst Haeckel. It is published in March. He continues lecturing at *Die Kommenden*, whose leadership he assumes after the death of Jacobowski. Also, he gives the Gutenberg Jubilee lecture before 7,000 typesetters and printers. In September, Rudolf Steiner is invited by Count and Countess Brockdorff to lecture in the Theosophical Library. His first lecture is on Nietzsche. His second lecture is titled "Goethe's Secret Revelation." October 6, he begins a lecture cycle on the mystics that will become *Mystics after Modernism* (CW 7). November-December: "Marie von Sivers appears in the audience...." Also in November, Steiner gives his first lecture at the Giordano Bruno Bund (where he will continue to lecture until May, 1905). He speaks on Bruno and modern Rome, focusing on the importance of the philosophy of Thomas Aquinas as monism.

1901: In continual financial straits, Rudolf Steiner's early friends Moritz Zitter and Rosa Mayreder help support him. In October, he begins the lecture cycle *Christianity as Mystical Fact* (CW 8) at the Theosophical Library. In November, he gives his first "Theosophical lecture" on Goethe's "Fairy Tale" in Hamburg at the invitation of Wilhelm Hubbe-Schleiden. He also attends a tea to celebrate the founding of the Theosophical Society at Count and Countess Brockdorff's. He gives a lecture cycle, "From Buddha to Christ," for the circle of the *Kommenden*. November 17, Marie von Sivers asks Rudolf Steiner if Theosophy does not need a Western-Christian spiritual movement (to complement Theosophy's Eastern emphasis). "The question was posed. Now, following spiritual laws, I could begin to give an answer...." In December, Rudolf Steiner writes his first article for a Theosophical publication. At year's end, the Brockdorffs and possibly Wilhelm Hubbe-Schleiden ask Rudolf Steiner to join the Theosophical Society and undertake the leadership of the German section. Rudolf Steiner agrees, on the condition that Marie von Sivers (then in Italy) work with him.

1902: Beginning in January, Rudolf Steiner attends the opening of the Workers' School in Spandau with Rosa Luxemburg (1870-1919). January 17, Rudolf Steiner joins the Theosophical Society. In April, he is asked to become general secretary of the German Section of the Theosophical Society, and works on preparations for its founding. In July, he visits London for a Theosophical congress. He meets Bertram

Keightly, G.R.S. Mead, A.P. Sinnett, and Annie Besant, among others. In September, *Christianity as Mystical Fact* appears. In October, Rudolf Steiner gives his first public lecture on Theosophy ("Monism and Theosophy") to about three hundred people at the Giordano Bruno Bund. On October 19-21, the German Section of the Theosophical Society has its first meeting; Rudolf Steiner is the general secretary, and Annie Besant attends. Steiner lectures on practical karma studies. On October 23, Annie Besant inducts Rudolf Steiner into the Esoteric School of the Theosophical Society. On October 25, Steiner begins a weekly series of lectures: "The Field of Theosophy." During this year, Rudolf Steiner also first meets Ita Wegman (1876-1943), who will become his close collaborator in his final years.

1903: Rudolf Steiner holds about 300 lectures and seminars. In May, the first issue of the periodical *Luzifer* appears. In June, Rudolf Steiner visits London for the first meeting of the Federation of the European Sections of the Theosophical Society, where he meets Colonel Olcott. He begins to write *Theosophy* (CW 9).

1904: Rudolf Steiner continues lecturing at the Workers' College and elsewhere (about 90 lectures), while lecturing intensively all over Germany among Theosophists (about a 140 lectures). In February, he meets Carl Unger (1878-1929), who will become a member of the board of the Anthroposophical Society (1913). In March, he meets Michael Bauer (1871-1929), a Christian mystic, who will also be on the board. In May, *Theosophy* appears, with the dedication: "To the spirit of Giordano Bruno." Rudolf Steiner and Marie von Sivers visit London for meetings with Annie Besant. June: Rudolf Steiner and Marie von Sivers attend the meeting of the Federation of European Sections of the Theosophical Society in Amsterdam. In July, Steiner begins the articles in *Luzifer-Gnosis* that will become *How to Know Higher Worlds* (CW 10) and *Cosmic Memory* (CW 11). In September, Annie Besant visits Germany. In December, Steiner lectures on Freemasonry. He mentions the High Grade Masonry derived from John Yarker and represented by Theodore Reuss and Karl Kellner as a blank slate "into which a good image could be placed."

1905: This year, Steiner ends his non-Theosophical lecturing activity. Supported by Marie von Sivers, his Theosophical lecturing—both in public and in the Theosophical Society—increases significantly: "The German Theosophical Movement is of exceptional importance." Steiner recommends reading, among others, Fichte, Jacob Boehme, and Angelus Silesius. He begins to introduce Christian themes into Theosophy. He also begins to work with doctors (Felix Peipers and Ludwig Noll). In July, he is in London for the Federation of European Sections, where he attends a lecture by Annie Besant: "I have seldom seen Mrs. Besant speak in so inward and heartfelt a manner...." "Through Mrs. Besant I have found the way to H.P. Blavatsky."

September to October, he gives a course of thirty-one lectures for a small group of esoteric students. In October, the annual meeting of the German Section of the Theosophical Society, which still remains very small, takes place. Rudolf Steiner reports membership has risen from 121 to 377 members. In November, seeking to establish esoteric "continuity," Rudolf Steiner and Marie von Sivers participate in a "Memphis-Misraim" Masonic ceremony. They pay forty-five marks for membership. "Yesterday, you saw how little remains of former esoteric institutions." "We are dealing only with a 'framework'... for the present, nothing lies behind it. The occult powers have completely withdrawn."

1906:   Expansion of Theosophical work. Rudolf Steiner gives about 245 lectures, only 44 of which take place in Berlin. Cycles are given in Paris, Leipzig, Stuttgart, and Munich. Esoteric work also intensifies. Rudolf Steiner begins writing *An Outline of Esoteric Science* (CW 13). In January, Rudolf Steiner receives permission (a patent) from the Great Orient of the Scottish A & A Thirty-Three Degree Rite of the Order of the Ancient Freemasons of the Memphis-Misraim Rite to direct a chapter under the name "Mystica Aeterna." This will become the "Cognitive Cultic Section" (also called "Misraim Service") of the Esoteric School. (See: *From the History and Contents of the Cognitive Cultic Section* (CW 264). During this time, Steiner also meets Albert Schweitzer. In May, he is in Paris, where he visits Edouard Schuré. Many Russians attend his lectures (including Konstantin Balmont, Dimitri Mereszkovski, Zinaida Hippius, and Maximilian Woloshin). He attends the General Meeting of the European Federation of the Theosophical Society, at which Col. Olcott is present for the last time. He spends the year's end in Venice and Rome, where he writes and works on his translation of H.P. Blavatsky's *Key to Theosophy*.

1907:   Further expansion of the German Theosophical Movement according to the Rosicrucian directive to "introduce spirit into the world"—in education, in social questions, in art, and in science. In February, Col. Olcott dies in Adyar. Before he dies, Olcott indicates that "the Masters" wish Annie Besant to succeed him: much politicking ensues. Rudolf Steiner supports Besant's candidacy. April-May: preparations for the Congress of the Federation of European Sections of the Theosophical Society—the great, watershed Whitsun "Munich Congress," attended by Annie Besant and others. Steiner decides to separate Eastern and Western (Christian-Rosicrucian) esoteric schools. He takes his esoteric school out of the Theosophical Society (Besant and Rudolf Steiner are "in harmony" on this). Steiner makes his first lecture tours to Austria and Hungary. That summer, he is in Italy. In September, he visits Edouard Schuré, who will write the introduction to the French edition of *Christianity as Mystical Fact* in Barr, Alsace. Rudolf Steiner writes the autobiographical statement known as the "Barr Document." In *Luzifer–Gnosis*, "The Education of the Child" appears.

1908: The movement grows (membership: 1150). Lecturing expands. Steiner makes his first extended lecture tour to Holland and Scandinavia, as well as visits to Naples and Sicily. Themes: St. John's Gospel, the Apocalypse, Egypt, science, philosophy, and logic. *Luzifer-Gnosis* ceases publication. In Berlin, Marie von Sivers (with Johanna Mücke (1864-1949) forms the *Philosophisch-Theosophisch* (after 1915 *Philosophisch-Anthroposophisch*) *Verlag* to publish Steiner's work. Steiner gives lecture cycles titled *The Gospel of St. John* (CW 103) and *The Apocalypse* (104).

1909: *An Outline of Esoteric Science* appears. Lecturing and travel continues. Rudolf Steiner's spiritual research expands to include the polarity of Lucifer and Ahriman; the work of great individualities in history; the Maitreya Buddha and the Bodhisattvas; spiritual economy (CW 109); the work of the spiritual hierarchies in heaven and on Earth (CW 110). He also deepens and intensifies his research into the Gospels, giving lectures on the Gospel of St. Luke (CW 114) with the first mention of two Jesus children. Meets and becomes friends with Christian Morgenstern (1871-1914). In April, he lays the foundation stone for the Malsch model—the building that will lead to the first Goetheanum. In May, the International Congress of the Federation of European Sections of the Theosophical Society takes place in Budapest. Rudolf Steiner receives the Subba Row medal for *How to Know Higher Worlds*. During this time, Charles W. Leadbeater discovers Jiddu Krishnamurti (1895-1986) and proclaims him the future "world teacher," the bearer of the Maitreya Buddha and the "reappearing Christ." In October, Steiner delivers seminal lectures on "anthroposophy," which he will try, unsuccessfully, to rework over the next years into the unfinished work, *Anthroposophy (A Fragment)* (CW 45).

1910: New themes: *The Reappearance of Christ in the Etheric* (CW 118); *The Fifth Gospel; The Mission of Folk Souls* (CW 121); *Occult History* (CW 126); the evolving development of etheric cognitive capacities. Rudolf Steiner continues his Gospel research with *The Gospel of St. Matthew* (CW 123). In January, his father dies. In April, he takes a month-long trip to Italy, including Rome, Monte Cassino, and Sicily. He also visits Scandinavia again. July-August, he writes the first mystery drama, *The Portal of Initiation* (CW 14). In November, he gives "psychosophy" lectures. In December, he submits "On the Psychological Foundations and Epistemological Framework of Theosophy" to the International Philosophical Congress in Bologna.

1911: The crisis in the Theosophical Society deepens. In January, "The Order of the Rising Sun," which will soon become "The Order of the Star in the East," is founded for the coming world teacher, Krishnamurti. At the same time, Marie von Sivers, Rudolf Steiner's coworker, falls ill. Fewer lectures are given, but important new ground is broken. In Prague, in March, Steiner meets Franz Kafka (1883-1924) and Hugo Bergmann (1883-1975). In April, he delivers his paper to the

Philosophical Congress. He writes the second mystery drama, *The Soul's Probation* (CW 14). Also, while Marie von Sivers is convalescing, Rudolf Steiner begins work on *Calendar 1912/1913*, which will contain the "Calendar of the Soul" meditations. On March 19, Anna (Eunike) Steiner dies. In September, Rudolf Steiner visits Einsiedeln, birthplace of Paracelsus. In December, Friedrich Rittelmeyer, future founder of the Christian Community, meets Rudolf Steiner. The *Johannes-Bauverein*, the "building committee," which would lead to the first Goetheanum (first planned for Munich), is also founded, and a preliminary committee for the founding of an independent association is created that, in the following year, will become the Anthroposophical Society. Important lecture cycles include *Occult Physiology* (CW 128); *Wonders of the World* (CW 129); *From Jesus to Christ* (CW 131). Other themes: esoteric Christianity; Christian Rosenkreutz; the spiritual guidance of humanity; the sense world and the world of the spirit.

1912:　Despite the ongoing, now increasing crisis in the Theosophical Society, much is accomplished: *Calendar 1912/1913* is published; eurythmy is created; both the third mystery drama, *The Guardian of the Threshold* (CW 14) and *A Way of Self-Knowledge* (CW 16) are written. New (or renewed) themes included life between death and rebirth and karma and reincarnation. Other lecture cycles: *Spiritual Beings in the Heavenly Bodies and the Kingdoms of Nature* (CW 136); *The Human Being in the Light of Occultism, Theosophy, and Philosophy* (CW 137); *The Gospel of St. Mark* (CW 139); and *The Bhagavad Gita and the Epistles of Paul* (CW 142). On May 8, Rudolf Steiner celebrates White Lotus Day, H.P. Blavatsky's death day, which he had faithfully observed for the past decade, for the last time. In August, Rudolf Steiner suggests the "independent association" be called the "Anthroposophical Society." In September, the first eurythmy course takes place. In October, Rudolf Steiner declines recognition of a Theosophical Society lodge dedicated to the Star of the East and decides to expel all Theosophical Society members belonging to the order. Also, with Marie von Sivers, he first visits Dornach, near Basel, Switzerland, and they stand on the hill where the Goetheanum will be. In November, a Theosophical Society lodge is opened by direct mandate from Adyar (Annie Besant). In December, a meeting of the German section occurs at which it is decided that belonging to the Order of the Star of the East is incompatible with membership in the Theosophical Society. December 28: informal founding of the Anthroposophical Society in Berlin.

1913:　Expulsion of the German section from the Theosophical Society. February 2-3: Foundation meeting of the Anthroposophical Society. Board members include: Marie von Sivers, Michael Bauer, and Carl Unger. September 20: Laying of the foundation stone for the *Johannes Bau* (Goetheanum) in Dornach. Building begins immediately. The third mystery drama, *The Soul's Awakening* (CW 14), is completed.

Also: *The Threshold of the Spiritual World* (CW 147). Lecture cycles include: *The Bhagavad Gita and the Epistles of Paul* and *The Esoteric Meaning of the Bhagavad Gita* (CW 146), which the Russian philosopher Nikolai Berdyaev attends; *The Mysteries of the East and of Christianity* (CW 144); *The Effects of Esoteric Development* (CW 145); and *The Fifth Gospel* (CW 148). In May, Rudolf Steiner is in London and Paris, where anthroposophical work continues.

1914: Building continues on the *Johannes Bau* (Goetheanum) in Dornach, with artists and coworkers from seventeen nations. The general assembly of the Anthroposophical Society takes place. In May, Rudolf Steiner visits Paris, as well as Chartres Cathedral. June 28: assassination in Sarajevo ("Now the catastrophe has happened!"). August 1: War is declared. Rudolf Steiner returns to Germany from Dornach—he will travel back and forth. He writes the last chapter of *The Riddles of Philosophy*. Lecture cycles include: *Human and Cosmic Thought* (CW 151); *Inner Being of Humanity between Death and a New Birth* (CW 153); *Occult Reading and Occult Hearing* (CW 156). December 24: marriage of Rudolf Steiner and Marie von Sivers.

1915: Building continues. Life after death becomes a major theme, also art. Writes: *Thoughts during a Time of War* (CW 24). Lectures include: *The Secret of Death* (CW 159); *The Uniting of Humanity through the Christ Impulse* (CW 165).

1916: Rudolf Steiner begins work with Edith Maryon (1872-1924) on the sculpture "The Representative of Humanity" ("The Group"—Christ, Lucifer, and Ahriman). He also works with the alchemist Alexander von Bernus on the quarterly *Das Reich*. He writes *The Riddle of Humanity* (CW 20). Lectures include: *Necessity and Freedom in World History and Human Action* (CW 166); *Past and Present in the Human Spirit* (CW 167); *The Karma of Vocation* (CW 172); *The Karma of Untruthfulness* (CW 173).

1917: Russian Revolution. The U.S. enters the war. Building continues. Rudolf Steiner delineates the idea of the "threefold nature of the human being" (in a public lecture March 15) and the "threefold nature of the social organism" (hammered out in May-June with the help of Otto von Lerchenfeld and Ludwig Polzer-Hoditz in the form of two documents titled *Memoranda*, which were distributed in high places). August-September: Rudolf Steiner writes *The Riddles of the Soul* (CW 20). Also: commentary on "The Chemical Wedding of Christian Rosenkreutz" for Alexander Bernus (*Das Reich*). Lectures include: *The Karma of Materialism* (CW 176); *The Spiritual Background of the Outer World: The Fall of the Spirits of Darkness* (CW 177).

1918: March 18: peace treaty of Brest-Litovsk—"Now everything will truly enter chaos! What is needed is cultural renewal." June: Rudolf Steiner visits Karlstein (Grail) Castle outside Prague. Lecture cycle: *From Symptom to Reality in Modern History* (CW 185). In mid-November,

Emil Molt, of the Waldorf-Astoria Cigarette Company, has the idea of founding a school for his workers' children.

1919:   Focus on the threefold social organism: tireless travel, countless lectures, meetings, and publications. At the same time, a new public stage of Anthroposophy emerges as cultural renewal begins. The coming years will see initiatives in pedagogy, medicine, pharmacology, and agriculture. January 27: threefold meeting: " We must first of all, with the money we have, found free schools that can bring people what they need." February: first public eurythmy performance in Zurich. Also: "Appeal to the German People" (CW 24), circulated March 6 as a newspaper insert. In April, *Toward Social Renewal* (CW 23)—"perhaps the most widely read of all books on politics appearing since the war"—appears. Rudolf Steiner is asked to undertake the "direction and leadership" of the school founded by the Waldorf-Astoria Company. Rudolf Steiner begins to talk about the "renewal" of education. May 30: a building is selected and purchased for the future Waldorf School. August-September, Rudolf Steiner gives a lecture course for Waldorf teachers, *The Foundations of Human Experience (Study of Man)* (CW 293). September 7: Opening of the first Waldorf School. December (into January): first science course, the *Light Course* (CW 320).

1920:   The Waldorf School flourishes. New threefold initiatives. Founding of limited companies *Der Kommende Tag* and *Futurum A.G.* to infuse spiritual values into the economic realm. Rudolf Steiner also focuses on the sciences. Lectures: *Introducing Anthroposophical Medicine* (CW 312); *The Warmth Course* (CW 321); *The Boundaries of Natural Science* (CW 322); *The Redemption of Thinking* (CW 74). February: Johannes Werner Klein—later a cofounder of the Christian Community— asks Rudolf Steiner about the possibility of a "religious renewal," a "Johannine church." In March, Rudolf Steiner gives the first course for doctors and medical students. In April, a divinity student asks Rudolf Steiner a second time about the possibility of religious renewal. September 27-October 16: anthroposophical "university course." December: lectures titled *The Search for the New Isis* (CW 202).

1921:   Rudolf Steiner continues his intensive work on cultural renewal, including the uphill battle for the threefold social order. "University" arts, scientific, theological, and medical courses include: *The Astronomy Course* (CW 323); *Observation, Mathematics, and Scientific Experiment* (CW 324); the *Second Medical Course* (CW 313); *Color*. In June and September-October, Rudolf Steiner also gives the first two "priests' courses" (CW 342 and 343). The "youth movement" gains momentum. Magazines are founded: *Die Drei* (January), and—under the editorship of Albert Steffen (1884-1963)—the weekly, *Das Goetheanum* (August). In February-March, Rudolf Steiner takes his first trip outside Germany since the war (Holland). On April 7, Steiner receives a letter regarding "religious renewal," and May 22-23, he agrees to address the question in a practical way. In June, the Klinical-Therapeutic Institute opens in Arlesheim under the direction of Dr. Ita Wegman. In August, the Chemical-Pharmaceutical Laboratory opens in Arlesheim (Oskar Schmiedel and Ita Wegman, directors). The Clinical Therapeutic Institute is inaugurated in Stuttgart (Dr. Ludwig Noll, director); also the Research Laboratory in Dornach (Ehrenfried Pfeiffer and Gunther Wachsmuth, directors). In November-December, Rudolf Steiner visits Norway.

1922:   The first half of the year involves very active public lecturing (thousands attend); in the second half, Rudolf Steiner begins to withdraw and turn toward the Society—"The Society is asleep." It is "too weak" to do what is asked of it. The businesses—*Der Kommende Tag* and *Futurum A.G.*—fail. In January, with the help of an agent, Steiner undertakes a twelve-city German tour, accompanied by eurythmy performances. In two weeks he speaks to more than 2,000 people. In April, he gives a "university course" in The Hague. He also visits England. In June, he is in Vienna for the East-West Congress. In August-September, he is back in England for the Oxford Conference on Education. Returning to Dornach, he gives the lectures *Philosophy, Cosmology, and Religion* (CW 215), and gives the third priest's course (CW 344). On September 16, The Christian Community is founded. In October-November, Steiner is in Holland and England. He also speaks to the youth: *The Youth Course* (CW 217). In December, Steiner gives lectures titled *The Origins of Natural Science* (CW 326), and *Humanity and the World of Stars: The Spiritual Communion of Humanity* (CW 219). December 31: Fire at the Goetheanum, which is destroyed.

1923:   Despite the fire, Rudolf Steiner continues his work unabated. A very hard year. Internal dispersion, dissension, and apathy abound. There is conflict—between old and new visions—within the society. A wake-up call is needed, and Rudolf Steiner responds with renewed lecturing vitality. His focus: the spiritual context of human life; initiation science; the course of the year; and community building. As a foundation for an artistic school, he creates a series of pastel sketches. Lecture cycles: *The Anthroposophical Movement; Initiation Science* (CW 227) (in England at the Penmaenmawr Summer School); *The Four Seasons and the Archangels* (CW 229); *Harmony of the Creative Word* (CW 230); *The Supersensible Human* (CW 231), given in Holland for the founding of the Dutch society. On November 10, in response to the failed Hitler-Ludendorf putsch in Munich, Steiner closes his Berlin residence and moves the *Philosophisch-Anthroposophisch Verlag* (Press) to Dornach. On December 9, Steiner begins the serialization of his *Autobiography: The Course of My Life* (CW 28) in *Das Goetheanum*. It will continue to appear weekly, without a break, until his death. Late December-early January: Rudolf Steiner refounds the Anthroposophical Society (about 12,000 members internationally) and takes over its leadership. The new board members are: Marie Steiner, Ita Wegman, Albert Steffen, Elizabeth Vreede, and Guenther Wachsmuth. (See *The Christmas Meeting for the Founding of the General Anthroposophical Society* (CW 260). Accompanying lectures: *Mystery Knowledge and Mystery Centers* (CW 232); *World History in the Light of Anthroposophy* (CW 233). December 25: the Foundation Stone is laid (in the hearts of members) in the form of the "Foundation Stone Meditation."

1924:   January 1: having founded the Anthroposophical Society and taken over its leadership, Rudolf Steiner has the task of "reforming" it. The process begins with a weekly newssheet ("What's Happening in the Anthroposophical Society") in which Rudolf Steiner's "Letters to Members" and "Anthroposophical Leading Thoughts" appear (CW 26). The next step is the creation of a new esoteric class, the "first class" of the "University of Spiritual Science" (which was to have been followed, had Rudolf Steiner lived longer, by two more advanced classes). Then comes a new language for Anthroposophy—practical, phenomenological, and direct; and Rudolf Steiner creates the model for the second Goetheanum. He begins the series of extensive "karma" lectures (CW 235-40); and finally, responding to needs, he creates two new initiatives: biodynamic agriculture and curative education. After the middle of the year, rumors begin to circulate regarding Steiner's health. Lectures: January-February, *Anthroposophy* (CW 234); February: *Tone Eurythmy* (CW 278); June: *The Agriculture Course* (CW 327); June-July: Speech [?] Eurythmy (CW 279); *Curative Education* (CW 317); August: (England, "Second International Summer School"), *Initiation Consciousness: True and False Paths in Spiritual Investigation* (CW 243); September: *Pastoral Medicine* (CW 318). On September 26, for the first time, Rudolf Steiner cancels a lecture. On September 28, he gives his last lecture. On September 29, he withdraws to his studio in the carpenter's shop; now he is definitively ill. Cared for by Ita Wegman, he continues working, however, and writing the weekly installments of his *Autobiography* and *Letters to the Members/Leading Thoughts* (CW 26).

1925:   Rudolf Steiner, while continuing to work, continues to weaken. He finishes *Extending Practical Medicine* (CW 27) with Ita Wegman. On March 30, around ten in the morning, Rudolf Steiner dies.

INDEX

Billing Address:

Gregory Nikkel
P.O. Box 11734
Bozeman MT 59719

Gregory Nikkel
P.O. Box 11734
Bozeman MT 5971

Shipping Address:

Gregory Nikkel
P.O. Box 11734
Bozeman MT 59719

Bozeman

Your order of April 07, 2014 (Order ID 116-1163092-8512246)

Qty	Item
	IN THIS SHIPMENT
1	What Is Necessary in These Urgent Times: Eighteen Lectures Held Steiner, Rudolf Paperback
	9780880106313

This shipment completes your order.

541978650 - 000

zon Fulfillment Services
Trade Street
ngton, KY 40511

For detailed information about this and other
orders, please visit your account. You can also
print invoices, change your e-mail address and
payment settings, alter your communication
preferences, and much more - 24 hours a day -
at http://www.amazon.com/your-account.

Returns Are Easy!
Visit http://www.amazon.com/returns to return
any item - including gifts - in unopened or
original condition within 30 days for a full refund
(other restrictions apply). Please have your order
ID ready.

Item Price	Total

rnach Janua $25.00 | $25.00

**Thanks for shopping at Amazon.com, and
please come again!**

and you're done.